Integrating Care for Older People

Integrating Care for Older People

New Care for Old – A Systems Approach

Christopher Foote and Christine Stanners

Foreword by Bob Kane and Rosalie Kane

Jessica Kingsley Publishers
London and Philadelphia

The photograph on the upper left of the cover appears by kind permission of Paul Windsor and Charan Singh Rai.
The photograph on the lower left of the cover appears by kind permission of Corinna Whitfield, L. Bull and J.E. Jones.
Every effort has been made to contact the relatives of those in the remaining photographs. The photograph on the top right was taken in Chicago by one of the authors and the subject gave her permission for it to be used in presentations about care systems. That on the lower right was taken in Hillingdon and the subject gave her permission for it to be used subsequently in a public exhibition. This was taken by Paul Windsor.

First published in the United Kingdom in 2002
by Jessica Kingsley Publishers Ltd
116 Pentonville Road
London N1 9JB, England
and
325 Chestnut Street
Philadelphia, PA 19106, USA
www.jkp.com

Copyright © Christopher Foote and Christine Stanners 2002

British Library Cataloguing in Publication Data
A CIP catalogue record for this book is available from the British Library

Library of Congress Cataloging-in-Publication Data
Foote, Christopher, 1939-
    An integrated system of care for older people : new care for old / Christopher Foote and Christine Stanners.
        p. cm.
    Includes bibliographical references and index.
    ISBN 1-84310-010-X (pbk. : alk. paper)
    1. Aged--Care--Great Britian. 2. Aged--Services for--Great Britain. 3. Integrated
delivery of health care--Great Britain. I. Stanners, Christine, 1935- II. Title.

HV1481.G7F662002
362.6'0941--dc21   2002018447

Printed and Bound in Great Britain by
Athenaeum Press, Gateshead, Tyne and Wear

Contents

List of Figures   6

List of Tables   7

List of Chapter appendices   7

Foreword   9

Preface: Introducing Emily: Problems in the current
               systems of care for older people   12

               Introduction   13

Chapter 1   The Roots of Discrimination   25

Chapter 2   Trying to Understand It All:
               A Systems Approach   46

Chapter 3   Implementation Models   67

Chapter 4   Assessment: Getting to Know
               the Older Person   89

Chapter 5   Preventing Crises: Health Promotion, Chronic
               Disease Management and Risk Management   110

Chapter 6   Putting it in Place: Some Solutions   134

Chapter 7   Information Systems: Connecting Places   167

Chapter 8   Involving the Users   190

Chapter 9   Evaluating an Integrated Care System   225

Chapter 10   Levers and Tools for Integrating Care   271

Chapter 11   The New Professionals: New Ways of Working
               Together for Integrated Care   305

Chapter 12	Changing Places: The Way Ahead for the Care of Older People	323
Chapter 13	Integrating Care at the End of Life	345
Epilogue:	Remember Emily? Meet Winifred	353
Appendix A	EPICS – A Profile of an Elderly Persons Integrated Care System in South Buckinghamshire	357
Appendix B	Other Models of Integrated Care	360
	Acknowledgements	368
	About the authors	371
	Subject index	373
	Author index	383

List of Figures

1.1	Problems with hospital admission viewed from a systems perspective	33
1.2	The vicious cycle of primary-secondary interface	37
2.1	Systems map of integrated care	48
2.2	Reinforcing and balancing loops	51
2.3	Contrasting machines and complex adaptive systems	59
3.1	The integrative whole systems model	70
3.2	Moving the older person line down	72
3.3	Moving the crisis line up	74
3.4	Reducing the number of critical events	76
3.5	The integrative care management model	77
3.6	Value of 'older person partnership'	82
6.1	EPICS organizational structure – EPICS-r-US	138
6.2	EPICS management and line management system	146
6.3	Setting up and sustaining an integrated care system	155
6.4	Setting up and sustaining an integrated care system (contd.)	156
8.1	Aims and objectives of a local Older Persons Action Group	203
9.1	The continuous evaluation process	230

9.2	Cycle of evaluation and strategy generation	232
10.1	PDSA learning cycle	293
10.2	Parallel and synchronous processes	302
11.1	Levels of communication	308
12.1	Communities for caring	340

List of Tables

| 2.1 | Emerging Principles | 61 |

List of Chapter appendices

5.1	The Parkinson's Disease Management Team	132
6.1	Topics Used in a Feasibility Study	158
6.2	Example Job Description for the EPICS Co-Ordinator	163
7.1	Integrated Care – Assessment Evaluation Processing	184
7.2	Example of Information Held on an EPICS Referral Screen	187
8.1	'Margin to Mainstream' Case Studies	217
8.2	Focus Groups	219
8.3	An Example of Outcomes from Focus Groups Convened to Consider the Issues of Managing the End of Life in Hospital	220
8.4	The Process of Setting up the EPICS Conference	221
9.1	Costings for the EPICS Project in South Buckinghamshire	254
9.2	Balanced Scorecard	256
9.3	GP satisfaction Questionnaire	258
9.4	Ongoing Quality of Service: Monitoring interviews with older people who had used EPICS	260
9.5	Questionnaire for Referrers	264
9.6	Glossary of Terms Used in Evaluation	267
10.1	Two Exercises which develop insights to your systems	301

This book is dedicated to the memory of Marjory Warren
and Lionel Cosin who sowed the seeds...

Foreword

We are pleased and honoured to write a foreword to this volume. We have heard bits and snatches of the evolution of the EPICS project in South Buckinghamshire for over a decade, but it is impressive to see it laid out so clearly. It is a story well worth telling, replete with lessons for many. For those who are sceptical about systems theory or believe systems theory is impossible to reconcile with an emphasis on the human being, Christopher Foote and Christine Stanners illustrate how a systems approach can be used in the service of putting the older person's interests, preferences, and basic humanity first. For those systems theory enthusiasts who give little thought to the people who pass through the system, the authors illustrate the emptiness of that approach. The book radiates a concern for the older person for whom the system is supposed to work and for those who labour in that system, but it also makes clear that without a systematic approach we are doomed to make little progress. Emily, lying on an emergency room gurney, provides a strong leitmotiv as the authors help us understand that we may not even be asking the right questions about why she is lying there in a state of unnecessary crisis.

This book fills an important void. At a time when most Western societies face a pandemic of chronic illness, the authors have pointed to an effective way to approach the necessary reorganization of health care. At a time when many depair about how to improve the healthcare system, viewing physicians as intransigent, this book suggests that it is possible (although not always easy) to secure doctors' co-operation in improving the care system. The recommendations are realistic. They do not call for a revolution, or even a reformation. Rather, they suggest how to build on the current infrastructure to make gradual but goal-directed modifications to bring our health and social service systems into more proper alignment with the realities of a world dominated by chronic illness.

The authors refer at one point to 'wicked questions', which can open the doors to new insights. Despite the title of this book, which implies a focus on the care of older people, we are tempted to ask what would happen if indeed the concept of age were eliminated. Should care be redefined to look at the generic issues of chronic disease and frailty regardless of age? Especially in the United States, where virtually the only group covered by universal health insurance is older persons, one might argue that age-based policies are anachronistic. The lessons of EPICS transcend a particular age range. They should be seen in the light of improving care in general. Obviously, not everyone needs a comprehensive approach to care all the time, but everyone would benefit from a care system that can react to problems quickly and efficiently, even if they arise rarely. All people with chronic illnesses should welcome a system that acts proactively to avoid catastrophes, not just reactively to deal with them when they arise. Everyone would welcome a system that was person-centred rather than disease-focused.

There is no shortage of books and articles telling us how to reform the healthcare system, but few can claim a base in the evidence of success. Theory is useful, but its use extends only so far. Academics are often accused of taking something that works in practice and seeing if it can work in theory. This book moves in precisely the opposite direction. It uses practice to undergird theory. As the authors note, no matter how much theory there is, and no matter how many reports are written, unless they are translated into improved outcomes for older people they can be little more than 'exhibits in the halls of academe or management'. This book is authentic. The authors have successfully merged an introduction to systems theory applied to healthcare with a real life experience. The authenticity is enhanced by their disclosing their failures as well as their successes. It is fascinating to follow the history of an amorphous creation and see it take shape. The precepts the authors offer from their own experience and their review of the literature become more credible because they are anchored in a real project that succeeded despite enormous obstacles.

The book's message is relevant for a variety of audiences. Students of healthcare can find valuable lessons about what it takes to make major change in practice among a variety of professional groups. They can see the importance of thinking outside the box, daring to ask big questions about the ultimate goal of care rather than more targeted operational questions that may doom them to simply defining their ruts better. Practitioners may take solace in discovering that it is possible to change major attributes of practice and actually feel better about oneself and more fulfilled. Policy makers will find themselves asking why this hasn't been done before, and perhaps may find themselves willing to take the new risks that go with change.

Despite the authors' own warnings that this is not a blueprint, we are tempted to cry out to these policy makers to read and replicate. However, certain truths must be faced. Mandating and funding such efforts may not prove as successful. In the United States there is a tradition of settlement of the western frontier. The first people to venture out into this wilderness were true pioneers, who laboured unceasingly to make the arid land bloom. Their hard work and determination established the frontier. But they were followed by a larger group of settlers, who needed clearer laws and rules of conduct to maintain the system begun by the pioneers. So too in healthcare are there pioneers and settlers. The approaches that work in the hands of creative and determined people may not support those who come next and need more codified rules. It will be interesting and informative to see how moving EPICS from a developmental project to a model for replication will affect it. How much can be learned and applied? How much needs to be learned anew each time? As the authors note, some wheels should be reinvented. How should systemic application of the EPICS concepts be achieved? Given the story told here it seems foolish to mandate creativity. There are valuable lessons to be gleaned from this volume, but perhaps the inspiration that comes from knowing that taking the other path can sometimes lead to a better way of doing things is the most important lesson to be learned.

Dr Foote notes that he had hoped to go to his grave with EPICS carved on his chest. He and his co-author, Ms Stanners, have, in fact, left a bigger legacy in the form of this book. We, another pair of physician/social worker collaborators, are grateful they wrote it.

Robert L. Kane and Rosalie A. Kane,
University of Minnesota School of Public Health

Preface

Introducing Emily: Problems in the current systems of care for older people

Emily lies in a corner of the accident and emergency department, worried and agitated and starting to cry. She's alone, her granddaughter who came to see her in hospital left three hours ago to collect her own children from school.

Her shoulder is still painful from where she fell on it and she hasn't had anything to eat or drink since breakfast. She did not want to come into hospital but the pleasant nurse said that they didn't think they could send her home to be on her own again and she would find a bed for her somewhere in the hospital by the evening. Her warden will look after the cat, but she has already said two or three times in the last week that Emily should be in a home. Emily doesn't understand this because the doctor who came to see her said he could not find very much wrong apart from the bruised shoulder and it wasn't broken. Hadn't she been going out to do her own shopping until two or three weeks previously? Her own doctor, whom she had seen two to three weeks before, had promised that he would try to keep her at home and see what he could do to improve her strength.

When the warden had found her on the floor early that morning she called the emergency doctor who said to send her straight to casualty. Why don't they ring my own doctor or that nice social worker who called last week and said she would look into it? They would know what is best for me. All her friends had said don't go to hospital because even if you come out they don't let you home. Now her own daughter was dead, her granddaughter could not have her and look after her own children, and she had so prayed that she would not go into a home.

Introduction

...one of the greatest opportunities that faces us this century is to respond to the needs of [the] ageing population and to harness effectively the contributions older people can and do make to society.

Tony Blair, UK Prime Minister

This book is about people. It is primarily about older people and especially those older people who need care and support at times of particular vulnerability. It is about emancipating older people from a history that has given them a bad press, and freeing them for a fuller and more productive life with greater choice. It is, in fact, a book about US ALL since we are all growing older. As Rabbi Lionel Blue has said: 'Older people don't go away. We become one.' (Better Government for Older People 1999)

The book is also about how people behave as individuals and in organizations. At its heart is the challenge to achieve a deeper understanding of the needs and aspirations of us all as we get older: an understanding that will result in changed behaviour and attitudes in both individuals and organizations providing care. Society must let go of the fear that older people are the problem and embrace the concept that, in fact, they can be the solution to the problem. Organizational behaviour must demonstrate trust in the older person. This is the key to developing new ways of working to achieve integrated systems of care.

This book is based on a case study of a project of integrated care for older people in South Buckinghamshire. EPICS (Elderly Persons Integrated Care System – see Appendix A for a description of the organization's function). The authors worked together as part of the EPICS team from 1995 to 1999. As a case study they believe that the experiences are of value to a wider public.

The authors hope that the book will have immediate interest for practitioners, planners and managers of care for older people, that it will have especial value for those managers who have responsibilities across care groups in both statutory and voluntary organizations, and that students and those in training will also find it useful and stimulating. Because some of the conceptual thinking is necessarily condensed it may be difficult to grasp on first reading, but it is hoped that the models and case examples will assist in the understanding of the complex structures and relationships in integrated care systems. The book offers practical guidelines and suggestions for those who are charged with the implementation of such systems, and it gives examples of ways of involving older users (and potential users) in the development and monitoring of services.

It is the authors' experience that the principles that they applied to this work with older people are transferable to other specialisms and client groups. For example, a consultant paediatrician attending a workshop on integrated working thought that the underlying principles which were being applied by the authors to the care of older people were directly applicable to the care of children. Also, from our knowledge of projects in other countries (in Sweden, New Zealand, the USA and France) it appears that the principles are transferable across cultural and political boundaries.

It has not been possible to validate EPICS through rigorous scientific methods. With the current emphasis on initiatives having to be evidence-based, the evidence of EPICS may seem tenuous. However, the project put great emphasis on continuous evaluation as a means of ensuring continuing improvement, which has to be the underlying goal for older people's care.

We have not addressed specific funding issues in relation to projects other than EPICS. The way innovative and integrative projects are funded is important. Current budgetary controls in the UK are divisive and constrain the integration of services. The flow of funding needs to be more flexible and imaginative. Shared budgets and joint funding are currently being promoted through legislation, but this is no guarantee that organizations will work in an integrated way. We believe that integrated care will not happen unless the other cultural and organizational issues raised in the book are addressed at the same time.

The great achievements of social policy and economic growth over the last 50 years and, in the UK particularly, since the introduction of the welfare state, have produced new problems in living with an older population. People are spending longer in retirement. They have greater expectations. They are better informed, partly due to their increasing familiarity with information technology. They are certainly much more knowledgeable on health matters. They have seen their rights enshrined in patients' and citizens' charters. New generations will be even more 'consumer oriented'.

With these changing attitudes there has never been a better time to rethink the way society values its older people. But we all know change is not easy. Older people find it difficult to change their expectations of how they will be treated. Professionals find it difficult to change because of fears and threats to their status and practice. But no matter how difficult, these changes have to happen. And they will.

The key to change is the ability to work together with mutual respect and trust. All those working towards an integrated care system have to develop shared values and a common purpose. And they have to develop that purpose and those values together. Managing change requires maturity and time. Attention must be paid to the losses as well as the gains. The current mechanistic way of responding to a wide variety of problems, with separate organizations and professionals from a range of disciplines all 'doing their own thing', appears to have failed. The reductive approach to problems simply produces compartmentalization, the exact opposite of integration.

The authors believe there is another way. The secret is to manage the parts whilst recognizing their position in the whole. Since the way something is viewed becomes the way it is perceived, current conceptual models need to change. The conceptual models used in this book are called 'complex adaptive systems'. This means 'a collection of individuals (or organizations) with the freedom to act in ways that are not always totally predictable who are interconnected, so that the actions of one will change the context within which the others operate' Plsek and Greenhalgh (2001).

There are important themes running through the book. Prime amongst them is the value of having older people in true partnership. 'Participation' is moving from a concept of consumerism to one of citizenship. This requires the recognition that ownership and provision of care are joint responsibilities between user and provider. There are other recurring themes:

- using systems thinking and modelling as the major tool for reform

- developing a powerful vision for what is to be done based on shared values

- the importance of information systems that inform *in a timely manner*

- the crucial role of evaluation in providing feedback so that the systems of care can learn, adapt and change

- truly knowing about the older person through the assessment process

- both personal and organizational development to be achieved through learning

- balancing the tension between the provision of care for the individual and care for the populations of older people
- the concept of 'community' as the corporate relationships of caring that bind together older people, their carers, and professionals in their localities.

The reader may feel that the scale of this change is too daunting even to attempt a start. We believe that applying complex adaptive systems thinking provides a more optimistic approach for those committed to redesigning care for older people in the twenty first century. Its core message is that big changes emerge from multiple small changes implemented concurrently or at least in quick succession. It has been shown that each individual can change the context and environment by 15 per cent (Morgan 1998) and therefore a sufficient number of people working together can have a major impact for change. Furthermore, if EPICS can do it in South Buckinghamshire, it can be done where you are too!

As this book is primarily addressing issues around integration and managing complexity, there are important topics concerning older people's care that have not been discussed, or have only been touched upon. We hope that the further reading sections provide sources for the reader wishing to pursue such topics in greater depth.

In the UK current government policies emphasize the central role to be played by older people in planning and monitoring their own care. The *National Service Framework for Older People* (NSF) (Department of Health 2001) is the blueprint for ensuring that the needs of older people are at the heart of the reform programme for health and social services. It sets out the standards that are to drive the management of an older population, focusing on:

- rooting out discrimination
- providing person-centred care
- promoting older peoples' health and independence
- fitting services around older peoples' needs.

Other countries would also appear to be moving towards similar standard-setting and implementation.

The authors hope the book will underpin the NSF and will be helpful in implementing the NSF standards, the NHS Plan and other recent government initiatives around 'Better Government for Older People' and partnership working.

Status of older people

The NSF provides descriptions of the status of older people in their life journey. These are very relevant to the discussion in this book. However, the authors feel that one important category has so far been ignored. They would extend the descriptions to include those older people who are at the end of their lives.

Those entering old age: People who have completed their career in paid employment and/or child rearing and are active and independent. (This is how the NSF describes it but they add 'this is a socially-constructed definition of old age, which, according to different interpretations, includes people as young as 50, or from official retirement ages of 60 for women and 65 for men.')

For these the goals of health and social care policy are seen to be to promote and extend healthy, active life and to compress morbidity (the NSF uses the term 'morbidity' to describe that period at the end of life spent in frailty and dependency).

Those in a transitional phase: People who are in transition between healthy active life and frailty. For these, the goals of health and social care policy are to identify emerging problems ahead of crisis and to ensure effective responses that will prevent crisis and reduce long-term dependency.

Those who are frail: People who are vulnerable as a result of health problems or social care needs. The goals of health and social policy are to anticipate and respond to problems, recognizing the complex interaction of physical, mental and social care factors which can compromise independence and quality of life.

Those at the end of their lives: People who are facing social, health and emotional issues in the last years or months of their lives. The goals will be the re-education and support of practitioners to work as partners with older people in facing these issues, and a new belief in the value of getting older.

This book examines the current situation facing users and providers of care. It considers the context within which care is being provided in the UK. In healthcare, this includes the deterioration of elderly care services, the use made by the media of reports of bad conditions for older people in hospitals and the inappropriate use of emergency services. In social services, it includes the increasing pressure to provide ever more resources, and the resulting raising of criteria levels for access to services. In the voluntary sector, the context includes organizations being driven by funding crises to provide services (controlled by statutory requirements) that are solely targeted at those in greatest need rather than at the preventive function of community support.

The book discusses how short-termism to provide quick fixes (for example funding to relieve winter pressures on services and hospital waiting lists and also whole systems support funding) has led to opportunistic development of initiatives without a longer-term strategy. It shows how the impact on services and users has been confused, wasteful and frustrating. It describes briefly the legislative context for change and problems in the current systems. It explores the 'vicious cycle' of care and the counter-intuitive and counter-productive drive towards the bottom line of financial accountability. It examines the 'silo' mentality amongst professionals and organizations, which works to keep areas of practice separate and forces organizations to become self-centred and lose their focus on the older person. It suggests that inevitably all this leads to age discrimination.

The first chapter looks at the roots of discrimination against older people. It traces the history of the Poor Laws in England, which fostered the image of dependency and shifted the burden of responsibility for care from the individual to the local community. It discusses how the values and systems of care derived from an agricultural society could not handle the needs arising within an increasingly industrial society. The result was that older people were admitted to Poor Law hospitals run by charitable institutions with a philosophy of 'doing unto' their patients. It is suggested that this was how the negative image of 'the elderly' developed, with loss of choice and control, associations with pauperism, lowered self-esteem, leaving an ingrained perception of the older person as a burden on society, rather than as an asset and enricher of it.

The chapter goes on to look at changes in the way health and social care has been delivered in the latter part of the twentieth century, resulting in a 'vicious cycle' of response. The chapter concludes with some practical exercises to address age discrimination within organizations.

Chapter 2 presents the view that bringing a systems approach to developing integrated care will enable the problems outlined above to be managed. It describes how systems work, and particularly aims to give some understanding of complex adaptive systems, stressing the organic nature of interactive relationships, that is, people are not machines. The power of complex adaptive systems is achieved through self-generated projects and the impact of small events precipitating major change. It therefore offers hope of change where people feel powerless to affect the rigidity of existing systems.

The chapter offers models for running workshops and training in understanding the way systems work and how everyone in the system interrelates.

Chapter 3 demonstrates the value of modelling in a systems context. Modelling is used as a method of visualising the impact a particular set of events can have on a system. It sets out implementation models with a set of simple rules for the development of integrated care systems. The modelling will help organizations with the implemention of the important principles in the NSF:

- listen to and act on the views of older people and their carers
- develop a shared vision and partnership working
- build strong leadership
- promote inclusive planning
- develop and implement a communication strategy
- ensure that local services are culturally appropriate, meeting the needs of increasingly diverse communities.

In this chapter the authors reflect on the impact of 'disconnectedness' in care and inappropriate care that does not involve the client in planning and decision-making.

The dependency levels of older people are modelled with diagrams showing how raising the level at which crisis occurs reduces pressure on the care systems and enhances the independence of the older person. Other models demonstrate how integrating systems for the individual with systems of managed care produces a 'managed population' of older people to make best use of resources, and to predict need and prevent crises. The chapter ends with a proposal for a civic model for the integration of care.

Chapter 4 addresses the critical function of assessment. It describes assessment as being itself a complex process and identifies the constituent parts and sub-processes and how these are connected. It stresses the importance of the comprehensive 'geriatric assessment' and emphasizes both the diversity of the assessment process (particularly between organizations) and the value of this diversity. The importance of having a system to ensure consistency and sustainability over time is underlined. The NSF has made its main plank for achieving person-centred care a single assessment process across health and social services in which the older person and their carer take a central role. The authors emphasize that assessment is a continuous process and not a one-off event, and that the tools used, such as the forms, are often confused with the process. Implementation of a single assessment process will require the development of integrated systems and the breaking down of professional barriers.

Chapter 5 discusses the systems approach to preventive care and risk management which leads to healthy communities.

> The NHS and local partners should re-focus on helping and supporting older people to continue to live healthy and fulfilling lives. They should work together in partnership to develop healthy communities which support older people to live lives which

are as fulfilling as possible (including leisure and lifelong learning). (Department of Health 2001, p.107).

Different approaches to chronic disease management that make the older person the 'expert' on their own care are discussed.

Chapter 6 considers solutions to problems involved in setting up integrated care and presents working models, including the 'virtual' organization of complex adaptive systems. Experience of the conflicts between health and social service values is shared. The tensions between organizations and people, and between expectations and reality, are explored. And the lesson 'not to seek perfection but to start the journey to improve' is shared. This sets in motion the reviewing and re-envisioning described in the book as the 'iterative' process.

The structural components of an integrated system are presented. Practical examples of initiatives and reasons why some of them failed are given. A flowchart shows how the process of setting up and maintaining an integrated care system is a continuous process.

Chapter 7 discusses the central role of information technology in providing the networks for achieving high-quality care for older people. Information technology has a standardizing function: for example, utilizing standard assessment processes so that appropriate decisions can be made for the 'managed person'; instantly making available guidelines to support decisions for 'managed care'; providing for equity in service provision by exposing areas of deprivation or over-provision as part of risk management and a 'managed population'.

Information enables people to take creative risks. It facilitates evaluation and enables flexibility in the system by providing the evidence of use and effectiveness of care.

The client database which was central to EPICS and the supporting services directory are presented. The system has now been adapted and developed by the programmers to include a single assessment process. Examples of the data collection systems are reproduced.

Chapter 8 describes methods of involving users (and their carers) and potential users in strategic planning and partnerships in service development. Practical examples of tried methodologies are offered under the headings:

- direct participation of users
- informed views of users

- community development
- local scrutiny and accountability.

Illustrative examples of national and local initiatives are described. Consultation with older people themselves as users and potential users was central to the integrated care model developed by the authors. A key concept was the fitting of services around older people, rather than requiring people to fit themselves into the services. Public and private consultation was the tool used to identify the real needs of older people. This concept has become a key standard in the NSF and readers will find some practical suggestions on making it happen.

Chapter 9 looks at the issues around evaluation in a complex adaptive system. The book emphasizes the critical importance of planning evaluation into all development and sets out models and methods that have been tried out. The difficulties and pitfalls of evaluating integrated care systems that are 'virtual' organizations (when much of the activity is about co-ordination and not direct service) are discussed, along with the relevance of qualitative as well as quantitative measures. The availability of proven evidence is variable, but the book suggests that the evaluation process itself produces evidence. A flowchart illustrates the process of evaluation, and a short glossary of terms used in evaluation is included at the end of the chapter.

Chapter 10 suggests levers and tools for implementing models of integrated care. Methods for developing a shared vision and promoting partnership working across professional and organizational boundaries are discussed. The critical importance of leadership in complex adaptive systems is emphasized and checklists are provided of the leadership skills that need to be developed.

Chapter 11 considers how complex adaptive systems need a new kind of professional as managers and practitioners. It considers how generic training and shared responsibility can help to develop the necessary skills. Some of the emerging issues about accountability and line management are discussed, as well as the conflicts and tensions that demand mature and flexible responses from professionals working in this new way.

Chapter 12 explores how new thinking and new ways of doing things can have a big impact on the shape and style of some of the structures that have traditionally been associated with older people's care. It suggests that innovatively designed structures can facilitate creative ways of working and reduce the stress normally associated with multidisciplinary and multi-agency team working. For the acute hospital, current methods of triaging and alternatives to admission need redesigning. Further expansion of specialist care into the community will provide an opportunity to break down the primary and secondary care interface.

Long-term care is one area where overall thinking and perceptions have moved on little from the workhouse ethos of long-term 'parking'. The central theme is that a redefinition of long-term care away from traditional institutional and nursing home care might resolve problems that currently bedevil the selection, transfer and admission of older people to such homes.

The chapter will ask how prepared the community really is to provide its own care; it will question how much of it at the moment is really an extension of hospital care over which community practitioners have relatively little influence.

Chapter 13 raises the taboo subjects of dying and death. Patients and their professional and informal carers find them difficult to discuss. Palliative and hospice care have become fashionable, and yet the needs of those dying in old age remain unrecognized. The whole issue requires public debate. The contention is that resolving issues around (and improving care at) the 'end of life' is the key to releasing and resolving the major tensions in providing high-quality care for older people throughout all their later years.

The Preface and the Epilogue tell two individuals' completely different stories, that of Emily and that of Winifred. Between them they demonstrate the contrast between much of the current reality and what is possible through integrated care.

Throughout the book the term 'older person' is used to describe someone who is over 65 and the term 'elderly' is broadly used to describe the generic group. A single older person is referred to as 'she' to follow the precedent set in Emily's story. In order to distinguish between the older person ('she') and practitioners, the latter are generically referred to as 'he'. The style of the book is pragmatic with signposts to further reading and website contacts. There is cross-referencing between sections in different chapters.

Key points are listed as headline points at the end of each chapter. In some chapters a short 'overview' summarizes the discussion. Other detailed descriptive material and example pro-formas appear as appendices at the end of chapters. Those relating to the whole book will be found in an Appendices section at the back of the book. These include brief profiles of other integrated care projects.

Writing this book, putting together the experiences of two very different people with two different professional backgrounds, has been a continuing part of our individual journeys. Common to both of us is a sense of privilege at having been able to build on the work of early visionaries, and an increasing respect for the hundreds of older people who have been the source and the resource for our work.

References

Better Government for Older People (1999) *All Our Futures: The report of the Steering Committee of the Better Government for Older People Programme* www.bettergovernmentforolder people.gov.uk/reference/pub161.htm

Department of Health (2001) *National Service Framework for Older People.* London: Department of Health.

Morgan, G. (1998) 'New directions in management: The art of using small changes for the large effects.' *Journal of Innovative Management 4*, 1.

Plsck, P.E. and Greenhalgh, T. (2001) 'The challenge of complexity in health care.' *British Medical Journal 323*, 625–628.

Chapter 1

The Roots
of Discrimination

When Buddha was still Prince Siddartha he often escaped from the splendid palace in which his father kept him shut up and drove about the surrounding countryside. The first time he went out he saw a tottering, wrinkled, toothless, white-haired man, bowed, mumbling and trembling as he propped himself along on his stick. The sight astonished the prince and the charioteer told him just what it meant to be old.

'It is the world's pity' cried Siddartha, 'that weak and ignorant beings, drunk with the vanity of youth, do not behold old age! Let us hurry back to the palace. What is the use of pleasures and delights, since I myself am the future dwelling place of old age.'

From The Coming of Age *by Simone de Beauvoir*

In this chapter we trace the roots of discrimination against the elderly through the Poor Laws and changes in social welfare in the UK. We discuss the underlying cases of current stresses in the systems of care for older people which reinforce the negative images of ageing, and suggest practical exercises to address prejudices within organizations.

About Emily

How has the situation described in the preface come about? Though this story is anecdotal it is typical of many similar stories of the care of older people. Often they feel let down, out of control and not able to have a say in what is to happen to them. They feel swallowed up by the system, powerless to do anything about it.

It would be easy to blame anybody or everybody, even Emily herself, for this situation. Newspaper headlines depict stories of emergency departments bursting at the seams with people waiting hours for treatment and lying on trolleys waiting for admission; hospital wards over-full, with significant numbers of people inappropriately admitted in the first place waiting to be discharged. Hospital waiting lists get longer because beds are not available for elective work. Resources and skilled people are inappropriately used to grapple with the all-consuming problem of 'emergency care'.

> *Often older people feel let down, out of control and not able to have a say in what is to happen to them. They feel swallowed up by the system, powerless to do anything about it.*

Social services have similar problems. Heavy demand for both residential and nursing home placements has stretched their budgets to a point where other services are threatened, particularly services that are preventive or that enable independence.

There are significant variations in the criteria used for admissions to nursing and residential homes across the country. This almost certainly indicates that in some areas a proportion of these admissions must be unnecessary. However, innovative attempts to change this are being made. These include such measures as step-down and step-up care: someone in a hospital, for example, might need care, but not in that high-level setting (step-down care); or high users of resources in their own homes can be moved into a higher level of care, for example sheltered housing or residential care, to reduce the level of their dependency. Because of the complexity of the problem co-operation is required from other agencies, particularly those providing healthcare. This is difficult to co-ordinate because other agencies have their own problems.

The historical roots

As ever, the past continues to dictate the present and the current culture of elderly care is embedded in history. In the Middle Ages care was very often dependent on the chance availability of religious institutions and their ability to provide outreach care. Increasingly, lay institutions were developed in larger towns providing care on a charitable basis. The Reformation, with the dissolution of the monastic system, left a vacuum of care until the Poor Law Act of 1601 put the onus and responsibility for care on the local community. It was never (as in other countries such as France) to be the legal responsibility of the family.

Strangely, perhaps, it was never intended that the responsibility for care for the older person should rest on themselves or other individuals. In an essentially agricultural society the responsibility was to be 'no blame–no fault'; a failed crop or harvest was too often beyond the control of the individual. So this Poor Law Act, incorporating the practice of previous centuries, enshrined the corporate and community care values that are still relevant today. Perhaps in small communities it was not such a great concern that the older person had their individual care institutionalized within the parish boundaries, nevertheless 'being on the parish' was a demeaning state for many.

The Quakers were at the heart of the workhouse concept in the mid-seventeenth century. Born of high ideals, workhouses based within parishes were to be communes of care and self-help where paupers could find work and employment. Over the years, the concept degenerated as more and more of the sick and disabled who could not work were housed there. In an agricultural society with no formal prisons some of these workhouses became, or were associated with, houses of correction for individuals convicted of smaller crimes. In the absence of a formal, universal pension system those elderly people who were deemed to be paupers were housed there too. So the workhouse was no longer a place to find work but a repository for 'unproductive' and needy members of the community.

The development of the Industrial Revolution saw the rise of ever-larger conurbations with which systems of care and the values derived from an agricultural community could not cope. The relaxation of the Poor Law and the ever-rising cost drove the Victorians to pass the Poor Law Amendment Act of 1834. This Act, in contrast to that of 1601, blamed the pauper, especially the able-bodied, for not working, even if work was not available. In an attempt to contain costs, outdoor relief was not to be given, and those requiring help had to be admitted to the workhouse and submit to its frequently harsh regime.

In further attempts to reduce the burden on society, the smaller parish-based workhouses were amalgamated into the larger Union Houses. The abolition of outdoor relief and funeral benefits resulted in families commiting many elderly people to the workhouse to die in order to qualify for a free funeral. In the absence of a prison system, the petty criminal would also be admitted for punishment and correction. Many other people without adequate means, and unable to cope in the community (such as vagrants and itinerants) would frequently be admitted to the Union House to end their days.

The development of Poor Law hospitals in the mid-nineteenth century, though an improvement in some cases for the sick and dying, still did very little to improve the lot of the elderly. In the absence of alternative means of support they were often admitted under pretext and remained there for years, some never to be discharged. Underpinning all this was the concept of charitable purpose that the hospitals and workhouses adopted. To the providers, this was 'doing good'. To the inmates, it was 'like it or leave it' and 'good is being done unto you even if you do not like it'.

> *The elderly have often come to typify a negative picture: one of loss of choice and control because society has taken that over. This has been reinforced by the associations with pauperism, lowered societal esteem and being a burden rather than a benefit to society.*

It is perhaps not surprising from this historical perspective that the elderly have often come to typify a negative picture: one of loss of choice and control because society has taken that over. These perceptions are reinforced by the associations with pauperism, lowered societal esteem and being a burden rather than a benefit to society.

In contrast, other societies that have not travelled this historical path have traditionally revered their elderly as repositories of wisdom, the baton carriers of values that ensure the continuation of their ways of life. (Readers might like to read Simone de Beauvoir, *Coming of Age*, chapter 2.)

There are heroes who have lit beacons to show the way of change. Marjory Warren, the 'mother' of modern elderly care, turned the West Middlesex Poor Law Hospital into the first unit to assess and then rehabilitate older people, enabling them to return to the community. She set the basic principles in the late 1940s that still apply today. Fergus Anderson looked at the elderly in the community in Glasgow and put the specialty of care on a sound academic footing in the 1960s. Lionel Cosin, a surgeon by training, transformed surgical and orthopaedic treatment by his innovative approach of early operation and then early mobilization of elderly patients. In Oxford in the 1960s he went on to introduce the concepts of respite care and day hospitals as ways of meeting the complex needs of the elderly and their carers.

Other heroes were Sheldon, who examined and questioned the health and living conditions of the elderly in the Midlands in the late 1940s and, of course, Lord Beveridge whose report in 1942 (*Social Insurance and Allied Services*) effectively changed the whole infrastructure of financial support. He introduced the principle of social insurance in post-war Britain, a socially inclusive concept embracing older people as well as the sick and unemployed.

How is it that despite these and other giants, there are the problems of today?

The current issues

Changes in the delivery of healthcare services

The 1970s and 80s saw a growth of geriatric units, many of them still sited in the old Poor Law hospitals, separated from the quickly expanding technology of diagnosis and treatment in the new hospitals that were being built.

There was a strong body of opinion that the elderly were being deprived of technological care, although evidence was accruing that they would benefit at least as much as younger patients from these more aggressive approaches. The evidence also indicated that these approaches shortened the length of hospital stays (Grimley Evans 2000). The solution was, and continues to be, to achieve the correct balance between access to 'high-tech' care and appropriate conventional 'geriatric' care. The right care to the right older person, at the right time and in the right place, is the key to a high-quality service.

> The right care to the right older person, at the right time and in the right place, is the key to a high-quality service.

Once the departments of geriatric care were established in acute hospitals, pressure grew to integrate the care of the elderly with other specialties, particularly general medicine. The premise was that as all adult patients were getting older there was little difference in the generality of care. What is more, the presence of the specialty enhanced the care of elderly patients throughout the hospital. The change of image achieved for geriatric practitioners through becoming part of mainstream practice improved recruitment to a specialty short of doctors.

Two other major developments influenced the nature of hospital care: the need to improve out-of-hours emergency care, and the reduction in junior doctors' working hours.

The improvement of emergency care out-of-hours was directed particularly at surgical care and the availability of more expensive, 'high tech' facilities, such as intensive therapy units. This enabled emergency surgical facilities to be reduced in number, providing fewer but larger and better-resourced units (National Confidential Enquiry into Perioperative Deaths 1999). As medical emergency care cannot take place without surgical support, the medical units followed the surgical ones into larger hospitals.

The other factor, the reduction in junior doctors' working hours, had to be achieved without extra doctors, and the only possible solution was to create larger teams with cross-cover on larger sites.

The outcome of both these factors was an increasing number of admissions of older people to large hospitals where they were treated mainly as acute emergencies even if this was not their primary need. Once acute elderly medical care was incorporated into the acute hospitals the very real financial pressures resulted in the specialized geriatric units being threatened and in many instances reduced to a shadow of their former selves (Bowman *et al.* 1999; Svanborg 1996).

However, the profile of older people needing care was changing too. They were growing older, and though generally more functionally competent there was an increasing number of very frail elderly people, many of whom were approaching the end of their lives. On the other hand, the younger elderly were better able to cope with the physiological stresses of illness. They got on their feet more quickly and seemed not to need the help of specialist geriatric units. This divergence, together with the overall reduction in geriatric facilities, made it necessary to reinvent specialist elderly care.

Society was changing also. Not only was the public better informed, but where previously it had accepted passively whatever was offered, it was now becoming much more demanding on services. The greater openness that was required from professionals and hospitals alike put care under scrutiny. The natural tendency to find someone, or something, to blame resulted in a greater number of complaints and legal actions for compensation.

There have also been changes in primary care. Significantly, general practitioners have given up providing 24-hour care personally and are delegating to deputizing agencies or doctors' co-operatives. Consequently, emergency care has been increasingly provided by doctors whom the older person does not know and, as importantly, who do not know the older person.

> *Emergency care has been increasingly provided by doctors whom the older person does not know and, as importantly, who do not know the older person.*

Together with rising patient expectations this resulted in a greater demand on hospital services, particularly on accident and emergency departments. In the absence of relevant information about past medical history, medication and the social setting of the patient, there has been an increasing tendency to admit the older person inappropriately into hospital rather than risk the consequences of sending them home in an increasingly litigious society (Ingold *et al.* 2000).

Even if the clinical decision would have been not to admit the older person, the extra care needed to support them in the community (either for medical or social reasons) was often not immediately available. So they would often be inappropriately admitted, most frequently to acute hospital wards where they were likely to have prolonged stays, which not only compounded their problems but also those of the hospital. If the medical and acute geriatric wards with staff used to dealing with such problems were full, the overflow was to surgical and other wards with less geriatric expertise (Health Advisory Service 1999). This was another potential cause of delayed discharge. In such a system it was increasingly difficult to maintain high-quality services across the whole hospital for care of the elderly. No matter how empathetic the staff were, the elderly were seen as an obstruction and a burden preventing the ward from carrying out its primary function.

Another factor within the hospitals has been the development of the accident and emergency units as the 'front door' of all emergency admissions. These became the triage centres for emergencies, assessing and prioritizing care needs. This funnelling of patients through the accident and emergency department resulted in delays and queuing with prolonged trolley waits and resultant likelihood of complications like pressure sores. If there were no facilities for complex assessments in the emergency departments to meet the needs of the frail elderly there was a tendency to admit the patient.

If through lack of a proper assessment the care team did not know the reason for the admission they would not know how best to care for the patient. As a result, the required care was not administered and the elderly patient's needs were frequently not met. Studies have suggested that between 20 and 30 per cent of patients over 75 years are admitted inappropriately to an acute hospital setting when their needs would be more appropriately met elsewhere in rehabilitation wards, non-acute hospital beds in community hospitals, or in residential homes (Coast, Peters and Inglis 1996). The evidence suggests not only that these patients remain in hospital longer but also that at any one time 30 to 40 per cent of the acute hospital beds are being used for patients who do not require acute hospital care (Fenn *et al.* 2000).

Because of poor community care some of those patients discharged were frequently readmitted and then discharged again on several occasions – the 'revolving door' syndrome. Chronic disease management of respiratory, cardiac and neurological problems could not maintain such patients in the community. Many of these patients were elderly and also added to the recycling of need.

Hospital bed managers, who were responsible for managing planned admissions from waiting lists, were having increasing difficulty in admitting these patients when the bed occupancy was so high and they were unable to predict sufficient discharges. The paradox of the situation was that many of the patients on the waiting list were themselves elderly and waiting for operations of proven benefit and cost-effectiveness

(South Buckinghamshire NHS Trust 1997). So, some older people who would have benefited from being in hospital were being denied admission. Moreover, whilst on the waiting list their condition would deteriorate and they would suffer further distress, both physically and psychologically. A few of these patients would themselves become emergencies and need admission for a complication or crisis arising out of their underlying medical problem.

Increasing financial pressure on local managers frequently resulted in services such as rehabilitation or community hospital beds (which appeared to be non-essential for emergency care) being reduced or cut (Nocon and Baldwin 1998). Some of the savings made were ploughed back into expanding the emergency services further. Perhaps it is not surprising that options for alternative care were not available and that everybody was sucked into acute care whether they needed it or not (Audit Commission 1997). The old saying 'If all you have is a hammer, everything looks like a nail ' is very apposite in this context.

Changes in the delivery of social care services

The social services, being part of local government, have a completely different set of objectives and constraints. They are accountable to the local electorate through council members, and their budgets are competing with other major community needs, such as education, policing, housing, roads and leisure activities. These financial differences are reflected in one of the major cultural differences between health and social care, in that those receiving social care are means-tested and charged. This inevitably results in bureaucratic complexity and can delay the delivery of social care to the detriment of the older person. Inability to respond in a timely manner increases demand on crisis management, adding considerably to the professional pressures and stresses on social workers. Moreover, the burden of this increased and unnecessary crisis management puts further strain on scarce resources.

The burden of the increased and unnecessary crisis management puts further strain on scarce resources.

Changes in social policy had big implications for both older people and the providers of services. The policy swung from providing incentives to older people to go into residential care to encouraging them to remain in the community in their own homes.

In local authorities support for older people had focused on the provision of residential care since Part III of the National Assistance Act of 1948 laid a duty on them to provide institutional care: 'The local authorities will have the duty of providing residential accommodation to be available for persons who need care because of age, infirmity, etc., irrespective of their means' (Section 21/1a). This provision by the authorities became familiarly known as 'Part III accommodation'. The provision was not free. A means test was applied to assess what contribution to the cost should be made by the resident. Guaranteed sums of 'unprotected' capital were to be disregarded until the sum exceeded £400. (In 2001 this sum was £18,500.)

The burden of the relief of destitution was to be lifted from local authorities and central government was to take the responsibility through the National Assistance Board.

Social services had responded to wartime priorities by developing specialist workers, often with special emergency training programmes. Consequently, cross-client group-working to develop care programmes within the family was difficult, and this created the image of older people isolated from their families and community.

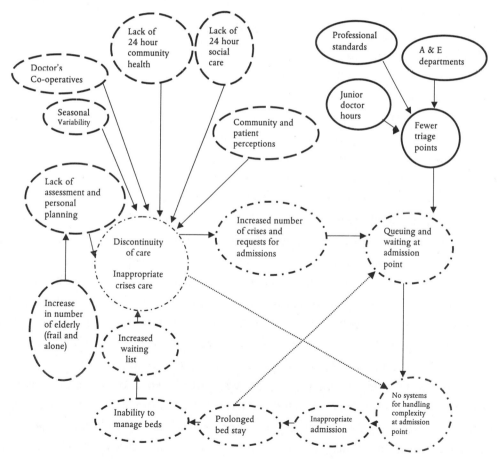

Figure 1.1 Problems with hospital admission viewed from a systems perspective

Over time the generic workers developed specialisms. Although they were able to work across client groups, child care cases attracted media attention, and scarce skills and resources were focused on this high-profile area of social work. As a consequence, teams for older people were largely staffed by social work assistants and not by fully qualified social workers. Although the quality of work was often high, this suggested a lower value was placed on work with older people, and the complexity of their problems and support networks was underestimated.

In 1968 the Seebohm Report had envisaged a more marginal role for voluntary organizations than the one they had played under the Poor Law Act.

In 1982 the Barclay Report addressed the need for the reorganization of social service departments to reflect both the emerging trends of working and the emphasis of the current government on promoting self-help. It envisaged the majority of caring being carried out by the informal sector of family, friends and neighbours, augmented by voluntary organizations. Statutory services were to offer only a minimal direct service.

This was of course quite the opposite of the spirit of the Seebohm reconstruction. Taken in the context of the sociological changes that were happening at the time, the assumption that 'the community' would be the main support seemed optimistic in the extreme. The lack of skilled social workers in the field and the reduction in the voluntary workforce meant that there was more pressure on older people to move out of their homes into residential and nursing homes, and there was consequently a huge escalation of investment in privately run homes.

This was another 'quick fix', which resulted in the government expenditure on payments to top up the shortfall between what the resident of a home was assessed to pay and the actual charges made to the home escalating out of all expectation. The government had to address alternative ways of continuing this explosion of cost in providing institutional care.

The Community Care Act 1990 introduced measures to remove the financial incentive to provide care in residential and nursing homes. The Act was a radical rethink of the role and responsibilities of the state in relation to social welfare – introducing the totally new concept of a *welfare market* as opposed to a *welfare state*. There was a shift in local authority social services from provider to enabler.

A new framework for managing care was introduced with the appointment of care managers. Their role was to try to overcome some of the organizational dysfunction by co-ordinating the various aspects of care on behalf of the client. Budgets were devolved to the care managers which allowed them some flexibility. However, the managerial constraints put on the care managers as budget holders were viewed by

> ... *introducing the totally new concept of a welfare market as opposed to a welfare state. There was a shift in local authority social services from provider to enabler. A new framework for managing care was introduced with the appointment of care managers.*

many as being a way of financial containment rather than facilitating client-centred care. There was also constant pressure to take the lowest tender in purchasing external services. The introduction of performance management concepts meant there was less flexibility in provision of, for example, home care.

Though assessment was seen as a core process in care management, its primary purpose became the assessment of need for which there were known resources, rather than providing a holistic understanding of the older person. Assessment was seen to be the key to a needs-led rather than a resource-led service. Certainly, this assessment process was not used in the context of risk management or of ongoing preventive social care (Social Services Inspectorate 1991).

In spite of the stresses in the system, community care was generally successful in being able to maintain people in their own homes for longer (mainly due to crisis intervention and long-term community care). It was, however, so successful that when those older people could finally no longer be looked after in the community, they had reached such a high degree of dependency they had gone beyond the level of care that could be provided in a residential home. (It is important to note that the Audit Commission (1997) has shown that there is considerable variation in the use of residential and nursing home accommodation across the country.)

External pressures on social services

Pressures from hospitals to transfer patients from 'blocked beds' put further stresses on the provision of community care. The growing number of frail, older people made yet further demands on the social services' budgets for long-term nursing home placements. Frequently this resulted in budgetary competition between community and institutional care.

The pattern of care within sheltered housing (now not only provided by local councils, housing associations and national voluntary organizations operating locally such as Abbeyfield and The Anchor Trust) was similarly changed. On the one hand, there was less pressure on traditional sheltered housing for the elderly; and on the other, the tenants remaining needed more intensive support and care, often in premises that were not designed for such dependency. This has required a rethink on

...when older people could finally no longer be looked after in the community, they had reached such a high degree of dependency they had gone beyond the level of care that could be provided in a residential home.

the use of these resources: creative solutions working in partnership with other voluntary organizations, health and social care have allowed tenants to remain longer in their own homes (Audit Commission 1997).

For example, The Anchor Trust has developed 'stay-put' schemes which draw on government grants such as HEES (Home Energy Efficiency Scheme) and Care and Repair Schemes to improve the security, insulation and heating in older people's homes.

The value of safety and heating in the home

A socially isolated older woman who never left her home had the benefit of improvements to her home through a Care and Repair Scheme: 'I just couldn't believe it. When it was done I just felt it was a dream. I waited so long: it had been in such bad condition...there were gaps in the windows, gaps in the floorboards, no indoor water, no indoor toilet, no electricity, just one plug and one light. Another thing, I'm never in now – I go to different clubs. I get out more. If you can understand me, I probably should have done that before, whereas I used to sit and sort of look at it.'

Paradoxically, the quality improvements to residential and nursing homes required by new legislation is currently driving providers out of the industry and reducing the resource available. The risk for the future is a two-tier system, whereby only those who can afford the new prices will go into the homes and those who can't will be deprived of the choice. Yet again there will be increased pressure on the rest of the care system such as hospitals and community care.

The vicious cycle of blame and dependency

With increasing demand on hospital beds and pressure to discharge people more quickly (in order to admit even more emergencies) hospital emergency systems became overloaded, fraught and strained.

The lack of suitable care alternatives meant that even more people had to be treated as emergencies overloading a precarious situation even further. Those people who were unable to leave hospital were a 'problem' to the system and pejoratively called 'bed blockers'. As in many stressed systems the problem was projected on to other organizations, such as social services or community services, which had no control over the cause of the problem and consequently could do nothing to alleviate the vicious cycle.

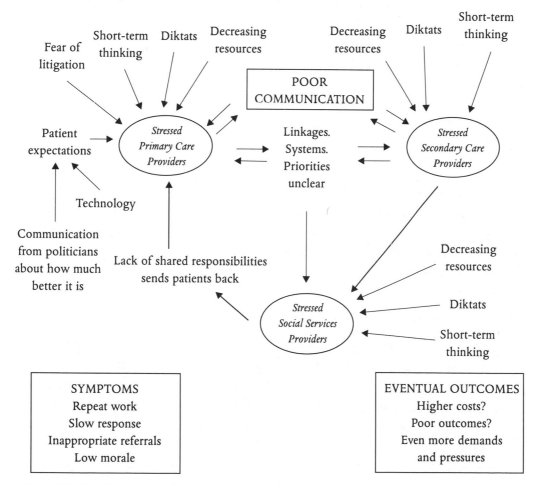

Figure 1.2 The vicious cycle of primary–secondary interface

These services were often not able to meet the immediacy of the demand from the hospitals. Hospitals were making themselves dependent on social services, and when their apparent needs were not met blame was apportioned and relationships became poor with increasingly defensive behaviour. In turn, the social services had need of healthcare organizations to help assess and rehabilitate some of the elderly people who were being inappropriately admitted to nursing homes. This widening gulf between organizations made it very difficult for them to co-operate in addressing problems that by working together would probably have been soluble.

This vicious cycle with its attendant worsening climate of blame and judgemental behaviour resulted in a range of organizational symptoms. For example, the lack of trust between professionals meant that they felt that they could not rely on assessments done by their colleagues in other disciplines. As a result they insisted on doing their own. The inevitable outcome was multiple assessments done on each individual older person.

To compound the situation, the value of these multiple assessments was further limited when they were not shared among or communicated to those who needed to know. This also built in delays before any action could be taken to meet the needs of the older person being assessed, so the response was inevitably slow. Referrals were sometimes made inappropriately to meet the needs of the organization rather than the older person.

The outcome of all of this was poor-quality service and even higher demands and pressures on the system. Waste and duplication resulted in even higher costs on the organizations' already stretched budgets. What was even more insidious was the poor morale which all this caused. The ever poorer relationships drove the vicious spiral down further with the resentment nearly always being projected on to the older person. Result: increasing ageist prejudice.

Creating a virtuous cycle of improvement

Addressing these problems lies at the heart of this book. They have arisen out of a complex and intricate network of organizational interactions – many of them quick fixes to address short-term political and financial goals. The solutions will need to be complex too. But fortunately the complexity of the solutions can be tackled by developing some quite simple rules to guide the planner. (See chapter 2, p.62 on systems and chapter 3, p.84 on implementation models.)

However, there is unlikely to be any significant change until the older person is fully included as an equal in society. This will need major changes in attitudes and in the way older people are thought of, and an end to age discrimination. This has to be

There is unlikely to be any significant change until the older person is fully included as an equal in society. This will need major changes in attitudes and in the way older people are thought of, and an end to age discrimination.

the first challenge to those committed to creating a new world for and with older people.

The National Service Framework for Older People has set the standards for rooting out age discrimination, developing person-centred care and involving older people in the planning and monitoring of services. Practical ways to realize these standards are offered throughout this book.

Meeting the challenge: Some practical exercises
Examine personal attitudes

Taking time to reflect on individual personal attitudes is the start of the whole process. Honesty without self-blame for subjective feelings is essential. The chances are that they are the result of a range of external experiences, and centuries-old influences. Identifying good experiences with older people and analysing why they were positive can be a basis for building on them. Other techniques that might help in staff development include:

- In a group setting ask an older person to recall experiences when younger and compare them with those of the group. This will give the group insight into their own ageing processes and help them to realize that the elderly are not a race apart.

- Also in a group, ask older people their experience of ageist attitudes, and how these have affected them.

- Arrange staff training in communication skills with older people. Being able to understand them and put yourself in their position goes a long way towards overcoming ageist attitudes. Include older people in the group.

- Specifically allow time in the busy routine of providing care to talk and listen to the older person however briefly. The experience can be humbling.

The time to talk

One quiet afternoon in a geriatric ward a white haired, neatly dressed older woman was sitting calmly, a smile on her face.

The social worker had been told she never spoke, always sitting calmly with the smile on her face. Nothing was known about her except that she lived alone. The smile protected her from revealing that she suffered from a deep sense of shame, as well as unbearable loss.

The social worker sat quietly with the woman and eventually asked about her family. In due course the woman spoke. She told that she had a son and a daughter. She spoke flatly, the smile in place. Then she said that she no longer had a daughter. Her son had murdered her in their front room.

Whether the story was true or not the social worker could not know, but she felt a deep and shocking sense of humility at the depth of experience in this quiet woman's life.

Examine the corporate values of the organization

The strategic and operational policies of an organization should reflect the values it has in relation to older people. An examination of these policies should be undertaken regularly in the form of an audit to ensure that older people are not being disadvantaged. Objective performance measures in relation to older peoples' care will highlight changes that are required. The overseeing of this information needs to be shared with senior board members, or cabinet members in social services, with older people themselves and any related advocacy groups. Areas that may be of specific concern are:

- Hospitals
    - waiting list monitoring and management
    - ward-based care policies to ensure high standards that give dignity and self-worth to the older person
    - resuscitation policy – will need sensitive consultation but is very important
- Social services
    - criteria for admission to services
    - systems for monitoring 'closed' cases, i.e. those where the critical incident has passed and no further support is being given

- ° purchasing policies for residential nursing and home care
- Voluntary organizations
  - ° aims and objectives of the organization
  - ° criteria for admission to services (ever under pressure to take those in greatest need only)
- Primary care
  - ° accessibility
  - ° continuity of medical care in nursing homes
  - ° screening assessment and risk management
- Generic issues
  - ° making care-related information available to the older person in a way they can understand and thus partake in the care processes
  - ° policies around accessibility of care both in terms of physical access and availability to older people.

Actively involve older people in deliberations

Involving the older person in policy making is not easy but is extraordinarily fruitful. It not only helps to find out their wants and needs at the earliest stages, but it has been our experience that it also promotes higher-quality care which is more cost-effective. Many of the solutions the older people suggested were simpler and less demanding than they would have been had the professionals alone been involved. The elderly are not a homogeneous group, and a diversity of methods is required to involve them. The retired business executive may be comfortable in a boardroom setting but a frail person in a wheelchair who is deaf and unable to leave home may have at least as much to offer in policy making! The National Service Framework for Older People is now making it imperative to involve older people in the shaping of the values of care in a locality. However, there are as many implicit barriers to including older people as there are explicit. For example, even though older people are invited to public meetings, reduced mobility and access can prevent their attending. (Lack of transport is often a major stumbling block.) And even when they do attend they may not be encouraged to communicate in a manner in which they can be heard or understood.

The experience in South Buckinghamshire of developing an integrated care system for the elderly was that involving the older person became the catalyst for changing services, and that this involvement was fundamental to creating shared values across agencies. It forged relationships through a common cause.

Older people are on the whole nothing but realistic and, as in the story above (p.40), have often been through hardships of which we are unaware. It was the experience of the project that their demands are rational and reasonable, mostly directed to making themselves more self-sufficient. (See chapter 8, p.212 on involving users.)

Ensure dedicated leadership to combat ageism

Leaders in any organization are the shapers and guardians of the values of their organization. Theirs is the responsibility to address ageism and involve older people for mutually productive benefit. On the other hand, if leaders promote these values but they and their organizations fail to live by them, then a culture of scepticism and mistrust will be engendered through a lack of integrity.

There is enormous incentive for leaders in all related organizations to be involved. Leadership can come from within the professions, voluntary organizations or cross-specialty teams, and is at least as important as that from the appointed organizational leaders. Cross-specialty teams can be particularly effective in combating ageism, not only because they have each other's support but also because they often have the right mix of skills to be practically effective. An individual clinician with, for example, a passionate belief in the older person, good communication skills and the right mix of courage and persistence can carry the banner as a champion for the older person and the services that support them. Leaders like this are often a thorn in the side of conventional management but they can be very effective if they act with integrity and have the skills to link well with other professionals and carers. (See chapter 10, p.285 for more on leadership in complex adaptive systems.)

Overview – What a fine mess!

Perhaps it is not surprising that the care of older people in this country has got into the state that it has. Centuries of British culture have demeaned older people and devalued their contribution to society. The collective responsibility which society has chosen to take in caring for the elderly has more often than not been viewed as a burden when competing priorities come into play. In responding to external and political pressures, the organizations providing care have frequently sought to meet their own individual needs rather than co-operate and jointly meet the needs of older people.

What is also apparent from all the above is the complexity of the problem which in turn reflects the complexity of need of the older person. Short-term goals and reactive short-term 'solutions' have only served to heighten the problem. This lack of systemic long-term thinking and planning has resulted in the current system that has failed to handle the complexity and immediacy of older peoples' needs.

The existing vicious cycle needs to be turned into a virtuous one. At the heart of this has to be new values and attitudes toward older people in our society. New ways of thinking and dealing with the problems are necessary. More of the old ways will only make matters worse. The paternalistic approach, no matter how well meant, has to be a thing of the past. Older people have to be involved as equals not only in planning the care systems but also in managing their own individual care. This approach is the key to undoing the vicious cycle and meeting everybody's needs. Not just the needs of older people and their carers but also, paradoxically maybe, the needs of society and its statutory organizations.

Chapter 1 – Headline points

- Often older people feel let down, out of control and not able to have a say about what is to happen to them. They feel swallowed up by the system, and powerless to do anything about it.

- The elderly have come to typify a negative picture, associated with pauperism, lowered societal esteem and being a burden rather than a benefit to society.

- The right care to the right older person, at the right time and in the right place, is the key to a high-quality service.

- Emergency care was increasingly being provided by doctors whom the older person did not know and who did not know the older person.

- The burden of increased and unnecessary crisis management put further strain on scarce resources.

- The lack of skilled social workers in the field (for older people) and the reduction in the voluntary workforce meant there was more pressure on older people to move out of their homes into residential and nursing homes; this led to a huge escalation of investment in privately run homes.

- The Community Care Act 1990 introduced measures to remove the financial incentive to provide care in homes. It was a radical re-conception of the role and responsibilities of the state in relation to social welfare – the development of a welfare market as opposed to a welfare state. There was a shift in local authority social services from provider to enabler.

- When older people could finally no longer be looked after in the community they had reached such a degree of dependency they had gone beyond the level of care that could be provided in a residential home.

- There is unlikely to be significant change until the older person is fully included as an equal in society. Major changes in attitudes and in the way older people are thought of, and an end to age discrimination are needed.

References

Audit Commission (1997) *The Coming of Age: Improving Care Services for Older People.* London: Audit Commission.

Barclay Report (1982) *Social Workers: Their Role and Tasks.* London: Bedford Square Press.

Beveridge Report (1942) *Social Insurance and Allied Services.* Cmd 6404. London: HMSO.

Bowman, C., Johnson, M., Venables, D., Foote, C. and Kane, R.L. (1999) 'Geriatric care in the United Kingdom: Aligning services to needs.' *British Medical Journal 319*, 7217, 1119–1122.

Coast, J., Peters, T.J. and Inglis, A. (1996) 'Factors associated with inappropriate emergency hospital admissions.' *International Journal of Quality in Health Care 8*, 31–39.

Fenn, A., Horner, P., Travis, S., Prescott, G., Figg, H. and Bates, T. (2000) 'Inappropriate bed usage in a district general hospital.' *Journal of Clinical Excellence 1*, 221–237.

Grimley Evans, J. (2000) 'Ageing and medicine.' *Journal of Internal Medicine 247*, 159–167.

Health Advisory Service (1999) *Not Because They Were Old: An independant inquiry into the care of older people on acute wards in general hospitals.* London: HAS.

Ingold, B.B., Yersin, B., Wietlisbach, V., Burckhardt, P. Burnard, B. and Bula, C.J. (2000) 'Characteristics associated with inappropriate hospital use in elderly patients admitted to a general internal medical service.' *Ageing – Clinical Experimental Research 12*, 6, 430–438.

National Confidential Enquiry into Perioperative Deaths (1999) *Extremes of Age.* London: NCEPOD.

Nocon, A. and Baldwin, S. (1998) Trends in the Availability of Provision.' In *Trends in Rehabilitation Policy.* London: King's Fund.

Seebohm Report (1968) *Report of the Committee on Local Authority and Allied Personal Social Services.* Cmnd 3703. London: HMSO.

Social Services Inspectorate (1991) *Assessment Systems and Community Care.* London: Department of Health.

South Buckinghamshire NHS Trust (1997) Surgical Waiting List Data 1996–97.

Svanborg, A. (1996) Chapter 7. In S. Ebrahim and A. Kalache (eds) *Epidemiology in Old Age.* London: BMJ Publishing

Further reading

de Beauvoir S. (1970) *The Coming of Age* (New York) W W Norton & Company

This book is still available via the web in the USA and it is essential reading for those interested in combating discrimination with age. Simone de Beauvoir was a philosopher and writer who not only treats the topic from an historical perspective but throws an important humanistic and anthropological slant on the issue. It is easy and compelling reading.

Thane P. (2000) *Old Age in English History: Past Experiences, Present Issues.* (Oxford) Oxford University Press

An erudite and wide ranging review of older people in English history. It provides an excellent base from which to understand the past in order to look to the future. It is extremely well referenced with a very good bibliography.

Webster C. (editor) (2001) *Caring for Heath: History and Diversity* (Buckingham) Open University Press

This book gives a thorough background of the history of healthcare in this country with in-depth review of the international scene. It gives an accurate picture of the current situation and some of the dynamics of care with very good illustration of older peoples' care.

Granshaw L. and Porter R. (editors) (1990) *The Hospital in History* (London) Routledge

Apart from the historical account of hospitals this book gives insights of the values, both of society and the hospitals, in providing care through the ages.

Ebrahim S. and Kalache A. (editors) (1996) *Epidemiology in Old Age* (London) BMJ Publishing Group.

This excellent book has short and pithy reviews of a wide range of epidemiological issues of general interest for all those caring for the elderly. These include the ageing process, health service usage, nutrition and quality of life amongst others. There is useful information relating to social care and support as well which will broaden its appeal.

Kirkwood T. (2001) *The End of Age* (London) Profile Books
Kirkwood T. (1999) *Time of Our Lives – the science of human ageing* (London) Weidenfeld and Nicholson.

Both these books will challenge you to change the commonly held views of ageing and their impact on society. As always Tom Kirkwood peppers science with common sense. Do not be put off by the title of the second book, it is written for the layman and is an engaging read. Both give hope and optimism.

Chapter 2

Trying To Understand It All

A Systems Approach

Everything in the world is connected.

> *Howard Norman, in* The Bird Artist, *1994*

The start of systems thinking is the ability to see something from somebody else's point of view.

> *West Churchman, Professor of Business Administration*

In this chapter we look at the problems created for managers and staff of health and social services by quick fixes and shifting blame. It is suggested that looking at the care of older people from a systems perspective will release managers and staff from the 'command and control' model of management which has failed to meet complex demands. The chapter considers how it is the spaces between the structures where interaction and creativity grow, and gives examples and metaphors to help clarify the systems concept.

The care of older people does indeed seem to be in a fine mess. Everybody is trying very hard to remedy the situation and make things work better. Everybody is pushing against the apparent barriers to make things work better. There is no lack of commitment on anybody's part; yet it is not unusual to hear managers say that they do not understand what is going on. They create more capacity by making more beds available. They hire more staff and bring in problem solvers such as bed managers and discharge co-ordinators. They introduce new concepts, such as intermediate care, to cure the ills of the system in the hope, perhaps, that this will be a panacea. Yet things seem no better; and in some respects are becoming worse.

Unfortunately, much of what has has been done has been quick fixes and short-term solutions to what are long-term problems. Combined with this is an element of fear that is generated when managers' necks are on the block to provide short-term political solutions. They have been told to get their act together without any guidance as to how this is possible: the analogy of the depressed person being told to pull himself together springs to mind. This fear has seemingly paralysed objective thinking and, together with diktats from above, has frozen innovation and any ability to understand the underlying problems. Each problem is viewed as discrete and not related to any other. As a consequence, they are managed separately, often providing solutions that are not consistent with overall goals.

It is human nature to reduce problems to their component parts and then produce isolated solutions. Although superficially logical, this mechanistic approach prevents insight into the connectedness of the parts and the realization that the solutions are most often not within the problem area itself but outside it. To see the connectedness it is necessary to see the parts as a whole system and understand what connects the parts and keeps them connected. In other words, 'the system'. This ability to view things as systems and understand how systems behave is the key to solving the conundrum that faces the care of older people at the present time.

This ability to view things as systems and understand how systems behave is the key to solving the conundrum that faces the care of older people at the present time.

The word *system* is much used and frequently abused. But it is an important word which is impossible to replace easily. A definition of a system is something that maintains its existence and functions as a whole through the interaction of its parts (O'Conner and McDermott 1997). For instance, if the problem was to provide healthcare in a sheltered housing complex for older people then the parts would include the older person, the warden, the community nurse, chiropodist, community physiotherapist, housing manager, and many more besides. What connects them is their shared purpose, the networks by which they communicate with each other and the benefits to themselves and the older person. This system works within its own 'virtual' or metaphorical boundary. Those people, organizations and structures that lie outside the boundary are termed as being in the 'environment'. However, they may well have very important influences on the systems. For example, in Figure 2.1, residential homes may not be part of the system of care in sheltered accommodation (i.e. they are in the 'environment'), but they may have an important impact on the system because they decide who they will accept as residents coming from sheltered accommodation.

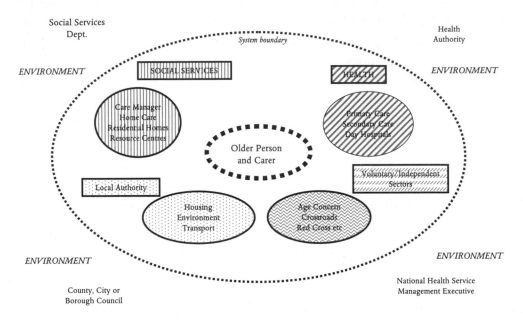

Figure 2.1 Systems map of integrated care

If the problem changes, then so must the constituent parts and connections within the system, as well as its boundaries. One of the important skills of the systems manager is to understand who needs to be included in the system, how to manage the connections and how to define and manage the boundaries. A responsibility of the manager is to look outside the system, across the boundaries, to see how the environment may affect the system. This may be through changes in legislation, the commissioning of services, external quality standards and the availability of skilled staff amongst others. In multi-agency care, one of the major challenges is how processes and people cross boundaries and how one system is connected to another.

> *In multi-agency care, one of the major challenges is how processes and people cross boundaries and how one system is connected to another.*

One system will often be connected to another: the system of care in sheltered housing is connected to the system of care in residential homes. These systems then also become subsystems of a larger system, that of combined care in both sheltered housing and residential homes. Systems can be viewed rather like a Russian doll, where one system is within another and another and yet another. Unravelling them is like stripping the layers of an onion. The skill of those managing care is the ability to envisage mental models of the systems and to understand them. The integrity and sustainability of a particular system relies on the involvement of these other system layers. As a rule of thumb, the direct interaction is with two system levels up and two levels down. (e.g. a level 3 social work practitioner will interact directly with his team manager and with the manager of the area office; he will also interact with social work assistants and the team clerk).

Addressing new problems with old systems has been a major source of the current vicious cycle within health and social care. Just tweaking the old system is never enough. If boundaries have not changed, if there is no new purpose and if there are no new parts, it is not a new system.

Defining the problem

Understanding the problem is the key to providing the solution. Frequently the symptom is viewed as the underlying problem, whereas it is only the manifestation of that problem. The older women lying on trolleys in the accident and emergency departments are seen as the problem at the time of admission – remember Emily. Solutions to that problem might include redefining the trolley as a bed, creating more trolley space, or trying to process admissions faster through the system.

These knee-jerk responses do not solve the real problem. The questions to be asked are: Why is Emily on the trolley, why has she been waiting such a long time and why are her needs not being met? Is it because some crisis has arisen and she cannot be cared for at home? If it is, then why has the crisis arisen? Perhaps it is because no one was truly aware of her condition and that she was at risk. Why was no one aware? The answer might be that nobody knew anything about her. This begs the question why. The answer to that could be that there was no assessment process that triggered access to care before her situation became one of crisis. From this analysis, the apparent 'trolley delay' problem can be seen to be really the root problem of a lack of knowledge of the older person on the trolley. Without this knowledge good early decisions cannot be made and crises prevented.

To be able to analyse problems like this, it is necessary to approach them within the context of a system. Whatever started the sequence of system failures is the real problem.

Sometimes, is not easy to identify the problem because of the way that systems are structured and relate to each other. This lack of clarity makes it difficult to see which system should be changed. For example, a well-documented problem for managers of hospital waiting lists is that of patients booked for pre-planned procedures having to be turned away on the day of treatment. This is because the hospital beds they need are also used for emergency care, and the two systems of planned and emergency care are very different. The waiting list system assigns a predicted length of stay to patients with known conditions who are to have predetermined procedures. Thus the demand is to a large extent predictable. By contrast, the emergency system is very unpredictable, in numbers, nature of the emergency and length of stay. Managing both systems together as one system, as often happens, makes *everything* unpredictable. It causes the previously predictable people on waiting lists to become unpredictable and less easy to manage. What is more, if they are kept on the waiting list long enough they in turn may become emergencies. The anxiety of being turned away may increase the risk of complications. Separating these two systems and managing them in different ways would benefit both systems.

The intuitive reaction of most people to a problem is to look for 'cause and effect'. When this involves individuals, and things are going wrong, the natural reaction is to apportion blame. Now the person becomes the problem. However, it is the system that should be examined, and focusing on the person diverts managers from looking into the real underlying causes. Systems thinking not only puts the 'blame culture' into perspective but will also create the solutions. Too often, people managing or working in the system are viewed as the problem. But 'firing and hiring' will rarely provide a solution to systemic problems.

> *Too often, people managing or working in the system are viewed as the problem. But 'firing and hiring' will rarely provide a solution to systemic problems.*

Another outcome of thinking mechanistically rather than systemically is assigning an inappropriate cause to an effect. The tendency is to look for something that has happened recently (and is therefore easily recalled) to be the cause of an effect. For example, the reason Emily is lying on the trolley in A&E may be ascribed to the immediate lack of beds rather than the lack of assessment that should have taken place weeks, if not months, before. In people's minds the delay in response can disconnect the cause from the eventual outcome. There is a danger that long-term problems and benefits are ignored in favour of short-term political solutions.

Systems and behaviour

Understanding of the way that systems behave will give further insight into what is going on around us. This insight will allow the design of better systems of care.

The behaviour patterns of systems are fairly predictable and are the result of two major systemic dynamic forces. The first is the *reinforcing loop*, the second is the *balancing loop*.

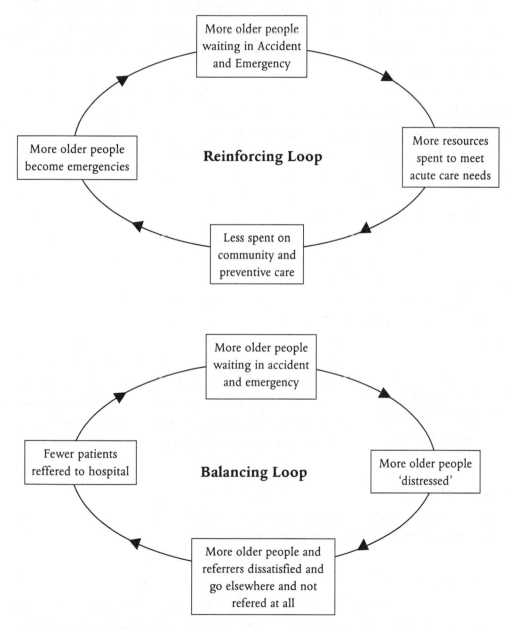

Figure 2.2 Reinforcing and balancing loops

The reinforcing loop will exponentially increase or decrease the outcomes of systems process. An example of the reinforcing loop (in the case of Emily on the trolley in A&E) might be that more resources are used to bolster the facilities and staff in the A&E department. This would leave less for community care. Fewer and fewer assessments can then be done. As a result even more older women would be sent to A&E for emergency care where they would have to be kept lying on trolleys. A similar model around the pressures on nursing home beds could be that more of the budget is spent on providing nursing home places and less on community care. This would result in more need for nursing home places thus reinforcing the pressures and stresses on the nursing home system.

The second systemic dynamic force is the balancing loop. The balancing loop generates forces of resistance that tend to counteract the underlying processes. It is a way in which the system regulates itself to avoid it getting out of control. There are many examples in human physiology and nature of these balancing loops. One is the way that glucose in the blood is very finely controlled to provide a balance between those processes that produce sugar and those that use it or store for future use. An example from the care environment might be that by increasing the number of day centre places to relieve pressure on residential care demand for those places may be so stimulated that they are quickly filled and the pressures on residential care return. To improve that situation the underlying reasons for the demand need to be addressed. In the fullness of time all new systems develop balancing loops and stabilize themselves.

One of the most important lessons to be drawn from the impact of these loops is that whenever new capacity is created new systems to manage the demand have to be put in place as well. Demand can create both reinforcing and balancing loops for capacity. Put another way, the availability-of-care system has two subsystems, that of available capacity and another of the levels of demand.

> *Whenever new capacity is created new systems to manage the demand have to be put in place.*

Systems archetypes

Of the dozen or so system behaviour models that exist, four or five account for most of the common behaviour patterns of systems.

Fixes that backfire

This is an archetype where there is tension between the results of a short-term solution and the long-term needs of the system. Junior doctors' hours is an example.

These were reduced by creating larger teams working for shorter periods. The objective was to reduce the number of hours worked to create more time for sleep and recovery as well as for improved training. It was hoped this would result in enhanced morale. However, there had been no change in the volume of work. If anything it increased, and it certainly became more demanding through greater use of technology and the need for new expertise. The reduction in continuity of care, the increased numbers of handovers and not being able to follow each patient through produced even more stress. The result was that junior doctors (though their hours were shorter) had to work even harder ending up just as tired and stressed. They had little opportunity to be trained or to learn. Research had shown that stress was not necessarily related to hours worked but to lack of sleep, poor diet and not having their work appreciated. It was important that their fear of mistakes was addressed and their training needs met (Firth-Cozens 1987). As a consequence, they were less satisfied and more left the profession. So those remaining had even more pressure put on them. The long-term result on the wider system may be that there are even fewer doctors in both the community and the hospitals. This will mean even longer trolley waits for Emily and other older people.

> *Inappropriate solutions create more pressure on the leaders and managers of teams further reducing morale and creating more problems.*

One of the paradoxes of fixes-that-backfire is that those who implement them are frequently aware that such short-term solutions are not going to work. But they are under such pressure that they will always take some action rather than do nothing. These inappropriate solutions create more pressure on the leaders and managers of teams further reducing morale and creating more problems.

To reduce the number of fixes-that-backfire, it is important not only to be aware of the root problem but also to have a systemic view of the problem that will enable appreciation of the scope and size of the impact of the fix. The fewer short-term fixes that are applied at any one time the better. Because everything is connected, the effect of several short-term fixes is multiplied rather than just being additional.

Not all short-term fixes fail and backfire. In systems that are understood, and where longer-term goals have been recognized, quick fixes are sometimes necessary to make the small adjustments required to keep an organization flexible and adaptable to external factors.

The limits to growth

No system can grow for ever. There are always limiting factors that will control its final size. Frequently, the limits to growth are such that the system is unable to fulfill its potential. These limits and the constraints they bring are often caused by other systems. Understanding this can allow them to be minimized to make the system as good as possible. A commonly met example is where community care is expanded and developed to help as many older people as possible stay in their own homes. These new schemes require more staff with new skills. They are not always available, and this limits the amount and type of care that can be delivered. The system that provides the staff is the limiting one to the new system of community care. In this situation recognizing the limiting factor of staff availability is the first step in reducing that as a constraint and so maximizing the potential of this new community initiative. Measures can then be put in place to make more staff available and minimize the limiting effect. Another example is that of managing hospital waiting lists and reducing the numbers of people on them. The temptation, often succumbed to in order to achieve numerical objectives, is to cherry-pick the easy cases first and so achieve early targets. The next time round, all the more difficult cases (those that need more time and skilled staff to deal with them) are left, so fewer can be handled and in the final analysis the goals are not met. The limiting factor is the availability of resources to meet the goal of overall reduction in the waiting lists.

In many limits-to-growth situations the reaction of some managers is to try to push the system even harder to overcome the barriers caused by the constraints. This situation can be recognized when pleas are made for the team to work even harder (and not smarter) or to get more older people through the same number of beds. This rarely works for any sustained period. The aim has to be to remove as many of the constraints as possible and let the system grow to its optimum potential.

> *The aim has to be to remove as many of the constraints as possible and let the system grow to its optimum potential.*

Recognizing the limiting factors through system thinking at an early stage and then managing them so they limit the new system as little as possible is the key to success.

Shifting the burden

This is a very common situation in care services at the moment. It describes how the responsibility for the solution to a problem is transferred from person to person or organization to organization. Often, the person or organization transferring the responsibility does not appreciate that they have themselves caused the problem or at least contributed to it. Nor do they realise that by causing the problem they have the solution within themselves. In such situations one organization then becomes dependent on the other to provide solutions to problems it has itself brought about and over which the latter has little control. This dependency results in addictive behaviour. As in other addictions this behaviour demands quick fixes, most of which backfire and make the problem worse. However, if the quick fix is not provided, the emotional ferment that bubbles up causes blame and bad feeling between them.

The classic example is where older people in hospital are deemed to need nursing home care and social services are expected to provide it instantaneously. To a large degree the responsibility for creating the need for nursing home care for these patients will lie with the hospital itself. In the first place, it encouraged the admission through its emergency care policies. Once in hospital some of the older people are then made dependent by the lack of structured services for them, and when they have been made dependent they cannot easily be discharged back into the community. Social services are unable to meet the needs as quickly as the healthcare system would like and are blamed for a problem that is not of their making. What is worse, the older person is also blamed and labelled a 'bed blocker'. As the problem has been largely caused by the hospital, the solution rests with the hospital also. It must find alternative ways to admit and care for these patients. It must provide specific and improved age-related services. And it must develop partnerships with other organizations such as those in the primary care system. All of these initiatives remain the responsibility of the hospital. Of course, the hospital may want to explore how many of these problems have been shifted to them unnecessarily. They may simply be feeding the addiction of others. But then, such is the way of systems thinking!

An example of shifting the burden on to one person is when, as sometimes happens, a single bed manager or discharge co-ordinator is expected to shoulder the responsibility for both admission and discharge policies. The rest of the clinical team and staff stand back and expect them to do this, even though they themselves are key players in managing admissions and discharges. The 'addiction' to bed managers and discharge co-ordinators means that the underlying deeper process problems within the ward and hospital do not get addressed. Perhaps it is not surprising that so few of these key staff remain in post for any length of time.

Putting in place solutions to counteract shifting the burden is not easy. It is never easy to persuade people or

> *It is never easy to persuade people or organizations who perceive they have a problem that it may be of their own making!*

organizations who perceive they have a problem that it may be of their own making! Again, the start has to be to understand the root problem that underlies the situation, how it is being created and who 'owns' the problem.

It is then necessary to persuade the 'owners' that they can become the solvers of their own problem. They then go from being dependent and addictive to being independent and able to solve their own problems. If they are sufficiently mature in their attitudes they will realize that by working constructively with their partners to solve problems they may create an interdependence which can unleash considerable growth.

Addictive behaviour also puts a limit on growth for each organization. To manage it takes time, understanding and a tight grasp on long-term goals and objectives. There are very few people and organizations who, given the right amount of fear and moral and professional pressure, will not revert to dependency and defensive behaviour.

A historical parallel: The tragedy of the commons

In the Middle Ages it was customary for villagers to graze their cattle on common land that was jointly owned. If there were only a few cattle there would be plenty of grass to fatten them all. But the temptation to put more cattle on the free common land was great. Consequently there was soon not enough grass to go round. The poorly fed cattle became undernourished and diseased, and in some cases died. With hindsight, fewer cattle grazing would have been better for everybody. This is a situation replicated in many systems today.

In its own way the accident and emergency department (with its attendant Emilys) is also a common. It is an area shared by the primary care physicians, the patients they send there and the hospital staff who use it as a reception centre and for initial treatment. With everybody using it for their own purposes, the resources are stretched to breaking point; and, when the reinforcement loops provide even more patients, the emergency department bursts its seams.

Community care could also be considered a possible 'tragedy of the commons'. Social services will use it to try to keep older people at home; not only because that is where older people want to be, but in order to reduce the number going into long-term nursing care. Pressure from hospitals and families to discharge older people back into the community also puts demands on social services. This shared use of community care may jeopardize both hospital and social care and cause the systems to crash to everyone's detriment.

> *There is a collective responsibility for all of those involved to find a solution.*

Facing up to the 'tragedy of the commons' entails getting everyone to understand the structures and processes that have brought this about, and to acknowledge that there is a collective responsibility for *all* of those involved to find a solution and that this process should include the older people themselves. Viewing this through the lenses of the other systems archetypes ('fixes-that- backfire', and 'limits-to-growth' and 'shifting the burden') and sharing responsibility will help unravel the problem and turn it around to the 'common' good.

Accidental adversaries

One of the facts of life is that two people or two organizations with a lot to gain from working closely together often become adversaries when the original intent was to co-operate as closely as possible and help each other. As in a marriage, it is very easy to make promises and statements of intent but more difficult to live them out. Stories abound of senior managers of separate organizations, sharing difficult situations, having heated arguments. And because each is an independent agent they may not understand the deep-seated needs of the other. This lack of shared understanding of the other's culture and beliefs (together with poor communication) causes them to develop separately, identifying only their own needs. In a 'tragedy of the commons' situation where there is competition for scarce resources, one party will accuse the other of intentionally obstructing their processes of care even if this was not intended by the other party in the first place.

When a social worker says that he won't work within the medical model and a nurse claims that a social work model is vague and indeterminate they, too, are acting as accidental adversaries. It requires all the skills of emotional intelligence to counter this adversarial situation. (The reader might like to read more on the concept of emotional intelligence: see *Working with Emotional Intelligence* by David Goleman (1998).) It is fundamental that the parties are made to understand each other's point of view and are able to put themselves in the other's shoes. To develop a common goal it is important to start by respecting the goals of the partner person or organization. A shared purpose built on common values and an openness of communication are essential ingredients in the solution.

Complex adaptive systems

Understanding how systems behave is important because no matter how well systems are designed, the nature of system structures will tend to allow people to revert almost as a default position to mechanistic and defensive behaviour patterns when they are stressed. It is a common experience that at workshops, often conducted in pleasant surroundings with few pressures, people find it easy to agree to joint working. But when they return to their bases, the everyday competing pressures are so great that all the good intentions fly out of the window and defensive behaviour becomes the norm again. However, if systems could be designed to minimize these adverse and limiting behaviour patterns then there would be a much greater chance of successful outcomes.

Current systems of care are very complex and easily change in subtle ways over which we appear to have no control. Yet there are many systems in nature and human physiology that demonstrate that complexity can be managed for mutual benefit. In the human body the brain, heart, kidneys, bones and muscles are are all structurally and functionally very different. Each works independently, but in co-operation, for the mutual benefit of the whole. They are connected by an intricate network of nerves and chemicals that send and receive messages to co-ordinate their separate functions. They have a common purpose: the survival, reproduction and fulfilment of their corporate structure – the human body. Another example in nature is the tropical rainforest. It teems with plant life and animals that live separately, yet they support each other so that each survives through their interrelationships. Changes in one subsystem will change the balance of the whole. Removing the trees will alter the micro-environment and cause many of the plants and animals to die and the whole system to crash. Each part is interdependent on the other.

Social systems are complex systems also. A family may have grandparents, parents and children, all with differing needs and all performing different roles but with a shared vision of being a family and providing a support network for each other. A sheltered housing complex may be an even more complex system incorporating the older resident, their carers and families, the housing department or housing association, a warden and an alarm system, the carers from the social services department, private domestic help and a variety of healthcare workers.

Apart from their complexity, these systems are also adaptive. Often they can change independently of each other to meet any challenges that the whole system of care faces.

With these examples in mind, we can define a complex adaptive system as a collection of individual agents all of which have the freedom to act in ways that are not always totally predictable, and whose actions are interconnected such that one agent's actions change the context for other agents. Other characteristics of complex adaptive systems are that their processes are non-linear, unlike machines, which tend to have linear processes. In complex adaptive systems small changes may have very big effects, both for better and for worse. For example, it only takes a relatively small proportion of the older people admitted to hospital to bring that hospital to a standstill if they are unable to be discharged. In complex adaptive systems it is not possible to predict and forecast in detail because of the non-linear structures. However, it is possible to know in broad terms the direction and purpose of the system.

> *In complex adaptive systems small changes may have very big effects, both for better and for worse.*

Changing a complex system means changing numerous things at once. This can only be done by several teams all instigating small changes that combined will have a major impact on the whole system. Another characteristic of such systems is that they are self-organizing and, when they start interacting, new behaviours emerge, some of which are unpredictable. To move the complex system forward, a series of small changes almost in the form of an experiment need to take place at the edges where the old meets the new, where stability is on the verge of instability.

♦ Organizations are not machines

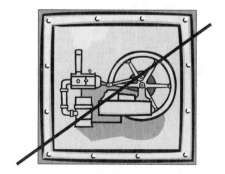

♦ mostly they are complex adaptive systems (CAS)

MACHINE =   *maximum* specification
             elimination of variation

CAS =   *minimum* specification
             purposeful variation

Figure 2.3 Contrasting machines and complex adaptive systems

Another characteristic of complex systems is that they produce 'attractors'. These are parts of the system that will naturally draw in energy from other parts of the system to create change. An often quoted example is that of the stone and the bird. Suppose that you wished to throw a stone at a target some distance away. This is a mechanistic process. The inanimate stone has no variable influence of its own and, given a skilful thrower, it will hit the target. However, if the stone were changed for a bird there would be an entirely different outcome: the bird would almost certainly fly off in the opposite direction under its own will when thrown. So how can the bird be got to the target? An obvious way would be to find something that attracted the bird so that it spontaneously flew there. That might be some corn to feed on, or possibly a bird of the opposite sex. The corn or the other bird is the attractor which brings the bird and its energies to the target.

This has important potential consequences in understanding how to manage change in a complex system. The independent agents in a complex system cannot be forced to change unless very threatened, but they can be persuaded to change if there is sufficient attractiveness in the change process to benefit them. Put simply, they will ask 'What is in it for us?' The manager of complex system change will ensure that there are always sufficient attractors for all the independent parties in the change process and so forestall much of the resistance to change.

All this has major implications for the way that systems are managed. It means letting go and trying not to figure it all out with every possible detail. The traditional command-and-control systems are too constraining. When designing new systems of care it means that not every activity requires detailed specification. Broad indicators will do. The inherent adaptability of the various parts will provide the detail that cannot be planned for. The new system emerges from the self-organizing and creative properties of complex adaptive systems.

Table 2.1 Emerging principles of extended scientific management

When you find yourself frustrated at the way things are and your past attempts to change them...

Principle	*Statement*	*Contrast*
New Metaphors	Look to complexity and living science metaphors...	...in addition to traditional machine metaphor.
Simple rules	Work with the notion that complex outcomes can emerge from good enough vision and minimum specifications...	...instead of always trying to plan out and guide things in great detail.
Appropriate clockware/ swarmware	Become comfortable using varying degrees of certainty and agreement to choose clockware when appropriate, and swarmware when appropriate...	...instead of fearing that chaos is the only alternative to planning and control.
Tuning from within	Learn to tune the complex adaptive systems you exist within by varying diversity, boundries, coupling, information flow, power differentials, anxiety, and the mix of cooperation and competition...	...instead of acting aloof and trying to 'kick the machine' to get it to work.
Non-linear change points	See paradox, tension, and seeming impossibilities as perhaps your best opportunity for real change...	...rather than avoiding and smoothing over these.
Exploring the environment	Launch many diverse experiments, reflect on what is happening, and keep moving in those directions that seem successful...	...instead of trying to figure out the 'one best way.'
Natural attractors and flows	Recognize and try to find ways to work with natural networks (e.g. cliques, rumor mill) and natural energy (what people seem drawn to) within your organization...	...rather than always relying on formal structures and programs.

From Zimmerman, Lindberg and Plsek (1998, p.44) with permission.

Many managers and professionals who put great faith in the traditional command-and-control methods can be critical of the apparent looseness of the change process in complex systems. They still believe that change can be controlled up front. Even though the complex system methodology seems to give untold freedom and appears random, it is in other ways very tight. Provided there are shared values, a genuine commitment to a common purpose and an evaluation and reporting system that gives feedback, the discipline in the system is self-discipline rather than an enforced discipline (Wilson and Holt 2001).

Put another way, 'feed-forward' (that is, up-front instructions) can never be as flexible and adaptable as 'feed-back' from which changes can be made. And it is feedback from which changes can readily flow. For instance, in the EPICS project (which was managed along the lines of complexity) the high standards set were met, project timetables were kept to, and at no time was the budget overspent.

Sometimes thinking through the complex ideas of complex systems can be difficult if we use normal 'machine-like' cause-and-effect language. The use of stories and metaphor is a useful way of describing and talking through complex ideas. The metaphor of the jazz band was one used in EPICS to describe some aspects of complex adaptive organizations. The members of any jazz band have a common purpose in wanting to play music together to please either an audience or themselves. They will play the same piece in the same key to agreed rhythms and they will start and finish together. But within this framework they have a chance to play independently and creatively. At the same time they support each other so that the piece works as a whole. The result is that the music is always changing and yet always giving pleasure. These jazz musicians have created some simple rules which they apply every time they play to allow creative and entertaining music. Simple rules are common to all complex adaptive systems.

Paradoxically, simple rules, all applied together, create the complex patterns of care that are needed to build a framework for a practical plan. A further example of simple rules in action is the complex traffic system of motorways. Here, the simple rules include access only for certain types of vehicle, overtaking on the right, slower traffic to keep to the left and all to keep within given speed limits. This accommodates an enormous variety of vehicles, driving to a large number of destinations, at various speeds using differing amounts of fuel and different schedules. By the same token it is possible to develop simple rules for the health and social care of older people which allow complexity to be handled and the complicated world of older people to be managed. (See chapter 3, p.84 on implementation models for the simple rules.)

> *It is possible to develop simple rules for the health and social care of older people which allow complexity to be handled.*

Does this mean that mechanistic ways of thinking and planning have to be totally abandoned? Certainly not. For predictable situations (such as a hip replacement) a predictable clinical pathway is extremely appropriate. Also, when evaluating aspects of complex systems, it may be appropriate to analyse them mechanistically. For example, it may be entirely appropriate to know the readmission rates after discharge or how much a particular intervention costs financially. However, if the evaluation is done on a multidimensional model then it can *reflect* complexity, even though each dimension may itself be simplistic and mechanistic.

As discussed above, there is a multiplicity of system frameworks and archetypes and even systems experts can philosophize for years (and they do) about how they all relate. If any one of the frameworks involves complexity then the whole systems framework must be complex, and moving between them requires adaptability. In EPICS a simple and pragmatic approach enabled the relationships to be partly understood and worked with. Another metaphor used was an elastic bag (the complex adaptive system) which attracted other systems into it. Some of these were linear, others multidimensional. It was possible to work with the whole bag or individual system parts within it. The elasticity of the complex adaptive system (the bag) kept everything within it in touch and connected, and the bag changed shape and became larger or smaller.

Managing the spaces

> *Bamboo's strength comes from its hollow stems. A cup is made of both bottom and sides. But its use lies in its emptiness.*
>
> Lao Tzu (6th century BC)

How can spaces be managed? Is this yet another paradox associated with complexity? In the EPICS project this concept was developed latterly to help people with getting things connected. Traditionally, managers and professionals have tended to focus on structures, buildings, people and guidelines, but complex systems rely more on relationships and interactions than on physical attributes only. As in physics, it is what you don't see that is important: the magnetism that pulls things together and the gravity that stops everything spinning off disjointedly into some unknown space. This metaphor of spaces is important as it defines the spaces in a complex adaptive system as compartments in which things happen. And what occurs in the spaces cannot be left to chance if the project is to survive and that is:

- a shared purpose based on the underpinning values and vision

- managed communication networks

- common language and definitions

- leadership that facilitates easy flow between the parts

- shared evaluation systems and outcome measures.

Overview

At the heart of shaping new care for old is the skill of being able to think in terms of systems. Systems exist whether they are liked or not. It is systems that have shaped the current patterns of care. It is no longer possible to ignore them and bury our heads in the sand. To understand the current situation it is necessary to review it through the lens of systems thinking. The behaviour of people, and thus systems behaviour, is the nub of the analysis. Even with the more enabling and liberating processes of complex adaptive systems, individuals are free agents within them and they have a habit of reverting to default positions of defensive behaviour whenever threatened with change.

Much can be done to improve the context within which people work, to allow them to express themselves in a more emotionally mature way and thus reduce the chances of reverting to unco-operative and untrusting behaviours. The science of complex adaptive systems methodologies removes many of the constraints on behaviour by fostering co-operation and trust. This is the only way complexity can be managed. The importance of understanding complex adaptive systems is that it makes possible what previously was seemingly impossible. Small changes in several areas at the same time can have, and do have, big impacts on the systems overall. Many of the present problems in health and social care have arisen out of a series of relatively small changes, often 'quick fixes that backfire', which were intended to solve perceived short-term problems. Conversely, small changes for the better appear to have an equally beneficial effect as is shown later in preventive care and the management of emergencies. Systems thinking therefore gives us a framework with which to move forward.

Chapter 2 – Headline points

- The ability to view things as systems and understand how systems behave is the key to solving the conundrum that faces the care of older people at the present time.

- In multi-agency care, one of the major challenges is how processes and people cross boundaries and how one system is connected to another.

- The insights from a systems approach help with the understanding of underlying problems and the design of better care.

- Too often, people managing or working in the system are viewed as the problem. But 'firing and hiring' will rarely provide a solution to systemic problems.

- Whenever new capacity is created, new systems to manage the demand have to be put in place.

- Inappropriate solutions create more pressure on the leaders and managers of teams further reducing morale and creating more problems.

- The aim has to be to remove as many of the constraints as possible and let the system grow to its optimum potential.

- It is never easy to persuade people or organizations who perceive they have a problem that it may be of their own making.

- There is a collective responsibility for *all* of those involved to find a solution.

- In complex adaptive systems small changes may have very big effects for both better and for worse.

- It is possible to develop simple rules for the health and social care of older people which allow complexity to be handled.

References

Firth-Cozens, J. (1987) 'Emotional distress in junior house officers.' *British Medical Journal Clinical Research Edition 259*, 6597, 533–536.

O'Conner, J and McDermott, I. (1997) 'Introduction.' In *The Art of Systems Thinking*. London: Thorsens.

Wilson, T. and Holt, T. 'Complexity and clinical care'. *British Medical Journal 323*, 625–628.

Zimmerman, B., Lindberg, C. and Plsek, P. (1998) Edgeware – Insights from Complexity Science for Healthcare Leaders. : VHA Inc.

Further reading

Skyttner, L. (1996) *General Systems Theory – An Introduction*. London: Macmillan.
An easy, flowing general introduction to systems thinking.
Checkland P. and Scholes, J. (1999) *Soft Systems Methodology*. London: John Wiley & Son Ltd.
Written by the masters of soft systems methodology, it addresses complexity issues through soft systems and gives some very practical applications such as 'rich pictures', which were found to be very useful in EPICS workshops.

Senge, P. (1992) *The Fifth Discipline: The Art and Practice of the Learning Organisation.* London: Century Business.

Senge, P., Kleiner, A., Roberts, C., Ross, R. and Smith, B. (1994) *The Fifth Dicipline Field Book: Strategies and Tools for Building a Learning Organisation.* New York: Doubleday.

Both these books are essential reading. The Fieldbook builds on and expands the basic tenets of systems thinking (the Fifth Discipline), personal mastery, mental models, shared vision and team learning as proposed by Peter Senge. They cover the critical gap between personal and organizational change.

Cohen, J. and Stewart, I. (1994) *The Collapse of Chaos: Discovering Simplicity in a Complex World.* London: Penguin.

Written by a biologist and a mathematician, this book lays out some of the basic principles of complex systems from the natural world.

Stacey, R.D., Griffin, D. and Shaw, P. (2000) *Complexity and Management.* London: Routledge.

The subtitle of this book is 'Fad or Radical Challenge to Systems Thinking?' And it does take a critical and philosophical look at complex systems. The truths from this generalist approach are easily applicable to health and social care.

Zimmerman, B., Lindberg, C. and Plsek, P. (1998) *Edgeware – Insights from Complexity Science for Healthcare Leaders.* Irving, TX: VHA Inc.

This is the only book the authors are aware of that is devoted solely to complexity and healthcare. It is easy to read and understand and is full of practical illustrations, albeit from North America, that are very relevant elsewhere. Its principles can be readily translated to social care. It is a must to read.

CHAPTER 3

Implementation Models

The significant problems we face cannot be solved with the same level of thinking we were at when we created them.

Albert Einstein

In this chapter we describe the process of modelling as one of the tools that can be helpful in understanding and developing systems of care. Six implementation models are presented, based on the experience within EPICS, with diagrams to illustrate the models. The impact on the systems of care and the quality of life of older people is discussed.

The previous chapter explained the importance of thinking systemically. It allows for systemic analysis and understanding of the underlying relationships between structures and the spaces between them. However, to move from an analytical stance to the actual generation of new systems is not easy. There is an enormous practical gulf between an individual understanding and learning about systems thinking and getting groups or teams of people to do the same. Even late on in a project, different perceptions of purpose, process and outcome can emerge in members of the team because they do not share a fully understood common view of the project and its goal. Frequently this is because the concepts and underpinning theories have not been shared and remain in the mind of the originator, champion or leader. In any case, the complexity of many of the issues around older people's care is very difficult to represent and communicate in conventional terms. An important tool that arises out of systems thinking is modelling. This can make some of the underlying tenets and

> *An important tool that arises out of systems thinking is modelling.*

structures more explicit and expose the interrelationship. It also allows these to be shared. Additionally it can test the assumptions and logic and check possible outcomes. A model can be defined as:

> an abstraction, a set of assumptions about some aspect of the world, either real or imaginary, intended to clarify our view of the object, process or problem by retaining only characteristics essential to the purpose we have in mind. It is a simplified conceptual or physical image that may be used to investigate the behaviour of a system or the result of an action without altering the system or taking the action. (Miser, Quade and Wiley 1985, p.119)

An example of such a model is a road map, which is a simplified depiction of the road system showing the relationship of the roads and how to travel between points within the map. If the purpose changes, for example from driving to hiking along footpaths, the model or the map must change either to a completely new map or to include additional information. The map allows directions to be given to others without actually having to take them along the route. The model is relevant to the relationships of the problem or the task being addressed, and as such will not contain data irrelevant to that problem. This may result in a simplification of the reality of the whole system. For example, the driving map may not include information about traffic lights, because the map is about direction and the route to follow and not about driving technique or the highway code or possible holdups on the route.

Models can take many forms and may have differing degrees of complexity. They can range from simple mechanistic models to complex adaptive system models with perhaps a high degree of metaphorical expression. The simpler mechanistic models tend to have a quantitative basis in that they use numbers, calculation and formulae. The classic example is financial modelling. Complex models tend to be more qualitative (to do with qualities and characteristics of things rather than just pure numbers) and are usually expressed graphically or even pictorially. Some situations demand that several types of model are used. For example, planning an assessment centre may be a very complex process with multidisciplinary staff, involving several agencies and multiple assessment tools. The processes may be modelled using graphics, flowcharts, feedback loops and other illustrative aids, but a simpler financial model may be needed as well to assess cost-effectiveness. (See chapter 7, p.237 and p.254 for more on evaluating cost-effectiveness.)

Modelling is often criticised when it depicts only a simplified version of the 'real-world' situation. This may be because the initial questions and problems have not been properly identified or addressed, or because the model cannot provide the answers and a new and different model is needed. However, the strength of models is that they give an understanding of systems and allow further questions to be asked and further models to be generated. This enhances the mind-maps that people generate to help them understand a problem. The process of individuals developing a model together allows these mind-maps to be shared (Miser, Quade and Wiley 1985).

> *The strength of models is that they give an understanding of systems.*

While developing the EPICS project, several implementation models were generated. (See the Introduction, p.13; chapter 6, p.141 and Appendix A, p.354 for a description of the EPICS project.) Some were undertaken prior to the project starting, others were created during the project to help understand what was happening. Modelling is essentially a process of continually reviewing what is happening.

> *Modelling is essentially a process of continually reviewing what is happening.*

Some models need changing and revalidating as the project progresses. New models are needed when the context and goals move on. The models described here are examples which may be of direct use to those already leading integrated projects. Alternatively they may provide a stimulus for the formulation of new models when an initiative is being planned. If they are used directly, it is important not to use them blindly but to ensure that they fit the context and situation for each individual project. There were five main models developed whilst setting up and running EPICS:

- the integrative whole systems model
- the integrative care management model
- the 'valuing the older person' model
- the simple rules model
- the civic model.

The integrative whole systems model

This was the earliest model used in EPICS and was particularly useful in helping with the understanding of the relationship between acute care, rehabilitation and preventive care. It gave insights into minimizing crises and making care situations more manageable. The model can be used in both health and social care settings.

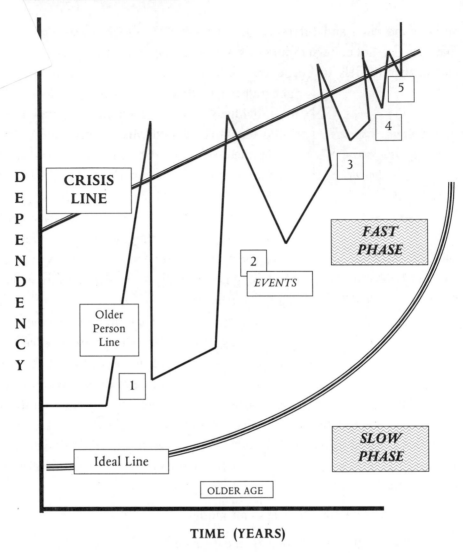

Figure 3.1 The integrative whole systems model

The vertical axis in Figure 3.1 is dependency, which can be measured in whatever units are appropriate to the context. They could relate to function or ability for example. The horizontal axis is time in years, starting at whatever age is considered to be the start of old age. Most people start their later years fit and well, actively involved in their families and communities and enjoying leisure pursuits. This is the 'ideal' older person line on the graph. People can remain like this for 10 to 20 years, only deteriorating when the physiological processes of ageing accumulate and they become increasingly dependent on others. This is irrespective of any disease process that may also be occurring.

However, many people start their old age being more dependent than the 'ideal'. This may be for a variety of reasons: because they have high blood pressure, they smoke, are diabetic, overweight or physically less fit because they take too little exercise, or they may be socially isolated. These people are more likely to have disease-related crises and can become acutely dependent, for example when they have a heart attack (Event 1 on the graph). In this example, the patient recovers (as most of them do) but is not quite as independent as previously, even if only through losing confidence. After a period of time they may then have a stroke (Event 2). On this occasion, they become dependent very quickly and are admitted to hospital remaining there longer. When discharged they are significantly more dependent than before the stroke. Over time, and in part exacerbated by their previous disease, they have a series of clinical events such as chest infections or urinary incontinence which, though less serious in themselves, in an older person with a chronic disability will make them even more dependent (Events 3, 4 and 5).

In the current systems many of the problems arise around the transfer from community systems to hospital systems and back again.

The care of these conditions is divided between acute hospitals and the community. The change from one system of care to another system is considerable and dramatic and may be catastrophic. (for more on this topic see *Catastrophe Theory in Systems Thinking* by Arnold (1998)) In the current systems many of the problems arise around the transfer from community systems to hospital systems and back again. If these are too unpredictable and too many the systems cannot cope and crises occur. Managers ideally would wish to manage the demand so that the systems are as stable as possible and interchanges between them are within the capacity of each of them. The change zone is represented by the crisis line in the model. Below the line are community systems. Above it are the hospital or other institutional systems such as nursing homes.

The model can be used to help think through possible strategies to put sufficient stability into the systems so that they can cope.

Using the model

The model can be used to help think through possible strategies to put sufficient stability into the systems so that they can cope. There are various relationships that can be further modelled to achieve this:

- moving the older person line down
- moving the crisis line up
- reducing the number of critical events.

MOVING THE OLDER PERSON LINE DOWN

If the crisis line remains unaltered in its present position but the older person line is moved downwards (as in Figure 3.2) there will be fewer occasions when incidents cross the crisis line. This will reduce the pressure on the systems. Moving the older person line down can only be achieved if the person becomes less dependent either actually or potentially.

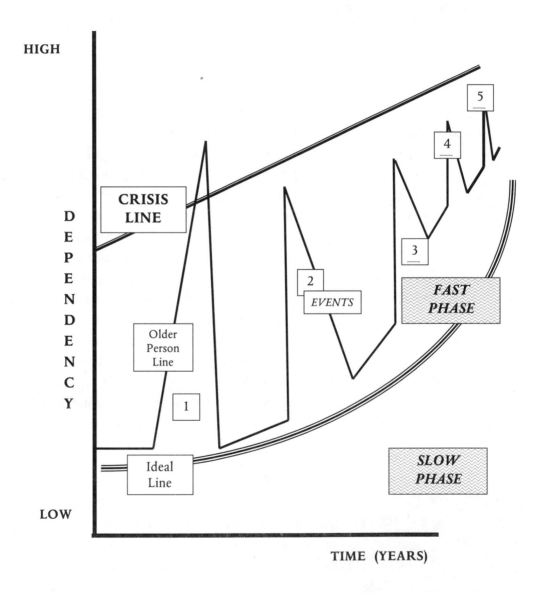

Figure 3.2 Moving the older person line down
Improving health by prevention and promotion at all ages

How can this be brought about? First, older people will need to start their old age fitter and with fewer risk factors. This means that they enter old age with fewer problems or potential problems. This immediately extends the dimensions of the problem: younger people become part of the equation and need to be persuaded to keep fitter to help prevent problems when they are older. Controlling their weight and blood pressure, eating a healthy diet, taking more exercise, stopping smoking and reducing alcohol abuse are all major lifestyle changes that can bring this about. As people get older, these lifestyle measures should be continued. In fact, they may be even more beneficial in old age. Eating a healthy diet with sufficient calcium and taking enough exercise will reduce the risk of osteoporosis; taking exercise has been shown to reduce the risk of falling. Stronger bones and fewer falls should together result in fewer fractures. Reducing malnourishment may improve an older person's immune system, both reducing and helping combat significant infections. Evidence has shown that controlling blood pressure (even in people up to 80 years of age) has a significant impact on reducing the chances of having a stroke (Collins and MacMahon 1994). The National Service Framework Standards 5 (Stroke) and 6 (Falls) emphasize the key importance of preventive programmes.

Good mental health is also important. Poor motivation and depression have been shown to be factors in reducing health in older people. They become less mobile and eat insufficiently thus jeopardizing their physical health. Being able to maintain good relationships and having contact with other people has also been shown to improve morale and probably reduce the incidence of depression (Blanchard 1996).

Exploring the model in this way shows that a whole range of people and systems that might not have been thought of initially need to be directly involved.

Exploring the model in this way shows that a whole range of people and systems that might not have been thought of initially need to be directly involved, for example, health promoters and educators, dieticians, local leisure and arts centres, swimming clubs, and so on. District councils will need to plan for safe streets and housing conducive to maintaining good social relationships, working in partnership with voluntary organizations and housing associations. Prime amongst the needs are transport systems that allow older people to participate in the normal activities of daily living, and giving them access to facilities for an active social life. In fact this whole systems model is stimulating the production of a community lifestyle model!

MOVING THE CRISIS LINE UP

If the crisis line (as in Figure 3.3) is moved up and the older person line with the individual events remains unchanged, fewer older people will cross the crisis line. This will reduce the number of crises and pressures on the person and the care processes as the person moves from one system to the other.

How can this be achieved? The simplest way would be to transfer some of the attributes of the hospital or institutional systems to the community or domiciliary systems. People currently go to hospitals for skills, expertise and the availability of

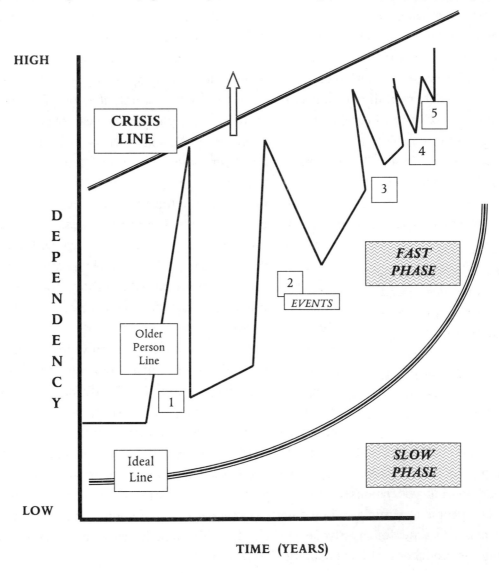

Figure 3.3 Moving the crisis line up
Bringing expertise to the older person in the community

technology that is not present in the community. If some of these were to be trans-ferred to the community, it could cope with the situation without making so many demands on the hospital itself. This could be achieved by training community-based staff in some of the skills and expertise of hospital staff.

Alternatively, bringing hospital staff out of the hospital (possibly on a flexible basis) could also make those skills and expertise available in the community. Similarly, technology could be transferred to the community. For example, dialysis for renal failure can be (and sometimes is) provided in the home. Implanted defibrillators would mean that older people would have certain heart rhythm problems (often potentially life threatening) treated automatically without having to go to hospital. Technical advances such as telemedicine have shown that it is possible to monitor and maintain people at high risk in the community, and that complex treatment programmes (that previously could only be carried out in hospitals) can be under-taken. For example day units, some of which are attached to community hospitals, can frequently provide treatment that previously would have required admission to an acute hospital. (See chapter 12, p.330 on alternatives to admission.) All these measures would reduce the need to cross the crisis line and change from one system to another when an individual emergency occurs.

Considering solutions in this way will naturally raise questions as to how these new services are to be structured. Roles and the networks and communication channels that will be necessary to underpin them will be scrutinized. Ultimately, of course, these considerations will result in designing a new system that will be better able to cope because there will be fewer crises.

REDUCING THE NUMBER OF CRITICAL EVENTS

If the number of critical events is reduced then obviously there will be fewer people likely to cross the crisis line (as in Figure 3.4). Many of the lifestyle and health promo-tion changes proposed above have been shown to cut incidents of heart attack, stroke, fractures and depression, and so reduce critical events. Other ways also exist to help reduce these events. For example, the taking of aspirin by those with known ischaemic heart disease reduces the incidence of heart attacks. Likewise, the use of aspirin by people who have had small strokes or transient ischaemic attacks will reduce not only their occurrence but also probably the number of major strokes. Older people with multiple problems often take multiple medications and may suffer significant side-effects, some of which may result in admission to hospital. Judicious prescription and regular monitoring of prescriptions can significantly reduce the number of critical associated events that are likely to result in crises. Both local and hospital pharmacists can play an important part in achieving this. This is yet another extension of the team concept and the shared skills that need to be incorporated into our systems thinking.

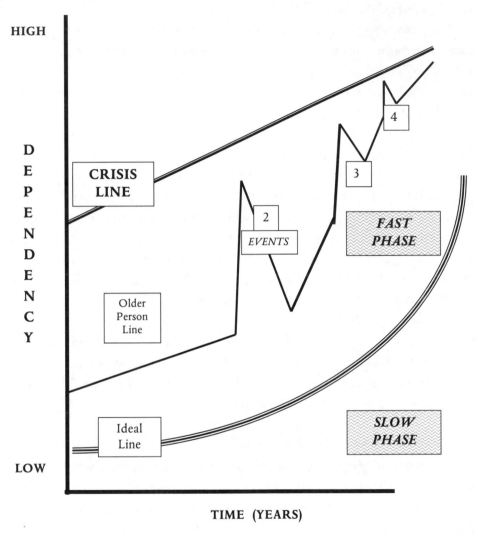

Figure 3.4 Reducing the number of critical events

Summary of the integrative whole systems model

This model demonstrates fairly simply the complex interactions that result in crises. It stimulates consideration of a wide range of solutions, from handling individual critical events to managing the demand on services by preventive health measures and healthy lifestyle changes. The model can also demonstrate to a wide range of organizations and individuals that their skills and resources are important in the system. It

> *This whole systems model demonstrates fairly simply the complex interactions that result in crises.*

may provide solutions which might not be immediately apparent if viewed from only a single professional or departmental point of view. As has been shown, the model invites questions and these will almost spontaneously stimulate the generation of further models which will give new insights into the problems and possible solutions.

The integrative care management model

Having viewed problems from the whole systems perspective there now arises the question of understanding how any necessary changes are to be implemented. Also, who will make the changes and by what methods? This model aims to give a perspective between the individual older person, the care they receive and the population or the care community of which they are a part (see Figure 3.5).

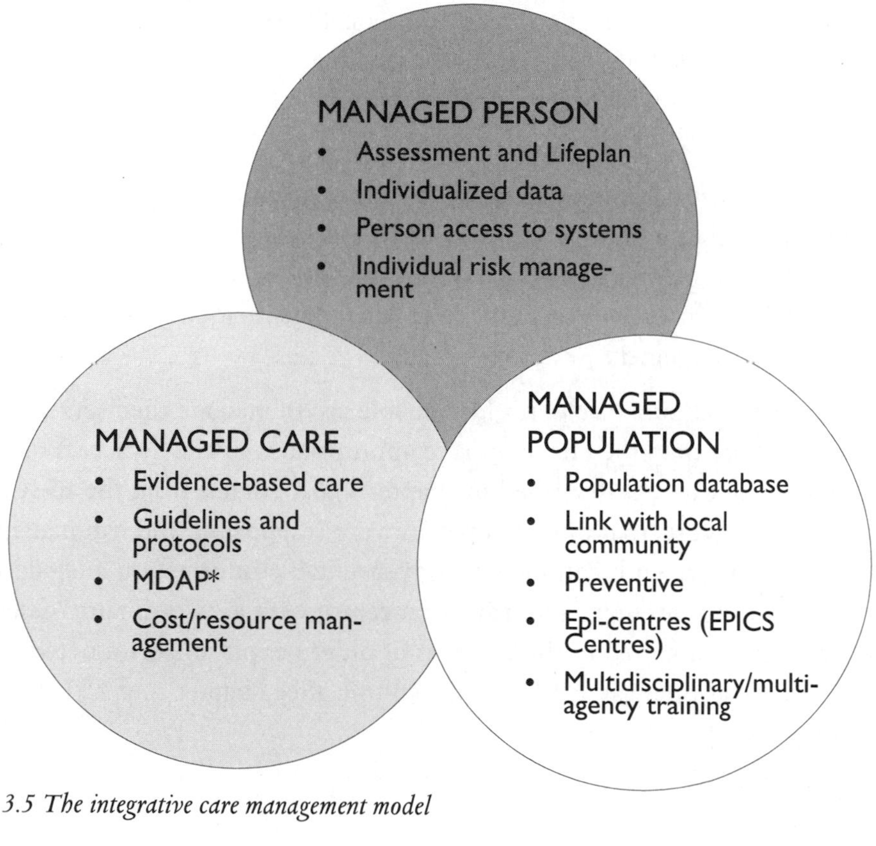

MANAGED PERSON
- Assessment and Lifeplan
- Individualized data
- Person access to systems
- Individual risk management

MANAGED CARE
- Evidence-based care
- Guidelines and protocols
- MDAP*
- Cost/resource management

MANAGED POPULATION
- Population database
- Link with local community
- Preventive
- Epi-centres (EPICS Centres)
- Multidisciplinary/multi-agency training

Figure 3.5 The integrative care management model

* *Multidisciplinary Assessment Panels*

The managed older person

Wherever possible the older person should manage themselves. This concept has to be at the heart of any strategy to combat ageism and develop a person-centred care programme. Some of the principal elements are:

- *Assessment and Lifeplan.*The assessment process, the process that provides knowledge about the individual older person, is at the centre not only of this model but of the whole system of care. It should include: consideration of the way an older person sees themselves spending the rest of their life; the health and social care problems that may be predictable; and the way they would like the end of their life to be managed. (See chapter 4, p.93 on assessment and chapter 13, p.347 on end of life.)

- *Data systems.* Once the assessment has been completed it needs to be filed in such a way that each individual older person can be uniquely recognized. The data should be individualized, and should incorporate as much relevant information from other locality systems to provide the widest possible knowledge of that individual. The older person should be able to interact with this data and provide much of it themself. At the very least they should have knowledge of it.

- *Individual risk.* This knowledge of the older person together with their known wishes and preferences should permit anticipation of likely future events. A large part of managing demand for the whole system is focused around risk management of the individual person. (See chapter 5, p.126 on risk management.)

- *Access to social care systems.* If older people are to manage themselves successfully then they have to have appropriate and timely access to the systems of care. As described in chapter 1, experience from the EPICS project suggests that older people are very responsible and can manage their own care with confidence if given suitable information and support. A one-stop centralized co-ordination centre with a co-ordinator/assessor who was committed to the interests of older people and who networked widely, was one way EPICS achieved this. (See chapter 6, p.151 'Putting it in place'.)

Managed care

> *Only evaluation can provide the feedback that leads to knowledge and improvements.*

It is evident that care processes have to be managed and that the way in which this is done is all-important if high-quality care is to be provided. Too often care is planned and delivered without evaluation. But only evaluation can provide the feedback that leads to knowledge and improvements. The following specific approaches to managing care were found useful in the EPICS project:

- *Designing structures relevant to meeting the needs of the older person.* Frequently, older people are required to use facilities that are inadequate because they are out of date or designed for other purposes or other people. Existing structures lead to processes being duplicated by teams and individuals who do not have the training and skills to carry out what is asked of them. A typical example might be an acute medical ward that does not have the facilities, staff or staff time to look after older people properly. It is not uncommon for older people to be admitted to hospital able to walk, but because the facilities and staff to maintain this level of ability are not available, they become bedbound and are said to require nursing home care. The provision of appropriate accommodation designed for older people's care (with staff motivated and competent to undertake that care) is crucial, whether in hospital or in the community. Multidisciplinary teams and cross-agency panels are all structures through which care for older people can be co-ordinated.

- *Justifying the rationale for planning and delivering particular types of care.* There is an increasing body of evidence in relation to the care of older people which gives guidance on what is useful and effective. Wherever possible the rationale for planning and delivering particular types of care should be justified.

- *Creating guidelines and protocols.* These provide a framework for teasing out the evidence to demonstrate the effectiveness of the care and making the processes available for others to follow. Planning care pathways can be of similar value and can provide consistency of care for some conditions, such as a fractured hip. Frequently, however, the complexities of care for older people make the use of care pathways difficult and not helpful beyond deciding progress through levels of care.

- *Ensuring the cost-effectiveness of the care being delivered.* This is part of the process of managing care. High-quality care should reduce waste and duplication. (See chapter 9, p.249 on evaluation and costing.)

The managed population

One of the underlying tenets of the EPICS project was that the population had to be managed as well as the individual older person. The elements of managing the population were seen to be:

- *Managing a database.* With knowledge of the population it is possible to identify groups within it who have different or special requirements. A prime example is people with different ethnic backgrounds who may have different cultural and physical needs. Knowledge of the total population of older people through a database allows the assessment of the fair distribution of resources. (See chapter 7, p.171 on applying information technology.)

- *Managing the spatial component.* Knowing who people are and where they are allows available services to be related to them effectively. Linking with communities and localities to improve the quality of life of older people is catalytic to providing flexible and innovative services. (See chapters 7, p.178 and p.181 on information systems)

- *Community prevention programmes.* The advantages of proven preventive programmes for the individual older person is self-evident, but their prevalence may be variable. Such programmes delivered through population-based schemes may have a considerable impact on the use of resources and managing demand. An example from a health promotion programme might be that lowering cholesterol levels throughout the population may have little beneficial effect on any given individual, but by encompassing the total population small reductions may have a beneficial effect on overall risk. This may in turn reduce the incidence of heart attacks within the population and relieve pressure on hospitals.

- *Managing risk.* Managing risk for each individual is very important in providing a client-focused service. However, managing risk across the *population* may be the best way of managing the resources and ensuring that they are available for the provision of acute care when an apparently unavoidable crisis does arise. It also gives the opportunity to identify some populations of people at risk. For example those at risk from hypothermia could be identified and then managed specifically to reduce the risk in cold weather.

- *Managing chronic disease populations.* These are also population groups and can be managed corporately with common guidelines and practice for each disease. A register with each one identified should be the backbone of their management. For example, in chronic chest diseases the use of this register and dedicated staff such as a community respiratory nurse could reduce the number of unneccesary admissions to hospital.

- *Training for population-based care.* Experience from the EPICS programme showed the value of training community-based teams in practical and simple population health techniques, such as managing the whole of a case-load rather than individual patients on it. Being able to identify all the carers in a given locality (including family members and other voluntary helpers) aided effective planning for training.

The value of this implementation management model lay in its providing for the implementation of the three important dimensions at the same time: need, demand and the provision of high-quality care. It addressed the complexity of care delivery in relation to the complexity of need.

The 'valuing the older person' model

The power of true involvement of the older person became increasingly apparent.

As the EPICS project developed, the power of true involvement of the older person became increasingly apparent. Involving the older users was initially intended simply to demonstrate respect and to dignify the older person. But over time, and after some early evaluation, the benefits to the systems of care delivery were apparent. Making older people true partners meant that more sensible use was made of resources. This freed up more resources to plough back into the services. The model evolved through trying to understand this interaction and to communicate the process to others.

Several assumptions were made for this model. The first was that most older people want to be as independent and self-sufficient as possible and, wherever appropriate, to be in charge of their own situation. The second was that providing rehabilitation, home improvement and assisted living is cost-effective and fosters the older person's independence. The third assumption was that there was a gradation of dependence from total independence to complete reliance on others. (See chapter 12, p.323 for a fuller discussion of these issues.)

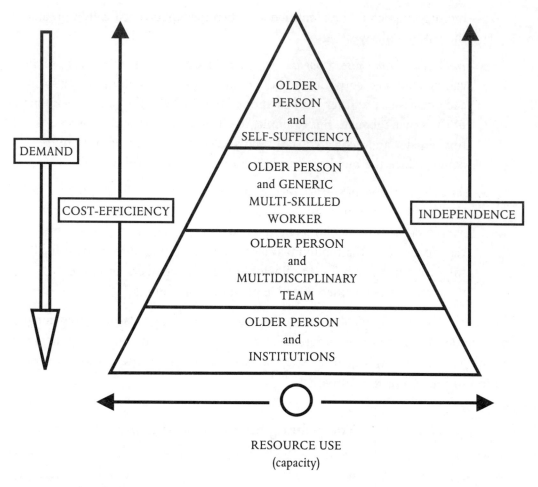

Figure 3.6 Value of 'older person partnership'

Levels of dependence

LEVEL 1: OLDER PERSON AND SELF-SUFFICIENCY

It is often assumed that older people are not self-sufficient and independent. Many of them are, and there is much to learn from them. They seek out information and use it to solve their problems independently. Many make few, if any, demands on the systems of care. They act as their own primary care assessor and co-ordinator. For example, if they have a headache they will diagnose and make their own prognosis by saying that if it is not improved within a couple of days they will go to see their doctor. They will undertake their own treatment by buying and taking a simple painkiller. They will reassess themselves to see if they are better or if they need to refer themselves to the doctor. Many do the same with regard to their own home care. If cooking becomes difficult, they buy prepared meals from the supermarket or seek information on home delivery services rather than ask for 'meals on wheels'. Better information, education programmes and support groups might improve their self-care skills even further.

LEVEL 2: OLDER PERSON AND THE GENERIC MULTI-SKILLED WORKER

At this level a multi-skilled generic worker can provide support in a variety of ways to promote re-enablement and rehabilitation. The experience is that many older people can remain independent with a little help and that only relatively low-level skills are required from the support workers to do this. When they have multiple problems they need a range of skills to be available at one time and a multi-skilled generic worker, supported by qualified supervisors, can do this very cost-effectively.

A care worker in an intermediate care system will be multi-skilled and will have the training to support an older person in their own home on discharge from hospital or day hospital. They will also be able to:

- provide personal care and simple nursing needs
- reinforce the prescribed physiotherapy and occupational therapy treatment programmes
- carry out ongoing assessment.

LEVEL 3: OLDER PERSON AND THE MULTIDISCIPLINARY TEAM

This is where a single multi-skilled worker cannot provide all the support needs. These have to be met by a team of more skilled professionals at obviously greater resource cost. For example, an older person may require highly skilled rehabilitation and have a nursing need such as a leg ulcer. There may also be a need for adaptions in the home, or financial advice.

LEVEL 4: OLDER PERSON AND INSTITUTIONS

This is where the older person requires help from a complex organization. This organization may be a hospital, nursing home or residential home where the costs are likely to be higher, although not always so. When the cost of a care package to keep one older person in their own home exceeds the cost of keeping them in an institution, there may be a perverse incentive to move them into a residential or nursing home, or even hospital. However, inappropriate use of these resources may have a cost to the whole system that is greater than the financial cost.

> *If the older person is inappropriately placed at a higher level of dependency than necessary, it is patently not cost-effective.*

If the older person is inappropriately placed at a higher level of dependency than necessary, it is patently not cost-effective. From the older person's perspective this reduces their independence and the role they play in managing their own care. From the provider's point of view it reduces the availability of complex care for those who genuinely need it. Much of the rationale in home care and step-down and step-up care revolves around these concepts. Moving people to the top level of independence not only improves their quality of life but reduces pressure on care systems and frees up resources for dealing with people with higher dependency levels.

The simple rules model

Complex adaptive systems were described in chapter 2, p.62 and the concept of 'simple rules' was introduced. These simple rules were formulated at a workshop organized by EPICS from the joint experience of 14 teams of people all working on various aspects of integrated care for older people and coming from a variety of care backgrounds (and countries!). The rules were validated against each one of the projects presented at the workshops; subsequently the authors have validated them against other older people's care projects that are working across care boundaries.

The simple rules provide another and most important model for implementation, helping to address the complexity of needs of older people and the complex networks of organizations and systems that meet those needs. The simple rules can be used not only to design systems from the start but also to refine them by acting as a checklist for integrated care projects already in existence. Of all the models that we have used this is probably the most inclusive and all-encompassing for implementation.

> *SIMPLE RULES FOR A BETTER SYSTEM OF CARE*
>
> - *user focus*
> - *networks of care*
> - *easy access*
> - *effective assessment*
> - *avoidance of personal crisis*
> - *easy information flow*
> - *blurred boundaries*
> - *continuous feedback.*

- *User focus.* This involves proactively learning about older people, their carers and community, their needs, values, aspirations, and definition of quality of life. These should drive the systems of care. This does not mean that the professionals can abandon their obligation to educate and develop the skills of older people and the systems.

- *Networks of care.* This means building networks of service that place more emphasis on the older person's needs than on organizational boundaries. It will encompass multidisciplinary learning and planning.

- *Easy access.* This means making access to information, advice and service easy. It should ideally be one-stop, always available when needed and timely and responsive to the older person's requirements. It will also mean easy access for practitioners who are working on behalf of the older person.

- *Effective assessment.* This asserts that rapid, effective and sufficiently detailed assessment systems are in place actually to mobilize services. It is essential that assessment processes are shared appropriately throughout the network of providers.

- *Avoidance of personal crisis.* This is achieved through education and the development of preventive practices that activate intervention and help as early as possible. It is vital not to let things get to crisis point.

- *Easy information flow.* This is produced by creating systems that allow information to flow so easily that once someone in the system of care knows something about an older person, everyone else in the system who needs to know can have access to it. This information will, of course, be within the constraints of agreed protocols on confidentiality. One measure of the success of information flow will be how much the older person knows about their care and its delivery.

The power arising from sharing, with its joint responsibilities and joint access to a diverse range of skills, is very strong.

- *Blurred boundaries.* This involves finding ways to share budgets, resources and ways of working to blur current organizational boundaries within legal and statutory constraints. The power arising from sharing, with its joint responsibilities and joint access to a diverse range of skills, is very strong and should lead to innovative and creative solutions.

- *Continuous feedback.* This is essential to sustain a dynamic system. Building in evaluation and feedback loops to review the whole system continually permits flexibility of practice in both creating and containing change.

Apart from helping to design and implement systems the simple rules can be used as part of the evaluation system. Each simple rule could be used as one of the dimensions in a multidimensional evaluation system, thus completing the feedback loop. (See chapter 9, p.238 for more on evaluation.)

The civic model

As EPICS evolved over the first four or five years it became apparent that many of the teams were no longer working solely within their unitary professional models of care.

> *A unifying, superordinate model of care which encompassed the whole system and reflected some of the relationships of those involved was required.*

The medical team was assuming some of the role of the social worker and the social worker some of the responsibilities of the medical team. Moreover, the skills in truly involving the older person were developing throughout, and none of the professional models current at the time included the older person as an equal. The whole process of care had become even more complex as the other local government agencies, the voluntary sector and finally the community became involved.

A unifying, superordinate model of care which encompassed the whole system and reflected some of the relationships of those involved was required. It also had to reflect the complexity and the totality of all those involved and the adaptive way the teams were now working. This new model was to include the current unitary professional models and not just replace them. This was partly because it was too professionally threatening for people to let go of them completely, even if it were legally possible, but also because their very diversity was a strength to the professional relationships and the older person's care. In fact, now it had to be expanded to include other models from the voluntary sector and the community, even if these were not always explicit. They all needed to be sitting fairly comfortably within a unifying system or model. In other words, a civic model. This is not to say that tensions did not exist within the civic model, but it provided a safe environment in which they could be constructively and positively addressed.

The civic model was based on the following assumptions:

- that the older person had a responsibility for their own well-being, and in accepting this executed a responsibility to the community

- that the local community had a responsibility to the older person not only to enable them to fulfil their personal goals but also to provide care and support to ensure that quality standards of care were met

- that care was based on communities that provided mutual support through the residents, local companies, spiritual groups, voluntary and professional organizations and local councils

- that there was a community network that could create and maintain the shared values that were made explicit

- that there was equitable access to appropriate care for all in the community irrespective of age, gender, disability or ethnicity.

The civic model as described here evolved from working practices rather than shaping them from the start. But it was useful as a mental model to develop our joint working further. (See chapter 8, p.201 for examples of the civic model.)

Overview

The evolution of these models was an iterative process that was found to be most helpful in creating integrated working across organizational boundaries. The models provided mind-maps that could be shared to develop a common understanding. Like all models, these have tended to simplify reality so that it can be understood while still allowing for complexity. All of these models could be developed further but, if used by others, need to be validated for the context in which they are to be used.

Chapter 3 – Headline points

- The strength of models is that they give an understanding of systems.

- Modelling is essentially a process of continually reviewing what is happening.

- In the current systems many of the problems arise around the transfer from community systems to hospital systems and back again. An important tool that arises out of systems thinking is modelling.

- The model can be used to help think through possible strategies to put sufficient stability into the systems so that they can cope.

- Exploring the model in this way shows that a whole range of people and systems which might not have been thought of initially need to be directly involved.

- Only evaluation can provide the feedback that leads to knowledge and improvements.

- The power of true involvement of the older person became increasingly apparent.

- If the older person is inappropriately placed at a higher level of dependency than necessary, it is patently not cost-effective.

- The power arising from sharing, with its joint responsibilities and joint access to a diverse range of skills, is very strong.

- A unifying, superordinate model of care which encompassed the whole system and reflected some of the relationships of those involved was required.

References

Blanchard, M. (1996) 'Depressive Illness.' In S. Ibrahim and A. Rilach (eds) *Epidemiology in Old Age.* London: British Medical Journal Publishing.

Collins, R. and MacMahon, S. (1994) 'Blood pressure, anti-hypertensive treatment and the risks of stroke and of coronary heart disease.' *British Medical Bulletin 50,* 272–298.

Miser, H.J., Quade, E.S. and Wiley, C.E. (eds) (1985) *Handbook of Systems Analysis: Vol. 1. Overview of Uses, Procedures and Practice.* Chichester: John Wiley & Son.

Further reading

Arnold, V.I. (1998) *Catastrophe Theory.* New York: Springer Verlag.

Senge, P., Kleiner, A., Roberts, C., Ross, R. and Smith, B. (1994) *The Fifth Discipline Fieldbook: Strategies and Tools for Building a Learning Organisation.* New York: Doubleday

This book gives some useful examples of modelling, particularly some of the 'flight simulator models' using computers to act out scenarios of complex interactions in business and service settings.

Chapter 4

Assessment

Getting to Know the Older Person

Single assessment is about working together – it is not the bit of paper.
Joan Elliott, Senior Social Services Manager,
Buckinghamshire Social Services

An exercise in imaginative empathy is important for approaching the assessment tasks
in a spirit of humility. One cannot capture the essence of a human being through a
standardised assessment tool, and it is the height of hubris to imagine one can.
Rosalie Kane (Kane and Kane 2000)

In this chapter we look at assessment as a complex process which builds the knowledge base about individual older people and populations of older people. This knowledge should result in focused, high-quality care to individuals and good community-based preventive and risk-reduction programmes. The chapter emphasizes the importance and value of involving the older person in all stages of the assessment process. It also stresses the tension for practitioners between conforming to a standardized system and their wish to use their independent professional judgement. We suggest that this is the most appropriate way to gain their commitment to a sustainable assessment process. The chapter discusses the selection and use of assessment tools as a way of facilitating the implementation of an assessment process.

It may be surprising that, despite their complexity, there are only three core processes in both health and social care – assessment, treatment and care. Though there are myriad other processes they all fall under one or other of these three major headings.

This is suggestive of complex adaptive systems behaviour and it is likely that some simple rules can be derived.

- *Assessment.* This is the process of enquiry that provides information from which decisions are made and action may be taken. Though assessment is often thought of as a social term, in its broadest meaning it includes clinical diagnosis.

- *Treatment.* This is the process whereby some transaction takes place to alter the condition of the older person, usually following some form of assessment. The term has a strong medical implication but again in a wider sense, it involves giving attention to people's needs, and this would certainly fit with a social context.

- *Care.* This is the process whereby concern is expressed and shared, people are looked after and considerations about safety are made. It is more than just the physical act of looking after someone.

Of these three core processes it is logical to implement the assessment process before the other two. The cultural issues and practical implementation are very similar to those of the other processes and once they have been addressed in assessment it may then be easier to implement the other processes. The complexity of the assessment process is very real, particularly if it is applied in a truly holistic manner. There are numerous stakeholders involved and many contextual situations to be considered.

The assessment process has grown out of the current systems of opportunistic and reactive care. Because of this it is often perceived as a 'one-off' exercise that involves an individual person and an individual practitioner. It is like one person taking a snapshot of another, whereas the story and journey of an older person is much more a video or film that shows changes over time, with a cast that is constantly varying and where the older person is the only actor whose presence is guaranteed throughout. Because of this 'one-off' assessment the assessment *process* is often equated with the tools that are used to undertake it. It is much more about the giving and receiving of information, the analysis and understanding of that information, the sharing of the knowledge and wisdom that results and

> *Assessment is the process of enquiry that provides information from which decisions are made and action may be taken.*

> *Assessment is often perceived as a 'one-off' exercise that involves an individual person and an individual practitioner.*

> *The assessment process is often confused with the tools that are used to undertake it.*

the ability to trigger appropriate change. It is also about the subsequent storage of the information to build a knowledge-based service that can handle the complexity and allow adaptability.

The value of the assessment system, no matter how imperfect it may be, is in giving some consistency and a framework to the whole process of care. Though the assessment system is open to bias, the tools are imprecise, and outcomes are at risk of exploitation, it is the only method available to provide a systematic approach. It is the key to providing some qualitative and quantitative measurement of care, thus ensuring equity and access to services.

The involvement of the older person in assessment

If the assessment process is the key to integrated services, the way older people are involved will set the style of that involvement for the other processes of care. The older person is the expert on themselves, particularly on their current and past experiences (see chapter 8, p.198 on involving patients as experts). The physical and emotional distress is theirs and nobody else's.

The failure to recognize this and 'listen' to older people has meant that physical and psychological conditions such as pain, anxiety and depression are often not recognized. These symptoms are difficult to recognize by observation alone, in fact can only truly be communicated by older people themselves. Even in the highly expert world of the hospital, the technical and scientific data that arise from the laboratories only has a meaning in the context of the individual person's physical and social situation. This insight can only be obtained effectively if the older person is made an active partner in the process. Looked at from the point of view of the other professional experts, this personal and contextual background and knowledge of the older person has to give added value and credibility to what they are doing, thus enhancing the mutual worth of all the contributions.

The fact that older people do not want to share everything about themselves with the assessor should not be interpreted as an indication of lack of self-awareness or concern. This is a trap for the unwary. It may not be until confidence and real trust has been established that they will divulge, if ever, details which they consider to be personal and sensitive.

There are important practical aspects in the involvement of older people:

- Simple, sensitive communication is a prerequisite. The use of language that everybody can understand is essential. Even older people with significant memory loss can play an active part in the assessment process. They still sustain valuable insights into their condition.

- The assessor must be aware of physical barriers such as hearing loss and impaired vision.

- The assessor needs to be sensitive to the capacity of the person being assessed. They may feel more comfortable with a slower pace of assessment. The frail older person may tire easily, and this may account for any reduction in performance.

- The development of trust and confidence is very important. The person being assessed will need to know the purpose and likely outcomes of the assessment. The confidentiality must be made explicit, and how any information that arises is to be handled should always be explained. Their permission to proceed is essential.

- A good assessment is a multidimensional process. Not only should the assessor discover information about the older person but the older person should be able to discover more about themselves. In turn, they should be given the opportunity to assess the systems they are being assessed by. They must know how they may benefit and get value. It is only through their appreciation of the potential benefits to themselves that they can take a meaningful part. Their long-term commitment to the whole process is an essential component of the assessment. To foster this commitment, methods of reporting back to them and keeping them informed should be set up. The assessor should also provide the opportunity and time to encourage questions and give feedback.

- The patient or client should hold records of their own assessment processes.

Some assessment tools encourage participation whereas others by the very nature of their structure do not. Those that rely directly on observation alone, as do some of the behavioural and activity-of-daily-living tools, make it more difficult to involve the older person. On the other hand, tools with a lot of freeform which provide for a descriptive account from the older person, such as those favoured by social workers, require significant participation. A criticism levelled at these relatively unstructured assessment tools is that they may not be consistent and are difficult to quantify for comparison at a later date. As a holistic assessment cannot rely on any one tool, the secret is to get the right balance between the two types of assessments. The tick-box type of assessment form may tend to depersonalize the older person unless the questions are set and given in such a way that the older person is truly involved. This relies very heavily on the communication skills of the assessor to promote discussion.

The ultimate involvement would be if the older person could design and carry out

> *The ultimate involvement would be if the older person could design and carry out their own assessment.*

their own assessment. To some extent this already happens intuitively. People set themselves standards relating to their quality of life and then reassess themselves to see how they are doing. Again, it will depend on the empathetic communication skills of the professional assessor to give these a framework and make them explicit. Assessment tools have been checked for their reliability when performed by the older person and it has been verified that there are some assessments the older person can carry out very effectively for themselves.

Lifeplan

Lifeplan was a project developed as part of the EPICS assessment process. It was an attempt to change the whole approach to assessment by altering the nature of the relationship between the older person and the assessor. Most assessments are traditionally carried out in a professional versus client/patient model. The Lifeplan was to create an ambience of partnership, and the outcomes were to be a mutual covenant with obligations on both parties. It was to be the framework for a dialogue. The principal aim was to optimize the quality of life for the older person, according to their wishes and by their standards, and wherever possible put some fun back into their lives.

Lifeplan was not itself a tool but was a basket for a whole range of tools. It included a full medical and mental health assessment as well as social, environmental and dietary assessment tools. Risks were explored and how they could be managed. The older person could also be given information on practitioners such as dieticians, chiropodists and alternative therapists. Part of the process entailed making the older person aware of local amenities such as exercise groups, clubs, churches, specialist shops, continuing education and cultural pursuits. The intention was to help them to integrate with a community. This was consistent with the civic model of care that was evolving in EPICS through this period. (See chapter 3, p.86 on implementation models and chapter 8, p.201 on involving the users.)

The prime focus was on the older person's expectations of their own lives. The 'obligation' on the older person was that they should try to live their life to the full and as healthily as possible and be able to make a contribution to the life of the community. The 'obligation' on the assessment system was that it should help the older person to achieve the identified life goals wherever possible.

A central theme of the Lifeplan was to anticipate the future as much as possible and make contingency plans, as part of a health and social preventive programme. Inevitably, this meant addressing end-of-life issues and the way that older people would wish to handle the end of their lives. Many older people seem to be able to look at this to a greater or lesser extent, and have already internalized many of the issues. Put in the context of 'living life to the full' until the approach of the end of life, this did not seem unduly depressing. And for some it was a release valve for deep emotions. Discussion sometimes centred on the making of a living will, and if one was made, it was important for the assessment system to record its existence so that it would be available for those concerned with supporting the older person through the terminal stage of their lives.

The concept was very challenging to many professionals. Most of those invited to pilot the assessment would not participate. Initially some of the assessors who did undertake the work found it difficult either to raise or discuss end-of-life issues and sought support in doing this. There is an amusing story of the excellent practice nurse who had found it difficult, one day bursting into a room, with a grin from ear to ear, saying 'I have done it! It was easy! The patient brought the subject up!'

The changing relationship between the assessor and the assessed in discussing end-of-life issues also presented a challenge. Training and support for the assessor are essential and time consuming. To date there is only one GP practice that continues to develop the model and it is carrying out a long-term evaluation on behalf of its primary care trust.

The purpose of assessment

The purpose of assessment is:

- to make a summative appraisal of the individual's situation or diagnosis; this will also help in predicting the likely future possibilities (in other words, provide prognostic clues), which is helpful in both medical and social assessment for risk management

- to identify any needs or required treatments; in social care the major emphasis has become one of deciding the eligibility for care and as such assessment performs an important role in the gate-keeping process to available resources; this puts greater emphasis on the financial and cost implications in assessment than is relevant in healthcare; this can be an important cultural difference between health and social care that may put pressure on relationships

- to evaluate the benefits of any social or health intervention on an individual person; if an assessment is repeated over time it may demonstrate if change has occurred as a result of any intervention carried out as part of a therapy or care plan.

There are several reasons for undertaking assessments:

- to prevent breakdown in either health or social care; this will be largely preventive and may involve screening as well as any direct preventive assessment tools

- to deal with incipient breakdown; this is more likely to involve those at higher risk and will include people in chronic disease management programmes

- to deal with actual breakdown; this will essentially be crisis management in most instances

- to monitor ongoing need and care

- to manage quality, ensure standards are being met and measure improvements in care

- to undertake research.

The stages of an assessment process

Assessment is essentially an iterative process that can start anywhere in the assessment cycle and be repeated as many times as necessary. It is not a simple linear process as many perceive it to be. It is truly complex. It has been suggested that there are four types of assessment (NSF Standard 2):

- contact assessment

- overview assessment

- in-depth assessment

- comprehensive old-age assessment.

This approach implies that these are distinct and separate assessments and that the person's assessment moves inexorably from one to the other and that the assessor should do the same.

In the EPICS project a different approach was taken. This was that there was only one assessment process, which varied for each individual according to their need. The four levels of assessment were looked upon as stages within one complete assessment process.

The context of the assessment process

Place

Like everyone else, older people live in a wide variety of settings and environments with which they interact. Many of their needs will arise as a result of these interactions. A person who is in their own home may have completely different requirements from somebody confined to a bed or chair in a nursing home or hospital. A different set of assessment tools may be required in different settings. Some tools may not valid for multiple settings. For example, it is said that the Barthel Index, which is a frequently used functional assessment in rehabilitation settings, is not valid in the community setting, and another tool – the Community Dependency Index – has been developed for this and is claimed to be more appropriate (Eakin 1995). Sometimes it is just that the tool has been validated in the one setting only and there are no data on an alternative, rather than it having been shown that it cannot ever be used in that setting.

> *A different set of assessment tools may be required in different settings.*

For many older people the choice of venue for the assessment is crucial. For those who are frail the only relevant setting is the one in which they live. If they have memory difficulties then the assessments are better done in an environment they know and are not threatened by.

What adds to the complexity of the assessment process for older people, especially if they are frail, is the very complicated care pathway that takes place (often in a relatively short time) when they become unstable or have a crisis. They may start in their own homes, be seen in a hospital emergency department, admitted to an acute ward, transferred to a rehabilitation or intermediate care setting and then back to their own homes or an institutional setting, and then followed up in a day unit or as an outpatient. The complexity and potential for confusion are self-evident. The person's needs are constantly changing and multiple assessment tools may be required; and all the providers will need to network the information. This immediately raises the question of how the spatial components of assessment are handled and geographical information systems may be a solution. (See chapter 7, p.181 for more on information systems.)

The initial stages of the assessment process (collecting basic information and enquiring into the person's needs) can be carried out anywhere including over the phone. But as the assessment progressively requires more complex tools and a more multidisciplinary approach it may best be done in a setting such as a day hospital or resource unit where it would be expected that all the necessary team were working.

Time factors

Time is another important contextual issue for the assessment process. Practically, the time of day when the assessment is carried out may be relevant: for example at the end of a busy day the older person may be tired and perform less well. Equally, the assessment process has to be aligned to the current need or planning. An assessment done last week, month or year may not take into account more recent changes and cannot be assumed to be relevant to the present.

> *Time is another important contextual issue for the assessment process.*

For those planning the assessment system, the timing of an assessment is significant. Assessments have a financial and resource cost and prudent planning will aim to maximize the benefit to individuals and groups of older people. The frequency of the various assessments needs addressing.

Who should be assessed?

Answering this question is like opening a Pandora's box. Ultimately, it can only be answered once the strategy of older peoples' care and the operational issues are resolved. One of the simple rules that evolved from the EPICS and complex systems concepts was that it was necessary to know 'a little about everybody and a lot about a few'. (See chapter 3, p.84 on implementation models.) The 'little about everybody' usually consisted of a minimum data set and any other information from any screening assessments such as over-75 checks. Where available, this information was easily obtainable. (See chapter 9, p.238 on evaluation.) For the 'lot about a few' most of the data came from contact assessments when clinical, social or life events occurred. In EPICS the elderly population was assigned to one of three groups:

- *The low-risk group.* This group was by far the largest and consisted mainly of the fit elderly of any age who were independent. Much of the effort in assessment was to enhance lifestyle and to put in place any preventive healthcare following screening.

- *The at-risk group.* These people were characterized by two or more of the following: usually being over 80 years old, living alone, with reduced mobility, having a history of falling, being recently bereaved, having recently been discharged from hospital, and being on multiple drug therapy (a surrogate marker for multiple pathology). The aim was that these older people should be reviewed and monitored regularly (several times a year) by both the EPICS and the community teams, using a variety of methods including telephone calls and volunteers. Many of this group were directed to active therapy and rehabilitation programmes in the community.

- *The interface group.* This group was so called because the members were assessed as being at the interface of community and institutional care. They were identified by extreme frailty, being housebound, suffering from significant chronic disease and being unable to manage in the community without major (i.e. twice daily or more) input from the home care team or family carers. This group was inherently clinically and socially unstable. Maintaining them in the community required that the systems could respond to crises very quickly at any time of day or night. Usually this involved the rapid response team. In EPICS the contact with the nursing homes was only being slowly developed, but it would be possible to consider older people in nursing or residential homes being assessed for possible return to the community as being in this interface group as well.

This structured categorization of the elderly was helpful in targeting resources appropriately. It also provided the framework for the use of a wide variety of creative methods to address the needs of a community of individual people at the same time.

The ability to capture information on any of the care systems so that it became part of the knowledge-base for any individual older person was extraordinarily helpful. The benefits were that time was not spent seeking information that already existed and that where new information was required it could be accurately targeted.

Who should do the assessments?

Much unnecessary time and effort is currently taken with the replication of assessments for some people. This means that others who need them do not get them and the failure of provision for others that need them. Stories are legion of a single older person at home being assessed by a succession of professionals because these professionals are not communicating with or trusting each other (Social Services Inspectorate 1998). With appropriate training it is possible for a professional in any discipline who has knowledge and understanding of assessments from their own practice to be able to do an assessment that includes multidisciplinary components such as simple functional mental health and social tools. If this can be agreed between the team and one of the professionals, accountability can be satisfied, duplication can be eliminated and more older people who require assessments can be targeted.

For complex assessments and those older people who require highly technical diagnostic skills and equipment the team will necessarily be more extensive. It will include the older person and their carers, social workers and medical specialists including geriatricians, specialist nurses and paramedical staff. This kind of assessment is probably best done in a setting such as a day hospital or hospital outpatient clinic. In most cases this will not entail admission to hospital.

Ensuring the sustainability of the assessment system

The history of assessment is littered with attempts to implement new assessment schemes that have immediately failed or have survived only a short time and then withered. The early attempts to undertake over-75 health checks in primary care in the UK and the difficulties of implementation of assessment and care management in social services are two examples (MacLean 1996). The mandating of assessment to be undertaken by practitioners for bureaucratic, financial and resource allocation is a sure recipe for the assessment system to be corrupted or not complied with fully. In some instances, these mandated assessments are done by proxy. They are often delegated to inappropriate staff who may be untrained, such as students or newly appointed care assistants. In the USA staff are frequently hired specifically to complete the forms (Stuck *et al.* 1993). For assessment to have any enduring value it is vital to ensure the commitment of the older person and the practitioners to the whole process and its application (Kane and Kane 2000).

Ownership

It has been said that assessment is the professional thumbprint of the individual members of the multidisciplinary team. Many teams have been disrupted or work dysfunctionally because of disagreements in choosing and then using assessment tools consistently. Assessment is a very personal way for the professional to express themselves in their work. That expression is dependent on the culture of their profession and their own personal and professional values. To make the assessment system work across professional and organizational boundaries this must be recognized and then accommodated. Too often the assessment process is an attempt to get practitioners to conform, and this is especially so in those that are mandatory assessments. This ignores the strength that the diversity of the professional cultures can give to truly reflect the complex nature of needs of the older person. The secret for those leading in the development of the assessment process is to balance the advantages of the diversity of professional cultures with the advantages of consistency in application and the requirement for some bureaucratic conformity – a tension that absolutely begs for a complex adaptive systems approach.

A team that has already worked through the development of shared values, created mutual respect and sorted out the roles and competencies for each team member will find this a lot easier, but not necessarily straightforward. It is always surprising to see what new or potential conflicts arise when the practicalities of application of an assessment system are to be put in place. Tensions that have been masked by compromise come to the fore when practice becomes a reality. Frequently the implementation of an assessment system is the first time that a team feels the need to face up to the tensions of professional diversity. In which case this is as good a field of discovery and experiment as any.

The 'toolbox' approach

In the EPICS project a conceptual model was used to help provide some conformity and still value diversity through the 'toolbox' approach. The teams found it relatively easy to formulate the early stages of the common assessment jointly, provided that they knew they were able to have some professional choice and judgement when they felt it appropriate. The inclusion of a minimum data set, a statement from the older person as to their own perceived needs and an initial functional, psychological and social assessment was then straightforward. The concept of the 'toolbox' then came into its own.

The idea was that each professional could identify a specific assessment tool that they had chosen by agreed criteria and they thought necessary for specialist technical assessment. This was then metaphorically put in the toolbox. Though specific tools were owned by the individual professional or team, the toolbox was owned by everybody. Usually, but not invariably, the assessment tool was used by a member of the professional team owning it who then reported on it. However, the obligation of that professional team was to ensure that the criteria for choice of the tool were fulfilled, and that any necessary training outside the professional discipline was provided; also that all the other team members from different professions shared in and understood the results so that the tool had a value for everybody. Examples of such tools ranged from specific measures for Parkinson's disease and nursing dependency scores to continence and falls.

This layered approach to assessment seemed to satisfy the professional's need to conform while remaining able to practise using their own judgement in any given situation. It allowed each individual practitioner to exercise some degree of independence and at the same time to fulfil their responsibility to the rest of the team. It also allowed the flexibility to meet the needs of each older person.

The relevance of the assessment process

Within EPICS, and other integrated care projects, the relevance of the assessment as perceived by the professional assessor is crucial to the completion and continuation of the whole process. The key skill of the assessor is to recognize what questions need to be asked through the assessment process that are relevant to the needs of the older person, and then to apply the appropriate tools to get the answers that will have a real impact for the better. If the process and the tools fail to do this, they lose their credibility and a degree of professional cynicism arises. If the tool is not seen to be useful, it will be abandoned by one means or another, no matter how much pressure is brought to bear on the professionals by the authorities.

To understand the relevance of an assessment the assessor must first understand all the potential needs of the older person and the possible interventions that are available to meet those needs. They require insightful knowledge. These insights will need to extend to the whole range of options arising from multidisciplinary and cross-organizational working. Likewise, the training and team development programme should provide the opportunity for all this to be shared.

Resource implications

Sharing resources

Any successful assessment process requires resources. If these are not properly planned for and made available it will put inevitable strain on the whole implementation and put both the credibility and integrity of the managers at risk. The resources for an integrated system can also be integrated and shared. In EPICS the pooling of training resources, enabling multi-skilled practitioners from all the agencies to do common basic assessments, was certainly viewed as cost-effective. Reducing unnecessary duplication of assessments and sharing information meant that waste was reduced and higher-quality care was delivered.

Time

Time is an important resource that has to be considered when planning. There are two aspects: first, to make time available officially for staff in their job plans; second, to design the assessments to fit into the time available in work schedules. The assessment has to be 'do-able' within the time constraints. If the assessment is too cumbersome and takes too long it will not be done. This is true in both healthcare and social work environments where the practitioners are under considerable pressure. In acute hospitals, assessments may need to be done in minutes rather than hours.

Information technology

Another resource often neglected at the start is the availability of information technology and support for the electronic networking and storage of assessment information. At an early stage the problems of working across organizational IT boundaries and confidentiality issues must be embraced. (See chapter 7, p.177 on information technology.)

The relationship of the assessment process to the management of care

In both health and social care it has been demonstrated that there is greater compliance (both initially and over time) with the assessment process if the assessors also have some control over the identification of the resource that relates to the assessed need. In social work this has been achieved through the care management model. In this the social worker not only assesses but also plans and reviews the care delivery, though not actually delivering direct care. Previously, the assessment had been designed to match people to services, rather than identify needs, and this led to difficulties in completion and consistency in the assessment (Social Services Inspectorate 1991).

In healthcare, patient outcomes following assessment are improved if the clinicians who do the assessments also implement and have control over the recommendations. The combination of assessment and sustained control of clinical management appears to be the most effective way to improve patient care.

The lesson from both health and social work is that assessments done in isolation from the care delivery process are likely to fail (Rubenstein *et al.* 1984).

The analysis and implementation of assessment outcomes

Carrying out the assessment is only half the overall process. The other half is the analysis and interpretation of the information that arises. Frequently this is not given as much priority as the choosing and the completion of the assessment tool and is another reason that assessment gets a bad reputation. This failure to put in place mechanisms for decision analysis is another reason why assessments fall by the wayside and are unsustainable over time. The more the information from an assessment is seen to be used and to be useful, the more likely it is that the professionals will continue to value and use it.

Who should do it?

The analysis and decisions arising from an assessment can be undertaken by an individual, a single professional team or a multidisciplinary team. The single individual has the advantage of speed of reaction, especially if they have done the assessment themselves. However, they may be biased by their past experiences, limited knowledge and the culture of their professional background. Some of this can be overcome by the use of guidelines and protocols and suitable training. Decisions from a single professional team have some of the same complications, but there is likely to be a wider variety of experiences and more knowledge.

Multidisciplinary teams can provide a more holistic approach to the evaluation of the assessment and ensure that important domains of care are not ignored; for example, any rehabilitation that might reduce any handicap or disability as identified by the social work team. On the other hand, multidisciplinary team decision-making can be notoriously cumbersome and slow, particularly if decisions can only be taken by the team jointly, and they meet only periodically. There are ways this can be overcome with good team-working and trust. Some teams can work well with both prospective and retrospective reporting and discussions. An agreed framework for working together with clear boundaries for each member to make delegated decisions outside meetings may be useful. Allowing the team to function by networking is also a possibility that can be considered.

Decision-making must be planned for

The important point is that this decision-making rarely works if left to chance alone. It depends on being planned for and being explicit. This aspect of the assessment process must be positively managed. A good evaluation and monitoring system of both the assessment outcomes and the process itself, using planned evaluation meetings and providing time to reflect together on the whole methodology, will enhance the team assessment skills. This whole feedback loop fosters continuous learning.

Training

Training is frequently the catalyst to create and bind together the assessment process across professional and organizational boundaries. It is too often neglected in the desire to get quick results. Practitioners need to have a deep understanding of the purposes and limitations of the tools they use. Fields for training include:

- the selection and use of individual assessment tools
- how to communicate with the older person and prepare them for being truly involved with the assessment process
- how to communicate and work with other professionals in conducting assessments, especially to develop an ambience of trust
- how to analyse and understand the outcomes of the assessment
- how the assessment decision-making process links with the other care processes (Department of Health 2001).

Selecting the assessment tool

The selection of the assessment tool is usually the first consideration given in the implementation of any assessment system. It has been deliberately placed towards the end of the chapter to make the point that, unless all the other factors above are in place, no matter which tool is chosen the assessment system is likely eventually to break down and fail.

There are literally hundreds of assessment tools for the elderly in existence, and more are produced on an almost daily basis. This alone indicates that there is no perfect tool that covers all potential aspects of patients' needs and addresses the contextual issues of time, place and reason for undertaking the assessment. The temptation to be prescriptive and to advise a single tool because it is administratively easier not only demonstrates a lack of insight into the assessment process but is a recipe for sure long-term failure. Although the National Service Framework has recommended moving towards a single assessement process it has not given a definitive model, believing that the process of generating a model unique to the locality will ensure it is 'owned' and used. The EASYcare model and the Home Care MDS (minimum data set) have been developed to achieve a common, if not a single assessment (see Further Reading for examples).

The method developed in the EPICS project was to view the assessment process as requiring a variety of tools to be used flexibly. The selection of tools for each individual older person would be almost unique, rather like the contents of a shopping basket. This metaphor of the shopping basket can be extended further. The shopping usually includes those things bought and used every week (such as sugar, coffee, milk, washing powder, etc.) and other things that, for example, will fit into that week's menus. It is unusual for two shopping baskets to contain the same goods, and so it should be for the assessment process if the individual needs of each older person are to be met.

In selecting an assessment tool it is necessary to take into account whether it shows reliability, validity and reponsiveness:

- *Reliability*. This indicates whether the tool is consistent in producing similar results when performed by different people and on different occasions.

- *Validity*. This indicates whether the tool is measuring what it was intended to or not. It will include whether the components of the scale or tool cover all aspects of the condition being assessed, and whether those components can actually be measured with any accuracy. Another important criterion of validity is the ability of the tool to predict subsequent change in a person's status at a later date.

- *Responsiveness*. This is the capacity of the tool to measure change either over time or because of some intervention. The change over time is usually due to the person's condition or situation naturally improving or deteriorating. The intervention may be some therapeutic measure or a social care input. The responsiveness of a tool is particularly important if it is to be used to measure outcomes.

The domains of care

The domains of care describe the component areas within the assessment that together make for a holistic process. The domains are not only programme-specific (that is, related to preventive measures or improvement of mental or physical health or other conditions) but may also be discipline-specific. For example, at the stage of contact and initial assessment, the assessor may assess for all the domains using tools chosen by or with other professionals. But for more in-depth and complex assessments, the assessment of each domain may be undertaken only by the discipline or organization that is acknowledged to have the appropriate skills and experience. This is another operational issue that needs clarification and understanding between the multidisciplinary team members. If not addressed it is a potential point of conflict.

Even at the most superficial level the use of a stated range of domains has value in providing a checklist to make sure that the whole-person approach has been considered. At a deeper level, it provides a framework for selecting the appropriate tools and connecting them together, thus ensuring that, combined, they provide for an all-encompassing and inclusive system of information gathering.

The National Service Framework for carrying out assessments suggested domains and sub-domains of care (see box).

The domains and subdomains of care

- User's perspective
    - problems and issues in the user's own words
    - user's expectations and motivation around improving the quality of life and end-of-life issues
- Clinical background
    - history of medical problems
    - history of falls
    - medication use and ability to self-medicate
- Disease prevention
    - history of blood pressure monitoring
    - nutrition
    - immunization history
    - drinking and smoking history

- ○ Exercise habits
- ○ History of cervical and breast screening
- Personal care and well-being
  - ○ personal hygiene
  - ○ dressing ability
  - ○ pain symptoms
  - ○ oral and dental status
  - ○ foot care
  - ○ tissue viability, especially of skin
  - ○ mobility
  - ○ continence and difficulties with bowel and bladder function
  - ○ sleeping patterns
- Senses
  - ○ sight
  - ○ hearing
  - ○ communication
- Mental health
  - ○ cognition dysfunction including memory status
  - ○ depression, reactions to loss, and other emotional difficulties
- Relationships
  - ○ social contact and networks including relationships and interests
  - ○ care arrangements from family, organizations and voluntary and neighbour support
- Safety
  - ○ abuse and neglect
  - ○ personal safety particularly in relation to the immediate environment
  - ○ public safety and the risks posed by the older person to others
- Environment
  - ○ care of the home and managing domestic tasks such as cooking, shopping and cleaning
  - ○ accommodation and heating
  - ○ financial competencies and financial provision
  - ○ access to local facilities and services

Overview

Assessment is an extremely powerful process that is pivotal in facilitating multidisciplinary and cross-organizational working. Even more importantly, properly configured and sensitively used, it is a very potent method of truly involving the older person. For them it can facilitate greater insight into their own needs and demonstrate the availability of choices in designing their own care. It ensures that they are incorporated as partners in both the process and delivery of care. This approach is not inflationary – quite the opposite: it is very cost-effective.

Assessment will achieve its maximum impact when the information it produces can be stored and managed to provide knowledge of both individuals and communities. From this an intelligent response to actual and anticipated needs can help reduce clinical and social risk for all older people. The assessment system is in itself a complex adaptive process. The emerging, self-organizing processes harness the commitment, capabilities and energy of the older person to manage and control their lives. Assessment, like learning, is a lifelong practice for the older person and those connected with them.

Chapter 4 – Headline points

- Assessment is the process of enquiry that provides information from which decisions are made and action may be taken.

- Assessment is often perceived as a 'one-off' exercise that involves an individual person and an individual practitioner.

- The assessment *process* is often equated with the tools that are used to undertake it.

- The ultimate involvement would be if the older person could design and carry out their own assessment.

- Time is another important contextual issue for the assessment process.

References

Department of Health (2001) *The Single Assessment Process: Guidance for Local Implementation.* London: HMSO.

Eakin, P. (1995) 'The Community Dependency Index.' *British Journal of Occupational Therapy 58*, 17–22.

Kane, R.L. (2000) 'Mandated assessments.' In R.L. Kane and R.A. Kane (eds) *Assessing Older People.* Oxford: Oxford University Press.

Maclean, T. (1996) *The Assessment Process.* In C. Clarke and I. Lapsley (eds) *Planning and Costing Community Care.* London: Jessica Kingsley Publishers.

Rubenstein, L.Z., Josephson, K.R., Wieland, P.G., English, P.A., Sayre, J.A. and Kane, R.L. (1984) 'Effectiveness of a geriatric evaluation unit: A randomised clinical trial.' *New England Journal of Medicine 311*, 1664–1670.

Social Services Inspectorate (1991) *Care Management and Assessment: Practitioner's Guide.* London: HMSO.

Social Services Inspectorate (1998) *Care Management Study.* London: Department of Health.

Stuck, W.E., Siu, A.L., Wicland, G.D., Adams, T. and Rubenstein, L.Z. (1993) 'Comprehensive geriatric assessment: A meta analysis of controlled trials.' *The Lancet 342*, 1032–1036.

Further reading

Bowling, A. (1997) *Measuring Health – A Review of Quality of Life Scales.* Buckingham: Open University Press.

Though not specifically written about older people it is still completely relevant and contains valuable scales and advice.

Bowling, A. (2001) *Measuring Disease.* Buckingham: Open University Press.

This contains very useful, disease-specific assessments and scales that are valuable for choosing tools to add to the more general assessments.

Clarke, C. and Lapsley, I. (eds) (1996) *Planning and Costing Community Care.* London: Jessica Kingsley Publishers.

This book gives a very useful background following the community care legislation of the early 1990s. The chapter on assessment for social work is excellent and puts it in a care management context.

Kane, R.L. and Kane, R. (eds) (2000) *Assessing Older Persons – Measures, Meaning and Practical Applications.* New York: Oxford University Press.

The 'bible' on assessments with a very nice balance between well-documented and researched tools and practical wisdom on their application. It is very comprehensive and easy to read.

Sheffield Institute for Studies on Aging (1999–2000) *EASYcare–Elderly Assessment System.* University of Sheffield, UK. Website: www.bbr-online.com/easycare

EASYcare is a system for rapid assessment of an older person's physical, mental and social well-being focusing on quality of life rather than disease. It has been developed primarily to help practitioners improve the care they provide for older people. In addition EASYcare can be used to measure population case-mix, needs and outcomes to help with service management, resource allocation, research and policy making. The system has been tested on several sites in Europe and in Northern Ireland.

Streiner, D. and Norman, G. (1995) *Health Measurement Scales – A Practical Guide to Their Development and Use.* New York: Oxford University Press.

This is a much more technically oriented guide for those who wish to understand how to devise scales. But it does give real insight to the whole process very clearly.

Chapter 5

Preventing Crises

Health Promotion, Chronic Disease Management, and Risk Management

Every system is perfectly designed to produce the results it does. If you do not like the results then you must change the system.

Paul Batalden, Director of the Institute
for Leadership in Healthcare,
Dartmouth, USA

In this chapter we consider the benefits to older people and to organizations of preventing crises using a complex adaptive systems approach. Examples are given of situations where failure to integrate has had a bad outcome for the client or patient, and of other situations where there has been an attempt to bring a systemic response with a better outcome for both the older person and the organization. Different approaches to chronic disease management are discussed with examples from specific programmes. The chapter focuses mainly on examples from healthcare, as this is where studies have mostly been documented.

It is obvious that crises and emergencies should be avoided if at all possible. And yet most healthcare systems are focused on dealing with emergencies. Much of the healthcare resource is spent on them, and so is much of a healthcare professional's training. There is also a general cultural expectation in the population at large that healthcare and emergencies are virtually synonymous, a perception reinforced by the flashing blue lights and sirens of ambulances speeding through the streets. Two of the most popular English-speaking television shows are of dramas in emergency rooms or casualty departments. Certainly, for older people, the current systems of care direct them to the emergency systems even if they do not need them. There is no doubt that most older people benefit from admission to acute hospitals for care but not necessarily all of them. Accepting that they do have other care needs, about 20–40 per cent of older people who are admitted to an acute hospital could be managed in an alternative setting. (See chapter 1, p.37 on the roots of discrimination.)

There is accumulating evidence that it is possible for older people to manage their own care or to be managed by others in ways that reduce the chance of crises. However, it is unlikely that any single intervention is going to have significant impact. Most studies suggest that multidimensional interventions are necessary, which involve diagnosis, assessment, rehabilitation, psychosocial and environmental input from multidisciplinary teams and organizations. Crisis prevention in older people is complex because they have multiple needs and multiple inputs are necessary to achieve change. It would seem a fertile area for a complex adaptive systems approach that also provides an integrative approach for the older person.

In considering crisis prevention the following topics will be discussed:

- frailty prevention
- disease and accident prevention
- chronic disease management
- rehabilitation
- reduction in acute hospital distress
- clinical and social care risk management.

Frailty prevention

Frailty is that condition typified by the combination of disease processes, with the physiological de-compensation associated with ageing (such as decreased muscle strength) resulting in functional limitations and handicap in relation to the environment in which they live. It is a multidimensional definition and not just due to a disease process or to age alone. According to Stuck *et al.* (1999), the main risk factors for loss of independence by older people living in the community are:

- impaired thinking, e.g. memory loss or confusion.
- depression

- more than one disease

- bodyweight (too much and too little)

- walking difficulties

- social isolation

- low level of physical activity

- poor self-perceived health

- smoking

- vision impairment

- no alcohol use compared to moderate use

These risk factors are complex in the sense that they can be both independent and dependent on each other. For example, people who are depressed are more likely to be inactive and therefore more socially isolated. As a result it has been found that multiple risk factor interventions are more successful than those done singly. There is increasing evidence that this helps reduce the risks of falling, improves mood, maintains independence and keeps older people out of institutional care for longer. When the costs have been examined it has usually been shown to be cost-effective in reducing demand on health and social care budgets. However, it is probably necessary to continue the interventions over time to maintain benefit. Once there is a tendency to frailty it will always be present and the effects of training and improvements will disappear if the intervention is not continued in some form. Consistent with complex adaptive system modelling, small changes with more than one intervention have been shown to be successful in producing and maintaining improvement.

> *It has been found that multiple risk factor interventions are more successful than those done singly.*

A number of key interventions have been shown to be effective:

- improving physical activity including walking, improving muscle strength, balance gait and the ability to transfer (for example from bed to chair/toilet, etc.)

- assessing and improving hearing and vision

- managing social isolation and depression

- assessing and managing dementia

- advising and giving support in maintaining adequate nutrition
- counselling for and stopping smoking
- screening and counselling for problem drinking
- optimizing medication, particularly psychotropic drug use and polypharmacy
- improving safety in the home and the use of over-the-counter medications.

The implementation of such programmes is not easy but has been shown to be worth the investment. However, it is imperative to engage the older person in the whole process (which entails convincing them of the value of their involvement), because otherwise it will fail. Ideally the older person should be in charge, or at the very least be influential in designing and implementing some of the programmes themselves. Also peer support is probably essential to maintain their involvement over time. Making it fun and enjoyable is an important ingredient for success, which is why activities such as dancing and bowls have been so popular, combining, as they do, physical and social activity. Leisure centres that provide facilities for activities in the form of a club and also offer eating and restaurant areas seem equally popular. Some of these leisure facilities also provide screening clinics as part of the service. They have skilled health and fitness instructors who are able to provide personal training programmes for older people after initial screening. The value of some of these programmes has been recognized by the fact that GPs are providing free access to fitness training on prescription.

It is unlikely that these schemes can be made to work for any length of time if they use a medical or even a social care model. A health promotion model is more appropriate. But it is still important to involve primary care teams in the referral process and thus keep them aware of the benefits available to older people in the local community. If such a programme is to be successful it needs to involve the whole community, often with the local authority taking the lead.

The Meadow Larks

At Rectory Meadow surgery, a GP practice in South Buckinghamshire, the Meadow Larks are a group of older people who have been assessed as being frail and at risk by any member of the primary care team. Many of them are lonely and isolated and sometimes recently bereaved. At one of two weekly meetings they and a volunteer from Extend, a charity promoting exercise and movement to music for older people, run the club which is held in the surgery premises. They organize their own transport, pay a small subscription and make their own mid-afternoon snack together. Apart from the exercise involved, they socialize and provide some mutual support and supervision for each other. They have a series of talks from other older people and healthcare workers on a wide series of health issues ranging from holidays to nutrition and teenage sex (the latter they say is to understand their grandchildren). Through the surgery networks they are connected to the EPICS system and other community projects. This group has become so successful that it is difficult to meet the demand and to find ways of expanding it without taking over the surgery premises completely. A small-scale evaluation confirmed that it is much appreciated by the older people and that they continued to 'network' outside the actual meetings. What is more, the members of the Meadow Larks, have made significantly less use of the services of the primary care team than had been the case previously.

For those leading the development of integrated services the first steps are to identify and network with those organizations that are responsible for community health and safety, either by inviting them to the various project groups or, if that is not possible, finding a way to join other programmes (providing speakers is usually productive!) on to theirs. The experience in most of the integrated care schemes known to us is that we are pushing on open doors. It is enlightening to see the creativity that diverse groups can bring to improving community care when they work together.

Disease and accident prevention

It is well recognized that some of the diseases associated with older people are preventable. Even those that are not preventable can be managed in such a way that the impact of the disease is minimized. Primary prevention to reduce the occurrence of disease remains the responsibility of the primary care physician and GP. Influenza vaccination is accepted as being of value to all older people and pneumococcal vaccine to most (particularly certain high-risk groups such as those in institutions or with chronic lung or heart disease). Other interventions include screening for carcinoma of the breast or colon, hypertension and diabetes and falls prevention (Patterson 2000).

Secondary and tertiary prevention is focused on minimizing the effects of diseases that already exist, for example early screening for cancer, identifying the complications of diabetes or identification of osteoporosis in an older person with a fracture. Secondary and tertiary prevention may also lie with the primary care team but frequently involves specialist care as well. There is considerable evidence that many of these well-proven prevention programmes are not consistently put in place and the benefits are denied to the older person (Muir Gray 1997). This may not be surprising if the delivery of primary care and preventive care are viewed as two different systems rather than a single system. Generally speaking, the essence of primary care is still the management of the individual patient on an opportunistic and reactive basis, whereas disease prevention and screening are based on the proactive management of populations or groups of people. The two systems require different behaviours from the systems themselves, the professionals involved and the older person.

> *There is considerable evidence that many of these well-proven prevention programmes are not consistently put in place and the benefits are denied to the older person.*

A disease prevention model requires:

- *The selection of clinically relevant and effective prevention strategies.* This will benefit from advice and help from both epidemiologists and public health physicians.

- *A knowledgeable and receptive population of older people who are prepared for and able to partake in the disease prevention programme.* This will require the help of health educators, the local media, libraries and older persons organizations, such as Age Concern, as well as disease-specific organizations, such as those for diabetes or Parkinson's disease. NHS Direct has an important role to play, and the increasing use of the internet by the older person would be another way to involve them through the use of local community internet services. (see chapter 7, p.178 on information technology.)

- *A population-based information and screening system (such as the one piloted by EPICS) that can identify target groups who could benefit from the prevention strategies.* This could be built on current databases of primary care practices or locality-based information systems. Central to this process are information specialists, computer technicians and clerks to record and input data.

- *A multidisciplinary primary care team that is both knowledgeable and competent to understand and undertake the disease prevention programmes.* They and the appropriate specialists need to be involved in the planning supported by the practice mangers. Multidisciplinary training will help the team approach and so involve the trainers.

- *Links into secondary care where laboratory or other investigative procedures (such as colonoscopy) are required.* This will also facilitate appropriate and timely intervention when this is needed.

- *Community preventive programmes to be in place at the start.* If they are not available the implementation process should be questioned and probably not proceeded with. Community pharmacists, opticians, private therapists and other staff, practitioners in alternative medicine, staff at leisure centres and day centres and volunteers may all be catalytic in making this happen, apart from the traditionally recognized health and social work staff usually associated with older people's care. The more creative the solutions the greater will be the array of people potentially involved, and this can appear alarming.

- *The necessary structures for staff to facilitate and network all these disparate groups into a cohesive whole.* They will require adequate facilities to counsel and advise (for example, a sufficient number of telephone lines). A decision support system may be particularly helpful to the clinical staff.

The sustainability of the whole process will depend on sufficient feedback to all those involved: the older person about their own care; the locality groups about community health; the professionals about their performance and the success of the prevention programmes. And do not forget that the commissioners need to know they are purchasing cost-effective prevention. All this depends on a robust evaluation and reporting system that needs to be agreed by all and put in place before the programmes start. (See chapter 9, p.250 on evaluation.)

The whole process is in fact another complex adaptive system involving different people in different places doing different things towards a common end. This will need to be integrated and self-organizing and will require complex adaptive behaviours and leadership.

Chronic disease management

Chronic disease is a significant burden for older people, their carers and the health and social systems that support them. It is estimated that upwards of three-quarters of older people over 65 have at least one or more chronic diseases, and this number rises with age. This burden has a big impact on the suffering of older people and will not only threaten physical activity but also increase psychological distress, social isolation and stress on carers. The de-conditioning and depression which chronic diseases bring about result in a vicious downward spiral of dependency. There is an increasing body of evidence that structured interventions can have a major impact in improving the well-being of the older person, reducing stress on carers and rationalizing and reducing demand on health and social care systems (Elkan *et al.* 2001; Wagner, Austin and Von Korff 1996).

> *The de-conditioning and depression which chronic diseases bring about result in a vicious downward spiral of dependency.*

In keeping with the complex adaptive system approach it has been suggested that multiple small interventions will result in a significant improvement for a given individual. It will also have a very major impact on the use of care resources, particularly for unnecessary hospital admission (Von Korff *et al.* 1997).

A significant minority of acute hospital admissions are for older people with acute exacerbations or worsening of chronic diseases that were in fact predictable. Many of these people have recurrent admissions (usually under different medical teams) without the chronicity of their conditions being properly addressed – the so-called 'revolving door syndrome' (Chapter 1, p.33).

The range of diseases that can benefit from chronic disease management is growing. The evidence for the success of some of the programmes is now so overwhelming that it is surprising that they are not being universally implemented.

Currently, the various components of the chronic care system appear to be in 'silos' with strong boundaries around them. What chronic disease management there is, is based in the community and often isolated from, or with difficult access to, the expertise of secondary care. There are examples of good systems (especially around diabetes), but older people, particularly those in institutions, have considerable difficulty in accessing even these services. Diseases where chronic disease management programmes have been introduced include:

- chronic lung diseases

- heart failure

- coronary artery disease

- diabetes mellitus

- a wide range of malignancies and cancer

- renal failure

- Parkinson's disease

- strokes

- arthritis

- mental health conditions, including depression and dementia.

This list is by no means exhaustive but does demonstrate the wide range of conditions that need to be considered.

Expert systems in chronic disease management

Older people benefit from chronic disease programmes, and some programmes have older people registered with them. However, a major criticism sometimes levelled at these programmes is that they focus on single disease processes whereas older people frequently have multiple diseases. Also, it is felt that older people's care should be more holistic and address the multiplicity and complexity of their condition. This point is well made in the light of current good practice for older people's care. At the same time, chronic disease management is becoming increasingly sophisticated and requires more and more expertise. So it is unlikely that it can be easily and completely undertaken by generalists, no matter what their discipline.

Within the EPICS project this apparent tension and paradox, which appeared to be a block to improving the quality of care to older people, was tackled by considering it from a systems approach. The notion of expert systems was introduced to facilitate modelling for chronic disease management. 'Expert systems' is a concept borrowed from computing and information technology. It involves systems that are able to provide intelligent decisions, based on knowledge that is specialized to that system and through decision support tools. For example, in the management of chronic obstructive pulmonary disease (COPD) the expert system will ideally include the hospital medical specialist, the specialist respiratory nurse, the respiratory therapist, the pharmacist, the general practitioner, practice nurse and community nurse with specialist experience, as well as the technician who manages the equipment in the home.

Together, this team provides a wide array of experience and knowledge involving most, if not all, aspects of the care of COPD. They will use their own dedicated information systems (albeit connected to others) as well as guidelines and protocols (the decision support tools) to help in consistent decision-making. They are likely to use technology (to measure oxygen and carbon dioxide levels as well as breathing capacity) that might not be available to the generalist. And between them, they will have the skill to report X-rays and specialist scans. They will evaluate across the team to provide the expert feedback that they need to improve and validate their service. This feedback will be shared by everybody *including the patient.* In other chronic disease management processes, such as dementia care, the experts will also include psychologists, social workers and care managers with special expertise.

Central to all this is the older person and their carers. They will be essential to the system as individuals but also as 'experts about themselves'. They will then become experts in the management of their own disease. (For further information on patients as experts see chapter 8, p.198.) In this model, the bulk of the care is provided by the older person and their direct carers; followed by the primary and community care teams supported by the secondary care teams.

In South Buckinghamshire, Parkinson's disease was the first chronic disease management programme to be undertaken for older people that involved linking hospital specialists with the community staff. The specialist nurse in Parkinson's disease was the link person who co-ordinated the services. By basing the Parkinson's disease services for older people within the day hospital and the geriatric outpatients' clinic it was possible to link these to the generality of care needed for the older people. (For an example of an initiative in which the patient became an expert see the description of the Parkinson's Disease Management Team in Appendix 5.1, p.132.)

In the EPICS scheme we were able to replicate this to a large part in diabetes care, showing that the expert system model is a way of providing integrated care across the primary/secondary care interface. The expert system concept lies comfortably within overall complex adaptive system thinking. This chronic disease management process reflects the simple rules developed for integrated systems. (For a description of the simple rules model see chapter 3, p.84.) The expert patient is not only at the heart of the system but has easy access to the rest of the system. The other members of the team providing the networks of care also have easy access to each other. Information is shared easily from a common database which is built on recurring and effective assessments. This chronic disease management will reduce the risk of crises. The database and monitoring systems provide feedback about both patient care and team performance. The multidisciplinary nature and cross-organizational teams certainly blur current boundaries of care, which is one of the basic simple rules.

Linking the expert systems to each other and to the generality of care was the problem facing those involved in pushing forward the development of the EPICS systems. The first stage was to recognize and accept that it was indeed a complex system and could not be reduced to a traditional simple linear model. Once viewed in this light the constraints and hurdles of traditional thinking seemed easier to overcome. There was no way that the specialist departments that were components of the chronic disease management programme would give up control of their own domains. The hospital specialist teams, the primary and community care teams all wished to retain control of their areas. This meant that there was little danger of the EPICS team developing a central command-and-control management style.

> *Linking the expert systems to each other and to the generality of care was the problem facing those involved in pushing forward the development of the EPICS systems.*

It took time to generate a joint purpose and philosophy but shared ownership was successfully achieved. It was generally accepted that it was not necessary to try to think of everything all at once, but to keep moving forward, experimenting as the project evolved, doing things bit by bit around those pieces of the jigsaw that were already in place. The secret lay in connecting, communicating, getting feedback and then reflecting on the whole process together. The key factor in making the system self-organizing was sharing information with decision support systems and improving access for all parts of the system.

> *It was generally accepted that it was not necessary to try to think of everything all at once, but to keep moving forward, experimenting as the project evolved.*

Rehabilitation

Rehabilitation is at the very heart of the ethos of care for older people. The objectives of rehabilitation are the restoration of function, capability, physical and mental health and, as a consequence of all this, regained independence (Nocon and Baldwin 1998, pp.5–11). When it is not possible to restore function fully, rehabilitation should aim to maximize the older person's capabilities and, where chronic medical conditions are concerned, to prevent unnecessary deterioration that will in turn hasten dependence.

Partly due to market pressures within the NHS, recent years have seen a reduction in the number of rehabilitation beds and staff. This is particularly true in acute hospitals. This has resulted in the virtual abolition of long-term care for older people in NHS-controlled beds (Nocon and Baldwin 1998, pp20–23). Day hospital and outreach rehabilitation have been similarly cut back. This is almost certainly a major factor in the rise of emergencies referred to the acute services. On the other hand, it has been estimated that if morbidity and disability rate can be reduced by a modest 1 per cent per year then publicly provided formal care costs could be reduced by 30 per cent (or £6.3 billion per annum) by 2030, with proportionate shorter-term gains on the way (Continuing Care Conference 1998). This approach to balancing limited capacity with long-term demand requires vision, long-term thinking and planning in contrast to the current short-term, quick fixes approach.

Traditionally, rehabilitation has been implemented following an acute event such as a stroke or hip fracture, and in these cases it has been shown to have a positive effect. But rehabilitation can also play an important role in chronic disease management. It may restore function lost through de-conditioning from long-standing chronic diseases such as cardiac failure, pulmonary disease or neurological diseases such as Parkinson's Disease. In all of these conditions it has been shown that rehabilitation, as part of a complex package of interventions, can improve well-being and reduce crises that result in admission to hospital (Applegate *et al.* 1990; Rubenstein *et al.* 1984).

For the elderly, particularly the frail elderly, rehabilitation is unlikely to be effective without it being part of a complex package of interventions that includes a complex geriatric assessment (Sinclair and Dickenson 1998). Such an approach can reduce death rates by 35 per cent and readmission to hospital by 12 per cent. The complex care package will also include clinical care for other chronic medical conditions and appropriate social and environmental interventions. For the optimum improvement in chronic conditions the rehabilitation also needs to be ongoing and consistent over time.

There is an enormous opportunity to improve rehabilitation services for older people. But it will require more than just financial investment. The whole thinking and approach to rehabilitation will have to change (see chapter 12, p.331). Central to this change will be the true involvement of the older person so that they set their own goals and aid their own therapy and do not just rely on intermittent input from trained professionals. By the same token, rehabilitation services need to be more responsive and flexible to the needs and situation of the older person.

Reduction in Acute Hospital Distress

Many older patients gain enormous benefit from admission to hospital. Access to diagnostic facilities, planned orthopaedic and ophthalmic surgery and stroke management are all examples of this. Given the right clinical and psychological support, older people do well even with the most advanced technological interventions such as cardiac surgery. However, for some older people hospital care is fraught with danger and hospital is a hazardous environment (Calkins and Naughton 1999). Divorced from their familiar surroundings, in a stark clinical environment with much activity and noise they are easily agitated and disorientated.

Acute hospitals are organized around providing swift, 'high-tech' treatments with rapid turnover. For the frail elderly these interventions are not always appropriate (Lefevre *et al.* 1992). Their need is for expert assessment that takes into account their multiple pathology, as well as their social and environmental needs. In hospital, they are often in less than adequate facilities, their dietary and fluid needs may be ignored and staff may not be sufficient in numbers or training to care for them properly (Health Advisory Service 1999). All of this results in unnecessary dependency and poor outcomes.

The older patient's psychological needs are also frequently neglected. Depression is often overlooked and is a major cause for morbidity in acute hospitals (Koenig *et al.* 1988). Depression reduces the older person's motivation and has a direct impact on their rehabilitation capabilities. Delirium is the presenting feature of many acute illnesses of the frail elderly and the significance of this is often not appreciated (Rockwood *et al.* 1994). The acute confusion is often inappropriately treated with drugs and the underlying acute condition overlooked, such as infections or metabolic conditions.

The results of surgery in older people can be very rewarding provided the conditions are satisfactory. A recent study (NCEPOD 1999) has shown care needs to be given in the following areas:

- Correct fluid management (taking into account the older person's physiological status) supervized by an experienced team.

- A team of senior surgeons, anaesthetists and physicians (working closely together) is needed to assess physical status and operative risks and be closely involved in all aspects of care.

- The experience of the surgeons and anaesthetists needs to be matched to the technical demands of operating on the older patient.

- Appropriate post-operative care must be available. This should include high-dependency support and intensive care.

- Sufficient daytime theatre and recovery facilities should be available to ensure no patient waits more than 24 hours once fit for surgery.

- Recognition that older people require adequate, safe and skilled pain relief pre- and post-operatively.

- Recognition of post-operative complications that are more common in the elderly (particularly gastro-intestinal complications).

Poor discharge procedures often compound what has been a poor experience of acute hospital stay. Likewise, poor integration of acute hospital care with community-based support and follow-up may negate any benefit that the hospital stay has brought about.

Too often the hospital stay results in unnecessary long-term dependency. One study has shown that 23 per cent of patients had been dependent prior to admission and 42 per cent were dependent at the time of discharge. Though some of this was due to the disease such as strokes, others were due to less than adequate care processes (Hirsch *et al.* 1990).

Many of these adverse events are avoidable by redesigning systems of acute care for older people. (See chapter 12, p.326 on acute hospitals.) Selecting the right patients for the care available may be important too. More refined assessment techniques are now able to predict the functional loss in older people during hospitalization and at three months post-discharge (Sagar *et al.* 1996). As well as advanced age, reduced cognitive function and loss of independence on any one of the six instrumental activities of daily living (IADL), delirium, malnutrition, pressure sores and recent falls all predicted a poor outcome. It is possible that older people who fall into these categories should be cared for in specialist facilities other than acute hospital wards that have no expertise for older people's care.

Balancing the undoubted benefits of hospital for some against the proven risks for others, whilst at the same time improving the quality of care for all older people in hospital, is the Gordian knot that needs untying.

Clinical and social care risk management

Everybody who is concerned with the social and healthcare business, and that includes the older person and their carers, is involved in risk management. Even in the most straightforward situation it is complicated, but with the complexity of integrated care (involving multidisciplinary input across organizations) this scale of involvement can be a daunting prospect. Nevertheless, it is a very important underlying principle that cannot be ignored. At the worst it can drive people into their professional and organizational silos and become a difficult cultural barrier to cross in the integration process. Social workers may have a completely different view of risk management from healthcare workers. The social work perception of risk in a needs-based service for older people is the failure to meet an assessed need when the resources to meet it are not available. Risk management in healthcare has grown from the need to minimize complaints and the risk of litigation. The risk of litigation and the costs of compensation that arise from it have been an enormous incentive to eradicate potential errors in treatment. However, designing high-quality care for the older person from the start through integrated care will prevent the errors from arising in the first place and should significantly reduce the risk of litigation.

Lack of shared responsibility and risk-taking in a nursing home

Mrs J was a 92-year-old widow living in a nursing home locally with known carcinoma of the colon and secondary cancer in her liver. She had not been able to walk or care for herself for some weeks. One weekend she became more confused, developed a fever and started coughing. The nursing home staff requested a visit from the 'on-call' doctor from another practice who had no previous knowledge of her. On his arrival he diagnosed a chest infection. The care plan in the home included nothing about the management of her malignancy and nothing about her wishes or those of her family. Her only daughter was away for the weekend, and attempts to contact her by telephone were unsuccessful. The on-call GP said he was reluctant to accept responsibility for any decision about whether to treat. At this point the nursing staff said they were unable to continue to manage her in the home and that they could not accept further responsibility. The bed manager at the local hospital agreed to accept her for admission but did point out that the wait in the accident and emergency department for a bed in the ward would be several hours. Mrs J died in the hospital 36 hours later.

For the purposes of the EPICS project the potential benefits of clinical risk management were divided into two parts:

1. *Involving the older person.* This centred on delivering quality healthcare through integrated care, focusing on improving access to services, reducing delays wherever possible, and on health promotion and preventive care. As a result the risk of any particular crisis arising decreased for any individual older person.

2. *Involving the organizations delivering healthcare.* This focused on:

    •   improving their ability to manage demand so that even if there were a crisis for the older person it should not necessarily be a crisis and a risk for their resource management as well

    •   reducing the likelihood of complaints and litigation by providing a more acceptable service and removal of errors in care delivery.

In EPICS, risk management was viewed from another context, that of preventing crises and providing the highest quality of care. In fact, the taking of responsible risk when it meant fulfilling the older person's wishes was encouraged. Sometimes these risks were not taken by an individual practitioner because they felt that the outcome of an untoward happening following on from taking a risk was not in their control.

Improved access to any of the service systems meant that responsible risk could be taken. By taking the risks jointly, practitioners felt more empowered to take the risks the older person was wanting to take for themselves; and they as practitioners felt less likely to be personally blamed if things went wrong. The experience was that under these conditions things were much less likely to go wrong in any case. In fact, any untoward event could be recognized early, and because of improved access to all parts of the system the crisis situation could be avoided and no blame attached.

Example of a responsible risk
taken by the professional team

Bessie, a single woman in her early 80s, had been in a geriatric unit for a year. Her home circumstances appeared to be too unfavourable for her to return home to live alone. She was mildly confused and living in a past which held only her mother and father. She often thought she was at home and talking with them. She had no relatives. She had suffered a stroke, but was now walking with a frame and was able to dress herself.

Her home was virtually unaltered from when her parents had lived in it, with no heating or hot water. Situated on the bank of a river, it had an outside lavatory round the back. The path to it was overgrown. Her iron bed with a big feather mattress was up a steep, narrow staircase. Bessie would not consider living in a residential home, nor moving from this house. Nor would she spend any money to have heaters installed or any other alterations.

The hospital consultant, the community psychiatric nurse, the occupational therapist, the hospital social worker and care manager all felt it might be possible for Bessie to manage at home. However, heating and a bed downstairs were requirements for any attempt at rehabilitating Bessie in her own home.

The hospital social worker found that Bessie was known to a solicitor who had attended her parents and he came out of retirement to talk with her to win her confidence. She finally gave him power of attorney and heaters were purchased and a single bed and commode installed downstairs. After a year in hospital, frail and confused Bessie went home for a trial 36 hours. Neighbours took responsibility for checking Bessie in the day.

Back home in her familiar surroundings Bessie was less confused . She remained at home. The professional team had taken a real but responsible risk in helping Bessie to live as she wanted to.

Footnote: Bessie had the last word. She had the home carer bring her feather mattress down to put on the new bed!

EPICS encouraged a culture of responsible risk-taking through high-quality assessment, easy access to services and information and a responsive review system. A strategy of total risk avoidance will result in some instances in the delivery of unneccessary care. For example, if the risk involved sending Bessie home (see box) had not been taken, she would have remained in a hospital bed or nursing home.

> *EPICS encouarged a culture of responsible risk-taking through high-quality assessment, easy access to services and information and a responsive review system.*

The importance of information to clinical risk management

The EPICS information system was an essential tool. Without it, the risk management programme would not have been possible. The central population register was at its heart – older people were categorized by risk factors (see chapter 7, p.169 on information systems) and then put into one of three groups:

- *Lower-risk group.* The people in it tended to be younger than in the other groups and were essentially fit and well. This group constituted the majority of those on the register. The aim was to direct health promotion and preventive programmes towards them. (Note: It was usually from this group that the older EPICS volunteers were recruited.)

- *Higher-risk group.* This group was older, frailer and usually living alone or, if married, with a spouse of similar age. They were usually already known to one or more service agencies but were living independently in the community. This group had more frequent assessments and tended to access EPICS more.

- *Interface group.* This group was living at home or in sheltered accommodation but was usually receiving maximum packages of care with home care visits up to three times a day, and not infrequently night care as well. They were poised at the interface between being able to continue at home and needing long-term institutional care. These older people frequently needed the help of the EPICS team to tide them over short-term crises.

The database used in the information system allowed categories and combinations of risk factors to be selected and groups of older people to be identified. For example, every winter it was used to identify those people over 80 years, living alone, known to be at risk of hypothermia during a cold spell and to make sure they were coping and warm. Usually this meant nothing more than a telephone call and a support visit from a volunteer.

A concern that arose later with regard to risk management related to the pathway or journey that the patient had taken or was taking through the care process. Even if there were predetermined care pathways, the individuality of each patient and the customization of care often meant that the care was not following any recognized pattern. In this situation it was imperative that the record system was able to track back and find the 'care trail' no matter who was involved and where. The record-keeping system had to cover the single, whole, or ongoing care process. It was essential to identify clearly the individual practitioner's contribution and the practice for which they were professionally accountable.

There is much to be said for joint record keeping (see chapter 7, p.182 on infor- mation systems) on a common central electronic system that includes a laptop or handheld recording device for all to use. Wherever possible a print-out of records should be held by the patient or client. (In the future it is possible they too may have their own computer or digital TV system linked with the integrated care system.)

In EPICS the locality co-ordinator updated the 'care trail' on the central computer, but each of the professionals kept their own individual records. Though this initially appeared to be a bureaucratic burden, the plan was to make the system available to involved practitioners through an intranet so that they could make direct entries. This would have made it possible for everybody to know the care programme as it happened.

Overview

Historically, clinical risk management has had a very poor and negative image especially amongst clinical staff. It is associated with complaints and litigation, and compliance, none of which lie easily with the basic values of clinical care. For many it appears threatening, even if it is supposed to help contain those threats. However, there is a positive way of looking at risk management. Measures can be taken to reduce risk by identifying it, taking steps to minimize it and recognizing that easy access to other appropriate help (possibly admission to hospital or a short-term bed) is available if needed. In a culture of no risk-taking there will be an inappropriate over-provision for the majority of older people to protect the minority at highest risk.

> *In a culture of no risk-taking there will be an inappropriate over-provision for the majority of older people to protect the minority at highest risk.*

Identifying the risks for any given older person and apportioning them between the professionals in the team makes them less daunting. What appear to be 'unacceptable' risks for any one person or organization to take unilaterally become acceptable risks when taken together with others. This process of respecting the other team members' responsibility in risk-taking (and importantly, not abusing it) and supporting other team members was a very cohesive factor in maintaining team integrity and respect. Rather than constraining risk-taking, it enhanced it. Central to all this is that the older person and their family will share in the responsibility. Their wishes, how much risk they wish to take in any given situation and what type of care they want will be an essential part of risk management.

Chapter 5 – Headline points

- It has been found that multiple risk factor interventions are more successful than those done singly.

- There is considerable evidence that many of these well-proven prevention programmes are not consistently put in place and the benefits are denied to the older person.

- The de-conditioning and depression which chronic diseases bring about result in a vicious downward spiral of dependency.

- Linking the expert systems to each other and to the generality of care was the problem facing those involved in pushing forward the development of the EPICS systems.

- It was generally accepted that it was not necessary to try to think of everything all at once, but to keep moving forward, experimenting as the project evolved.

- EPICS encouraged a culture of responsible risk-taking through high-quality assessment, easy access to services and information and a responsive review system.

- In a culture of no risk-taking there will be an inappropriate over-provision for the majority of older people to protect the minority at highest risk.

References

Applegate, W.B., Miller, S.T., Graney M.J., Elan, J.T., Burns, R. and Akins, D.E. (1990) 'A randomised controlled trial in a geriatric assessment unit in a community rehabilitation hospital.' *New England Journal of Medicine 322*,1572–1578.

Calkins, E. and Naughton, B.J. (1999) 'Care of older people in hospital' In E. Calkins, C. Boult, E.H. Wagner, J.T. Pacala (eds) *New Ways to Care for Older People.* New York: Springer Publishing Company.

Continuing Care Conference (1998) 'Preface' p. v. *Fit for the Future: The Prevention of Dependency in Later Life.* London: Continuing Care Conference.

Elkan, R., Kendrick, D., Dewey, M., Hewitt, M., Robinson, J., Blair, M., Williams, D. and Brummell, K. (2001) 'Effectiveness of home based support for older people: Systematic review and meta-analysis.' *British Medical Journal 323*, 719–725.

Health Advisory Service (HAS 2000) (1999) *Not Because They are Old: An independent inquiry into the care of older people on acute wards in general hospitals.* London: HAS 2000.

Hirsch, C.H., Sommers, L., Olsen, A., Mullen, L. and Winograd, C.H., (1990) 'The natural history of functional mobility in hospitalised older patients.' *The Journal of the American Geriatric Society 38*, 1296–1303.

Koenig, H.G., Meador, K.G., Cohen, H.J. and Blazer D. (1988) 'Depression in elderly hospitalised patients with medical illness.' *Archives in Internal Medicine 148*, 1929–1936.

Lefevre, S., Feinglass, J., Potts, S., Soglin, L., Yarnold, P., Martin, G. and Webster, J. (1992) 'Iatrogenic complications in high risk elderly patients.' *Archives of Internal Medicine 152*, 2074-2780.

Muir Gray, J.A. (1997) *Evidence-based Purchasing and Commissioning in Evidence-based Healthcare.* London: Churchill Livingstone.

NCEPOD (1999) *Extremes of Age: The report of the National Confidential Enquiry into Perioperative Deaths.* London: NCEPOD.

Nocon, A. and Baldwin, S. (1998) *Trends in Rehabilitation Policy: A review of the literature.* London: Kings Fund Publishing.

Patterson, C. (2000) 'Health promotion, screening and surveillance.' In J. Grimley Evans, T.H. Franklin Williams, B. Lynn Beattie, J-P. Michel and G.K. Wilcock (eds) *Oxford Textbook of Geriatric Medicine.* Oxford: Oxford University Press.

Rockwood, K., Cosway, S., Stolee, P., Kydd, D., Carver, D. and Jarrett P. (1994) 'Increasing the recognition of delirium in the elderly patient.' *Journal of the American Geriatric Society 42*, 252–256.

Rubenstein, L.Z., Josephson, K.R., Wieland, G.D., English, P.A., Sayre, J.A. and Kane R.L. (1984) 'Effectiveness of a geriatric assessment unit: A randomised clinical trial.' *New England Journal of Medicine 311*, 1664–1670.

Sagar, M.A., Rudberg, M.A., Jalaluddin, M., Franke, T., Inouye, S.K., Landerfeld C.S., Siebens, H. and Winograd, C.H. (1996) 'Hospital Admission Risk Profile (HARP): Identifying older patients at risk for functional deline following acute medical illness and hospitalisation.' *The Journal of the American Geriatric Society 44*, 251–257

Sinclair, A. and Dickenson, E. (1998) 'Findings – what the systematic reviews show' pp.18–19 *Effective Practice in Rehabilitation: The evidence of systematic reviews.* London: Kings Fund Publishing.

Stuck, A.E., Walthert, J.M., Nikolaus, T., Bula, C.J., Hohmann C. and Beck, J.C. (1999) 'Risk factors for functional status decline in community-living elderly people: A systematic literature review.' *Social Science and Medicine 48*, 445–469.

Wagner, E.H. Austin, B.T. and Von Korff, M. (1996) 'Organising care for patients with chronic illness.' *The Millbank Quarterly 74*, 511–544.

Von Korff, M., Gruman, J., Schaefer, J., Curry, S. and Wagner, E.H. (1997) 'Collaborative management of chronic illness: Essential elements.' *Annals of Internal Medicine 127*, 1097–1102.

Further reading

Calkins, E., Boult, C., Wagner, E.H. and Pacala, J.T. (1999) *New Ways to Care for Older People: Building Systems Based on Evidence.* New York: Springer Publishing Company.

The topics of health promotion and prevention together with risk management are covered well by this book from the USA. It provides very stimulating reading and a range of interesting ideas for older peoples' care with as good a literature and evidence base as is possible.

Prevention of Dependency in Later Life Group (1998) *Fit for the Future: The Prevention of Dependency in Later Life.* London: Report of the 'Continuing Care Conference'.

This excellent report from the Continuing Care Conference has not received the recognition it deserves and gives a well-researched and argued case for disease prevention and rehabilitation in the UK. Copies are still available via Help the Aged, London.

APPENDIX 5.1

The Parkinson's Disease Management Team

The rudimentary Parkinson's Disease Management Team was given a boost by the appointment of a new neurologist with a special interest in degenerative diseases of the brain and who was eager to expand and network his services. There was already a general practitioner with expertise in Parkinson's Disease (PD) management who linked with other GPs in the community interested in PD care. A geriatrician with an interest in PD also ran regular clinics for older patients with PD separately. Even though a PD liaison nurse had also been recently appointed the service seemed disjointed. There was no consistency of provision and an element of chance in any given older patient receiving the service they needed. The problem was mutually recognized. At several meetings of all those involved, a shared purpose, based on agreed values, was shaped and an outline implementation process agreed. Almost inevitably no new monies or resources were available, so they had to think creatively about sharing resources. Two of the major issues were:

- How does everybody benefit from the expertise of the new neurologist?

- How can a more holistic service be provided to those older patients with PD and other chronic diseases?

The key worker throughout the early stages was the PD liaison nurse. She undertook a number of tasks:

- To survey and identify all the patients with PD in South Buckinghamshire, done from hospital and primary care records as well as personal contacts. From this a population database with clinical details of as many individual patients as possible was generated.

- To create an information system on a centralized computer and replicated on the personal hand-held computer which she took with her to update the information on each patient contact.

- To formulate at clinical staff meetings guidelines for the management of PD. These were to be shared by all the staff, departments and primary care practitioners.

- To develop networks for PD care with the acute hospital wards, the accident and emergency department, the primary care teams and GP surgeries. These also linked with both the neurologist's and the geriatrician's clinics. The PD nurse held a nursing clinic in parallel with the geriatrician's clinic to facilitate joint consultation when necessary.

- To establish a patients' Helpline to improve patient access.

The Department of Care for the Elderly improved access to their department by arranging for one day per month to be devoted to PD care at the day resource unit at the local community hospital. Both the neurologist and the liaison nurse were encouraged to refer patients directly if they felt there was a need for a complex geriatric assessment for any older patients with multiple medical needs not already known to the department. The care of the patients was easily shared between the consultant neurologist and the geriatrician in a way that most appropriately met the patients' wishes and needs. For example, during the day unit phase the geriatrician might supervise and when that phase was completed there was a choice to refer back to either the neurologist's or the geriatrician's clinics.

Because the day resource unit was a central component of the EPICS fast track assessment service, and connected to the rapid response team, any emergencies or urgent assessments for PD patients were directly linked and could be undertaken at any time. On the day allocated for PD work, the liaison nurse, the geriatrician and the therapists ran parallel clinics whilst the day unit staff undertook more generalist assessments. Not only could patients be seen jointly, but a case conference with the social worker and the EPICS central co-ordinator at the end of the morning brought everything together. The whole process was co-ordinated by the nurse in charge of the day unit. The system allowed for great flexibility. Each member of the team would see some PD patients throughout the month in their individual practice. But they would also network as necessary with the rest of the team at any time. Those GP practices that ran their own shared care clinics for PD had access to the help and advice of the day unit either directly or through the liaison nurse.

The involvement of patients in their own care was much easier in this flexible scheme that could offer genuine choices. Patients were encouraged to be involved in training to manage their own drugs wherever possible. The local Parkinson's Disease Society became a user forum for discussion, training, self-help and support and an advocate for improving services. It very quickly became part of the care network.

Chapter 6

Putting it in Place

Some Solutions

There is nothing so difficult as turning a good idea into action.

Goethe

To find the problem is the same as finding the solution.

Rittel and Webber, systems analysts

This chapter addresses some of the practical issues involved in implementing EPICS. It describes the importance and value of the stakeholders and the stakeholder systems and explores the need to have a wide diversity of stakeholders to create innovative solutions. It confirms the importance of developing wide networks and managing relationships. It gives a model for the structures required for implementation. It emphasizes the importance of the one-stop service and the involvement of the older person through a telephone link. The chapter includes a flowchart that offers a practical guide to implementation.

No matter how much theory there is, no matter how many reports are written, unless they are translated into improved outcomes for older people they can be little more than exhibits in the halls of academe or management. This has to be the grand challenge for all who have the vision for change. The journey is full of potential pitfalls, and if there is no blood, sweat or tears, despite all the excitement, it is unlikely that profound change is occurring.

Sometimes there are moments of overpowering doubt within the leaders as they are pressurized to meet short-term goals with quick fixes. And everybody at some time feels stressed when faced with the possibility of leaving their professional comfort zones. For the innovators it does require a persistence and doggedness, mixed with more than a little mental courage, to continue. However, have no doubt that it is all worth it. For those teams and organizations who have achieved it, the benefit of knowing that they are more effectively helping older people and the fulfilment of a positive and rewarding environment to work in are more than compensation.

For everybody putting these changes into place there is a very steep learning curve. Even if the professional has done it elsewhere, the uniqueness of the new situation (with fresh colleagues and different communities and care organizations) always provides new and unforeseen challenges. Working within complex adaptive systems means allowing freedoms that inevitably result in some mistakes and errors.

> *Working within complex adaptive systems means allowing freedoms that inevitably result in some mistakes and errors.*

Because nobody really knows the best way forward through all this complexity, there is no mistake-proof prescription for success. The secret lies in 'chunking' the project with multiple small ongoing changes at the fringes that can be more easily corrected if mistakes are made. The feedback loops (see chapter 2 on systems, p.54) that keep a check on the effects of these changes and give understanding of the outcomes are the lifelines in a sea of uncertainty.

The aim of this chapter is to give a general direction of travel for those implementing the changes. It is not intended as a specific itinerary to be followed rigidly in the order below, but it is probably advisable to follow the general route. The implementation process has to be an iterative one. As the project moves on to a new phase that phase has an impact on what has gone before. As a result, the previous stages may have to be modified, which in turn impacts on stages both before and after that. Sometimes, it truly is two steps forward and one back. But, in the systems context, this is the adaptive component of change, the built-in factor for fine tuning. And in the end, long-term sustainable goals are achieved sooner and the mechanism is in place for continued change thereafter.

'Changing ourselves'

In the early stages of the EPICS project, every mistake that it was possible to make was made. There was no clear path forward and the project team blundered on, only surviving on good will. However, the team was determined to stick with it and was also prepared to learn and give time to reflect on what was happening. The team was fortunate to have two excellent facilitators who helped them keep on track by means of systems thinking and through understanding of the dynamics of both system and personal behaviour. This all took time, with many days of workshops and personal learning. In the end, and despite all the agonizing and effort, everybody agreed that the benefits of doing this were very real, because, as the project slowly gained momentum, each stage thereafter was completed more easily and faster. An additional benefit for many of the team was that the insights and knowledge gained could be applied in other professional situations as well. Perhaps it should not have been the surprise it was when some realized the positive benefit it also had on personal lives outside the team. Complexity was creeping up behind us and we did not know!

The initial stages

Identifying the champion

Most such projects need a champion: someone to support and argue for the project from the very start. Usually it will be someone of sufficient professional and personal credibility to have the ear of those in charge and persuasive enough to sway peer professionals. The EPICS project started in 1985 with a potential conflict between the GPs who ran the local community hospital and the local department for the care of the elderly. The problem was access to beds when the latter's bed numbers were reduced for financial reasons in order to keep the community hospital open. The GPs were very jealous of their beds and admitting rights but, on the other hand, the beds had to be used in such a way that the impact of bed closures on the elderly care beds was minimized. How could the beds be shared in such a way that the GPs retained apparent control while the service to the elderly was improved?

After some swallowed pride on both sides, a scheme was devised that satisfied all parties. The elderly patients would be assessed by the team for the care of the elderly prior to admission to the community and day hospital and given a care plan. But, once admitted, the GPs were in charge of looking after them.

This not only improved the care for the older person but the nursing staff at the hospital were delighted with the support. It also resolved the care of the elderly department's problem of providing day-to-day medical cover with insufficient staff stretched over three other sites. The initial pilot worked so well that it seemed obvious that it could be expanded (especially as, once assessed, not all the potential patients needed admission). Out of this grew the concept of EPICS – it provided a vision of a future system that someone thought well worth championing.

Ultimately, a good champion should do himself out of the job, because everybody involved becomes so enthused and committed that they all assume the role. If the project relies on only a single champion over the long term, it will fail. Failed projects make champions into martyrs.

Identifying and involving the stakeholders

This is a fundamental process which needs great care and attention. Get it wrong and the project will only survive months, if it ever gets off the ground at all. A stakeholder is defined as anybody who has any interest or involvement in the project. This definition is useful in reinforcing the all-encompassing nature of stakeholder involvement, but in practical terms it needs to be broken down to be manageable.

INVOLVE ALL KEY ORGANIZATIONS

At the start of the project all the key organizations should be involved, preferably through their senior management, who have the authority to commit their organization wholeheartedly to the project.

Stakeholders come in all shapes and sizes. Some are organizations such as local government, trusts, patient groups, older people's clubs. Others are professional groups or individual people. At the start of the project all the key organizations should be involved, preferably through their senior management, who have the authority to commit their organization wholeheartedly to the project. It is not always easy to truly engage chief executives and senior managers who see themselves burdened with a whole range of other problems, and who often have different agendas involved with short-term targets.

PRESENT SOLUTIONS NOT PROBLEMS

The skill is to present senior managers with solutions rather than problems. They have quite enough of the latter already. Demonstrate how the older care project can significantly impact on other services, improve the whole system and help solve their major problems.

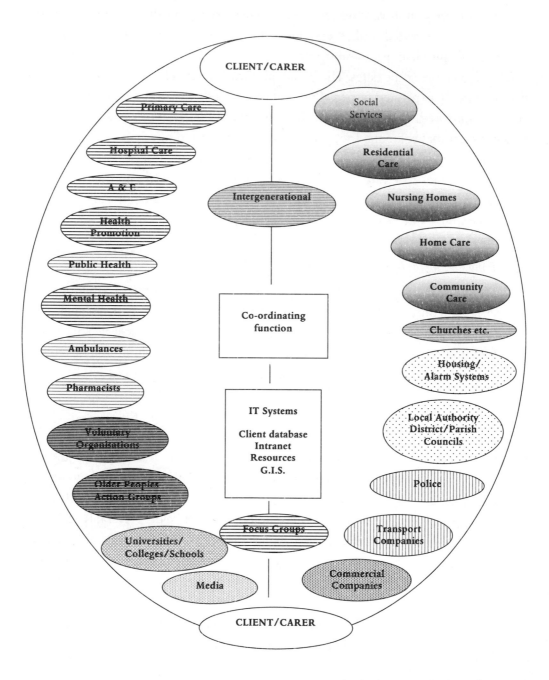

Figure 6.1 EPICS organizational structure – EPICS-r-Us

N.B. All of these stakeholders included representatives from both the private and statutory sectors where relevant

Identify some possible short-term gains that are early 'pay-offs'.

Stakeholders are busy people, and getting their attention, even for a short time, is sometimes tricky. The secret is to prepare thoroughly. Identify some possible short-term gains that are early 'pay-offs'. This is the 'honey to get them to the pot'. Rehearse presenting your case in two minutes flat. Literally two minutes, so that a chance encounter can be turned into a golden opportunity. And a short appointment can be an extremely productive one. Have the project and the important outcomes put on one side of A4 paper (and no more) for them to read. It is surprising how this exercise can crystallize the thinking of the team.

FOSTER VISIBLE COMMITMENT

Having got senior people involved, do not assume they are committed to the project. Their involvement may be motivated by other reasons, such as the need to satisfy some national agenda which has to be implemented. If this is the case, they will often send a deputy to meetings. The sustainable success of any major cross- or multi-organizational project that is going to have a big impact depends on the visible support of the various chief executives and their relationships to each other. And always remember, they are human beings too, and may need help and support in doing this.

A colleague from another area remembered attending hours of meetings directed at getting a consensus view on a strategic issue. The local authority held a strong view. It appeared after the discussions that a way forward had been agreed which was acceptable to all stakeholders.

Several days later an article in a local newspaper reported that the view of the authority had prevailed. The newspaper had been briefed by an officer from the authority.

CONFIRM THE OLDER PERSON AS A MAJOR STAKEHOLDER

The power of the involvement of the older person and their organizations needs to be harnessed at a very early stage.

The power of the involvement of the older person and their organizations needs to be harnessed at a very early stage. There is often a lay, non-executive director from one or other of the organizations who is older and is prepared to be involved. And certainly there will be an older person's organization such as Age Concern, or retirement associations, or clubs which may readily provide a representative. Carers' groups may wish to be represented too.

IDENTIFY AND RECRUIT 'DOERS'

To complete this early group, identify and bring together some of the influential professional people from across all the organizations. Try to single out the 'movers and shakers', the people who get things done. Because they are active doers they are usually easy to involve and welcome the opportunity to contribute. However, they also value their time, so their involvement needs to be productive. Their experience and wisdom from their previous work can be a stabilizing influence. But be cautious, these people sometimes have agendas of their own. If these can be aligned to the project it can be strengthening, if not they can become a barrier.

> *Try to single out the 'movers and shakers', the people who get things done.*

As the project develops, it is almost inevitable that some new stakeholder organization or person has to be approached and asked to join. This is part of the iterative process and the project leaders need to be sensitive to the need constantly to review the involvement of new stakeholders and what role they will play. These new stakeholders will be helped by an induction process first to understand and then to help the values and purpose of the project to evolve.

The more diverse the stakeholders, the greater the chance there will be of creative solutions. The more creative the solutions required, the more diverse the stakeholders need to be.

Recognise 'Neglected' stakeholders

Beyond the obvious stakeholders in health and social services (for whom the initial problems seem to be the most pressing) there seems to be a consistent pattern among the stakeholders who are asked to join at a later stage or are even forgotten completely.

LOCAL HOUSING ORGANIZATIONS

The EPICS experience (and that from elsewhere) is that these can be powerful agents for change. Increasingly they are being creative in the ways housing (particularly sheltered housing) is used to integrate community services. In many areas in the UK the housing department also runs the community-based alarm service for older people. The databases associated with this and the linking of alarms to rapid response services can enormously enhance both. There has been at least one attempt to base a complete integrated care system on a community alarm service. (See Warwick EPICS in Appendix B, p.362 at the end of the book.)

AMBULANCE SERVICES

Almost without fail the ambulance services are neglected in integrated projects at the outset. Working alone, they have pioneered information and service systems to meet emergency situations, and they are rapidly gaining expertise in triaging in older patient's homes with databases created for their own use. Their paramedics are already multi-skilled and use increasingly sophisticated technology (such as telemedicine) in their work and the way they interact with hospitals. The flexibility of the new integrated services will depend heavily on the ability to move either care to the patient or the patient to care. The ambulance services are already 'working in the spaces' (see chapter 2, p.63).

> *The flexibility of the new integrated services will depend heavily on the ability to move either care to the patient or the patient to care.*

POLICE

All of the older person focus groups organized by EPICS asked, first and foremost, for improved safety. They wanted to feel secure both inside and outside their homes. Police security arrangements have a major role to play in improving security and reducing the incidence of crime against older people. Community policing is a powerful network with considerable information and knowledge of older people at its command. It is usually the police, for example, who will find and look after vulnerable older people wandering in the street in the early hours. Frequently they will take them to the local accident and emergency department, whereas linking them directly to the rapid response services of an integrated care system could provide an alternative way of dealing with the situation, an alternative that is better for both the older person and the hard pressed A&E department.

COMMUNITY PHARMACISTS

Local community pharmacists are providing an ever-widening range of services within localities. These range from giving health advice to providing equipment, as well as the traditional role of preparing prescriptions. Even where prescriptions are concerned, they are preparing them in ways to improve compliance (such as using special boxes with tablets in marked daily compartments). They are also overseeing some aspects of drug safety, a substantial cause of error in healthcare. Because they are so intimately part of the locality and the local shopping facilities they have great potential in making services and help more accessible.

LOCAL LEISURE FACILITIES

Many of the leisure and activity centres have both the facilities and trained staff (health and fitness instructors, for example) to play a major role in health promotion and preventive disease management for older people. What the professionals see as healthcare the older person will see as leisure. (See chapter 5, p.112 on preventing crises.) The leisure centres offer a wide variety of activities (including swimming and dancing) in bright and lively settings far removed from the traditional venues of care; and, as participants, older people are included as part of the wider community.

LOCAL CHAMBERS OF COMMERCE

Most older people will use shops local to them, but without transport they are not always accessible. Local businesses and local authorities can do much to remove these and other constraints to make shopping easier. There is an enormous opportunity for local shopping facilities to be flexible. There are examples of shopping malls and streets being opened specially for older and disabled people at Christmas time, which could be extended to other times of year. In the decades to come the increasing numbers of older people will make them an influential customer group so that there will be a mutual benefit in exploiting this kind of opportunity.

Chambers of commerce also hold registers of the commercial enterprises in the locality. This can be a useful source for identifying and involving traders to provide services relevant to older people.

LOCAL BUSINESS AND INDUSTRY

EPICS in South Buckinghamshire forged very successful ties with several local businesses. These helped by sponsoring particular initiatives, for example the cost of the phone line and calls for the phone link. One big international company with its headquarters in the locality provided training opportunities with both facilities and equipment. Another printed the reports of the older peoples' conferences and a handbook of local community services. What is more, they encouraged their staff to help as volunteers, something many felt drawn to because they had elderly parents or relatives living within the community. All this activity was mutually advantageous as it enabled the businesses to behave as good corporate citizens (and to be seen doing so) and put something back into the community whose goodwill they were dependent upon.

LOCAL RELIGIOUS ORGANIZATIONS

As part of the community values system religious organizations can play a very important role in helping set values and mobilize support. They may have a network that
already includes helping older people and that can be extended. In South
Buckinghamshire the 'Churches Together' group took on running the telephone
links once the older person no longer required active support from the EPICS team
(see below). Parish councils in some areas have an active community-based support
network for older people.

LOCAL COMMUNITY LEADERS

These key people can help in setting values and ensuring that the particular needs of
their communities are brought into the system through proper representation. This
will include any ethnic communities or those where special needs require representation, for example in rural areas. There are numerous other community groups who
have been prime movers in helping shape community care, such as the Red Cross, St
John's Ambulance, the WRVS and the Women's Institutes, and they too can help set
the values in older people's care.

THE PRIVATE AND NOT-FOR-PROFIT SECTOR

It is very easy for the statutory organizations to feel that the burden of care is entirely
theirs. Much of the care that is already delivered is through private and charitable
organizations, yet they are rarely included meaningfully in the early stages of locality
planning. They are a significant part of the whole system of care and provide much of
the stock of resources. They need to be encouraged to be part of the whole.

This list is by no means complete. The opportunities for an integrated care system to
demonstrate its inclusiveness are virtually boundless. As an example, post offices,
where so many older people go for their pensions, are an important source of information, and there are numbers of innovative schemes centred on them. In some cases
these are providing benefit screening for older people with
a direct line to the Benefits Office for them to follow up any
entitlement.

> *Stakeholder involvement is itself complex and a very important subsystem within the whole system.*

Stakeholder involvement is itself complex and a very
important subsystem within the whole system. Managed
dynamically it is an extremely important networking tool
that gives enormous power to the project overall. It is the
way in which organizations and people remain connected

to the project and continue to feel ownership at whatever level they are involved. The major challenge is to balance the agenda of the project against the agendas of the stakeholders so that joint working does not become a political melee.

Developing the structural framework of an integrated care system

Some organizations using the complex adaptive system approach have managed with very loose, informal structures. Because of the large numbers of people and organizations (spread out over a large area) involved in EPICS, we continued with the rather more formal structures that we started with, but gradually loosened them to be more flexible.

Project board

There is a need for a group that is responsible for the strategic direction of the project and within which the senior executives can network. There are two choices:

- The first is to piggy-back the function on to an existing organizational group, such as a modernization board or a local implementation team. The risk is that if the group is dealing with a range of projects it is not sufficiently attached to the specific integrated care project and the senior managers do not have intimate experience of the implementation themselves. The focus may not be clear, and it becomes difficult to sort out ownership problems. On the other hand, senior managers do sometimes view this as an easier option administratively and a good use of their time. There is also the opportunity of strategically integrating it into other major projects.

- The alternative is the 'single project board'. This can be very focused and remains connected to the project. The board needs to meet only three or four times a year and, if adequate reporting and evaluation systems are in place, the meetings need not be long. (See chapter 9, p.237 on evaluation.) It is also easier to keep the whole board in real contact with the project through their participation in workshops, visits to care sites and hearing the views of the users and professionals involved.

Steering groups

These were locality-based teams of wide stakeholder involvement including users and carers to implement integrated care, essentially working around operational issues. Each was chaired by a senior manager from any one of the organizations involved, with the chairship rotating. They created local strategy and were directly involved with implementation. These groups met regularly every six to eight weeks. By ensuring that a wide spread of agendas was being met, the attendances were remarkably good. These groups became executive groups as the projects became established, and took on an operational and development function.

Locality groups

This was the forum where the practising professionals and volunteer team leaders and user representatatives met to plan, and to deal with day-to-day issues. Crucially, they also provided feedback to the steering group and the project board on the matters arising and the outcomes of the actual care processes. These locality groups met monthly, but most of their work was done outside the meetings through the networks of care. Again, the chairship rotated through each professional group. They were given the authority to organize themselves and to be as flexible and open to change as possible.

Development groups

Much of the development of the processes was done by those directly involved in delivering care. This made the best use of their unique knowledge of any problems with the implementation of care and their grass-roots knowledge of the locality. Equally importantly, it ensured that they had genuine 'ownership' of the processes they were responsible for. The membership of these groups came from across all the other groups. It included some board members and other experts co-opted from IT, finance, social services development teams, and so on, and representatives from housing associations and voluntary organizations. Some of the issues addressed by the different development groups were:

- a common assessment process
- flexible transport, co-ordinating resources from the community
- applying information technology
- involving users
- evaluation
- strategy

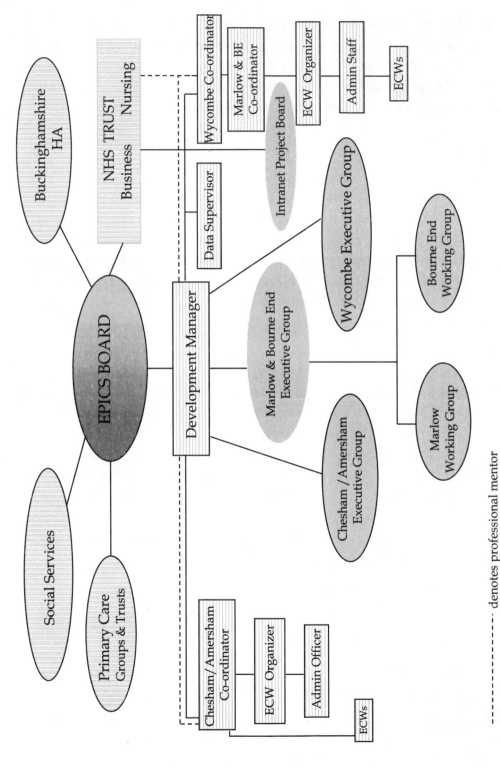

Figure 6.2 EPICS management and line management system

- Epi-centres (using facilities in, for example, sheltered housing complexes with residents and EPICS volunteers trained to provide an information service for the local older community, and where therapies and health promotion programmes could be focused)

- preparing a feasibility study and project initiation document (PID) when rolling the project out to other areas was planned. (See Appendix 6.1, p.158 at the end of this chapter.)

The whole process was dynamic with considerable cross-linking at all levels across the development groups. All played a part in developing the mission statement (see chapter 10, p.274 on levers and tools).

Aligning the total organization

In the early days of EPICS (when funding was very limited) the team was very dependent on existing support services to carry out the essential bureaucratic tasks involved in hiring people, paying salaries and selling the services. There were no funds to support this kind of activity, so much depended on goodwill of others to provide these functions. To make things run as smoothly as possible (even though 'approval' had been sanctioned by the board) the project manager and others would 'sweet talk' the relevant departments into helping when they were already busy. This contact blossomed further when the team realized that the support services' expertise could be used profitably if they were directly involved in project planning from the start, instead of just being approached to provide a service once the project was up and running. For many of the staff of the support services this was the first time they had been so directly drawn into the early stages of a project. It was something they clearly appreciated.

- *Trust Finance Department.* The Trust's finnance department was particularly helpful in guiding the project through the maze of joint-financing both across internal departments and across organizations. The insights they brought to the project were of great help. Their advice and suggestions for the evaluation of the cost-effectiveness of the project were particularly valuable. (See chapter 9, p.254 on evaluation.)

- *Commissioning.* In the days of the internal market in healthcare the 'product' had to be marketed and sold to GPs and their managers (even though representative GPs were involved in the project from the start). The Director of Commissioning for the health trust assisted us with advice and by brokering arrangements so that everybody got ' best value'. He too appreciated his early involvement.

- *Human resources.* Employing people to work across professional and organizational boundaries is never straightforward. For many of us it was a unique experience, and employment law appeared a minefield. Contracts and job descriptions had to be drawn up extremely carefully, on the one hand fulfilling legal obligations and on the other not stifling creative working and restricting the flexibility of integrated working.

- *Public health.* From the outset EPICS had identified the need to manage populations of older people. Much of public health work is in managing the health of populations of people. The expertise and guidance of public health physicians and epidemiologists was instrumental in helping set up the demographically based information systems and in the evaluation. The public health physicians had knowledge of the variety of funding opportunities and helped draft applications.

- *Public relations departments.* There was always news and information that the project wished to get out to the public, telling them about new services or involving them in some way in the project. Through the various public relations departments of local statuatory, commercial and voluntary organizations, access was available to in-house newsletters and to the local media. The project had made its own contacts with some local newspapers, but these public relations departments were instrumental in introducing EPICS to national and local radio stations and TV. They helped with the presentation of information leaflets and the advertising of workshops for the older people. In one area the public relations department got so involved with a major focus group workshop for older people that it agreed to run the ensuing older people's conference on behalf of the local council.

Networking with these support departments was vital to the project, particularly in the early stages, because it embedded the project in all the organizations' infrastructures and so made the project more robust. It also meant that there were allies dotted around who were invaluable in difficult times. However, the nature of most support departments within health and social services is to be introverted and low-profile; they tend not to come looking for you. The message is 'Go find them and engage them'.

Managing networks

Communications and networking is one of those soft issues that does not appear to give quick results. Accordingly it is often put on the 'back burner'. Even when it is acknowledged as being necessary it is often left to chance. With luck there may be some of the right people in the right place with the right networking skills. The maxim is that in major redesign projects, if the perceived time and resource demanded for good communicating and networking is calculated, and then multiplied by ten, it would still be insufficient. This 'managing of the networked spaces' can be critical to the success of integrated care and networked projects.

> *The maxim is that in major redesign projects if the perceived time and resource demanded for good communicating and networking is calculated, and then multiplied by ten, it would still be insufficient.*

The early planning must include a clear strategy and purposeful policy for networking and communication. Simple things such as the circulation of lists of relevant telephone numbers and e-mail addresses, newsletters, strategically placed noticeboards, can all be achieved with a little determination. It is invaluable to get information into guidelines, protocols, clinical and social care handbooks, and patient leaflets and information packs. Libraries, community centres, post offices and the council offices are all happy to have leaflets, and it is important to see that advice-giving agencies such as the Citizens' Advice Bureaux have good information on the project.

Talks to community groups, not only those for older people, are useful for disseminating information and winning volunteers. In South Buckinghamshire, EPICS volunteers were very effective in telling of their experiences to community groups and gave some of the talks. It was rare to return from these meetings without something significant to add to the project. The time was extremely well spent.

The personal touch

Despite all the benefits of electronic communication, our EPICS team found face-to-face discussions and meetings absolutely indispensable and productive.

A regular programme of visits to hospital wards (including accident and emergency departments), GPs surgeries, community nurses' meetings, social service panels and conferences was undertaken. The effort was always greatly appreciated. The EPICS team was always happy to be involved in induction processes. For junior doctors this meant regular six-monthly presentations in the hospital. But for other staff one-off visits to the EPICS co-ordination centre were regular occurrences.

It was the custom always to make visitors welcome when they came to the co-ordination centre, no matter how busy it was. Only an emergency had higher priority. The coffee pot became EPICS networking logo.

Designing networking into the structure

We found from our own experience of EPICS that it was sometimes possible to design the structure so that it facilitated important networks. Every opportunity to network had to be anticipated. Putting the EPICS co-ordinator in a community hospital in the centre of the town made it possible for all kinds of people from all kinds of organizations (including users and potential users) to drop in for information. (For a job description of the EPICS co-ordinator see Appendix 6.2., p.163) The co-ordinator was able to liaise directly with the day resource unit sited in the same building. As the GPs' surgery was next door, both doctors and community nurses found it easy to keep in direct touch. It was extraordinary how much important and relevant information seemed to be exchanged on what seemed to be such an informal basis. Yet another example of complex adaptive system processes at work.

An out-of-hours network

The ambulance service had vacated an old ambulance station in the centre of the town. A local doctors' co-operative took over the premises for their out-of-hours service, and the ambulance service managed the telephone network on behalf of the doctors when patients rang in out-of-hours. They also provided both driver and car to take the doctor on his calls. Some months later, the night-nursing service moved into the same building when they could not find a suitable base elsewhere. When the EPICS project later rolled out to the same area and was looking for a base of its own, it seemed a golden opportunity to move into the same location. The rapid response team could be sited there and network with the GPs, the night nurse and the ambulance services.

The EPICS day team was also on site for handovers as the night services came and went. Despite it seeming such an ideal set up, the authorities demanded such an exorbitant rent that it appeared beyond EPICS's minimal budget.

Desperate negotiations ensued for months whilst EPICS worked incessantly to persuade all concerned of the advantages of the total network. Eventually, good sense prevailed and the rent came down. EPICS moved in with great celebrations (to which the authorities were naturally invited) and the service moved from strength to strength.

Key features of the EPICS in South Buckinghamshire

One-stop service

The facility for the older person, their carers and the professionals involved to make only one call to seek help for their problem was one of the most valued aspects of the integrated service that was EPICS. It was the immediate, practical and outward sign that the service was 'joined up'. Everyone who contacted EPICS put great store by being able to get straight through to the service and get an immediate helpful response. When the referral was made directly by a personal visit to the centre or the day hospital, it was dealt with just as promptly. This aspect of the service was continually monitored and evaluated because, with so high an expectation, the standard could not be allowed to slip. If anything was the EPICS hallmark, this was it.

Making sure that everybody knew the EPICS 'one-stop' number was critical. For the use of older people hundreds of small, fluorescent, sticky labels were distributed with the EPICS call number on them to be stuck on their phones. (See chapter 9, p.244 on evaluation.) GPs and other call centres had to have the number easily available. The hospital telephone switchboard and the ward clerks were very helpful in diverting and arrange calls to EPICS on those occasions when people did not have the number and also the social services duty and emergency teams.

Criteria for success for a one-stop call centre

- easy access
- direct contact with the co-ordinator
- the confidence that comes from being helped by somebody who already knows about them (This was often reflected in the older person's willingness to take advice and help over the telephone when appropriate.)
- the professionals' appreciation of referring to a service with no 'handoffs' between assessment and urgent care provision that is, the same people dealt with both.(This enabled the professionals to take measured risk in their own professional field that they might not have otherwise done.)
- no charge to the user
- no duplication of service provision

The co-ordinator taking the call would do so in front of the computer and as the older person's name was mentioned she was able to bring up the current information from the database. Frequently she knew more about the older person than the caller and this gave enormous credibility to the service. The telephone request prompted a more formal assessment in about 64 per cent of the calls. Another very valued part of the service was that no forms had to be filled in for referral by anybody. Form-filling was felt to be a constraint which would cause bureaucratic delay and a barrier to a quick response. An end-of-episode form was generated, but in the format of a report to the primary care team. This was done automatically on the computer immediately after the intervention was completed.

The older persons' telephone link

This was a very important network in linking older people to EPICS. It was distinct from the 'one-stop' call centre though it was connected to it. It was the brain-child of a group of volunteers who managed it themselves. The telephone and the cost of using it was sponsored by a local business and it was housed in the project office with the volunteers coming in on a rota basis. The clients were referred by the co-ordinators following an assessment. The volunteer would ring at a regular agreed time, mostly once weekly, although it could be daily according to the need. The volunteers provided support and confidence for the older person, and it was a regular check on their situation. The volunteers had been trained and always had the immediate help of a professional, usually the co-ordinator. They also attended six-weekly support meetings with their volunteer team leader and the EPICS co-ordinator.

A very useful outcome was that EPICS was able to support some of the frailer older people who were at risk, but could essentially manage, when their carer or family went away on holiday. This prevented the need for a temporary admission to a residential home or other more expensive care as it gave the family the confidence to go away knowing their older relative would have a link to help through a regular friendly call. Another valuable benefit was that the rapid response team could be withdrawn sooner in the knowledge that the older person was going to be 'supervised' on the telephone and did not require a period of observation to see if they deteriorated afterwards. The co-ordinator found it helped her and was another 'pair of eyes and ears' allowing her to concentrate more on the newer referrals. The volunteers were very sensitive to changes in the voices and manner of their telephone 'link', and frequently a problem was averted by swift referral by the volunteer to the co-ordinator.

Another benefit was that some of the clients would accept help and advice from the volunteer whereas they had refused help from the social services or would not want to bother the community nurse or doctor. The client often gained confidence to accept help from the professionals.

The service became so successful that clients had to be 'discharged' from it to take on new ones. For some of those who were isolated and relied on the contact for social reasons this was very distressing (and for the volunteers who had sustained the link). The local churches agreed to take on the contacts with these people on a long-term basis and organized fund-raising to pay for the calls made. They also had direct access to the EPICS project office but made the calls from their own homes. They were trained by the EPICS team, and their team leader attended the EPICS support group. The volunteers knew they had instant access to the EPICS co-ordinator if a problem arose. The model for community development was an effective one.

Sustainability

There are many examples of health and social care projects that are started but fail some months later and are not sustained. These projects are often driven through the vision and energy of one or two people who are not fully engaging the whole system of care and its associated organizations. When these people either leave or simply give up because the barriers to maintaining the project over time are too great, the projects peter out. (See chapter 10, p.281 on levers and tools.)

The pressure for instant results, short-term solutions and quick fixes undermines the processes of sustainability. The temptation to cut corners and not put in place the underpinning core processes is great. These processes are viewed as being of little productive value, the 'touchy-feely stuff' that is the antithesis of mechanistic, command-and-control methods of working. The metaphor of a house and its foundations is very apt in this context. When the house is finished, the foundations, the footings and the plumbing can no longer be seen. Yet, without them, the house cannot survive for long.

Summary of process

The major ingredients for a sustainable integrated care project are:

- Identify everybody who has an interest or stake in the project.
- Gain the unstinted commitment of chief executives and senior managers.
- Truly involve them all in some way or other so they feel ownership.

- Ensure that everybody is a winner and has a pay-off.

- Align all parts of each organization so that they support the project and they change in response to new demands from the project.

- Develop a clear purpose based on shared values.

- Put in place ongoing training and development and devote sufficient time to it.

- Develop robust information systems that pass information across boundaries.

- Plan a dynamic evaluation system that is the springboard for further change and improvement in the project.

- Balance the pressure for short-term gains against the need for achieving long term-goals.

- Celebrate frequently.

These guiding principles may seem daunting but unless the first steps are taken and there is movement they are of no consequence. Do not waste time trying to design the perfect integrated care project. It will not turn out that way in any case, but is likely to have a completely different shape even if it has predictable and desirable qualities. There was no way that anybody in EPICS could have predicted that what started as a way to assess and manage a community hospital bed system would ultimately emerge as a major community redesign project.

All of this can only work if the right conditions exist for self-organization and there is the trust on which to base it. Certainly the rigid control mechanisms that many managers and care organizations seek will only engender constraints and a constraining behaviour that ensures that nothing really changes.

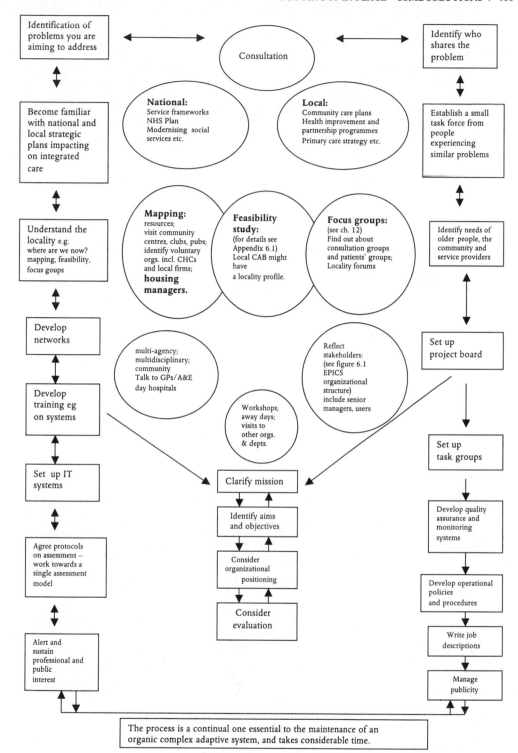

Figure 6.3 Setting up and sustaining an integrated care system

Identifying stakeholders:
- Meet with managers at the
  highest level
- COs and chairs of the health authority,
  hospital and primary care trusts and
  voluntary organizations
- Cabinet members, portfolio holders,
  commissioners in social services
- Housing managers, district and local
  councillors
-local MPs

Remember
**IT
ALL
TAKES
TIME**

Consider organizational
positioning i.e. where the project
is to be located organizationally:
- Within the health service?
- Within primary care?
  e.g. intermediate care
- Within social services?
- Within the voluntary sector?
- As an independent charity?
  etc.

Remember
**SENIOR
MANAGEMENT
OWNERSHIP
ESSENTIAL**

Remember
**USERS
AT THE
CENTRE**

Remember
NETWORKS
NOT
HIERARCHIES

Set up quality assurance and
monitoring systems including:
complaints procedures,
equal opportunities policy,
confidentiality policy

**INCLUDE
ALL USERS**

Clarify lines of
accountability
across agencies
and disciplines

Develop referral
protocols

Set up communication systems
Chart information flows on the basis of
who needs to know what & when:
1. to carry out the functions of the
   project
2. to monitor the processes
3. to provide information on the
   outcomes for users & practitioners
4. to inform strategic planning &
   development

Keep the project dynamic:
- Have regular case reviews with a
  representative group of
  practitioners, users and managers
- Have an annual review of aims,
  objectives and performance at a big
  meeting of all stakeholders with
  small group work on particular
  issues or cases
(See ch. 7)

Construct a
development plan

Consider publicity:
- create a corporate image
- produce user friendly
  information
- provide information packs
  for the media

Recruiting and keeping
staff and volunteers:
- have a user on the interview
  panel or meet the candidates
  informally
- keep paid and unpaid staff
  informed and use their ideas
- provide regular support
  meetings and appraisals

Blow your
own trumpet

Alert and sustain public
interest
- Events such as conferences,
  newsletters and bulletins,
  talks, open days, getting
  articles in journals, local radio
- Publish an annual report

Figure 6.4 Setting up and sustaining an integrated care system (cont'd)
The process is a continual one essential to the maintenance of an organic complex adaptive system

Chapter 6 – Headline points

- Working within complex adaptive systems means allowing freedoms that inevitably result in some mistakes and errors.

- At the start of the project all the key organizations should be involved, preferably through their senior management who have the authority to commit their organization wholeheartedly to the project.

- Identify some possible short-term gains that are early 'pay-offs'.

- The power of the involvement of the older person and their organizations needs to be harnessed at a very early stage.

- Try to single out the 'movers and shakers', the people who get things done.

- The flexibility of the new integrated services will depend heavily on the ability to move either care to the patient or the patient to care.

- Stakeholder involvement is itself complex and a very important subsystem within the whole system.

- The maxim is that in major redesign projects if the perceived time and resource demanded for good communicating and networking is calculated, and then multiplied by ten, it would still be insufficient.

APPENDIX 6.1

Topics Used in a Feasibility Study

1. **The locality**: the place and the people.

    - geographic area of operation by wards and postcodes (include a map with boundaries marked)

    - description of type of locality e.g. rural, light industrial, housing range, areas of deprivation etc.

    - population profile including ethnic mix

    - co-terminosity between health and social care providers

    - primary care groups and trusts, hospitals and health clinics

    - GP practices

    - social services offices

    - relevant voluntary groups.

2. **Background and purpose**

    - purpose of the study

    - background: how the project proposal has been formulated.

3. **The need for the project and how it was identified**

    - population predictions

    - disability profile of proposed client group

    - admissions to hospitals and care and nursing homes and numbers of respite care admissions

    - information on numbers where discharge from hospital has been delayed because there is no support in the community

    - continuing care: predictions on future demand

    - outcomes from consultation and any workshops

(Statistical data can be requested from health authorities, social services, county, borough or city offices and from district and parish councils.) Hospital finance departments and GP practice managers can be asked for numbers of patients registered, or admitted to hospital, etc.

4.   Opportunities

Survey the current provision and propose how the project could relate to and provide benefit for the providers:

- GP practices
    - ° identify numbers of patients and predict numbers of referrals to the project
    - ° estimate the potential benefits to GPs such as care packages co-ordinated from one referral point; rapid response to provide care in the home
- Day hospitals
    - ° numbers of places that could be made available to the project and numbers for whom the project might facilitate earlier and safer discharge
- Community hospitals
    - ° support facilities which could be made available to clients through the project
    - ° numbers of inappropriate admissions that the project might have been able to prevent and number of beds 'blocked' that the project might be able to shift
- possibility of outreach in clubs and day centres that would have reciprocal benefit
- sheltered housing centres as a source of giving and receiving information
- alarm call systems which are a potential source of referral to the project and could be of benefit to the users in providing instant access to information and support. Could be of mutual benefit in developing a client database and IT network
- existing voluntary services that could provide support to the project and which often have difficulty in getting referrals through lack of information on the part of the professional providers
- independent services such as 24-hour home care; handyman services (Support available to clients through the project and the project would be a source of referral for these agencies)

Similarly:

- local council developments
- partnership initiatives
- potential sponsorship and donations
- developments being planned by other agencies and organizations

Also to be considered are:

- changes in public policy and funding e.g White Papers on primary care; modernizing social services; continuing care, involving the users of services.
- initiative funding such as 'winter pressures' , 'waiting list reductions'.

5. Products from the project development process

- alternative models of integrated systems of care appropriate to the locality's needs will have been considered
- a preliminary costing exercise may have been completed
- a methodology for evaluating the outcome of the project will have been agreed
- an independent Project Management Assurance Group will have been set up.

6. Threats/constraints

For example:

- other integrated care systems in neighbouring localities
- public sector policy affecting purchasing strategies
- primary care trusts receiving funding to develop own services
- lack of quantitative evidence of cost-effectiveness of the project against the cost of other care systems/control groups.

7. Organisational Options

For example:

- Setting up as an independent charity:
  - ° *Advantages* such as tax relief: benefits from grants, payroll giving, trading (as in running a charity shop)
  - ° *Disadvantages* such as unpredictable funding; lacking the authority to co-ordinate professional members of the multidisciplinary team to provide assessment/treatment.

- Other options could be locating in one of health, social services or housing agencies. The advantages and disadvantages should be set out.

- Another option would be whether to set up with a co-ordinating function only, rather than as a provider. Again the advantages and disadvantages should be explored and stated.

8. Management structure

- The role and function of the project development group, any working groups and any quality assurance groups should be outlined

- Similarly the anticipated role and function of the committee or board of management and its membership, executive groups and possibly a financial management group.

9. Evaluation and monitoring

- pre start-up: any 'before' measurements that can be collected, such as admissions to hospital from the target population

- quality assurance of the project development: setting up a team representing users, business and technical (e.g professional) input

- monitoring outcomes: statistical records and regular reports to the management groups

- consumer satisfaction

- cost-efficiency.

10. Benefits

- to the users

- to the providers

- to the system.

11. Business plan

At this stage it is likely that setting out the options for the development and the likely outcomes with rough costings is all that can be offered, as below.

Model	Activity	Advantages	Disadvantages	Estimated costs
1.	Do nothing	No extra immediate costs	Lost opportunity; negative cost	£0.00
2.	Improve communications; develop common assessment; improve 'slow phase' care	Low cost (e.g. part-time co-ordinator)	No 'fast phase'; subsequent inappropriate care	£10,000
Etc.				

A recommendation can be offered for a particular model with more detailed costings. A summary of outcomes if this model is followed, including anticipated efficiency savings could be provided.

A project initiation document (PID) may be required after the feasibility study has been seen by the project board and managers and an agreement given on which model they want to adopt.

The purpose of a PID is to set out the scope of the proposed development, the timetable, the predicted costings and some management options. It will set out the project brief including reasons for setting it up, its objectives and projected outcomes. It will identify issues critical to the successful development of the project. The document should include the following headings:

1. Introduction   –The Project
                        – The Background

2. Project Brief

3. Opportunities

4. Products of the Development Initiative

5. Constraints, Threats or Opportunities

6. Organizational Options

7. Project Organization

8. Evaluation and Monitoring

9. Benefits

10. Business Plan.

Much of the information required can be summarized from the feasibility study.

APPENDIX 6.2

Example Job Description
for the EPICS Co-ordinator

Post Title:	PROJECT CO-ORDINATOR
Salary Scale:	Nursing Grade 'G' or equivalent
Hours:	37.5 hours per week or as appropriate
Location:	The Health Clinic
Accountable to:	The Project Manager
Purpose of Post:	To co-ordinate the resources of the community, statutory and voluntary services in response to the assessed need of people aged 65 and over referred to the project.
	To ensure that the users of the service are kept at the centre of planning and implementation

The post requires the post holder to be able to make autonomous decisions, often in isolation, regarding the welfare of clients and to advise the project careworkers on the management of the care of clients.

TASKS:
Assessment

1. To facilitate and where appropriate undertake assessment of the immediate needs of the older people and their carers referred to the project.

2. To arrange for multidisciplinary assessment in the local day hospital where appropriate.

3. To trigger the need for a community care assessment where appropriate.

Co-ordination and liaison

4. To ensure the client's wishes are central to the care plans.

5. To act as co-ordinator between the day hospital, community hospital, night nursing service, social and community services in providing a response to the assessed need.

6. To work in close collaboration with the day hospital staff offering operational and professional support.

7. To liaise with social workers, home carers, GPs, hospital consultants, district nurses, CPNs, health visitors, sheltered housing managers, voluntary agencies and volunteers in providing a timely, holistic response to the client's needs and feedback during and after the intervention.

8. To liaise with hospital ward staff and the accident and emergency department, regarding care and discharge of patients within the 'catchment' area for the project.

Strategic networking

9. To network with relevant organizations and build up knowledge of local resources.

10. To attend and facilitate, as required, meetings between practitioners and other people providing support to older people in the community.

11. To give talks as required.

12. To facilitate focus groups or action groups of older people as part of the commitment of the project to keep users at the heart of planning and monitoring.

Staff Management

13. To recruit, train and supervise the project careworkers:

- to manage the roster
- to allocate the work
- to receive feedback
- to advise on care

- to ensure they have the equipment they require

- to ensure they return timesheets

14. To co-ordinate the work of the project careworkers in order to avoid duplication and overlap with other agencies.

15. To negotiate with staff from other agencies over the handover of care.

16. To supervise the clerical assistants and data manager.

17. To ensure the volunteers recruited to the project are appropriately deployed, adequately trained and supported.

18. To ensure that health and safety standards are observed.

19. To ensure that policies and procedures are kept updated.

20. To deputize for the project manager as required.

Administration

21. To ensure the budget is sustained and to oversee the use of petty cash.

22. To ensure the records are kept up to date and to make the statistical returns and other departmental reports as required.

23. To respond immediately to a complaint, following the Trust's policy and to keep a record of accolades received by the project.

24. To ensure the security of the office and confidentiality of records.

IT Management

25. To liaise with the clerical and data assistants and the data supervisor, the project manager, the IT consultant and the Trust's data centre in developing and maintaining the systems.

26. To ensure the client database and the resources database are kept up to date.

Monitoring and Evaluation

27. To ensure an individual annual appraisal of performance is carried out with staff and, wherever possible, volunteers.

28. To assist in an annual review of the project.

29. To assist in the monitoring and evaluation of the outputs and outcomes of the project.

30. To assist in setting and monitoring quality standards.

31. To participate in and initiate appropriate continuing development of the project.

Other Duties

32. To undertake whatever other duties are agreed with the project and business managers.

Further reading

Davis, C., Finlay, L. and Bullman, A. (eds) (2000) *Changing Practice in Health and Social Care.* London: Sage Publications.

The chapters in this book cover a wide range of organizational and professional issues in relation to changing to a more integrated work-style. The book balances the tensions between social and health care creatively.

Ovretveit, J., Mathias, P. and Thompson, A. (eds) (1997) *Interprofessional Working for Health and Social Care.* London: Macmillan Press.

There are instructive chapters around teams and team behaviour, and an interesting one on how involvement of the person changes the polarity of relationships between professionals.

Senge, P., Kleiner, A., Rogers, C., Ross, R., Roth, G. and Smith, B. (1999) *The Dance of Change – The Challenges of Sustaining Momentum in Learning Organizations.* London: Nicholas Brealey Publishing.

From the stable of the Fifth Discipline, *this describes in very general terms the barriers to change. There is a lot of helpful advice and approaches that are worth knowing before you start. It is all about integrating.*

Chapter 7

Information Systems

Connecting Places

Man can live by information alone.

Anon

Information, in the technical sense is surprise value, measured as the inverse of expected probability.

Richard Dawkins

In this chapter we stress the importance of information systems underpinning the other processes of care. We consider the practical aspects of constructing and managing the database as well as the requirements for data collection. Issues around confidentiality and older people's involvement are stressed. The value of linking disparate systems and processes electronically is highlighted, and we point out the need to evaluate the information system itself.

Knowledge is an awareness and experience of things that allows decisions to be taken and hence actions undertaken. Other things being equal, the better the knowledge the better the decision is likely to be, and this applies both to individuals and organizations. In complex adaptive systems where control has been distributed rather than centralized, and where this freedom allows agents to act separately but towards a common goal, knowledge has to be distributed throughout the system. Knowledge is what co-ordinates the separate agents, provides the cohesion and prevents systems from falling apart. For example, knowing what the purpose of the system is and then how the system is performing through evaluation gives the system both shape and

> *Knowledge is what co-ordinates the separate agents, provides the cohesion and prevents systems from falling apart.*

direction. No system can survive without knowledge, and the more complex the system the more important shared knowing becomes.

Knowledge comes from information – it is the result of information being assimilated and then used – feedback and reflection then further qualify it for use on another occasion. Information in turn depends on data. Data is the raw facts as they exist – numbers of people, nursing home places, money in budgets – and on its own usually meaningless. When data is analysed and synthesized to help provide answers to questions, it becomes information. There is often confusion between what is meant by data and information, but they are separate and each moves from one to the other. Acquire data, put it in a context of enquiry, and it becomes information; use the information to make decisions and act, then review the outcomes and this becomes knowledge and learning has taken place. Knowledge in turn results in further questions being asked, this requires more information, which in turn requires the production of additional data.

Information and information systems are to a complex adaptive system what the nervous system is to the body. Without the nervous system the body would not be able to capture data through the senses, analyse it in the brain and then act on the information by sending messages to the muscles or the heart and lungs, as, for instance, when someone was to run inside from a thunderstorm. Without the central nervous system the muscles would be unco-ordinated, the heart would not beat sufficiently quickly to provide enough blood flow and the person would not be able to see where to go. The result would be somebody lying in a very wet heap on the ground. This is what metaphorically happens to so many new projects where information is not valued and thought unnecessary. And, as with the nervous system in the body, the information systems have to be in place before the action begins.

Information systems and EPICS

Once the very early concepts and ideas of EPICS had been roughly thought through (see chapter 2, p.61 – 'a good enough vision'.), the very first scheme the team addressed was the information systems needed for EPICS to function properly. It was not until a further 18 months had passed that the pilot service was actually started. There were two early questions to be asked:

- What information and information systems do we need to develop the project?

- What information and systems do we need to run the project?

These two questions overlapped to some extent. For example, when asking questions about the demography and numbers of older people within the locality, it was realized that the databases from which this information was extracted could become the basis for the client management database to run the project when it went live.

The information systems to develop the project were relatively simple and consisted of gathering data by phone and correspondence, putting it into a computer and analysing it, often graphically. The information was then sent to the steering group and the development team for them to discuss and ask further questions. The team needed to know the existence of other relevant information systems in social services, healthcare, the local authority and the voluntary sector and have some idea of the type and quality of the data available. At this time the possibility of other stakeholders in the system having access to the data was not considered.

Understanding the care processes

The next stage was to gain some understanding of the care processes in the various agencies that were already in place and that needed to be integrated.

The project manager spent time mapping out these processes and the way they interfaced with each other to track the flow of older people through the current systems. EPICS itself had no such care systems yet; the plan was to grow the information systems and the EPICS care delivery systems together in an organic manner. The steering group was very conscious that the information systems had to fit the care delivery processes and not the care delivery fit the information systems. To this extent, the information systems had to reflect the uniqueness of EPICS. It was not going to be possible to buy an 'off-the-shelf' product. The team used standard spreadsheets and databases to 'grow their own'.

> *The information systems had to fit the care delivery processes and not the care delivery fit the information systems.*

Constructing the database

It became clear as the operational and information requirements were planned that there was a need to know about both individual older people and the population of older people if both care delivery and risk were to be managed. Also, one of the questions raised by the steering group was how to evaluate the quality of care being deliv-

> *The first practical task was to set up a database that at least provided a register of all the older people in the area.*

ered. If access to services, relevance to the need of the whole community and equity were to be addressed (as well as cost-effectiveness and efficacy), the information systems would have to provide data about whole populations. So the first practical task was to set up a database that at least provided a register of all the older people in the area. Any further information available at the outset was a bonus.

The project manager approached what was then the local Family Practitioner Committee who agreed in principle to provide the database from their system. However, it would still be 'owned' by the local GPs' practice whose patients were the main body of the older population under consideration. The GPs were represented on the steering group but felt that issues of confidentiality were paramount. Consequently, they were somewhat guarded about sharing their own practice data. It was something they were considering for the first time. The social services and voluntary bodies on the steering group were also concerned about giving information on their clients and about the confidentiality issues around who would have access to the information.

Possible alternative sources of population data

As the EPICS project progressed, and as it networked with other projects in other parts of the country, other sources for database information were recognized apart from those held by primary care:

- The census data contains a population-based system which (provided it is fairly recent) may help.

- The local authority often has a register of older people using their alarm-call systems. Though these are not related to an overall population they often contain the names and other details of several thousand older people deemed to be at risk of one sort or another. The staff are linked to the older people and sometimes family and carers by phone.

- Some local hospital departments for care of the elderly (as in South Buckinghamshire) maintain a register and database (linked to the hospital systems) of all older people who are seen as patients.

- In some areas the ambulance trusts keep population-based data. For example, in Berkshire the ambulance trust keeps a total population database to help its crews and paramedical teams. Another in Surrey has a list of all frail older people who are cared for by a carer. (If the carer becomes ill, the ambulance crew will look for alternatives to inappropriate hospital admission for the older person.)

- Age Concern and other charitable organizations have mailing and contact lists through which they can distribute information in some areas.

> *It is important to know the purpose for which the original list was collated if it is to be used in another context, so that any biases and potential errors can be recognized.*

The value of these other databases was that they provided very useful subsets of older people who were in high-risk groups to add to a master register.

The GP database revealed inconsistencies and needed validating and correcting if it was to be used for the purposes of delivering care rather than just used for management purposes. It is important to know the purpose for which the original list was collated if it is to be used in another context, so that any biases and potential errors can be recognized.

Managing the database

At this stage, the first project manager who had considerable information system expertise left and a new project manager was appointed. The steering group advised that the new project manager would focus more on service delivery development. To balance up the project demands a part-time external IT consultant was appointed and quickly became an integral part of the team. He spent many hours with the nurses, co-ordinators and social workers refining both his and their understanding of what the information needs were. He ran role-playing sessions for the practitioners and users across agencies. This led to a shared understanding of the information flow and what each agency needed to know to carry out their tasks. The process was not without its stand-offs! The IT consultant continually emphasized the need to clarify business practices and procedures within individual agencies. He said the programme relied upon these being made explicit.

He was able to customize the computer screen so that the information could be accessed in the way that each user found most helpful. All this effort paid dividends in getting those who were going to be using the system involved and committed to working with it from the start. It also helped to improve the quality of their data input.

The management responsibilities for EPICS were seen by the system provider as:

- providing a functional specification
- providing a database definition

- installing and commissioning any database upgrades

- providing any onsite day-to-day management

- providing first-line support to any extension site

- managing meetings

- managing user expectation

- being available for project review and development meetings

- appointing a project board

- appointing a project manager.

A project board was planned with a chair, a senior technical representative and senior user. A project manager for the system was to be appointed. Quality assurance was to be monitored through a user assurance co-ordinator, a technical assurance co-ordinator and a business assurance co-ordinator.

Data collection

If the data collected was to be relevant and the basis from which useful information could be generated, it had to reflect the other processes of care delivery. Initially, a hypothetical set of referrals were worked on to see what might be needed. Even after this the team were not exactly certain what might be necessary, and there was some redundancy in the data collection. But as the data system itself was evaluated, any data not used for day-to-day practice was pruned from the database. Inevitably some was added as the project evolved and information requirements changed. The management of the whole system was dynamic and iterative.

The questions asked to ascertain type of data to be collected were:

- What information is needed about the older person to deliver personal care?

- How can the information system support the care planning?

- How can the information system help in the evaluation of the EPICS project?

- How can the information system help in the management of the project?

- How can the information system help in clinical risk management?

- How can the information benefit the older person?

WHAT INFORMATION IS NEEDED ABOUT THE OLDER PERSON TO DELIVER PERSONAL CARE?

A minimum data set was essential. Much of this came with the GPs' register, but a lot of time was spent validating it (for example, birthdays changed the age, but the records did not automatically update). Assessment data linked in with the assessment process was recorded whenever it was collected within the EPICS system and from wherever else it could be retrieved. This was broken down and recorded as assessment domains. (See Appendix 7.1, p.184 for an example of the development of the assessment element in the system.)

Social information included details of family and other social networks, and how contact could be made with them if necessary. Details of home accessibility for both the older person and care staff were included as was information for use in emergencies (where keys were kept and by whom, etc.). Information on care needs and what care was currently being delivered, by whom and at what times, was essential.

HOW CAN THE INFORMATION SYSTEM SUPPORT THE CARE PLANNING?

The information system made reference to current and previous assessments to give a picture of previous incidents and interventions and what had been successful or unsuccessful. A list of care-planning options was available on the drop-down boxes

---

The Community Resources Database

This was the brainchild of a younger volunteer who was herself disabled. She and a group of other volunteers spent two years developing an electronic database which contained a wide and diverse range of community-based information. Amongst other things, it listed shopping, recreational and service facilities that were oriented to help older people, transport and taxi services, and other support and self-help groups.

The series of lists and drop-down boxes could be triggered by a keyword relating to a condition or disability (e.g. deafness) or to a facility (e.g. a lunch club). It also cross-referenced and provided a range of local services that might benefit a person with that condition. The headline data could then be interrogated for more detailed information including contact numbers and person, eligibility, opening times and access, etc.

The volunteers kept the system updated by accessing electronically other community data systems.

The database provided the information for a small handbook directory which was distributed to older people in the locality – and practitioners – as a joint project with the district council.

on the computer screens. This was seen as a decision support in that they provided a checklist of what was available (see Appendix 7.2, p.187).

Future developments of the system were planned which would trigger access to guidelines and care pathways. To this end a database of all the community resources, both formal and informal, was constructed by the volunteers.

HOW CAN THE INFORMATION SYSTEM HELP IN THE EVALUATION OF THE EPICS PROJECT?

The data collected was aligned to the multidimensional evaluation model (see chapter 9, p.238 on evaluation). This meant collecting data on care outcomes, patient satisfaction, costs and process evaluation including evaluating the information system itself. This data was monitored over time.

The information system was configured to produce regular reports. These were usually delivered monthly for the local management groups and quarterly to the project board. The early reports were quite basic – the number of referrals and their source, the number of users currently 'on the books' and actively being managed and the rate of referrals. As time progressed, the reports and evaluation became more sophisticated.

HOW CAN THE INFORMATION SYSTEM HELP IN THE MANAGEMENT OF THE PROJECT?

As the project developed and as careworkers were employed, the information system allowed the co-ordinators to maintain timesheets and work programmes. From these, reports could be generated to give a picture of costs and work flow. The real-time information generated allowed the sensitive, simultaneous monitoring of both care delivered and the resources required to do it.

HOW CAN THE INFORMATION SYSTEM HELP IN CLINICAL RISK MANAGEMENT?

The computer consultants (working with the clinical team) identified the risk factors that they were able to extract from the database and allotted people on the database into risk groups (see also chapter 5, p.126 on risk management):

- age over 85 years
- living alone
- history of falls
- confusion and cognitive impairment
- recent bereavement

- multiple drug therapy
- recent discharge from hospital.

The team used a simple non-weighted scoring scale for the risk. The greater the number of items the higher the risk. Unfortunately there was insufficient staff to review the entire list regularly, but the 'at-risk' group were reviewed and screened on each occasion they were referred or the data entry was updated. The community staff (both health and social services) were then notified of the changes and telephone contact was made with the individual and their carers. Although this monitoring was, of necessity, limited it was felt to be useful as a way of prioritizing the time and resources of the team when an older person required help to avert or manage a crisis.

HOW CAN THE INFORMATION BENEFIT THE OLDER PERSON?

The older person will not have to give basic information repeatedly if the information is shared with, and made available to, all those involved in assessing, planning and implementing care. Practical details about their circumstances will be known, therefore the care plans will be relevant to their needs. They will get a more accurate assessment because the information system facilitates a systematic approach, and a swifter and better co-ordinated response can be organized because of the availability of networked information.

The older person will get accurate information about themselves and, through the community resource database, up-to-date information on facilities and services available.

Friday 4.45pm

A neighbour rang to say Jane was stuck in her chair, her knees having locked. The neighbour did not have a key but she had seen the EPICS number in the Age Concern newsletter and rang. The EPICS co-ordinator looked up the client's name on the computer. The system showed details of the client's family and a keyholder. She contacted the keyholder, arranged for a care worker to be there within 15 minutes and contacted the GP to ask for a visit.

The computer record showed that this had happened to the client before. On that occasion she had been taken to the A&E. This time, with the care worker's help, the GP was able to treat the knee and get the client on her feet again. The care worker was able to stay with Jane and help her get to bed, and visited the next morning to help her to get up.

> The likelihood otherwise of mobilizing social services at 4.45pm on a Friday was doubtful, and it was also unlikely that the GP would have made a home visit without the EPICS support.
>
> That being the case, the patient would almost certainly have ended up in A&E again, with the probability of admission because there was no one at home to be with her. The instant availability of information about the patient's circumstances and the previous episode was crucial in the successful handling of this older person's problem.

Capturing the data

Once the register was in place, the clinical information it held was updated monthly from a floppy disk supplied by the primary care team. Initial efforts to carry out the update electronically had failed for technical reasons. But, as it turned out, the primary care staff felt more in control of the situation handing over a physical disk, so that method was continued. Latterly, when the GPs felt more trusting and confident and the computer systems were upgraded, consideration was given for this to be done electronically through an intranet system.

The central EPICS co-ordinator was a very important agent in capturing the data. She or one of her colleagues took all the referrals by telephone sitting in front of the computer, and having brought up the older person's details on the screen quickly validated the minimum data set and entered any new information directly. Because of the ease of access there were very few high-risk people not already known, and there were very few occasions following referral when there was not some useful information about them on the system. From the outset of the project it was decided that there would be no referral forms to be filled in. Form-filling was felt to be a major barrier to older people self-referring and it would be a bureaucratic delay in the whole process. However, the people who seemed most appreciative of this direct referral were the social workers, GPs and nurses.

From the outset of the project it was decided that there would be no referral forms to be filled in.

A part-time computer assistant logged hospital inpatient and discharge data for older people from the area as well as accident and emergency attendances. Data from the day hospital was to be electronically transferred. The co-ordinator attended the multidisciplinary team meetings of the local community hospital and entered the data directly after those meetings. The social workers provided information about delivery of social care.

In retrospect, and with all the advances in computer networking, this appears technically very crude but it was very effective. The direct costs were about £15,000 per annum including the development and computer support costs. The ease of getting relevant, reliable and validated data meant that more and more people were either abandoning their own systems or using EPICS as well. As any contact was viewed as a two-way information exchange and an opportunity to gather as well as give information, the more people that used the system the better the data and information on it.

Confidentiality

Legal and technical aspects (registering the systems for data protection and putting in the necessary access checks, such as passwords and levels of information accessibility) all had to be put in place but were relatively straightforward.

What was not expected was the professional minefield that arose when sharing information across agencies was first discussed. The sharing of information was seen as an enormous threat by virtually all the professionals involved. The implication was that if somebody else had the information they could undertake that particular role and the original owner of the information would be redundant to the system. Posturing and protestation were common to all the professional groups in one way or another.

> *The sharing of information was seen as an enormous threat by virtually all the professionals involved.*

It took all of the 18 months or so that the information systems were being developed before the confidentiality issues were resolved, and then only just in time for the system to go live. It was one of the older lay people on the steering group who recognized the potential of the system for older people's care. Her staunch advocacy of the system eventually brought the professionals round to agreeing to take the 'risk' of trusting each other. She was the catalyst for changing views and moving the whole process up a gear. It also helped that the steering group gained increasing confidence as it saw the information system being developed and understood the workings of the protection systems.

As well as professional barriers there were institutional barriers to the sharing of information. These centred on the accountability that each professional had to their own parent organization, enshrined in their contracts. There had to be joint understanding and tolerance of these issues.

Involving older people in information systems

There is a myth that older people are technophobes and that they neither want to learn nor are capable of learning how to use computers and other modern equipment. This has not been the experience in EPICS, or elsewhere for that matter. (Brownsell *et al.* 2000). Overall older people are little different from the rest of the population and appear to have at least as good an understanding of the importance of information systems and their relevance to their own lives.

Computer Training in Slough

Age Concern Slough run regular training sessions for older people to learn how to use computers and get on to the internet. There is a small training unit where three or four people can learn together. Though there is skilled help available, most of the training is done by other older people who have been through the scheme themselves. This means that the pace of the learning is suited to them and they do not get so easily flustered as when somebody younger trains them. The older teachers are acutely aware of the problems having been through the programme themselves.

There is a real buzz in the unit and it is difficult to get the participants to stop and talk to visitors. What is equally valuable is that they have formed themselves into a support network outside the programme. They also benefit from the links they make with family and friends, who in turn benefit from this.

As the EPICS information system was being developed, the steering group wanted to know how acceptable the locality-wide information system was to the older people themselves; in particular, how many of them did not want to be part of it. The local Age Concern was asked to be the independent assessors and agreed to send out a questionnaire to all older people in Marlow with one of their regular newsletters. This contained details of the system, how it involved the older people and the possible consequences. Out of the 3500 older people contacted (those registered with the local GP practice) only eight replied saying they did not want their names to be included on the register.

Connecting the systems

The increased value from connecting all the databases in the locality that held information about older people soon became apparent. This link provided:

- improved communication between primary and secondary healthcare, between health, social services and the local authority

- better and easier access to the information with 24-hour availability

- wider sharing of the information which would enhance decision-making and risk management

- stimulation for a single assessment process and facilitation of its common use

- more efficient capture and collection of basic data, which only had to be entered once

- increased confidence in the system for all users.

The intranet

A project plan was drawn up to develop a pilot study for an intranet link between the EPICS co-ordinators, the department of elderly care in the hospital, the accident and emergency department, social services and three GP practices. Funding for three years was obtained through the health authority from joint finance funding. Following a competitive tendering process a software provider and a network management consultant were appointed. After thorough discussion between all the stakeholders several major hurdles were encountered:

- The NHS trust in whose facilities the project was located spent months scrutinizing the security and fail-safe processes and awaiting assurances from the service providers drawing up the contracts.

- GP surgeries had similar anxieties about security. They were also concerned that their current systems would not connect directly to the intranet and they would end up with separate systems that involved double entry of data.

- The social services department had similar concerns as the GPs over confidentiality and double entry of data. Their systems had been designed for the purposes of care management and could not network with the projected EPICS intranet.

After months of meetings and discussions, and reassurances from the IT consultants that the technology existed to ensure security, some of the GPs and social workers were persuaded of the benefits of an intranet link. However, it was at this time that the NHS Net was planned and about to come on line. The NHS trust decided that it would wait for this to provide the link and the intranet project plan was shelved. (It is planned that a modified version will be brought on-stream in 2002.)

Evaluating the IT system

To evaluate the effectiveness and value of an electronic system it is necessary to put in place performance measures for cost benefits and functionality. Although the intranet did not become operational at the time we were involved, the measures for monitoring its performance had been agreed.

To determine cost benefits the following measures were to be used:

- reductions in telephone queries
- time saved through receiving information faster
- time saved through receiving more accurate information
- time saved through receiving more complete information
- analysis of audit trails
- comparisons of paper forms against electronic transactions
- cost savings in postage, delivery and stationery
- cost and time savings through reduction in use of faxes
- cost savings in reduction of wasted requests and other transactions.

The functionality of the system was checked by asking these questions:

- How many times has it crashed?
- Do the users like using the system?
- Do the users find the system easy to use after training?
- Is the documentation comprehensive and helpful?
- Is the help desk reliable?

Future networks

Geographical information systems

> To evaluate the effectiveness and value of the electronic system it was necessary to put in place performance measures for cost benefits and functionality.

In the early days of EPICS, when thinking about whole populations, it became apparent that the structures of community and community care were both diffuse and 'virtual', and that there would be some value in having a better understanding of the spatial relationships both of need and the availability of resources. The supposition was that this could be a decision-support tool for care mangers in planning for, and making available care. As an example, it might be helpful to a care manger or rehabilitation manager who is delivering care in the community to older people suffering from a stroke to know where they were and what their needs were in relation to the resources in the community. This would apply not only to the official healthcare and social care resources, but also to the informal care and other services available. It was expected this would allow more individualized solutions for each older person's problems.

A system was chosen which could be developed to integrate with other information systems within the Community and Health Trust, and could relate to other agencies such as GP practices and social services. This was an off-the-shelf package 'Paradox Relational Database' which was then developed into a tailor-made programme by a small firm of IT consultants. The result was a geographical information system with superimposed digitized Ordnance Survey mapping that could focus down to individual houses and streets. This was simulated for about 60 hypothetical older people using several scenarios with a range of practitioners. They felt it had enormous potential benefit. Unfortunately funding was not made available to implement the system, despite the promise seen by the steering group in facilitating cross-boundary working.

Well-developed systems already exist in epidemiology and healthcare planning based on postcodes, but these were not spatially sensitive enough to deliver individualized health and social care. Also, a geographically based information system exists in the USA for the delivery of preventive care in communities (Plescia, Koontz and Laurent 2001).

Electronic health records

There are also exciting pilot projects elsewhere in the country that could have major benefits in networking information. The concept of data stores or data warehouses, which has been used commercially for some time, can be applied to health and social care systems. Current health and social care databases are used to bring together temporarily on to a central computer all the relevant data about any given older person for use by a practitioner at any time. After use, the data is 'returned' to the data warehouse whence it came and the central computer emptied. There are 16 pilot sites in the UK that should be providing some early evaluated information in a year or so.

Whether these electronic records will provide both individual and population-based information for clinical risk management remains to be seen. (For other references to particular electronic systems please see Appendix 7.1, p.184.)

Overview

Information systems are critical to developing and managing the complexity of older people's care. Information and the knowledge that flows from it are the context in which productive relationships are built. The ability to pass this information through the system depends on the individual and corporate communication skills of all those involved. Good communication and information systems rarely happen by chance alone. They emerge when the conditions of common purpose, shared values and shared enquiry have been established. Nevertheless, the structures of the information system, the hardware and the commonality of data inputs and outputs have to be managed in a very real and practical way as well.

The future is full of the expectation of all that modern computing technology may be able to offer. The greatest benefits are likely to come not directly from technical improvements, important though these are, but from the way that information is shared and used. Connections and networks will allow organizations to become 'intelligent' and more 'brain-like'. For older people this ambience of shared knowledge and networking offers the best opportunity for direct involvement in their own care. And when their expertise is added to the system, it will be a very powerful tool for progress.

From the EPICS experience the following lessons were learned:

- Understanding the current care and business processes and in what way they may need to change is a very important initial problem for the team to address. This takes time and effort. But without this, it is likely that the processes will be made to fit the information system rather than the other way about.

- The best way to get early commitment from stakeholders is to involve as many of them as possible as early as possible and to identify very clear advantages and payoffs for everybody. For managers, some short-term gains may be important to keep them connected.

- The more user-friendly IT is, and the more relevant it is made in helping people in their work, the more likely it is to be used.

- There needs to be a common data and information language throughout the system so that people can easily 'talk' to and understand each other. In practical terms this means some common assessments and other inputs, agreed reporting methods and consistent methods of data collection. A local glossary (with shared definitions of data) linked with a user manual has been found to be helpful.

- The system needs to be actively and creatively managed with technical and user support.

- The information system itself needs to be evaluated regularly to ensure the iterative processes of confirming the purpose, appropriate implementation and relevant evaluation are in place.

Chapter 7 – Headline points

- Knowledge is what co-ordinates the separate agents, provides the cohesion and prevents systems from falling apart.

- The information systems had to fit the care delivery processes and not the care delivery fit the information systems.

- The first practical task was to set up a database that at least provided a register of all the older people in the area.

- It is important to know the purpose for which the original list was collated if it is to be used in another context, so that any biases and potential errors can be recognized.

- From the outset of the project it was decided that there would be no referral forms to be filled in.

- The sharing of information was seen as an enormous threat by virtually all the professionals involved.

- To evaluate the effectiveness and value of the electronic system it was necessary to put in place performance measures for cost benefits and functionality.

APPPENDIX 7.1

Integrated Care – Assessment Evaluation Processing

An approach to processing assessments submitted by agencies to a central pool of information.

The following information comes from Interactive Online Solutions (IOS), a software design company which was associated with the initial system introduced to support the Elderly Persons Integrated Care System in South Buckinghamshire. An Integrated Care Solution has been developed using a number of clients' requirements to construct a method of collecting information related to older people. The system is applicable to any client group or population.

The target is to get a single method of assessment which all agencies can use in a consistent manner and in doing so will be able to perform overall risk analysis on the person that is being assessed. Expanding this, by collecting information in a central pool, the analysis can be applied to groups of people (e.g. disabled, older people, children). Extending this to location analysis results in a complete picture being formed of individuals within their environment.

The skills to be developed in implementing the system lie in the collection, storing, retrieval and presentation of this information to professionals who can interpret the results and so take life-enhancing decisions for the people being cared for.

Much work has gone into developing an approach to meet the goal of an integrated assessment form. The findings have been that everyone who performs an assessment needs particular information for their own purpose. Across the agencies there is a common core set of information, and this tends to be relatively static data (e.g. surname, date of birth).

The actual assessment data capture is dependent on the question asked. The question in one assessment may be similar to that in another but the assessor will have an objective in mind related to their own field and the answer recorded may be quite different.

The idea of implementing an integrated assessment into an organization is not realistic until the agencies are able to identify a common interpretation of the measures used. Performing a risk analysis on multiple assessment forms may also show a great variation in results although the risk factor (e.g. mobility) might be common.

So what approach are we taking at this early stage? It is best highlighted by an example:

1. A person is assessed by agencies A and B a number of times.

2. From each assessment the risks are calculated and decisions made (e.g. A calculates risk R1 and R2; B calculates risk R1 and R3).

3. Each agency would be able to identify their own trend lines.

4. If we take risk R1 – this is identified by agency A and B – by mapping the results on to the same output (e.g. a graph) the trend line for each agency can be identified. In an ideal case the trend line will be identical even if the values recorded by each agency are different.

Basically we are looking at like risk across the agencies and comparing the trends.

The system requires professionals who can use this method of recording in their environments. By analysing the trends, a true integrated assessment can be put into practice. Once in place, the risks and interpretations can be easily seen and the organization can move towards a common assessment procedure that can gradually be implemented within the recording system and data structures.

On-line Communications and Newton Software. (Formerly Interactive Online Solutions) Website: www.ios-net.co.uk

Other data systems relating to the care of older people

CareDirect

This scheme is being piloted in the West Country but is accessible throughout the UK. It is a web-based network that can provide information about care facilities to either the public or professional practitioners about health and social care facilities in the localities they serve. It will also provide information about specific disease states such as strokes, and using care pathways to advise on optimum treatment. Website: www.caredirect. gov.uk

Bettercaring

Launched on 1 May 2001, this national system (a subsidiary of the Stationery Office) provides the most comprehensive online database of over 20,000 local authority and independent registered care homes. The site is designed to help care professionals and the general public find appropriate care home places easily and quickly. It will also provide a nationwide directory of charitable and other support services. Website: www.bettercaring.co.uk

Care Standard Systems Ltd

This system has been recently developed to provide care home managers with the means to comply with all the requirements of the new Care Standards Act. It includes a recording system which will capture the day-to-day care interventions for individual residents and build up a continuing picture of the resident's care pathway. The model could be applied to other environments. E-mail: info@support4care.com

APPENDIX 7.2

Example of Information Held on an EPICS Referral Screen

Paradox for Windows - [CLIENT DETAILS]		
Client Record Actions Form Exit		

Client Reference : 1   Status : REG   Risk : LOW   Area : DH

Title : Mr

Forenames : John

Surname : Moore   Initials : J

Preferred Name : John

Date Of Birth : 18/01/1921

Age :

Deceased :

Marital Status : M

Sex : M

Type	Address Line 1
H	12 High Street, Marlow
R	The Residential Home

Category	Reference	Name
AUX	1	
DN	2	Miss Ellen Smith
HC	1	Mrs Astle Walters

Admission	Discharge	Event	Referral	
11/04/1995	12/04/1995	EPICS	GP	Dr Edwe
20/05/1995	01/06/1995	AE	WGH	
01/12/1995		EPICS	DN	Jane Gr

Contacts   Risk

Personal

Detail   Query

Address

Event   Return

1 of 3447 [:DATA1:CLIENT.DB]   Edit   Field

Mental Health	
Cognition and dementia, including orientation and memory	
Mental health including depression, reaction to loss, and emotional difficulties	
Relationships	
Social contacts, relationships and involvement	
Caring Arrangements	
Safety	
Abuse and Neglect	
Other aspects of personal safety	
Public Safety	
Immediate environment and resources	
Care of home and managing daily tasks such as food preparation, cleaning and shopping	
Accommodation	
Level and management of finances	
Access to local facilities and services	
Risk factors	
Age 85 +	
Lives Alone	
Major Illness	
Falls	
Loss Vision/Hearing	
MMT -8	
Recent hospitalisation	
Bereavement	
House Move	
Depression	
Reliant on carer	
+ 4 medications	

References

Brownsell, S.J., Bradley, D.S., Bragg, R., Catlin, P. and Carlier, J. (2000) 'Do community alarm users want telecare?' *Journal of Telemedicine and Telecare 5*, 4, 199–204.

Plescia, M., Koontz, S. and Lautrent, S. (2001) 'Community assessment in a vertically integrated health care system.' *American Journal of Public Health 91*, 5, 811–814.

Further reading

Smith J. (2000) *Health Management Information Systems: A Handbook for Decision Makers.* Buckingham: Open University Press.

There is very little about technology in this book but it more importantly relates information to decision making and strategy development. The chapter on 'Intelligent applications of health information systems' is worth the book alone.

Wilson D. A. (1999) *Managing Information.* Oxford: Butterworth Heinemann.

This is a very generic book the principles of which are easily translated into health and social care. It stresses the importance of making the information systems the slave and not the master of the underlying business processes.

Cropper S. and Forte P. (1997) *Enhancing Health Services Management.* Buckingham: Open University Press.

This book underlines the role of decision support systems in care. There are important chapters on spatial decision support, activity and capacity planning, queue management and system dynamics and community care amongst others.

Boisot M (1998) *Knowledge Assets: Securing Competitive Advantage in the Information Economy.* Oxford: Oxford University Press.

This book goes beyond information to knowledge. It puts it into a context of complexity and culture of organizations. It requires careful reading but this is moré than repaid by the understanding of the information needs of complex adaptive systems.

Chapter 8

Involving the Users

Our ideas have been listened to but have they been heard?

Member of a user panel in Camden, 1996

We cannot benefit from patient feedback unless we are ready to hear what patients have to say.

Thomas Delbanco (1996)

In this chapter we consider the relationships of the older person to the systems and how these might be fostered both individually and as groups and communities. We review briefly the approach to the legislation framed to involve users in consultation and service planning – an approach which changed from the consumerist to the partnership model. The partnership between user and provider is explored, and the development of the civic model is discussed. We look at ways of involving older users and potential users that have proved successful in EPICS and in other local and national initiatives. These include: older people's conferences and panels; government-sponsored initiatives such as From Margin to Mainstream and Better Government for Older People; the Debate of the Age carried out by Age Concern; local action groups; a national advisory group for older people; the use of focus groups and citizens' juries; and the involvement of older people in project development as volunteers.

The experience of developing an integrated care system with older people has demonstrated that making them the central focus was the key to integrating agencies, reducing conflict, getting best value for money, and developing purpose and direction.

The older person is at the centre of their own personal complex adaptive system, and lives with the uncertainty and unpredictability that are characteristics of these systems. They are accustomed to making assessments of their own capacity and resources. They are experts in managing their own disabilities. Shared knowledge, mutual trust and respect between them and other 'stakeholders' within their system can produce effective solutions to sustaining their independence and achieving personal fulfilment. It can also enable them to take responsibility for decisions that are made as part of the solution. The development of true partnerships with providers and planners of services can enable older people to influence how systems are managed to mutual benefit. There have been a number of national initiatives in both the public and voluntary sectors that have made a real attempt to bring authority and power to the views of older people. The challenge is to bring the views effectively into the strategic planning, care delivery and monitoring processes.

> *The challenge is to bring the views of older people effectively into the strategic planning, care delivery and monitoring procesess.*

Early approaches to involving users were modelled on concepts of consumerism and enshrined in Citizens' and Patients' Charters. They laid the emphasis on the right to complain, seeing the key requirements for the empowerment of citizens as information, choice, accessibility and redress when things go wrong. The new trend is to make users (and potential users) partners in care, sharing the responsibility for planning, delivering and monitoring services both as individuals and as representative groups.

Legislation

Present government legislation is attempting to achieve this partnership by providing formalized ways for older people to be involved at all levels in planning and delivering care, and in developing community services.

The National Health Service and Community Care Act 1990 emphasized the need for the involvement of both users and carers in the assessment process for care in the community services, and also in the planning process that is now continuously undertaken by local authority social services departments in the annual community care plan. There was also a commitment to involve users in the monitoring of the services. The Griffiths Report and the government's response, the White Paper *Caring for People*, both emphasized the importance of users gaining independence and control over their lives (Griffiths 1988; Department of Health 1989).

In the 1998 White Paper *Modernising Social Services* (see also chapter 1, p.32) it was said that the 'third way' for social care proposed by the government 'moves the focus away from who provides the care, and places it firmly on the quality of services experienced by, and outcomes achieved for, individuals and their carers and families' (p.4).

The NHS Plan (2000) recognised that accessing the experience of those who use health and other services, in particular social care services, is one of the best ways of identifying where failures of co-ordination have problematic and sometimes damaging effects.

In March 2001 a new commitment to older people for person-centred care and an end to discrimination was enshrined in the *National Service Framework for Older People* (Department of Health 2001b).

Public consultation and the NHS

There has been a commitment from the Department of Health to consult with users of health services for a number of years but in 1998 an important paper *In the Public Interest – Developing a Strategy for Public Participation in the NHS* set out some guidelines and models (NHS Executive 1998). The key concept was that public participation should become an integral part of the NHS: 'We need to move to a situation in which public participation is no longer a "bolt-on" but a core purpose of the service' (p.2). Some of the 'pay-offs' were seen as:

> *'We need to move to a situation in which public participation is no longer a "bolt-on" but a core purpose of the service.'*

- using patient's experience: 'Patients' experience could play a valuable part in the education of health professionals and in the evaluation of health policy and services.'

- reducing inappropriate usage: 'by involving people and enabling them to access better information, the use made of health services will be improved, engendering neither over nor under use. A failure to involve people is likely to increase inappropriate demand at an individual level, and to lead to services being designed on the basis of perceived rather than actual need' (p.4).

- improving cost effectiveness: 'Public participation may help control the cost of health services, and is likely to improve cost effectiveness.'

- finding new solutions by working with communities: 'Working with communities provides an alternative perspective that can lead to new solutions.'

Partnership was seen as the key to overcoming fragmentation between services and policies, particularly partnership between statutory agencies and the public to overcome the dominance of provider interests.

The EPICS experience was that another pay-off which could be added to the list was 'deflecting conflict'. Agreeing the client was the most important person in the system meant the focus on professional issues shifted. By focusing on the older person, a common purpose was generated to which everyone could subscribe. Professional protective behaviours were minimized. Furthermore, users would not need to resort to a complaints process to achieve the service they wanted.

In the late 1990s 'partnership' was seen as the key to overcoming fragmentation between services and policies, particularly partnership between statutory agencies and the public to overcome the dominance of provider interests. Local authorities had a responsibility to consult with users and with carers in drawing up their community care plans, but health authorities did not have a similar statutory requirement.

The journal *Action Points*, published by the NHS Confederation (Henderson 2000), supporting the New NHS Plan (Department of Health 2000) said:

> Patients are the most important people in the NHS. The aim of the plan is to redesign health services around the needs of patients and to involve patients and carers at every level of health care. Patients must have more influence over the way the NHS works (p.1).

A discussion paper *Involving Patients and the Public in Healthcare* was produced by the Department of Health in September 2001 (Department of Health 2001a). This spelt out more clearly the government's intentions to give authority to the users of services through new structures. It spoke of the outdated model where patients, their carers and their representatives campaign to be heard from outside the NHS, and of the aim to ensure that 'the voices of citizens, patients and their carers, are on the inside influencing every level of service' (p.5). For years the community health councils had been 'campaigning from the outside' and there was much public concern when the government announced its intention to replace them with new systems. Whilst the determination to put patients at the heart of service development (and with legal authority) and to empower citizens in the formal scrutiny and monitoring of services is welcomed, there is some anxiety that in the future the power will lie in the hands of statutorily convened organizations, and that the independence of grass-roots representation might be compromised. This will no doubt form part of the debate following the publication of the discussion paper. A warning was certainly given in the government paper against the new structures becoming dominated by a small number of organizations or articulate individuals (see comments under 'Problems in consultation' p.209).

The new structures proposed include statutory 'patients' forums' (with a voluntary membership) and VOICE, which will be a statutory organization with paid staff to facilitate the forums. The staff of VOICE will be employed by the local authority to keep it at 'arm's length' from the NHS. The NHS Plan proposed the establishment of a patients' forum in every NHS and primary care trust. Half the membership is to be drawn from local patient groups and voluntary organizations, while the other half will be randomly drawn from respondents to the trust's annual patient survey. The members will elect a representative to be a non-executive member on the local trust board. The guidance said the forum should have a clear remit and explicit evaluation criteria should be established from the start, a point that has been emphasized in this book. (See chapter 9, p.251 on evaluation.) It is proposed in the discussion paper that there will be one VOICE for every strategic health authority and it will co-ordinate the work of the patients' forums and ensure that the citizen's voice is heard as well. Local VOICES will be represented at a national level through the Commission for Patient and Public Involvement in Health. Every NHS organization will be required to publish an annual account of the views received and the action taken as a result. This will be published nationally as a patient prospectus.

The NHS Plan included, in the action points, the establishment of an independent local advisory forum or 'citizens' panel' chosen from residents of the area, to provide a sounding board for determining priorities and policies, including the health improvement programme.

In the report commissioned by the NHS Executive Quality and Consumer Branch, the Institute for Health Service Manager and the NHS Confederation (1998) four key policy areas were identified in which public participation needs to be developed:

1. in health improvement programmes and in relevant areas in the context of health action zones

2. in the development of primary care groups

3. in the context of the NHS working in partnership with other agencies to ensure better co-ordinated care

4. in the context of commitments to improve the processes and outcomes of clinical governance.

This report recommended four models which, taken together, constitute elements of an overall strategy for developing public participation. We have added a model and have provided examples to illustrate all five.

1. Direct participation of users

2. Informed views of users

3. Community development (the civic model)

4. Local scrutiny and accountability

5. Transactional process.

Model 1: Direct participation of users

This involves engaging user and voluntary groups in decision-making at local and national levels and building partnerships at the individual level between clinician and patient. The model is illustrated here by examples of initiatives promoting the involvement of older people in planning and implementation of services at both local and national levels. The individual relationships of older people with professionals are seen as important enough to be represented in a separate model (Model 5).

Local initiatives

With EPICS, early attempts to bring older users directly into the executive management group were not successful. They were either 'silent' members or focused on very personal issues which were felt by the practitioners and managers to be inappropriate at the level of executive decision-making. It was not recognized that they might be disempowered by the defensive behaviour of the professionals, who frequently use exclusive language and knowledge. (This is the very problem that the new national structures for participation aim to address through training.) The direct representation of older people on the executive management group was through the chair of the Age Concern Group running a day centre on the site.

Involvement of service users at the more operational levels was much more successful. A multidisciplinary working group met monthly to report on practice issues. This included an older service user, a volunteer representative, the organizer of the local volunteer bureau, a sheltered housing manager, a GP, the day hospital manager, an occupational therapist and physiotherapist, community social worker, hospital social worker and a community psychiatric nurse. The older person representative was often turned to for an opinion when contentious issues arose. The group had a rotating chairship, and the chair became a member of the executive group. It was hoped that an older user would take that role in due course.

Another group met monthly, convened by Age Concern, to which any representative from the EPICS working group was invited. This was an opportunity to review the health and social situation of the older people attending the day centre. It was also an opportunity to exchange information on both community issues and individual older people living in the locality who had been noticed to have a problem. It was a very effective process in preventive care.

Another effective way of directly involving older people was through their role as volunteers. The EPICS experience was that direct participation of older volunteers affected the way services were delivered. The volunteers had the ear of the older users and were mostly older people themselves. They informed the planning and assisted in monitoring services. They acted as a conduit for two-way information. Through their networks they were able to keep the professionals informed on what was happening in the community and how well the public understood the aims and goals of EPICS. What is more, the professionals sought their advice.

They assisted in publicity programmes and gave talks about EPICS to their own communities. They ran a help desk at the council's High Street information centre, the EPICS information service and the phone link with isolated older people. They were a vital part of the complex adaptive system: EPICS-r-us.

National initiatives

There have been a number of well-funded projects committed to empowering older people to have a real impact on the way community care is managed.

'From Margin to Mainstream' was a project established in 1992 by the Joseph Rowntree Foundation, one of a number concerned with the development of user- and carer-centred community care. Over a period of two years the Office for Public Management supported users, carers and staff in four local case-study sites. The objective was to enable users and carers to be involved from top to bottom in all local authority activities around the planning, management, service delivery and quality improvement of community care: 'from "them and us" to "us and us"'.

> The 'end' towards which users and carers are working is change – change in services, change in ways of delivering services, change in the thinking and attitudes within community care organizations. (Office of Public Management 1993, p.6)

The participants in the project 'challenge the assumption that services are products delivered by skilled staff informed by users' and carers' views'. Instead they support the evolution of a collaborative relationship between users, carers and staff. They describe the partnership as 'a group of people who have agreed a common aim and who will pool their resources in order to achieve it' (p.6). This definition stresses mutuality, shared risk and interdependence. It emphasizes that the concept is one of equality: 'partnerships are relationships between equals'. (For details of the projects studied and the outcomes see Appendix 8.1, p.217; for planning exercises and a checklist on setting up a project with users and carers see Appendix 8.4, p.221.)

> *Partnerships are relationships between equals.*

The authors of the 'From Margin to Mainstream' report made the final observation that in spite of the commitment of the users and staff it still seemed to be difficult to translate the learning from these experiments into the mainstream of public service and delivery. They also made the point that user and carer involvement initiatives for joint-working projects between authorities often founder because individual managers leave or change roles. Also individual users and carers 'burn out' and their skills and knowledge are lost. They suggest that 'there should be enough points of connection to make sure that many people within an organization are learning from exchanging ideas with users and carers at all points of service planning and delivery, making involvement proof against staff turnover' (see chapter 2, p.51 on systems behavoiur). The integrative approach to involving users modelled throughout this book would facilitate this interaction.

> *Often user and carer involvement initiatives for joint-working projects between authorities founder because individual managers leave or change roles.*

Model 2: Informed views of users

This model involves developing opportunities to engage with the informed views and experiences of citizens about health and health services. There are now the formalized structures to empower patients and citizens in patients' forums, which have been described above, but there is a new recognition of the value in using the patient as a resource.

Patients as experts

Current government thinking emphasizes that 'patients should be part of the process of developing education programmes'. A paper published in 2001 by the Department of Health, *The Expert Patient: A New Approach to Chronic Disease Management for the 21st Century* (Department of Health 2001c), says that the knowledge and experience held by the patient has for too long been an untapped resource. The idea was introduced in the White Paper *Saving Lives* (Department of Health 1999) and several self-management programmes (for people suffering from arthritis, multiple sclerosis and manic depression) have been evaluated. Results for patients have indicated:

- reduced severity of symptoms
- significant decrease in pain
- improved life-control and activity
- improved resourcefulness and life satisfaction.

The 'pay-offs' for service providers have been noted as:

- improved communication between GP and patient
- fewer visits to and from GPs
- more effective use of services.

(See chapter 4, p.91 on assessment for further reference to patients as experts (Department of Health 1999))

Citizens' juries

It was recommended in the NHS Executive (1998) paper *In the Public Interest* that citizens' juries should be used as a way of raising the standard of public debate on controversial health issues, such as whether health services should be provided free of charge to those who adopt health-damaging lifestyles. It also suggested that the method could be used to monitor a range of public policies in terms of their health impact; and to explore the values and priorities that underpin health improvement programmes and objectives.

Citizens' juries bring together a representative group of citizens (usually 12–15) to consider in depth an issue where a recommendation is required. They usually meet for between three to five days, during which time they hear evidence from witnesses, question them, and then discuss the issue before offering a recommendation. The members of the jury receive a small fee.

Members are given background information about the subject, and hear evidence from expert witnesses according to a set agenda. As well as answering jurors' questions, witnesses are allowed a set length of time to address the jury about the topic. Jurors are able to cross-examine any witness and are given the opportunity to call their own witnesses later in the proceedings.

Trained moderators guide the discussion to ensure that witnesses keep to time and answer jurors' questions. They will also ensure every member of the jury has a chance to express their views. An article in *Health Perspectives* suggests that health authorities will need to show how the recommendations of a jury will influence their decision-making.

> There is a danger, foreseen by Community Health Councils, that the exercises could be manipulated by a health authority to get the answer they want with a public seal of approval. (Association of Community Health Councils for England and Wales 1996, p.4)

As with all consultative processes there is a cost attached to running a citizens' jury. In South Buckinghamshire, for example, where a jury met for four and a half days in 1997 to consider the issue 'Should Buckinghamshire Health Authority fund treatment from osteopaths and chiropractors for people with back pain?', the cost was estimated to be around £15,000.

The 'Debate of the Age' carried out by Age Concern England as its millennium project set up 12 citizens' juries.

One, in Norwich (November 1998), debated the issue 'Should non-clinical factors be taken into account when prioritising NHS Services?'

Another, in Dundee (September 1998), considered 'Whose responsibility is it to provide and to pay for long-term care?'

A third, in Telford (October 1998), was asked to consider 'Should we be able to choose how and when we die? In what circumstances, if any, should people be assisted to die? Who should decide whether or not to assist?'

Focus groups

These have become an increasingly popular method for obtaining the views of con-sumers, particularly favoured by the present government. For example, focus groups of older users and their carers were used extensively in developing the National Service Framework and the National Care Standards.

The focus group is a small group discussion focusing on pre-determined ques-tions, appropriate when the issues are complex. It is an opportunity to look at issues in depth. The goal is to generate information about a carefully defined research issue by exploring individual motivations and attitudes. The discussion is open-ended, directed and interactive – problems with communication and understanding require careful and sensitive handling (Barrett and Kirk 2000). See Appendix 8.2, p.219 for a fuller account of how to run a focus group.

An example of how powerful a focus group can be in bringing about change in policy and practice was demonstrated in South Buckinghamshire. The local hospital and community NHS trust had set up a task group to look at how the end of life was managed both in the hospital and in the community. The consultant physician who had been the champion of EPICS drew together a small group including the hospital chaplain, a volunteer from a local hospice, a representative of the local bereavement association who had also been the project manager for EPICS, a nurse on one of the elderly care wards and a retired physiotherapist, who is a volunteer at the local hospice. It was agreed that the views of local older people should be sought. Two focus groups were convened: one a group of EPICS volunteers who were all over 65 and the other a group of individuals self-selected from a local Older Persons Action Group.

The first group (who knew each other quite well) quickly slipped into very personal and profound issues about their wishes around their own deaths, and those of their spouses. They recounted good and bad experiences and their doubts about whether they really wanted to make their own final decisions. They used the discus-sion to say how they felt the end of life could be managed with a choice of hospital (in an open or in a side ward), a hospice, or in their own homes.

The second group, who did not know each other, initially saw the problems around the end of life, and the decisions involved, as being theirs alone, and they wanted to be in charge. Later in the discussion they were able to explore the complex-ity of the issues and how they would involve their families and other support.

Both groups put forward suggestions. These were written up by the facilitator and presented to the task group. The impact of the direct views was immensely powerful. The ideas were formulated into a recommended code of practice and presented to the

Trust board. The direct views were appended. The recommendations were adopted as a practice and policy guide for managing the dying both in the hospital and in the community. (See Appendix 8.3, p.220 for the emerging guidelines.)

Some groups that meet together as a focus group have developed a sense of purpose which has led them to extend the role of the group. A focus group of older people in central London which grew into a self-activating group was convened initially to discuss the issue of whether older people would use a counselling service devoted exclusively to the needs of older people. A voluntary organization in Camden had planned to set up a counselling service specially for older people. Before investing time and seeking funding it was agreed that it should be established whether older people would find such a service relevant to their needs. A focus group was brought together at a local GP surgery where there was a link worker who visited older people in the community. She advertised the need for participants and a self-selected group of people over 65 was established. The group was facilitated by a younger woman who was training in psychotherapy. Her supervisor acted as her professional mentor.

The group members all came from a very localized community but did not know each other. They met for an agreed number of sessions. At the end of that time they decided they wanted to continue to meet as a self-support group. They used each other as co-counsellors. They had become their own complex adaptive system. They had demonstrated that they could and would use counselling as a therapy and that age had no significance.

The facilitator whose role was ended said the experience had been personally moving as she observed the developing trust between the group's members and between them and herself. She said she felt a sense of privilege at having shared in the life experience of these older people.

The organization set up a counselling service.

Model 3: Community development

This model is concerned with mobilizing communities to become participants in both defining problems and developing solutions to health and social service issues. It fits with the civic model of implementation described earlier in the book where complex interaction between the community and the individual depends on mutual acceptance of responsibility and the development of shared values. (See chapter 3, p.86 on implementation models.)

Locality forums

The White Paper *The New NHS* recommended the establishment of locality forums to contribute a non-statutory viewpoint to strategic planning and health improvement.

In Buckinghamshire, the Health Authority said:

> The agenda will be to consider issues concerning the environment, economic welfare, community infrastructure and community safety. The Forums are essentially consultation and reference groups with some planning and developmental capacity. Their prime focus is on determining local needs and priorities from a non-statutory user's and carer's viewpoint. (Spargo 1999, p.1)

LOCAL INITIATIVES

Critical locality links are with primary care groups and trusts, 'health for all' programmes and district councils. In Buckinghamshire the main points of value for primary care groups (and trusts) in setting up locality forums were seen as:

- They are inclusive and offer a fast track to public involvement and consultation.

- They represent the most effective route for engagement with voluntary organizations, users and carers.

- They carry the full commitment and support of all the district councils, trusts, the county council, community health councils, councils for voluntary organizations and the health authority.

- They will provide a sharp focus on local needs and issues.

- They will cross-reference, through co-membership, with strategy groups and will be fully represented on the Partnership Forum which brings together a range of related planning activities.

- They represent and tap into a very comprehensive network of resources, communication links and consultative mechanisms.

- They will provide fast-track information and an opportunity to test out responses and reactions to proposed consultation.

- They are established as standing groups, and so are not time limited or project-based, thus enabling long-term relationships to be established.

- They have a broad-based remit spanning health and social welfare with a particular geographical focus on public health issues. They will be able to carry forward specific pieces of community development where practicable.

In South Buckinghamshire the locality forums are supported by community development officers from the local district councils. They are proving to be successful in fostering confidence in 'ordinary' citizens who are not the usual in-groups to become active participants. The members of the forums read consultative documents and make written responses both at local and national levels. They are developing skills in presenting their views. Representatives from the locality forums become members of the high-level partnership forum where senior managers from health and social services, and the voluntary sector, commissioners and local authority cabinet members review strategic plans and outcomes.

OLDER PERSONS ACTION GROUPS (OPAGS)

Following conferences for older people set up by EPICS in different areas in South Buckinghamshire, it was resolved to form Older Persons Action Groups (OPAGs) to take forward the proposals and challenges to the authorities responsible for environmental, health and social services and to local commercial companies. Representatives

---

Our aim is

> To raise and take forward issues that are important to local older people

And our objectives are

- Working alongside local authorities and service providers
- Raising awareness of the varying needs of the older people in the community
- Organizing social events to promote networking and information exchange
- Promoting the personal development of members through the acquisition of new skills
- Working towards affiliation to BGOP (Better Government for Older People)

[We are a voluntary group]

[We focus on the needs and problems of the older members of our community]

We meet quarterly at .... (Free Membership)

Figure 8.1 Aims and objectives of a local Older Persons Action Group

of the OPAGs attend the locality forums so that there is a link of informed citizens right through to the high-level strategic planning forums.

Initially the groups were chaired and guided by the EPICS co-ordinators, but they soon became self-governing. However several of the EPICS volunteers have become members of the OPAGs and two-way feedback into EPICS is maintained through their membership. Members of the local OPAGs found that there is a national OPAG, although in this case the initials stood for Older Persons' Advisory Group. The local groups are planning to send representatives to the national group.

Examples of issues taken up by Older Persons Action Groups in South Buckinghamshire

Pharmacy and the Asian community

One of the problems raised by older members of the local Asian community was that they had to rely on their grandchildren to read the instructions on their medication.

This was raised with the community pharmacist who said it would be possible to print instructions in both English and Urdu and that she would look into the availability of software immediately.

Pay-off for the provider. It was perceived as good preventive care and therefore good professional practice.

Access to local small shops

A local small business threatened by the supermarkets in the neighbourhood approached the OPAG with a proposal to run a regular minibus service to bring older people to his shop, and others nearby. He also agreed a delivery service but felt older people enjoyed the experience of going shopping in a village shop environment.

Pay-off for the provider. The shopkeepers gained regular customers and goodwill in the locality.

Example of the two-way process where providers seek the views of the users

Uneven pavements and ill-placed street lamps and pedestrian crossing

The local district council and the security officer for the police approached the OPAG and were invited to a meeting to discuss the safety and security issues raised (and published) at the older persons conference.

An action plan was agreed as a result.

Pay-off for the provider. The authorities were seen to be responsive to community needs.

Electronic Government

The district council, charged with developing new government proposals for bringing information to citizens where they are most likely to find easy access asked if one of their officers could attend a meeting of the local OPAG to find out where they currently go for information.

The officers asked for suggestions for siting computers or TVs, and asked the members to ask all their contacts and feed the information back through the OPAG chairperson.

Pay-off for the provider. Easy direct consultation with older citizens.

Primary care groups and trusts

The White Paper *The New NHS* said that primary care groups and trusts should be encouraged to play an active part in community development.

> Community development can make an important contribution to assessing the health needs of local populations, through community participation in both defining and collecting information on local health needs. (Department of Health 1997).

In order to ensure that users are adequately represented, the health authority, and primary care groups and trusts need to know which user, patient and carer groups exist in their area and, in partnership with local authorities, should have the responsibility for supporting the development of such groups locally. In South Buckinghamshire one of the primary care trusts is funding the expenses of the local OPAG in partnership with the local council. The council provides meeting rooms and secretarial facilities free of charge, and the trust supports the costs of transport and carers.

'Better Government for Older People'

A two-year action research programme 'Better Government for Older People' (BGOP) had been set up in 1998 with the aim 'to improve public services for older people by better meeting their needs, listening to their views and encouraging and recognizing their contribution' (Better Government for Older People 1999, p.4). The programme provided a

> ...test-bed for some of the key concepts and questions within the modernisation and improvement agenda: how to achieve more integrated strategies and policies between different levels of government; how to balance short term remedial action with longer term prevention; how to achieve more citizen-centred and responsive services; how to increase the active involvement of users of services; how to improve the quality of practical outcomes at the front-line. (p.21)

Twenty-eight pilot projects were set up to involve older people in creating better services and communities that work for older people. The outcomes are being evaluated and the report *All Our Futures* (Better Government for Older People 1999) comments on the value of partnership working with citizens.

> This Report illustrates a real example of joined-up government in action. By consulting and listening, we can make a real difference to the lives of older people. By engaging and involving them in strategic planning and policymaking, we can ensure our services are delivered in the right way. The Prime Minister, Tony Blair (p.3)

The programme is being evaluated by Warwick University (Hayden and Boas 2000) and their Evaluation Report *Making a Difference* claims that as an action-research programme BGOP has been committed to learning – as much from difficulties as successes: 'The learning from pilots has shown the importance of effective political leadership and the need for local authorities to invest in staffing capacity for the management of change.' (p.107). These points have been made strongly elsewhere in this book. (See chapter 10, p.281 on systems and leadership.) The report suggested that community development might be difficult for health service professionals and managers to grasp. This is because, it says, in many ways it is the antithesis of the way they have been trained as experts or leaders. The point was made that it is essential to partnership working that the staff group and particularly the senior staff feel empowered. Only then will they be committed. A similar view emerged from the Dyfed pilot in the 'From Margin to Mainstream' initiative when staff were afraid of consulting with the public: 'they were afraid of being shouted at or criticised'.

The evaluation of the BGOP programme has shown that while the goal may be achievable (i.e. to listen to older peoples' views and include older people in strategic planning and development of services), 'the *mechanisms* are not in place in all areas, not sufficiently *sustainable* in *most*, not *fully developed* in any to deliver this ambition' (Better Government for Older People, p.4).

A BGOP network was launched in March 1999 to share knowledge and experience. It has 170 local authorities already affiliated and is growing. (See the BGOP website at www.bettergovernmentforolderpeople.gov.uk)

Model 4: Local scrutiny and accountability

This model is concerned with developing more effective systems for ensuring public scrutiny and public accountability at both a local and a national level.

Lay membership of primary care groups and trusts is part of the commitment of the government to involving citizens in planning, monitoring and scrutinizing services. This is another role that was undertaken by the community health councils but the government believes that elected members of the local councils will have an authority through the ballot box which will make them more effective.

The councillors will undertake a scrutiny role through the local authority's Overview and Scrutiny Committee. They will be able to call NHS executives to account in a face-to-face meeting twice a year.

Earlier examples of the involvement of citizens in a real way in monitoring quality have been demonstrated through the Social Services Inspectorate.

Lay assessors

AGE CONCERN HILLINGDON

In the mid-1990s the inspection of residential homes became a prime area for the involvement of members of the local community. Lay people were trained to go into homes alongside the social services inspectors. An early model in the London Borough of Hillingdon (1992/3) used the local Age Concern to develop a team of older people to act as independent assessors, visiting with the inspectors but with equal responsibilities to inspect records, procedures, etc. They were primarily concerned, however, with the quality of life of residents. It became evident that the lay members of the team brought a different perspective to the professional inspectors and often made contact more easily with the residents.

The model was piloted further on nursing homes in the private sector. The proprietors of the homes welcomed the more independent status of inspectors from outside the health authority and felt the model was successful because they were recruited, trained and supervised under thoroughly professional and accountable management. Such was their trust that they invited the lay assessors to make unannounced visits.

CAMDEN AGE CONCERN

Another model was developed in the London Borough of Camden with self-selected lay assessors (recruited by the local authority through advertisements) being given induction training and ongoing support facilitated by the local Age Concern. The role of Age Concern was seen as:

- providing objectivity and independence for the lay assessors
- providing public accountability
- providing expertise.

The aims of the induction training were:

- to provide the lay assessors with enough background material to understand the philosophical, legislative and managerial context of residential care in Camden
- to provide the opportunity to enhance listening and observational skills in order to feel at ease in the residential setting and able to communicate effectively with the residents.

'It is important that "training" should not destroy the freshness of the lay assessor's view as a citizen looking at the quality of life of another citizen.' (Stanners 1994, p.3)

A NATIONAL INITIATIVE

The government's intention to enable users to have an influence at all levels has been demonstrated by the appointment of a lay person (who also happens to be a wheel-chair user) to chair the new Social Care Institute of Excellence, SCIE (pronounced 'sky'). This is the counterpart of the National Institute of Clinical Excellence, NICE. Membership is half lay people and half professionals.

Model 5: Transactional process

This model reinforces the concept of person-centred care. It concerns the building of partnerships at the individual level between older person and practitioner. The individual becomes the partner of the professional in planning, implementing and evaluating their own care. The professional facilitates the user in making choices, and interacts with them in a way that is mutually agreed to be appropriate. The whole process of assessment, lifetime planning, self-managing is inherent in the model. Particular initiatives in EPICS that fostered the 'transactional' process included the day hospital and the EPICS care worker service.

Older people were referred to the day hospital, where EPICS had a place reserved daily; there they would have consultations with a range of practitioners on the day and a care plan would be agreed. The client satisfaction evaluation programme carried out by EPICS showed that some day patients were bored once their assessments and treatments were completed. The day hospital changed its policy. Each older person attending could decide whether they wanted to be there all day or whether they preferred to go home once the treatment was completed. They decided when they would arrive (transport permitting), whether they would stay for lunch and which activities they would participate in. Consultation as part of the evaluation had been an effective tool in promoting choice and putting the older person in control.

The EPICS care worker service was managed so that the client was in control of the way care was provided. The client agreed with the co-ordinator what support would be most effective, and when it should be provided. The care workers had discretion to carry out whatever tasks were appropriate at the time to suit the needs of the client. The care plan was left with the client. The experience was that neither client nor care worker exploited the freedom that the system allowed.

Another 'transaction' between the user and the service was the access to the EPICS service. If an older person identifies a need, and it takes several days for them to be seen for an assessment, it is the service needs that are being met rather than the older person's. The swift, one-stop access helped the older person to retain control.

Problems in consultation

One of the difficulties encountered in consulting with formally constituted groups (as, for example, in voluntary organizations) is how to avoid the 'party line' – the problem of the 'professional consultee'. This aspect was noted above (p.193) in the reference to the discussion paper *Involving Patients and the Public in Healthcare* (Department of Health 2001a). There is also a problem in maintaining a 'freshness' in the points of view of representatives. There is a fine line between empowering lay people through giving them 'training', and avoiding institutionalizing them into identification with professional values. Those charged with providing 'training' for older people to foster the confidence and knowledge needed to enable them to fill the roles of advocate, critic and innovator, and to act as partners in service and strategy development, should be aware of the difficulty. In the examples of trained lay assessors given

There is a fine line between empowering lay people through giving them training and avoiding institutionalizing them into identification with professional values.

above the policy was established that they should only serve for a period of four years.

Another problem in bringing lay people into joint working is to match the objectives of the user representatives and the professionals participating in a group. As happened in the case of EPICS given above, where the older person was not enabled to play an effective executive role, the professionals may be concerned with plans for implementation, or strategy development, and may become frustrated at the use of the time for the more personal concerns of the users. The users may be alienated by the use of the private shorthand language used by the professionals and the sense that their concerns are not being valued. The proposal to provide 'training' for lay representatives through VOICE is an attempt to redress this inequality, but the professionals will need to accept responsibility for removing the barriers created by the use of jargon and other exclusive behaviours.

There is a challenge in finding ways of reaching those individuals who are not members of groups or are not represented by groups, or whose voices have not already been heard. The locality forums seem to be achieving some success as noted above, and ways that EPICS found effective are discussed below.

Funding and resource costs

The BGOP evaluation report makes a point of saying that 'engagement with older people, and even consultation, requires resourcing if it is to be effective and inclusive' (Hayden and Boaz 2000, p.26). The cost of implementing consultative processes should not be underestimated. Room hire, subsistence and transport costs should all be taken into account, as well as the staff and time for facilitation and administration. To ensure that opportunities for consultation and participation are fully inclusive it may be necessary to provide personal care, or to pay for a carer to be with a frail person at home whilst the permanent carer can attend meetings. Signers, interpreters and loop systems may all have to be provided depending on circumstances.

> *Engagement with older people, and even consultation, requires resourcing if it is to be effective and inclusive.*

It is also important to be aware of the time and cost implications of recruiting members to the group. An experienced practitioner in the USA, Delbanco (1996) suggests that a list of 100 potential participants will produce 10 group members. He also says that recruiting one person to a focus group requires 17 telephone calls. An example of the unanticipated time costs in bringing a group together is provided by the experience of Camden Age Concern in central London.

Camden Age Concern set up a model which would bring some very elderly and frail people together in a panel to discuss issues of concern to them, with a view to empowering them to face the local authority. Eight people were identified through discussion with the agency's welfare team. The facilitator wrote first, then visited and identified a time and place for the panel meeting. He then set up transport facilities and wrote again to inform all members of the arrangements. He had been promised the assistance of a member of the social services department, but was then told that current workloads precluded this. The first meeting was cancelled owing to extremely adverse weather conditions. Attempts to reconvene the meeting within two weeks failed because of prior arrangements and health issues for most of the group. Planning for the project had started in February (1994) and the first meeting of the group finally took place in August. Only three older people attended. One could not come because she had to wait in for her home help whose schedules were unpredictable. One did not come because the driver could not find her block. Others had prior commitments. A second meeting was set for a month later but one member's health had deteriorated and another had to attend hospital after a fall. New members were recruited to attend subsequent meetings. The facilitator commented:

> ...the actual setting up of the panel took longer than anticipated. Much discussion took place with potential panel members, both about the panel and the reasons for establishing it, the venue, transport arrangements, etc. This was mainly carried out over the telephone, although four of the people involved were seen as well. Further time was necessarily taken up negotiating venue/transport issues. It is also worthy of note that in a number of telephone conversations with some of the people concerned other issues were raised, and the facilitator became involved in other matters relating to welfare and other concerns of the people to whom he spoke. (Schneerson 1994, p.26)

There may be a potential conflict of interest between empowerment and resources.

It has not been easy in the past to secure funding for consultation, and it should be recognized that there may be a potential conflict of interest between empowerment and resources, which may make the process of consultation with providers a less-than-honest or wholehearted process.

The concern of the legislation is with empowerment in relation to services and with a shift in the balance of power between users and professionals, while on the other hand local authorities must operate within resource constraints. (Parsloe 1994, p.114)

Sharing resources

Finding another organization with a 'shelf-project' (that is, a project that has been formulated previously, awaiting an opportunity for enactment) can be a useful way to secure resources and funding. It can also avoid 'consultation fatigue', described in the NHS Executive (1998) paper *In the Public Interest* as a danger where different agencies separately seek to engage with the same people and there is no effective partnership working. Organizations sometimes have a small allocation of funds for an unspecified project and can work together to produce an event, which could, for example, launch an initiative. Ownership of the product will be promoted and publicity secured by pooling resources.

> *Finding another organization with a 'shelf-project' can be a useful way to secure resources and funding.*

EXAMPLE 1: A CONFERENCE FOR OLDER PEOPLE

In South Buckinghamshire a local district council had funding to run an environmental health event but had not settled on a focus for the project. EPICS was being extended into the area, and it had been decided that an opportunity for the older people in the locality to meet to identify and discuss their needs would be popular, and would help create an agenda for action by both the district council and other stakeholders in the integrated care system. A joint working group was set up with representatives of all those with an interest in setting up such a conference (see Appendix 8.4, p.221 for detailed information on the process). Planning began nine months in advance but was barely long enough. The conference was given the title 'Growing Old, or Older and Growing?', a quotation from Carl Rogers, an American psychotherapist. Older people had been recruited as discussion group leaders. In advance of the conference they were enabled to learn, or to enhance, their group-work skills in a workshop run by the trust's training officer, a mutually enjoyable experience.

At the conference VIPs were only to be allowed to stay for the opening addresses as every available place was given to an older person. Professional staff were limited to one per discussion group, to act as scribes and raconteurs. The local press was very interested in this approach and in the policy to limit the attendance of professionals. They came to photograph the training session and reported: 'This approach to put older people at the heart of planning and implementing services, supported by the professionals, underpins the philosophy of integrated care.' They and also the local housing association each printed a small pro-forma for people to register their interest in attending. (The importance of feeding clear information to the Press cannot be over-emphasized. A briefing sheet before the event and a pack of essential information to hand out to them at the conference proved invaluable in achieving accuracy in reporting and getting the essential messages across.)

A model that was found to be effective in setting the agenda for the conference was to run a series of focus groups to identify some common themes of concern to the local older population (for a definition of a focus group and description of its func- tions see Appendix 8.2, p.219). Here again partnership with another project was effective. A local university was researching the needs of older people and planning a series of focus groups in the area. The researcher and the project manager for the integrated care project ran the focus groups together. These were mostly located in local clubs for older people. One was also held in a day centre and one was in a sheltered housing complex. In an attempt to reach Asian elders, the focus group leaders attended a mother-and-baby clinic run by an Urdu-speaking health visitor; the young women were invited to bring their parents and grandparents to a meeting. Unusually, both men and women from this older group of residents attended, later becoming participants in the conference where they were given a written translation of the issues and opening speeches. An interpreter was also provided.

The focus groups highlighted six areas of concern to become the topics for discussion at the conference. These were:

- accident prevention
- health
- home care
- leisure
- information
- transport.

At the conference itself each small group, consisting of ten older people with the facilitator and scribe, was invited to select one or more of these topics to discuss. The key fact emerging was that the older people's *perception* of their needs was different from those perceived by professionals, the *solutions* were the same, but the *implementation* was different. For example, the professionals identified the need for exercise as part of a healthy lifestyle. The older people identified their need as getting out and about. The professionals saw the solution formalized in health promotion programmes and exercise classes, the older people said that if public transport was improved, and if the pavements were repaired and levelled, and if the street lighting was adequate and positioned where *they* found the need, and if chiropody services were easily available, they would take exercise in going out, walking to the shops and the library, going dancing, and so on. This divergence in the perception of need by professionals and users was identified by Ross (1994), who observed:

> Some of the activities that are thought most likely to promote an active, independent older age are not necessarily thought of as 'services' at all but as opportunities for learning and keeping fit and healthy, volunteering and paid employment... (p.119)

She also made the point that

> ...most people, but particularly those who have long experience of being refused and ignored, have rather modest needs...people should be given what they actually want as compared to what 'professionals' think they need. (p.119)

The experience of EPICS and the perception of the government is that if older people are consulted and included as partners their demands for services will be realistic.

> *Older people 'should be given what they actually want as compared to what "professionals" think they need.'*

EXAMPLE 2: WORKING IN PARTNERSHIP

A second model of a conference that was successful in South Buckinghamshire concerned an Agewell programme and the local Health Promotion Unit, who were each looking for an opportunity to further a particular objective.

During 1997–98 Health for All (HFA), a multi-agency initiative in South Buckinghamshire, had commissioned Oxford Brookes University to carry out an assessment of older people's health and health-related needs. Agencies managing the project included EPICS, Age Concern, social services, Bucks Community Action, the Buckinghamshire Health Authority, the South Buckinghamshire NHS Trust and district councils.

The initiative examined what older people thought of the services provided by health and social services and voluntary organizations, how easy they found it to use the services and what could be done to improve them. The study involved consultation with groups of older people as well as interviews with professionals from statutory and voluntary organizations. When the report was finished (Skinner and Bartlett 1998) the Health for All Steering Group set up Agewell, a multi-agency project group to take forward the study's recommendations. One of its projects was to set up a conference with EPICS in response to the recommendation from the focus groups that older people should be included in consultation and planning processes.

The Integrated Care Project was preparing to launch a further development in the area, and wanted to secure publicity for this. Its volunteers had also prepared a directory of services generated from a database which they had developed over several years. They wanted the opportunity to run the draft directory past potential users; the conference facilitated this objective.

The conference therefore achieved multiple aims with pooled resources and greater impact than one initiative would have achieved on its own. The conference was attended by 120 older people and 50 professionals.

FOLLOW-UP FROM THE CONFERENCES

It was agreed that the report of the conferences, which recorded all the issues raised, would be sent to all the statutory and voluntary organizations concerned locally, regionally and, in some cases, nationally. In each case local businesses printed the documents at no charge. The local Member of Parliament distributed copies to the front bench of the government and to shadow ministers.

Action groups were set up to take the issues forward: the OPAGs described above (p.202).

Overview

The older person is at the centre of their own personal complex adaptive system. They are experts on their own situation and can inform both the individual practitioner and the other stakeholders in the systems of care on what will be best for them. The language of consumerism in the legislation has changed to one of partnership but it is still a challenge to bring the views of the older user into the system. Partnership implies shared responsibility, but there will be a need for a cultural change in professional attitudes for this to be a reality.

Older people are a heterogeneous group, and there are a wide variety of ways they can be involved in the care systems. These include direct participation, providing informed views, encouraging communities to identify problems and find solutions. Older people have a key role to play, together with the professionals, in ensuring high-quality standards of care and opportunities for personal fulfilment.

Making the older person a partner in service design has been shown to lead to cost-efficient provision, in that it is what the older user wants, and the older user is a responsible consumer.

In EPICS, sharing and working closely with the older person became part of the culture. The professionals learned that they would not be devalued, or lose their authority. In fact they were more highly valued by the older people. The older people in turn felt more valued by the practitioners and learned to work as partners in their own care. Everyone was a winner.

Chapter 8 – Headline points

- The challenge is to bring the views effectively into the strategic planning, care delivery and monitoring processes.

- We need to move to a situation in which public participation is no longer a 'bolt-on' extra but a core purpose of the service.

- In the 1990s 'partnership' was seen as the key to overcoming fragmentation between services and policies, particularly partnership between statutory agencies and the public to overcome the dominance of provider interests.

- Partnerships are relationships between equals.

- User and carer involvement initiatives for joint-working projects between authorities often founder because individual managers leave or change roles.

- There is a fine line between empowering lay people through giving them 'training', and avoiding institutionalizing them into identification with professional values.

- Engagement with older people, and even consultation, requires resourcing if it is to be effective and inclusive.

- There may be a potential conflict of interest between empowerment and resources.

- Finding another organization with a 'shelf-project' (that is a project that has been formulated previously, awaiting an opportunity for enactment) can be a useful way to secure resources and funding.

- People should be given what they actually want as compared with what 'professionals' think they need.

APPENDIX 8.1

'From Margin to Mainstream' Case Studies

The four 'From Margin to Mainstream' local case-study sites were Dyfed, Hereford and Ware, Sheffield, and Sutton.

Dyfed

Objectives

- developing user-run information services
- user participation in planning, and strategy development
- monitoring and evaluating services participation in training.

The outcome was the development of CATCH UP (Co-operative Action to Change and Hurry Up Progress), a co-operative of people with disabilities, carers and associates. The group extended their own model of user-run information services into other localities. It took an active part in community care planning at all levels (including the top). It helped in rethinking assessment processes, drawing up new complaints procedures, and delivering, as well as receiving, training.

Hereford and Ware

Objective

- to involve older people with mental health problems and dementia and their carers in consultation.

The outcome was the creation of a resource network of carers and real dialogue between social workers and carers about thorny problems. It also led to a reversal of attitudes held by the social workers both about the people with mental health problems and about the carers being too involved to be effective as consultative partners.

Sheffield

Objective

- for people with disabilities to be able to influence planning and purchasing of community care services.

The outcome was that a user-led network drew up and disseminated a Charter for People with Disabilities. They set out their own business plan and invited the local authority to discuss it. Subsequently they continued to meet regularly with managers within the social services, health and housing to influence planning and purchasing of community care services. A user has been appointed as a development worker (with users involved in the appointment, and drawing up the work plan).

Sutton

Objective

- consultation with users about a new day centre.

The outcome was the development of a user-managed learning centre for people with disabilities, with a user-led board offering the service as an independent provider under contract to the local authority. Other developments included working with GPs to extend carer consultation in primary care.

APPENDIX 8.2

Focus Groups

A focus group is:

- a small group discussion with a facilitator, usually limited to 8–12 people
- an open-ended, directed, interactive discussion focused on predetermined questions.

Steps in planning a focus group:

- What issues do you want to study?
- What questions do you want answered as a result of the focus group?
- Who wants the results?
- What characteristics should all focus group participants share?
- What costs should be anticipated?
- To whom will you present the results of the study?
- How will they be used?
- How will you present the results?
- How will you ensure the participants have feedback on the results?

The group members will be individuals who have been actively recruited to participate in the focus group and who share key characteristics: for example older people who are active enough to attend a luncheon club, but require transport to get there, would be a useful group to target when transport is an issue for discussion.

There may be an observer who can note the responses of the group members, the points of agreement and disagreement and any bias that may have entered the discussion. The observer will not participate in the discussion.

The success of the group can be very dependent on the facilitator who should be skilled in small group dynamics and take a neutral, non-biased position. He or she will guide the discussion but will not ask leading questions or bias the discussion.

APPENDIX 8.3

An Example of Outcomes From Focus Groups Convened to Consider the Issues of Managing the End of Life in Hospital

Principles of care

The art of living well and dying well are one.

Epicurus

Death is one of the attributes you were created with; death is part of you
Your life's continual task is to build your death.

Michel de Montaigne (16th century essayist)

- Every patient has a right to a comfortable and dignified end to his or her life that will affirm its quality and value.
- They should be able to spend their 'End-of-Life' in a manner that reflects how they have lived, i.e. to live until they die.
- Every patient has the right to the support that will help them to feel in control at the end of their lives, and to be central to all planning that involves them.
- Every family member has the right to support that will help them to experience the parting as positively as possible.
- The values and customs of the patient and family must be kept at the heart of any decision-making process.
- The dignity and privacy of the patient and their family must be of primary concern.
- The patient and their family must have speedy access to accurate information and expertise.
- The patient should have access to the level of information appropriate to their needs and desires.
- The patient should have access to any emotional and spiritual support they wish, which should continue to be available to the family, friends and carers after the death.

APPENDIX 8.4

The Process of Setting up the EPICS Conference

Working group

A joint working group was set up with representatives from the following: the district council's environmental health department, their catering department and a retired member of their transport department. Older people were represented by one person with reduced mobility who had been an organizer for Dial-a-Ride, a resident of a sheltered housing complex, a retired employee of a local commercial company with IT skills and a representative of the local volunteer bureau.

A local district councillor and the Integrated Care System's project manager and administrative assistant carried out the planning and the implementation.

A local commercial sponsor had agreed to print and distribute a report from the conference and sent a representative periodically.

Food, premises and facilities

The company who provided Meals-on-Wheels in the locality undertook to provide a hot meal free of charge. The council donated the use of the council chamber and adjoining meeting rooms. They also provided a special loop system to facilitate group discussion for people with impaired hearing. People with impaired vision had a volunteer dedicated to them for the day. Volunteer care workers assisted with any personal needs.

A nationally famous actor living locally (himself an older person) opened the conference together with the local Member of Parliament. A local student of photography took the photographs for the conference report.

Publicity

Advance notices, designed and executed by a volunteer with IT skills, were sent to all local voluntary groups with an interest in older people. They were posted in doctors' surgeries and hospital waiting rooms, libraries, council offices, newsagents, post offices, social services offices, offices of the benefits agency, CAB offices, community centres and churches. Most were delivered by hand.

Attracting a representative range of participants

A final list of two hundred older people who had expressed interest in coming had to be halved to one hundred. The list was scrutinized carefully to try to ensure a wide range of representatives, for example applicants from sheltered housing developments and clubs were limited to six per site. Couples were asked to come singly, one as a representative of the other, unless there was a special reason for them to attend together; people from different ends of the town where environmental problems might differ were identified.

Every applicant had a personally addressed letter explaining the need for selection and each of the people who were not able to attend was sent a form on which to write their issues. All two hundred were sent an interim and a final report. The postage was paid from the council's Environmental Health Project Fund.

This list of 200 names became a useful reference group for other organizations wishing to elicit views of older users. Although they had given their consent to be consulted on future issues, in the interests of confidentiality contact was made only through the EPICS organization that had run the conference.

Transport

As with all activities involving older users, transport is a key issue.

Cars and volunteer drivers were provided for all who needed them both before and after the conference. This operation required considerable planning and meticulous implementation. Each attendee received a letter telling them when and where they would be collected and the name of the driver. The letter also had a coloured sticker which identified which table they would be sitting at.

On the day of the conference the raconteur from each of the groups filled in a topic return form with issues and comments recorded.

Table 8.2 Topic Return Form

FEEDBACK FORMS FROM CONFERENCE DISCUSSION GROUPS

TOPIC:

GROUP No.	ISSUES ARISING	COMMENT

In the lunch break at the conference the issues arising and comments were collated by the raconteurs and group leaders and a summary was presented to the conference immediately after lunch, with the opportunity for further comment to be made from the floor.

A resolution was carried to take the issues forward by establishing Older Persons Action Groups and through the publishing and distribution of the conference report.

References

Association of Community Health Councils for England and Wales (1996) *'Citizens Juries.' Health Perspectives'*

Barrett, J. and Kirk, S. (2000) 'Running focus groups with elderly and disabled participants.' *Applied Ergonomics 31*, 6, 621–629.

Better Government for Older People, Report of the Steering Committee (1999) *All Our Futures* (www.bettergovernmentforolderpeople.gov.uk)

Delbanco, T. (1996) 'Focus group techniques in health care.' Paper presented at the Picker Institutes Second European Forum on Quality Improvement in Health Care. Paris.

Department of Health (1989) *Caring for People: Community Care in the Next Decade and Beyond.* White Paper. London: HMSO.

Department of Health (1997) *The New NHS.* White Paper. London: HMSO.

Department of Health (1998) *Modernising Social Services.* White Paper. London: HMSO.

Department of Health (1999) *Saving Lives: Our Healthier Nation.* White Paper. London: HMSO.

Department of Health (2000) *The NHS Plan.* Cmd 4818–1. London: HMSO.

Department of Health (2001a) *Involving Patients and the Public in Healthcare.* Discussion Document. London. (www.doh.gov.uk/involvingpatients)

Department of Health (2001b) *National Service Framework for Older People.* London: Department of Health.

Department of Health (2001c) *The Expert Patient: A New Approach to Chronic Disease Management for the 21st Century.* Discussion Paper. (www.doh.gov.uk/healthinequalities)

Griffiths, R. (1988) *Community Care: Agenda for Action.* London: HMSO.

Hayden, C. and Boaz, A. (2000) *Making a Difference.* An evaluation of the Better Government for Older People Programme. Warwick University. www.bettergovernmentforolderpeople.gov.uk

Henderson, A. (1994) Patient involvement in the new NHS. *Action Points 25*, December. London: NHS Confederation.

NHS Executive, Institute of Health Services Management, NHS Confederation (1998) *In the Public Interest – Developing a Strategy for Public Participation in the NHS.* London: NHS.

Office for Public Management (1993) *User and Carer involvement in Community Care: From Margin to Mainstream.* Briefing paper. London: Office for Public Management.

Parsloe, P. (1994) 'Balancing User Choice and Resource Constraints.' *Policy and Politics 22*, 2, 113–118.

Ross, K. (1994) 'Customer Caring?' *Local Government Studies 20*, 2, 188–189.

Schneerson, D. (1994) *A Report on the Issues concerning the Establishment of a Panel of Older People to consider Care in the Community.* London: Age Concern Camden.

Skinner, A. and Bartlett, H. (1998) *Age Well in Southern Buckinghamshire.* Report of a study on older people's services in Southern Buckinghamshire. Oxford Centre for Health Care Research and Development, Oxford Brookes University.

Spargo, J. (1999) *Locality Forums in Buckinghamshire.* Buckinghamshire Health Authority paper.

Stanners, C. (1994) *Summary Report of the Pilot Training Scheme for Lay Assessors.* Camden: Age Concern.

Further Reading

Philips, C., Palfrey, C. and Thomas, P. (1994) *Evaluating Health and Social Care.* Basingstoke: Macmillan.

Gives a succinct, jargon-free and honest overview of methods for engaging users in evaluation.

Pithouse, A. and Williamson, H. (eds) (1997) *Engaging User in Welfare Services.* Birmingham: Venture Press for the British Association of Social Workers.

A practical look at the reality of engaging users in the planning and delivery of services. It looks beneath the rhetoric and considers the way society fosters the disengagement of older people rather than promoting their status as consumers.

Chapter 9

Evaluating an Integrated Care System

In modern health and social care it is unethical not to be concerned with evaluation, and no longer acceptable to be 'evaluation illiterate'.

John Ovretveit, Professor of Health and Management, Nordic School of Public Health, Gottenburg, Sweden

There is nothing more difficult than providing the answer to a question to which the response appears obvious.

George Bernard Shaw

In this chapter we demonstrate the critical importance of evaluation in developing and sustaining integrated care systems. The purposes of evaluation are explored and examples given of different tools for evaluating complex adaptive systems. It is proposed that evaluation is an essential tool in the formulation and evolution of strategy and in the development of quality care. The steps in the evaluation process are identified, and we discuss some of the problems that arise when multiple agencies and activities are to be evaluated. The approach to costing adopted by EPICS as part of the evaluation is described. Terms commonly used in evaluation are appended.

The aims of evaluation

Evaluation is something that is occurring all the time, in everybody's lives. Judgements are continually made, for example as to whether somebody or something is liked or disliked. Mostly this evaluation is implicit and done intuitively without recourse to systematic analysis. It is buried in past experience with all the biases and baggage that this brings with it. It leads to the temptation to say 'I know. I do not need to know why I know. It is obvious.'

However, in setting up complex systems such as integrated care projects, there is no experience or knowledge base of such systems working from which intuition can spring. Evaluation is the only way to obtain understanding and deep insights into the processes. This can only be done through a planned and systematic approach. It is not always easy to get people to understand this because their previously learned behaviours in decision-making have been intuitive.

> *Evaluation is the only way to obtain understanding and deep insights into the processes.*

In some ways understanding what evaluation is about is easy. It is the answer to two apparently simple questions:

- *What is the value or worth of what is taking place?* This then raises the question to whom is it of worth or value? Is it the older person or their carers, or the practitioners, or the community or the service commissioners? In a person-centred system it must always have direct or indirect value to the older person but it may have variable impact on the others. However, the higher the quality of the service provided, the more everybody should be satisfied.

- *How will it be known what changes have occurred as the result of the interventions?* Put another way, how will it be known when the purposes have been achieved? This necessitates instituting processes of measurement, which will include collection of data, its subsequent analysis and then comparison with some predetermined standards.

Steps in evaluation

The purpose of an evaluation of a system of care is to provide knowledge that allows judgements and informed decisions to be made about the desirability for change. The above two questions mask the complexity of the underlying procedures needed to implement them. These more complex issues, in order of importance, are:

- identifying the issue or issues to be evaluated
- identifying the stakeholders

- understanding the problem and the context

- designing the evaluation and method of implementation

- data collection

- data analysis and reporting

- the report

- decision-making and planning for action.

IDENTIFYING THE ISSUE OR ISSUES TO BE EVALUATED

The issue may be a clinical or social intervention, a service or a policy, any of which may be raised by one or more of the agencies. It may arise for a variety of reasons, some planned and anticipated (such as an audit after guidelines have been introduced), others unplanned following an unforeseen event, such as a complaint or accident. The issue could be brought up by an individual from any one of the stakeholder agencies.

IDENTIFYING THE STAKEHOLDERS

This is a crucial step in setting up an evaluation. The stakeholders may be individuals, professional groups or organizations, all of whom have some benefit or 'pay-off' from being involved.

Each of these may have one of a variety of roles in the evaluation process, ranging from sponsors to users and evaluators. The people who will implement any changes following the evaluation are important members of the team even if they do not actually perform the evaluation. For any cross-disciplinary or cross-organizational issues it is even more important to recruit team members from all the involved disciplines and organizations at the earliest opportunity for the same reason. Without early involvement their commitment to the outcomes and motivation to change will only be half-hearted at best. The sponsors and those who have authority must accept responsibility for the evaluation outcomes if the integrity of the whole evaluation process is to be maintained. These ownership issues need to be addressed early and openly, and then must be kept under constant review.

> *The sponsors and those who have authority must accept responsibility for the evaluation outcomes if the integrity of the whole evaluation process is to be maintained.*

UNDERSTANDING THE PROBLEM AND THE CONTEXT

At this stage it may be necessary to refine the problem issue and be very clear what needs evaluating. If the presenting issue is only a symptom of a deeper problem, then identifying the real problem may be the start of the whole evaluation. An understanding of the overall processes involved is very helpful in knowing what is currently happening. Flowcharts, care pathways, process maps and guidelines already in place will all help to give informed insight to, and help map out, the present situation. A review of the literature to collect information about similar evaluations and any other evidence of effective interventions elsewhere gives essential background knowledge. At this stage it is possible to get some feel for the type and amount of intervention that may be necessary for any possible changes. Patently it would be unwise to prejudge the evaluation outcomes, but having some outline idea of what might be involved could have far-reaching implications to the stakeholders and particularly to the commissioners.

DESIGNING THE EVALUATION AND METHOD OF IMPLEMENTATION

The methods used are broadly divided into two categories – those that require qualitative tools and those that require quantitative tools.

Qualitative data is usually presented in a descriptive form that gives the experience of a person and their understanding and perception of that experience, expressed as far as possible in their own terms. Once the qualitative data has been collected, it can sometimes be quantified and given some form of numerical expression. On the other hand, quantitative methods both collect and report data in numerical form.

> Without the quantitative part of the evaluation which collects the patient-level information we will not be able to determine whether and how these processes of care produce different results in terms of health outcomes, functional outcomes, expenditures, service utilisation, satisfaction, quality of life and use of informal supports.

(PACE 1995, p.7)

Each method requires a separate set of skills and for the most part is carried out by different people. It is self-evident that the method and tools for the study need careful selection. How much of the evaluation is to be qualitative and how much quantitative are early questions that will dictate which tools are chosen from the wide range available. Two important areas (often not considered until the evaluation is under way, when they can impede progress) are those regarding ethical issues and confidentiality. For example, some audits and evaluation may need the approval of a local ethics committee or organization. Confidentiality has to be explicitly agreed. In any cross-boundary evaluation both these topics are more complex and require more time and effort to resolve.

DATA COLLECTION

At first sight this is another apparently straightforward process, but it is one that is full of potential pitfalls. The initial hurdle is to identify the type of data required. Once this has been agreed, the question of sample size needed for statistical analysis, how to collect the data and in what form, how the data is to be stored so that it can be analysed, are further challenges for the evaluators. It is usually at this stage that the difficulties in accessing databases and the incompatibility of information systems across all the agencies involved become frustratingly obvious.

DATA ANALYSIS AND REPORTING

It is not until all the data collected can be turned into meaningful information that the evaluation starts to have any intrinsic value. The planning for this stage of the evaluation is often neglected until the data is being or has been collected. But if the method of analysis has not been considered sufficiently early, the appropriate data may not have been captured.

> *If the method of analysis has not been considered sufficiently early, the appropriate data may not have been captured.*

An expert in evaluation techniques should be involved in the early planning stages. There may even be a need for a panel of experts if there are multiple outcomes and the evaluation is complex. For example, an evaluation may require people skilled in both quantitative analysis and qualitative analysis. If there are cost issues, an economist may be helpful; and obviously epidemiological and public health aspects will benefit from the assistance of experts in those fields.

THE REPORT

There is a need for a clear and easily understood report. Its distribution, together with any other information arising from the evaluation, is of considerable importance. If the evaluation is a form of monitoring, the timing and frequency of reports is also significant and may need to be fitted in with a schedule of planned meetings. The stakeholders are obviously the 'owners' of the report but may wish to have the report presented in a variety of formats so that they can all fully understand it.

> *There is a need for a clear and easily understood report.*

DECISION-MAKING AND PLANNING FOR ACTION

This has to be the *raison d'être* for the evaluation, and without it the evaluation has no meaning. This involves the active participation of all the relevant stakeholders and is not a function of the evaluation team alone. But these stakeholders may require help in fully understanding the limitations of the evaluation and how best to draw inferences from the report so that they make as logical decisions as possible on which to act. Finally, in the light of the decisions and any actions implemented, the stakeholders will need to consider the advisability of repeating the evaluation to see what effect, if any, the interventions have had. Evaluation has to be a way of life.

The success of any evaluation project depends on careful planning and attention to detail. The above stages of implementation are set out in the sequence that more or less fits the requirements of most evaluations. Nevertheless, they should not be implemented too rigidly in this order but should be sensitive to the context of the project. Certainly, it should be viewed as an iterative process with all the stages under ongoing review by the project team. As the project unfolds external and environmental changes outside the team's control will mean adapting the evaluation to meet those changes, so the process will always need to be flexible.

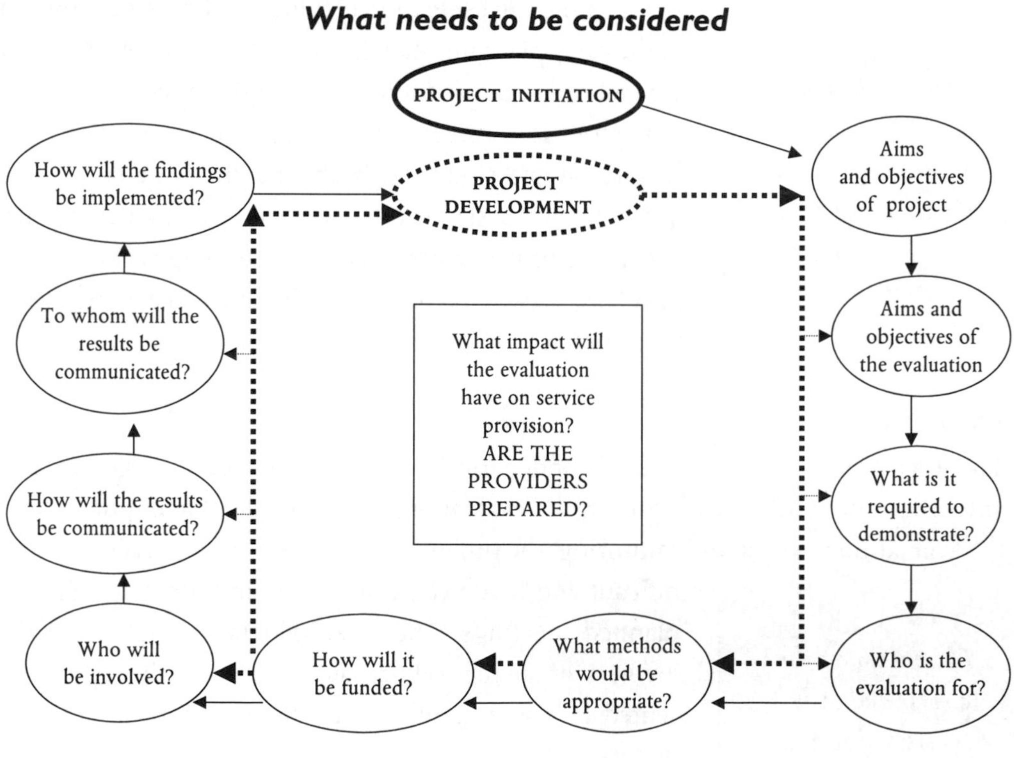

What needs to be considered

Figure 9.1 The continuous evaluation process

The benefits of evaluation – An example

Three years after EPICS had become operational in Marlow, the local management group were reviewing the routinely collected activity data and noted that the chart for night-time referrals had dramatically changed over the previous three months. The local GPs had always wanted a 24-hour service based locally to meet the acknowledged need at night. Whereas there had always been a number of referrals from 10pm to 8am, these had suddenly dropped to virtually nil. This was against a background of an ever-increasing overall demand from the referrers, including the self-referrals from the older people.

The initial reaction was slightly paranoiac and reflected the sensitivity of the EPICS team. The assumption was that the GPs were bypassing the EPICS system and sending the patients directly to hospital. The GPs themselves could offer no clues: each one of them was seeing only a small number of EPICS patients so they could not identify any obvious trends in their individual caseloads.

It was agreed that a clinical audit (carried out jointly with the local primary care practice) of all out-of-hours admissions to both the local acute hospital and the GPs' own community hospital might provide an answer. A four-month, retrospective survey of all out-of-hours admissions to both hospitals was analysed, against agreed criteria, by one of the GPs and a consultant geriatrician. Whereas a previous audit two years earlier had shown that avoidable admissions were still occurring, this audit showed no inappropriate admissions to hospital among the 160 patients admitted out-of-hours in the audit period.

There was no obvious reason for this change but possible explanations were:

- Demands for urgent and unplanned referrals for non-clinical emergencies for that day had been met during the day because of the improved accessibility and availability of assessment and care services provided by EPICS. Nobody was going to bed with unmet need.

- The GPs, who had been the major overnight referrers, may have unknowingly changed their referral patterns because of their confidence that their patient's need could be met by an early morning call or visit, and that most non-clinical emergencies could wait until then.

- The older people in Marlow themselves had sufficient confidence in the EPICS system that they were prepared to wait until the morning rather than refer themselves or call their GP for what they considered to be non-clinical urgent care.

Whatever the reason, the EPICS Executive Group together with the GPs reviewed the strategy of local care delivery and agreed that a local 24-hour service was no longer necessary. The resources that were released were used to provide more care workers at peak times to care for more dependent people, and to extend the catchment area.

This was an emergent behaviour in a complex system that was adapting. The feedback loops from the evaluation and monitoring systems were the method by which the team learned the need for changing the strategy.

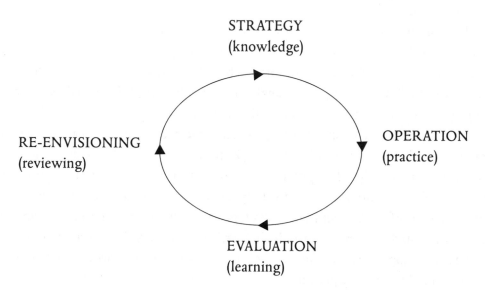

Figure 9.2 Cycle of evaluation and strategy generation

Where is the evidence?

The last decade has seen an increasing emphasis on providing evidence-based care. Initially, this was driven by the concept of internal markets to improve the commissioning of more cost-effective services. But in the last few years this purpose has been balanced by the use of evidence-based research as a tool to improve the quality of care for patients. The layers of evidence in descending importance are:

- systematic reviews with a meta-analysis of trials, some of which include randomized controlled trials

- individual randomized controlled trials

- individual trials that use proven statistical approaches that are well designed but not randomized

- descriptive studies including case studies and good practice
- opinion from respected practitioners or authoritative professional groups.

> There is a considerable cultural gulf between the agencies and their approach to evidence-based care.

There is a considerable cultural gulf between the agencies and their approach to evidence-based care. Healthcare has put considerable effort into it, including setting up reference and research validation centres, such as the Cochrane Centres, and electronic, web-based, databases such as Medline, which are all accessible by everybody, including the public (Muir Gray 1997). On the other hand, in the past the social services have focused very much on resource usage, particularly the cost of care, and the processes of social care delivery rather than care outcomes. As a senior social services development officer once remarked at an intermediate care evaluation meeting: 'All our council is interested in is how much it costs and whether it will get them votes.' There is now increasing emphasis being put on care outcomes through service planning, performance measures, best value reviews and joint reviews. (Sheldon and Chilvers 2000)

In designing cross-organizational evaluations it will be necessary to take into account any cultural differences. As in assessment systems, healthcare staff tend to have a greater propensity for quantitative evaluation compared with the social care staff who tend towards qualitative approaches. As initiatives such as intermediate care involve more and more practitioners from all the agencies, so the evaluation systems will demand an integrated approach to enhance joint working and the joint understanding of outcomes.

> No matter how good the methodology of the review or trial, there must always be some doubt as to the exact applicability of the data to the population or person under consideration for the current evaluation.

Systematic reviews

Evidence from systematic reviews and trials is very important in helping develop coherent strategies, rational operational policies and proper guidelines for care. It forms the anchor for much of the basis for the commissioning of care services. However, the trials have always been done somewhere else, at a different time on populations different from, but possibly similar to, those for whom the care is being planned. No matter how good the methodology of the review or trial, there must always be some doubt as to the exact applicability of the data to the population or person under consideration for the current evaluation.

In most situations all a systematic review of different systems can provide is a 'best fit' model (Sackett *et al.* 2000). There is still considerable room for professional and user judgement in making the final decisions. Where the decision does differ from the evidence or the available guidelines, provided it has systematically taken into account what evidence there is, this will still provide the most appropriate way to proceed for that particular circumstance. (Patently, if this happens too frequently the guidelines and evidence base need questioning and reassessing.)

Randomized controlled trials

Randomized controlled trials (see Glossary at the end of this chapter) are easiest in those situations where the inputs, in the form of types of people and the interventions, are few and straightforward, or where there are only one or two outputs that are both clear-cut and unambiguous. Most surgical, pharmacological and therapeutic trials fall into this category. Trials that involve multiple social and healthcare interventions and have a wide range of outputs are considerably more difficult. They require significant investment and time to complete. Isolating the intervention group from the control groups to prevent inadvertent 'contamination' by good practice in the control group (as occurs if the same staff are used in both groups, or even if there is just contact between the two teams) is not always easy. Perhaps it is not surprising that in the world literature there are only a handful of trials of integrated, whole systems, preventive programmes for the elderly that have been completed (e.g. Bernabei *et al.* 1998; Leveille *et al.* 1998).

Real evidence

For the most part, evidence-based data is a 'front end' tool in the care delivery process, used for setting it up and providing standards against which care can be subsequently evaluated. It can never be assumed that because the evidence is known this guarantees that optimum care is actually delivered to the older person. There is considerable proof that even if the evidence is known it is not always implemented (NHS Centre for Reviews and Dissemination 1999). So, as well as using traditional evidence-based information, there is

> So, as well as using traditional evidence-based information, there is an imperative for evaluation of the actual outcomes of the service being offered.

an imperative for evaluation of the actual outcomes of the service being offered.

Whether it be to individuals or populations of older people, what is needed is 'real people, real place and real time' evaluation that provides 'real evidence' to meet the needs of local people at the present time. Nor can we wait, continuing to provide the generally accepted poor standards of care for older people for the wrong reasons, until all the evidence-based data to plan the perfect service is available. In any case, it never will be. Things are always changing: yesterday's evidence may not be relevant to tomorrow's technology, societal values or expectations. But there is enough evidence of worth already available at least to get started.

> *The freedoms that complex adaptive systems demand should not be an excuse for the irresponsible application of new techniques and methods of care for older people.*

These tensions and paradoxes of evaluation are those of a complex system. They will need the techniques of complexity thinking and management to resolve. The freedoms that complex adaptive systems demand should not be an excuse for the irresponsible application of new techniques and methods of care for older people. Successful complex adaptive systems are not controlled from without. They control themselves from within, according to agreed values, shared purpose, adaptability, and the knowledge base built within them. Balancing the value and credibility of historic evidence against the imperatives of the present and against an unknowable future will always be a tension that is at the heart of a successful evaluation system.

Developing evaluation in EPICS

A mechanistic versus a complexity approach

To some, the implementation of an evaluation might seem fairly mechanistic even if the implementation is iterative and involves a variety of people across organizational boundaries. This impression is further strengthened when the evaluation reports contain sets of numbers taken from bureaucratic information systems and performance indicators, many of which have a money sign in front of them. Necessary though these may be on occasion, they fail to convey a picture of the complexity of care required for older people.

This tension of a mechanistic versus a complexity approach to evaluation took a long time to resolve during the evolution of the EPICS project. From early on, the project was developing as a complex system with emergent behaviours, and it often seemed that no one single person or group knew everything that was going on in terms of what was actually being delivered. This was heightened by EPICS being a 'virtual' organization, where the relatively loose structural and bureaucratic procedures made it more difficult to define and agree outcomes. The cross-boundary working provided 'soft' outcomes (i.e. those that are complex and not easily measurable) and not the traditional, more easily recognized 'hard' outcomes (i.e. those that are mechanistic and tend to be linear, and are more easily measurable). It was necessary to evaluate the performance of all the players in terms of communications, networking and achieving joint goals.

> *The integrity of the EPICS project as an integrated system depended on the feedback loops that an evaluation system could provide.*

There was a very real fear of the whole project disintegrating. Not only were the commissioners blowing hot and cold over the need for an evaluation but the EPICS team and project board had little idea of how to implement an evaluation system that embraced complexity. When the commissioners eventually said they would take the benefits of integrated care as a given and on trust (thus providing no funding for evaluation) they did the EPICS project no real favours. What was becoming increasingly apparent was that the integrity of the EPICS project as an integrated system depended on the feedback loops that an evaluation system could provide. Even if the commissioners did not want evidence, the EPICS teams did – in order to survive.

Exploration of the literature and advice sought from various experts was of little practical help in the mid-1990s. Even books on complex systems did not seem to address the situation in a way that was immediately of benefit. In the end, and after much joint reflection, a decision was taken to carry out a whole range of small evaluations at the same time using data that was available from the project database. This was partly because funds were not available from the project's revenue budgets to do anything else, and partly because the team were not certain what were the more important topics to address first. As the early data was analysed, it revealed a mosaic of information that gave a dynamic, and much broader (if still incomplete) picture of how the whole project was behaving.

Costing the project

Further internal pressure to develop the evaluation came from the EPICS Project Board, when it was proposed that the pilot project in Marlow should be rolled out to other areas. The health and social services sponsors on the board saw their scarce resources being diverted to the project, for which they needed justification. Also, there were plans for the commissioning process to change to locality purchasing by the GPs. They were concerned about the cost efficiency of the service they were buying because there was an imperative on them as locality purchasers to run a financially viable practice.

With the support of one of the health trust's financial managers a more robust costing method was developed. This was based on a banding system, graded by the level of input of care to each client from the rapid response team – a simple resource-usage grouping. It also costed out the time spent on assessment and co-ordination. When the locality-purchasing project was discontinued some months later, the EPICS team continued to use the cost measures developed, for planning and reporting to the Project Board. (For more details on the costing methodology see Appendix 9.1, p.254.)

User satisfaction monitoring

Shortly after this it was decided to set up a system to monitor clients' satisfaction with the EPICS service. To achieve an 'arm's-length' picture, as independent of the providing team as possible, volunteers, who were older people themselves, were trained to carry out a semi-structured interview using a questionnaire. For some of the clinical audits the trust's Clinical Effectiveness Department undertook the surveys and analysed them. For a one-off audit using critical incident techniques, a trained independent evaluator was brought in.

Sharing the information

The final lesson learned was that the more the information was shared the more value it had in helping create the necessary changes for EPICS to evolve and roll out to new localities. Moreover, those practitioners involved in EPICS recorded better-quality data because of their involvement in using the information themselves. It was important to present the information in ways that each of the user groups found helpful and easy to understand. For example, the Project Board responded enthusiastically when the EPICS team suggested that instead of long reports at their quarterly meetings, a series of charts that showed change over time graphically could be presented.

The 'attractors' of 'enquiry' and 'wanting to know' had become common to all the stakeholders. The experimenting with small changes from the small multiple evaluations (from which emerged a larger more comprehensive picture) was typical of a complex adaptive system. However, it was only in hindsight that the team appreciated that their way of working had demonstrated that they were using a systems approach.

Evaluating in multiple dimensions: The balanced scorecard

At the same time that the EPICS team were struggling with complexity, a system of evaluation was developing in the commercial world that provided a framework and model for the ideas developed in EPICS. It was the concept of the Balanced Scorecard (see Appendix 9.2, p.256 for additional information). This model proposed that any evaluation should be done in multiple dimensions at the same time or in the same timeframe. However, the model does have a temporal, or ongoing, dimension if it is repeated or if some monitoring tools are used. Also, change takes time and this may need to be reflected in the multidimensional evaluation.

The four major dimensions of the balanced scorecard were easily translatable into a care model:

- *Key process outcomes.* In health and social care this may be the numbers cared for or the results of treatment or care.

- *Customer satisfaction.* For the overall system, this usually implies that the customer is an individual or group of clients, patients or their carers. On some occasions when the internal processes are being evaluated the customer may be a care worker, nurse or some other professional worker involved.

- *Process complexity.* This dimension concerns the internal processes and how well the system works. For example, the ability to recruit sufficient care workers for the rapid response team could be a significant internal process to the whole system and require evaluating. Another topic area might be the way waiting lists are managed.

- *Financial or cost-effectiveness.* In the broadest sense this involved resource usage and value, but is often expressed directly in financial units or indirectly in some form of finance/resource ratio.

Making the shapes

What was appreciated later was that if it were possible to represent the project graphically by putting the outcomes on to the axes of a multidimensional model and joining together those points within the co-ordinates, they would form a 'shape'. This shape might be quite complex. However, these virtual shapes could be depicted metaphorically by some description implying an overall quality and perception. For example they might be described as good shapes, or bad shapes, or expanding or contracting shapes.

Relating this concept to care, a system of care that results in good and appropriate outcomes, happy and satisfied users and providers, carried out by a well-run organization, and with costs within budget could easily be described as being 'a good shape'. However, a change in only one of the dimensions could dramatically alter the overall shape. For example, in a situation involving the process complexity dimension, perhaps not enough care staff can be recruited. Although the care guidelines and all the other factors remain optimal, the outcome is that care cannot be delivered because there is no one to do it. Suddenly, the whole system is dramatically changed into a not-so-good shape, which may be a catastrophe for some (See *Catastrophe Theory* by V.I. Arnold.). As the EPICS team increasingly used the multidimensional approach, more of these intuitive complex patterns were recognized, giving insights into what was happening. There was a reality to this approach, because the evaluation of each dimension had been grounded on real data.

Balancing the tensions

The tensions involved in delivering on each dimension of a multidimensional model need to be weighed against each other (cost against care outcome, accessibility against staff availability, etc.) and balanced out. Hence the term 'balanced scorecard.' These multiple tensions reflect on the purpose of the whole system and naturally lead on to the need to keep the strategy under review, and help shape it in a repetitive process. This intertwining of vision and purpose with the evaluation, each impacting on the other, adds further value to the multidimensional approach.

> *The evaluation process using the balanced scorecard approach highlighted the tensions between the users, the practitioners and the managers in their expectations of the outcome of the service.*

The evaluation process using the balanced scorecard approach highlighted the tensions between the users, the practitioners and the managers in their expectations of the outcome of the service. The older people wanted a personalized service to meet their perceived needs, as a way of life. The practitioners were concerned with the professional issues of one-to-one care delivery and less with the wider population. Similarly, they had less concern over resource usage. The managers' main interests revolved around resource and financial issues, such as reducing numbers of admissions and budgetary constraints. This approach to evaluation exposed all the individual agendas, each valid in its own right, but needing to be brought together into a holistic common purpose.

> *A successful evaluation process will identify sufficient short-term gains within the longer-term framework.*

Another very practical point, and a cause of considerable tension, is the balance between, on the one hand, the short-term gains to solve immediate problems that beset managers, and on the other the need to take a longer-term strategic view that will result in sustained change. The real world puts very great pressure for immediate results on managers, such as meeting the 'winter pressures' targets each year, and unless these short-term issues are also addressed the managers may not give their wholehearted commitment to a strategy that gives results in the longer term. A successful evaluation process will identify sufficient short-term gains within the longer-term framework. Two examples in EPICS were:

- When rolling out the project to a new area the telephone link run by volunteers was put in quickly and with little cost to get a service started while the longer-term funding and planning issues were resolved. The value for this had been identified in the evaluation of the pilot project.

- The rapid response team of EPICS careworkers was set up relatively quickly to help address the hospital admission pressures while the longer-term preventive social and healthcare solutions were put in place and had an effect.

Evaluation tools used in EPICS

The evaluation tools used in EPICS vary according to the dimension of care being evaluated (see Calviou 1997). The dimensions of care are:

- care outcomes

- user satisifaction (older people and those referring to the system)

- process complexity

- financial and cost-effectiveness.

CARE OUTCOMES

Monitoring

- Admissions to hospital after an EPICS intervention drawn from the hospital database.

- The number of prevented admissions (estimated as a proxy), by asking the GPs what decision they would have made next if the EPICS service had not existed. If they said they would have sent the patient to hospital and if EPICS had instead provided care at home, it was assumed an admission had been prevented.

- The number of patients who had their discharge from hospital assisted by EPICS with the outcome that they were discharged earlier than predicted.

Outcome measures	
Was inappropriate admission to hospital/residential care prevented?	
Was earlier/safer discharge facilitated?	
How many bed-days were potentially saved? (Audit suggested 10 as an average)	

Clinical audits (see Glossary)

- Two major clinical audits were undertaken to look at the appropriateness of the admission to hospital of older people who had not been referred to EPICS. One audit was carried out, relatively independently, by the Clinical Effectiveness Department of the trust and the other by clinicians involved in EPICS.

USER SATISFACTION

Monitoring

- Users' (older people's) satisfaction recorded by trained volunteers on every sixteenth person referred to EPICS for whatever reason and by whatever method, using mainly qualitative techniques with a semi-structured interview and questionnaire. (See Appendix 9.4, p.260 for detailed information.)

- Users' satisfaction, applying critical incident techniques (see Glossary) performed by an independent evaluator trained in the methodology, as noted above.

- The professional users (referrers) were sent a short satisfaction questionnaire. This included both potential and actual referrers. (See Appendix 9.5, p.258)

Ongoing client satisfaction monitoring

A method for monitoring quality of service as experienced by the clients was devised in consultation with the Clinical Effectiveness Unit of the NHS Trust.

Every 16th client referred to the project (or the nearest one after, if for some reason it was not appropriate to the client's situation to interview them at the time) was seen by one of a small team of volunteers trained to carry out a semi-structured interview using a questionnaire.

Clients were assured of the anonymity of the replies, if that was what they wished, and were offered an addressed envelope to return the form to the project office.

The interviews included both those older people who had considerable input through the project and those who may have had a one-off contact.

Improvements to the service were made following these quality assurance interviews which, incidentally, were enjoyed by both clients and volunteers. One example was yellow labels with the contact number of the project to stick on the older person's telephone. These had been given to people who had received services co-ordinated by EPICS. Those interviewed suggested that it would be helpful if all older residents in the area could have one. A local firm donated the labels and Age Concern distributed them with their quarterly newsheet which went to every household in the locality where there was an older person.

Referrers' satisfaction

87 per cent of referrers said they were very satisfied with the service. The reasons they gave for not referring to another service were:

- the convenience and appropriateness of the service
- immediacy of response
- the service's community base and local response
- no similar alternative was available.

PROCESS COMPLEXITY

Monitoring

- Numbers of referrals by type of referral, e.g. for information, assessment, networking processes, rapid response.

Reason for referral	
medical	recent fall
	stroke
	UTI (urinary tract infection)
	post-operative
	etc.
social	withdrawal of carer support
	loss of confidence
	need for information
	social isolation

- Numbers of referrals by source and referrer. This included assessing the numbers of older people who self-referred or had been referred by a carer. This was taken as a proxy indicator of accessibility and the fact that the user was central to the referral system. The number of self and carer referrals rose over time to 25 per cent of the total, equal to the number from GPs.

Analysis of referrals	
Referrals	number
	source
	time
	number receiving careworker service
	time spent by careworkers per client
	time spent by co-ordinator per client

	duration of the intervention from the project
	average length of intervention
	average length of intervention by Careworkers
	number receiving Phone Link
	duration of intervention by Phone Link
Outcomes	referral on to other services (can be aggregated)
	no further intervention required

- Ease of access. To check that the objective of providing a 'one-stop shop' was being met, referrers were asked on the questionnaire whether it was easy to make contact and implicit in this was the single call (see Appendices 9.3, p.258 and 9.5, p.264). The initial evaluation showed that 5 per cent of all referrers had experienced difficulties in making the contact. The time taken from referral to contact assessment was monitored. This was to evaluate whether the assessments were conducted within two hours (the quality standard). The results showed that 80 per cent were conducted within an hour either by telephone or a personal visit. There was a negative feedback on the speed of response from one user out of the 31 interviewed in the critical incident evaluation.

Performance Measures	
How often do we advise G.P.s within 24 hours?	
How often do we send the summary within 5 days to G.P.'s and other involved professionals?	
Do we carry out an assessment within 2 hours of referral?	
Are we accessing the Day Hospital within 24/48 hours?	
Are we carrying out a client satisfaction interview on every 16th client as claimed?	
Are we collating and analysing the replies on the questionnaires?	
Are we consulting with older people effectively?	
Is our publicity material of a high standard	

Audit

- An audit was carried out by the local social services using retrospective data from a two-year period collected from their client database and EPICS database to see if there was duplication or overlap of services. This was to assess the effectiveness of the integrated system.

Interface between social services and EPICS

The analysis indicated:

- There was no duplication of services, i.e. similar services were not put in concurrently by both agencies.

- 39 per cent of episodes in which EPICS provided care supplemented an existing care package. This was usually because of a sudden change in need.

- 19.6 per cent of episodes were to enable social services to access services not provided by them, such as direct referral to the day hospital for complex assessments.

- 34.4 per cent were referrals in which EPICS provided a co-ordinating function with no direct service.

(Morgan 1998)

FINANCIAL AND COST-EFFECTIVENESS

Monitoring

- Costs per episode using the resource usage framework developed with the Trust's finance and commissioning departments.

- Management of budgets. Despite working within a complex adaptive systems context, and with the organizational freedoms this required, the budgets were never overspent over a five-year period.

Cost comparisons

- As part of the initial evaluation, comparative costings were estimated for the projected costs of prevented admissions against the actual costs of EPICS intervention. This used data from the trust's finance department and the medical records department to estimate costs and lengths of hospital stay. (See Appendix 9.1, p.254 for methods used.) The outcomes were reported in the Audit Commission's Report (1998) *Coming of Age: Improving Care Services for Older People*, as a Model of good practice, and also in the Report of the Royal Commission on Long Term Care (1999) *With Respect to Old Age*. What made the project of particular interest to these commissions was the potential cost saving demonstrated through using a system of integrated care.

The value compass

In the USA a multidimensional model has been developed, called the 'value compass', to help improve the clinical outcomes of well-defined groups of patients (Nelson, Batalden and Ryer 1998). This is used in conjunction with other quality improvement tools such as the PLAN–DO–STUDY–ACT cycle. (See chapter 10, p.291 on levers and tools.) Each of the four major compass points is a dimension of care.

- NORTH is the functional modality and includes physical function, mental health, social and role criteria, and possibly specifics (such as symptoms, e.g. pain) depending on the purpose of the improvement project.

- EAST contains issues around satisfaction with care delivery or perceived health benefits for the planned or delivered interventions.

- SOUTH encompasses the financial component in the form of costs, both direct and indirect if possible.

- WEST has within it the clinical elements that need to be measured (such as mortality and morbidity complications, also symptoms).

It has many of the same properties as the balanced scorecard in being able to reflect complexity. It is very much tuned to the clinical context and to the continuous improvement cycle.

Variation

It is rare indeed for any two systems to work in exactly the same way. Even mechanistic systems variably degrade and change over time. Those systems that involve humans in any way never perform with the same results twice running unless by chance. That things vary in biological and social systems is a constant. An analysis of any variation between two systems might demonstrate whether one or the other is more nearly achieving the aims originally planned. If there is a difference, why is it occurring?

- Why is there a several-fold variation of admission to residential and nursing homes across the country, those with the highest rates of admission having the longest waiting lists?

- Why is there so much variation in the take-up of welfare benefits by older people?

- Why is it that GPs have a several-fold variation in referring older patients to hospital for admission even after accounting for differences in patient population characteristics?

- Why do some hospital doctors vary in their interpretation of the same laboratory and radiological tests?

- Why is there a variation in performance indicators between hospitals?

- Why do similar hospital rehabilitation wards have varying lengths of stay with similar outcomes?

- Why is there so much variation in patient compliance to a given treatment?

Questions like this could easily fill the rest of the book – variation is so common. But it is continually ignored by managers and practitioners alike, even though it provides a very powerful analytical context in which to use evaluation tools such as the balanced scorecard approach. The variation is nearly always the end result of complex interactions, and it needs complexity tools to understand it.

TYPES OF VARIATION

There are two major types of variation, those that take place between two or more systems at the same time and those that occur within the same system but occur over time. The variation between systems can only be interpreted if the systems are comparable. For groups of people, it may not be easy to ensure that they are similar. They will need to be matched by sex, age, functional dependence, mental status and social background. With care, comparisons can be made to see if it is appropriate to continue analysis of the variations.

Variations that occur over time in the same system also have problems in data collection, recording and interpretation. The changes are plotted on a run chart at periodic intervals, similar to the temperature and pulse charts found at the bottom of a hospital patient's bed. Some variation is usually acceptable, as in the pulse rates on the patient chart. This is called common cause variation and it falls within a defined range. These common cause changes are generally predictable within the range, and are due

248 / INTEGRATING CARE FOR OLDER PEOPLE

to regular, natural and ordinary causes. However, when the changes are exceptional (that is, they fall outside the normal range for that process) it is likely that the causes are irregular and unnatural and are not inherent in the process.

However, the question then arises of how is it known when the result is outside the normal range of activity. This is usually managed by the use of control charts, which are 'run-charts' that have upper and lower limits that are set statistically, usually plus or minus three standard deviations of the mean. In simple terms, this means that if some event falls outside the upper or lower limits then there was originally about a 1 in 400 possibility of it occurring by chance. This makes it an indicator of being a special cause and thus worth investigating.

ANALYSIS OF THE VARIATION

Once the variation from either type is identified, finding the cause of it and understanding it is still not necessarily straightforward. The root cause will need to be identified and then a multidimensional analysis undertaken before the right intervention can be instituted. However, despite these difficulties the effort is usually well rewarded in providing information that stimulates change. An example follows of how looking at variations in the pharmacological regimes of two long-term nursing wards led to all-round improvements.

In South Buckinghamshire the nature and type of long-term care was being assessed at a local hospital just prior to the implementation of the 1990 Community Care Act. As part of an in-depth assessment undertaken by the Department of Care of the Elderly, the ward pharmacist produced figures, from her monitored data, that the wards were falling below the generally agreed target of having between 25 and 30 per cent of patients on no drugs at all. This was despite a three-monthly, consultant-led review of the drug charts. Further analysis showed that most of the increase in prescribing was due to the prescription of laxatives and sleeping tablets. After discussion it was agreed to see if there was any variation between the two wards concerned and whether this would give clues to the cause.

The specialist geriatric registrar, the two ward sisters and the pharmacist led the study. But all the day and night staff, including the social worker for the wards, were also involved. The two wards were compared by age and sex initially, and then a Barthel functional score, mini mental test scores and routine nursing dependency scores. From this it was demonstrated that the two wards were statistically comparable.

To most people's surprise there was about a three-fold variation between the two wards for the use of both laxatives and sleeping tablets. The initial reaction in the case of the laxative prescriptions was to say that the ward using least might have used more suppositories and enemas. However, when this was examined the opposite proved to be the case. The ward using most laxatives also used significantly more suppositories and enemas. During a facilitated meeting the nursing staff from both wards addressed the problem in a non-judgemental way. What was universally acknowledged was that there was clearly a different perception of the patients' needs between the two ward staffs, because there did not seem to be any major differences in outcomes such as constipation, impaction or incontinence between the two wards.

Similarly, where the sleeping tablets were concerned, it appeared that the night nursing staff on the ward using most sleeping tablets was more concerned that the noise some patients made might be keeping other patients awake. As a result they asked the resident doctor to prescribe more sleeping tablets for the patients. Because these patients were more sleepy in the morning it also heightened the perceived need for laxatives if they could not be taken to the toilet early enough. Again, independent observation on both wards showed no difference in the noise levels at night.

Because all the clinical and ward staff were involved in this evaluation from the start and felt they owned it, they took the initiative to review the whole management of nutrition, toileting arrangements and sleep requirements for both wards. The day staff wished to monitor the prescription of laxatives directly with the pharmacist and medical staff on a regular basis. Likewise the night staff on both wards sought ways to encourage sleep through non-pharmacological ways and manage the noisier patients without sedating them.

Follow-up assessments demonstrated that the outcomes were not only improved for the patients, but the drug bill fell and the nursing tasks became easier.

Unfortunately, the relatives had not been involved initially but the active relatives' support group on the wards became enthusiastic proponents of the new programmes when they joined the project later.

Nobody could have guessed at the outset that these would be the results from what appeared a simple exercise in variation evaluation. The shared ownership and the 'no-blame' culture allowed people to learn from each other. This was a complex adaptive system working at its best.

Reporting and presenting evaluation outcomes

You know when people are new to evaluation – they are surprised or complain when they discover that their service has no objectives, or vague statements of aspiration, or many conflicting objectives.

John Ovretveit, Professor of Health Policy and Management,
Nordic School of Public Health, Gottenburg, Sweden

Reporting is an important component of the whole evaluation system. Unless the outcomes are made known to the right people change will not occur. Feeding the information to the right people, at the right time, in the right place is the key to implementing change from evaluation.

At the outset of any evaluative process consideration should be given to how the results are to be communicated. Within EPICS there were three levels at which reports were made: the strategic level, the operational level and the practitioner level. These three levels were not mutually exclusive and compartmentalized, as the whole process was dynamic and organic, but they provided a model within which to work.

The reporting at the strategic level was to the project board. Quarterly progress reports and an annual report were presented, which were based on regular reviews.

An annual review (a broad band review) was carried out at the operational level. This informed the strategic process to review the need for change. It was not a static but an organic process of review with all the stakeholders. These included:

- users
- carers
- volunteers
- EPICS careworkers
- social workers
- a hospital social worker
- social services home carers
- district nurses and the community psychiatric nurse
- the day hospital manager
- occupational therapists and physiotherapists
- a hospital consultant, and the A&E consultant
- the GPs
- sheltered housing managers
- representatives from Age Concern, the Carers Centre, the Red Cross, the St Vincent de Paul Society and the local Volunteer Bureau
- the Director of Community Nursing and the senior nurse manager for the Elderly Care Directorate of the NHS Trust
- the EPICS co-ordinator, project manager and the data manager.

> *Focusing on the client enabled free discussion, without blame being apportioned to any one individual or department. The responsibility was shared and better practice was modelled.*

Performance was reviewed and objectives were set for achievement within the next year. The quality of service was reviewed through discussion of a selection of cases (anonymized). Mixed groups of professionals, clients and volunteers considered where good practice had resulted in an optimum outcome for the client, and where practice could have been improved to secure a better outcome for the client.

Focusing on the client enabled free discussion, without blame being apportioned to any one individual or department. The responsibility was shared and better practice was modelled.

At the practitioner level a series of case studies were reviewed half-yearly. These were carried out with a small group, usually a volunteer, GP, hospital consultant, day hospital manager, social worker, district nurse and the project manager and service co-ordinator. Named cases were reviewed in confidence, and again the responsibility was shared in a common aim to see where the system had failed the client. These meetings were highly valued by the participants.

Overview

The importance of evaluation cannot be overstated. It is critical in maintaining the integrity of the cross-organizational, multidisciplinary systems of care that are required for the delivery of flexible care that meets the needs of individual older people. The feedback that the evaluation process provides, plus the subsequent analysis and reflection, builds up the knowledge and understanding that moves projects forward and improves them. The evaluation processes must be considered and planned for as early as possible in the development of any project. Too often they are piggybacked on to projects as an afterthought.

Any care delivery system will always be enhanced by the knowledge of how effective it is in achieving its aims, because then its purpose and aims can be modified to achieve even higher-quality care. Evaluation then becomes an essential tool in the formulation and evolution of the strategy. The participation of all the stakeholders, including the older person and all the relevant carers and practitioners, gives the evaluation added strength ensuring better-quality data, more insightful analysis and a commitment to whatever changes are necessary.

The worth of an evaluation, and the sustainability of its process (so that enquiry and knowledge acquisition become part of the culture of the organization) is embedded in the way the evaluation is implemented.

- The evaluation must be providing answers to appropriate questions that address issues that are relevant to the context and the realities for delivery of care to older people.

- The evaluation should be aligned to other key processes in the delivery of care such as strategy development, clinical and social assessment processes, teaching and training and any other change mechanisms.

- The users must own the evaluation process and be involved throughout all the stages of implementation. They may need support in developing insights into its worth and practice.

- The outcomes need to be disseminated widely to everybody concerned, and in ways that they wish to receive the information.

- The potential change mechanisms necessary and the possible implications of that change need to be addressed at the outset and not after the results are available.

- The evaluation has to be feasible and 'do-able' within the resources and the time available for the outcomes still to be relevant. Particularly, the tools and methodology must be pertinent to the project objectives. Evaluation requires meticulous planning. If it fails for procedural reasons it does nothing to enhance the credibility of the whole process.

Finally, the evaluation process is itself complex and, in older people's care, is trying to facilitate the understanding of the complexity of care. The usual financial, performance indicator and traditional medical models of evaluation will no longer, of themselves, be sufficient. They tend to perpetuate the mechanistic approach to care and rarely involve the older person. There is an imperative to further develop multidimensional models of evaluation carried out in the same timeframe that can, on the one hand, reflect this complexity and, on the other, offer practical ways of providing solutions to improve the quality of care and, most importantly, reflect the older person's involvement in the care.

Chapter 9 – Headline points

- Evaluation is the only way to obtain understanding and deep insights into the processes.

- The sponsors and those who have authority must accept responsibility for the evaluation outcomes if the integrity of the whole evaluation process is to be maintained.

- If the method of analysis has not been considered sufficiently early the appropriate data may not have been captured.

- There is a need for a clear and easily understood report.

- There is a considerable cultural gulf between the agencies and their approach to evidence-based care.

- No matter how good the methodology of the review or trial, there must always be some doubt as to the exact applicability of the data to the population or person under consideration for the current evaluation.

- So, as well as using traditional evidence-based information there is an imperative for evaluation of the actual outcomes of the service being offered.

- The freedoms that complex adaptive systems demand should not be an excuse for the irresponsible application of new techniques and methods of care for older people.

- The integrity of the EPICS project as an integrated system depended on the feedback loops that an evaluation system could provide.

- The evaluation process using the balanced scorecard approach highlighted the tensions between the users, the practitioners and the managers in their expectations of the outcome of the service.

- A successful evaluation process will identify sufficient short-term gains within the longer-term framework.

- Improvements to the service were made following the quality assurance interviews, which, incidentally, were enjoyed by both clients and volunteers.

- Focusing on the client enabled free discussion, without blame being apportioned to any one individual or department. The responsibility was shared and better practice was modelled.

APPENDIX 9.1

Costings for the EPICS Project in South Buckinghamshire

The amount of contact time spent on each referral by the co-ordinator was analysed in each case. Two levels of activity were identified triggered by

1. a standard referral (66 per cent of cases) the process of which averaged 4 hours

2. a complex referral (34 per cent of cases) the process of which averaged 9 hours

A standard referral included an initial contact assessment, information giving, co-ordination of service response with other providers, volunteer support and follow-up.

A complex referral was a standard referral which included a complex assessment. It often included a comprehensive assessment in the day hospital. The hours included time spent on the co-ordination of initial care packages, networking with other agencies and administrative time.

The variable costs were calculated from the actual figures and fixed costs identified, which included accommodation, rental of pagers, on-call charges for care workers, etc.

The costs were spread over the number of referrals to produce an average cost per standard referral, which at 1996 prices was £180.00.

The add-on cost for services provided by the project's own care workers was calculated at an average cost of £128.00. The care worker service was used by 63 per cent of the referrals.

The average add-on time spent by the care workers for those referrals requiring the rapid response service was 15.6 hours. Some referrals had a higher, more intensive, level of support, some a more frequent but shorter length of visit. It was felt that calculating an *average* cost would provide the flexibility an integrated system relies upon for optimum performance.

From these calculations a cost relating to the number of referrals could be calculated, i.e. per 100 referrals

- 37 per cent would be calculated at the basic cost of £180.00

- 63 per cent would be calculated at the basic cost plus the add-on for the care worker service of £128.00.

The average length of the intervention was drawn from the database which recorded the date of referral to the project and the end-date. This averaged at 7.5 days of service.

A formula on which to base a contract for the co-ordination, assessment, and on-call service by care workers offered through the project was suggested by a health economist. To promote the service, this was sent to purchasers or commissioners so that they could quickly and easily see what they would get for their money.

FOR 200 REFERRALS YOU WILL GET:

- 1200 hours of assessment and co-ordination with other providers
- 1250 hours of volunteer support
- 84 hours of co-ordinated assessment in the day hospital
- 2000 hours of care worker support in the home
- 24 hour x 365 days of access to an on-call service

At a cost of ....

APPENDIX 9.2

Balanced Scorecard

The concept of a balanced scorecard to develop performance drivers was introduced in 1992 in America (Oliveira 2001). It was a method of carrying forward an organization's strategy using a set of measures to achieve and communicate a shared view of its future development. The scorecard is an aid in creating 'balance' among various factors which contribute to the overall performance within an organization. The balance adopted reflects the strategic choices of the organization or project.

The organization is viewed from four vital perspectives:

- financial

- internal processes

- learning and growth

- customer.

The balanced scorecard is intended to link short-term operational control to the long-term vision and strategy of the initiative. Strategy is seen as meaning the relationship between the project's vision and the operational plans to be followed on a day-to-day basis.

> It is based on three dimensions in time; yesterday, today and tomorrow i.e. what we do for tomorrow may have no noticeable financial or other benefit until the day after tomorrow. (Olve, Roy and Wetter 1999, p.7)

In a balanced scorecard outcome measures are combined with measures that describe resources spent or activities performed. Good scorecards will combine outcome measures with performance drivers, i.e. factors which will determine or influence future outcomes.

The primary function of the scorecard is to control 'company' operations. It furnishes a language for describing expectations and performance, then laying a foundation for discussions on how each individual can contribute to fulfilling the company's vision. The model should be viewed as an instrument for translating an abstract vision and strategy into specific measures and goals. Much of the strength of the model lies in the development process itself in which large numbers of employees participate in jointly analysing and discussing the company's situation and capabilities. Some change in behaviour may be required. Behaviour is governed by our values and attitudes, which in turn are based on previous experience. Often some form of external influence is needed to produce new experience – the balanced scorecard process can help in providing that.

Where the project works with a number of partners, as in an integrated care system, for example, the scorecard should include measures and goals for how these relationships are managed.

The process:

- define the context (e.g. social and health care for older people)
- describe its development and the role of the agency or project
- establish/confirm the company's vision
- establish the perspectives
- break the vision down according to each perspective and formulate overall strategic goals
- identify critical factors for success
- develop measures, identify causes and effects and establish a balance
- establish the top-level scorecard (senior management)
- break down the scorecard and measures by organizational unit
- formulate goals
- develop an action plan.

APPENDIX 9.3

GP Satisfaction Questionnaire

Dear Doctor,

You recently referred .... to EPICS.

As part of the EPICS monitoring programme we would be very grateful if you could complete Part I of the questionnaire below. If you have the time to fill in Part II it would be very helpful to our qualitative analysis.

Thank you,

Consultant Physician
Care of the Elderly
South Buckinghamshire NHS Trust

PART I

1. Was it simple to make contact with EPICS?

   i.e. the one point of access principle.

   YES/NO

2. Was your out-of-hours call using the EPICS pager responded to within 15 mins?

   YES/NO

3. Was the EPICS response what you wanted?

   YES/NO

   if not

   3.1 was it partially the response you wanted?   YES/NO

   3.2 was there a total failure?   YES/NO

4. Did the EPICS intervention prevent admission to hospital in your opinion?

   YES/NO

5. Did the EPICS intervention enable discharge from hospital to be arranged earlier?

   YES/NO

6. Did you get feed back on what was happening to the patient you referred to

   Verbal   YES/NO

   Written   YES/NO

APPENDIX 9.4

Ongoing Quality of Service
Monitoring interviews with older people who had used EPICS

Questionnaire

(To be used as part of a semi-structured confidential interview carried out with randomly selected clients on completion of their contact with EPICS)

1. Did you know the name of the Project before YOU had contact?

2. How did you hear about the Project?

3. If you or your family contacted the Project, how easy did they find the contact?

4. a) How well did you feel the Project understood what you were wanting?

    b) How did you feel the Project responded?

5. Did you have a visit from the Project's care workers?

    If 'yes' go to question 6. If 'no' go to question 7.

6. How did the Project care worker identify themselves to you?

7. How did you/would you feel about having a Project sticker left on your telephone?

8. How do you feel about the information you received from the Project?

9. Did you understand what help you were going to get through the Project?

10. How do you feel about the service/contact you received from the Project?

11. How do you feel you were treated? i.e. respect, courtesy, by your preferred name?

12. Is there anything you specially liked about the service/contact? or specially disliked about the service/contact?

13. Is there any way the Project could improve its service/contact?

14. Have you any comments not covered by the questionnaire?

Signature of client (optional) ....

Date of interview .... Name of interviewer.............................

During the time of the survey the questionnaire had been modified twice to reflect experience and the wishes of the interviewees:

1. to include a space for comments by the clients not covered by the questions

2. to add the date of the interview and the name of the interviewer and a space for the clients interviewed to put their signature if they wished.

Out of the 16 clients using the amended form, 13 chose to sign their name.

An example of the framework for analysing responses is given below.

PROCEDURES AGREED FOR CLIENT SATISFACTION INTERVIEWS

1.   The Co-ordinator will allocate every sixteenth client referred to the Project to be interviewed by a trained volunteer, as soon as possible after the completion of the contact with the Project.

2.   Referrals will include all the Project's services.

3.   Volunteers will be given:

  • the client's name

  • the client's address

  • the client's phone number

  • the date of the last contact with the Project.

Subsequently the volunteers were also given the reason for referral and any significant information which might assist the volunteer in making the contact with the client, e.g. 'hearing impaired' or 'slow to come to the door'.

4.   The volunteer will phone the client saying that they understand that they have recently had a service from the Project and would like to come to see if the client was satisfied and if they had any suggestions to make.

If they don't remember it was the Project it doesn't matter but the volunteer would still like to come. It should be stressed that this would be in confidence, that the person visiting is not employed by the Project, and that the answers would be written on a questionnaire, but the client's name would not be given. It is anticipated that the meeting would take about half an hour.

   The volunteer will advise the client that they will have an identity badge to show.

5.   On meeting the client the information about confidentiality in paragraph 4 should be repeated.

6.   On completion of the interview the volunteer should read out the answers written to check the client agrees.

The client should be reassured that anything that sounded critical will be seen as useful in improving the service.

   It does not matter if information is given about other services. These can be recorded too.

7.   The completed form should be put in an envelope addressed to the Project Co-ordinator and sealed in the client's presence, and the volunteer will return it to the Project office.

8. A volunteer should not visit a client with whom they have had contact in providing a service through the Project.

9. A periodic support meeting will be held with the volunteers engaged on this work and an independent facilitator. The Project Co-ordinator may also attend. If the volunteer has any concerns about a client they should contact the Co-ordinator immediately.

Summary of findings of a survey of 30 interviews carried out by two volunteers

- The survey demonstrates that the Project is providing a response to clients which is efficient, speedy and professional. Users of the service particularly valued the courtesy and respect with which they were treated, and the responsiveness to their individual needs.

- The communication between the Project and the clients was extremely effective, with the exception of one who had a severe hearing disability. (Training for staff and volunteers is being implemented as a result.)

- Publicity was seen as needing more attention, and the provision of written information about the Project was not consistent.

- Of the clients sampled, 66 per cent had received the care worker service, reflecting the pattern for the Project overall, where the statistics show approximately 60 per cent have care worker support and 40 per cent access information and other support through the Project.

Respondents commented on the value of the Phone Link and the quality of the volunteers, and on the promptness and friendliness of the careworkers.

APPENDIX 9.5

Questionnaire for Referrers

1. Have you heard of the Project?

2. How did you hear of the Project? (see example response analysis sheet below)

3. Have you ever referred to the Project?

   yes

   no

   tried but failed

4. If you have not used the Project, why not?

5. If you had tried to refer and failed, why did you fail?

6. How many times have you referred to the Project?

7. Reasons given for referral.

8. Did the service provide what was needed?

   yes

   partly

   no

9. If no, or partly, what was lacking?

10. Why did you choose to refer to the Project?

11. When you referred what happened?

   was it easy to make contact?

   was the response timely?

   was oral feedback adequate?

   was written feedback adequate?

   were staff helpful?

12. If it was difficult to make contact, why?

Example of ANALYSIS SHEET for Referrers
Question 2 How did you hear of the Project?

	CPN	Community nurse	GPs	Social workers	Housing	Day hospital	Hospital doctors	Hospital nurse
Word of mouth								
Formal presentation								
Written information								
Leaflet								
Poster								
Advertisement								
Other								

Comments were invited on:

- integration of the system and liaison between agencies
- communication between agencies in the system
- access/accessibility
- any changes which might improve the system
- any other matters.

APPENDIX 9.6

Glossary of Terms Used in Evaluation

audit (clinical)
> a method of measuring clinical (medical) outcomes against standards that have previously been set to see if the targets have been met; the outcomes are usually expressed in numerical terms

critical incident technique
> a technique in which people are asked about what happened at various stages of the intervention, collecting in their own words both what they consider to have been favourable and what they consider to have been unfavourable incidents

effectiveness the extent to which stated goals and objectives are being achieved

efficiency the relationship between the inputs (costs) on the one hand and the outputs and/or outcomes (benefits) of services on the other, i.e the ratio of total benefits to total costs

inputs the resources invested in specified official activities

meta-analysis a qualitative method of combining results of independent studies (usually drawn from published literature) and synthesizing summaries and conclusions from the studies. The analyses are used, for example, to evaluate therapeutic effectiveness and plan new studies in the areas of research amd medicine.

mission statement
> defines the business that the organization is in, or should be in, against the values and expectations of the stakeholders

objectives or goals
> state more precisely than a mission statement what is to be achieved and when the results are to be accomplished

opportunity costs
the satisfaction gained from undertaking the next best alternative activity on a preference listing, i.e. the total cost of a programme is the sum of benefits that would have been derived if the resources had been used elsewhere

outcome   the end-state which may or may not be the intended effect of specified inputs, outputs or processes: the impact of services upon intended beneficiaries

outputs   a measurable product attributable to an input or combination of inputs

procedure   accordance with formalized rules and regulations

process   a series of actions and interactions

processes   the ways in which activities are carried out

randomized controlled trial
a clinical trial for evaluating the efficacy of an intervention by comparing outcomes with a concurrent control group that has not received the intervention; the people taking part in the trial are selected by a random process

strategies   the principles that show how an organization's major goals are to be achieved over a defined time period; usually confined only to the general logic for achieving the objectives

structures   an organization's roles and relationships

vision   a challenging and imaginative picture of the future role and objectives of an organization, significantly going beyond its current environment and competitive position

References

Audit Commission (1998) *The Coming of Age: Improving Care Services for Older People.* London Case Study 12.

Bernabei, R., Landi, F., Gambassi, G. and Rubenstein, L.Z. (1998) 'A randomised trial of the impact of a model of integrated care and case management for older people living in the community.' *British Medical Journal 316*, 1348–1351.

Calviou, A. (1997) *An Evaluation of Marlow EPICS (Elderly Persons Integrated Care System.)* South Buckinghamshire: South Buckinghamshire NHS Trust.

Leveille, S.G., Wagner, E.H., Davis, C., Grothaus, L., Wallace, J., Gerfro, L.O., M. and Kent, D. (1998) 'Preventing disability and managing chronic illness in frail older adults: A randomised trial of community-based partnership with primary care.' *Journal of the American Geriatric Society 46*, 1–9.

Muir Gray, J.A. (1997) Appendix 1 – 'Sources of evidence.' *Evidence Based Healthcare*. London: Churchill Livingstone.

Nelson, E.C., Batalden, P. and Ryer, J.C. (1998) *Clinical Improvement Action Guide*. Illinois: Joint Commission on Accreditation of Healthcare Organisations

NHS Centre for Reviews and Dissemination (1999) 'Getting Evience into Practice.' *Effective Health Care 5*, 1, 1–16.

Oliveira, J. (2001) 'The Balanced Scorecard: An integrative approach to performance evaluation.' *Healthcare Financial Management 55*, 42–46.

Olve, N., Roy, J. and Wetter, M. (1999) *Performance Drivers*. Chichester: John Wiley & Son.

PACE – Programme for the All-Inclusive Care of the Elderly (1995) *Evaluation of the Total Longterm Care (TLC) Program*. Denver, CO: Total Longterm Care.

Royal Commission on Long Term Care (1999) *With Respect to Old Age*. (p.135, para.e) London: HMSO.

Sackett, D.L., Strauss, S.E., Richardson, W.S., Rosenberg, W. and Haynes, B. (2000) Chapter 7 'Guidelines' *Evidence Based Medicine*. London: Churchill Livingstone.

Sheldon, B. and Chilvers, R. (2000) *Evidence Based Social Care: A study of propects and problems*. Lyme Regis: Russell House Publishing.

Further reading

Arnold, V.I. (1998) *Catastrophe Theory*. New York: Springer Verlag.

Bowling, A. (1997) *Research Methods in Health: Investigating Health and Health Services*. Buckingham: Open University Press.

This book is more theoretical and gives insight to the development of tools. There are sections on the social aspects of disease and it shows the balance between qualitative and quantitative approaches well. There are chapters on questionnaire design and application and on focus groups that repay reading.

Olve, N., Roy, Jan. and Wetter, M. (1999) *Performance Drivers: A Practical Guide to using the Balanced Scorecard*. Chichester: John Wiley and Sons.

This book gives a clear account of the balanced scorecard. It puts the evaluation in a strategic context and shows how the two interact – one dependent on the other. The authors also describe the effect it has on the people and the organizations involved and the dynamic effect good evaluation has on all those concerned.

Ovretveit, J. (1998) *Evaluating Health Interventions: An Introduction to Valuation of Health Treatments, Services Policies and Organisational Interventions*. Buckingham: Open University Press.

This book provides a very good guide to the principles of evaluation that should be useful to not only those in the healthcare team but also to those from other agencies. All the illustrations are from healthcare but they are easily translated to other groups and there are sections relating to social evaluation as well.

Phillips, C., Palfrey, C. and Thomas, P. (1994) *Evaluating Health and Social Care.* Basingstoke: Macmillan.

This is a jargon-free, helpful book about the processes involved in evaluating and improving performance in public sector organizations. It emphasizes the value of the 'consumer voice'. It says that there is no single 'best' approach and suggests a range of approaches to evaluation.

Potter, J., Georgiou, A. and Pearson, M. (1994) *Measuring the Quality of Care for Older People.* London: Royal College of Physicians.

A useful book that has a very clear medical pedigree but nevertheless is valuable for the whole multidisciplinary team.

St Leger, A.S., Schnieden, H. and Walsworth-Bell, J.P. (1992) *Evaluating Health Services Effectiveness – A Guide for Health Professionals, Service Managers and Policy Makers.* Buckingham: Open University Press.

Though this book is approaching ten years since first publication it is still very pertinent and contains a lot of valuable information that is not collected together in any other book. It is very comprehensive without being difficult to read.

Chapter 10

Levers and Tools
for Integrating Care

Much is written on organisational change of a descriptive or ideological nature but the levers of change are rarely revealed.

David Billis, former Director of The Centre
for Voluntary Organization, London School of Economics

Go to the people.
Live amongst them.
Start with what they have.
Build with them.
And, when the deed is done
The mission accomplished,
Of the best leadership
The people will say
'We have done it ourselves'

Lao Tzu (6th century BC)

In this chapter we shall identify the particular tools – the 'levers of change' – required to develop a model of integrated care and the competencies necessary to achieve the objectives. We shall offer a few simple rules generated through the pooling of experience in many workshops and a 'process guide' to help those planning an integrated care project. The critical importance of leadership is discussed, and examples are given of ways to assess the range and balance of resources to provide a quality service.

The definition of a tool used here is something that is useful in carrying out a task or achieving a goal. As such it has a very broad meaning, and in fact this book itself could be looked upon as a tool. Certainly there are numerous tools to be found in other chapters. The most crucial of these is systems thinking itself. Understanding the current processes and their problems and then growing new systems is the cardinal skill in change and integration. (See chapter 2, p.46 on systems.) The other critical tool described in detail elsewhere is that of evaluation (see chapter 9, p.225 on evaluation), which provides the feedback so that systems can learn and adapt. Other important tools are project management and quality improvement skills but they are integral to the entire book and will not be addressed separately in this chapter.

This chapter is particularly concerned with tools that are the levers of change. In this context it is useful to remember that a lever is a tool that provides more movement with less effort.

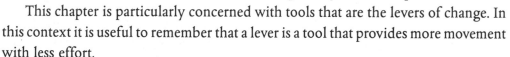

> ### *Tools that are levers of change*
>
> - developing a shared vision
> - creating shared values
> - leadership skills
> - team building
> - directed creativity
> - learning and training together
> - benchmarking and networking skills

Copying, as in painting by numbers, rarely results in true learning and understanding. To make a success of integrated care in a given locality it is important to have a deep knowledge of all the components and processes that go to make it up. At the very least, it is necessary to have an understanding of the current processes that are in place, and of how they might need to be changed. This not something that can be achieved by simply implementing a model from elsewhere. The rapid changes in external demands on care systems require the ability to adapt and remodel at any time – something that is difficult, if not impossible, if the method chosen is rigidly to implant a completed programme. The superimposing of a new system on an old one will cause the new system to take on all the faults of the old and cause both systems to degenerate to the lowest common factor. This is frequently the reason why new initiatives fail even if there has been some initial success. (See chapter 2, p.50 on systems.)

When EPICS held workshops for visiting teams they always contained a 'health warning' – do not copy what we have done but go away and do your own thing. (See also in this chapter p.297)

HEALTH WARNING

Do not blindly copy what we have done.
Select your own tools
(they may or may not be the same as ours)

AND DESIGN YOUR OWN MODELS.

There was always the temptation for the visitors to say 'We don't need to reinvent the wheel, let us just implement what you are doing'. But each community is unique. It has

> *Each community is unique, with different environments, populations and community facilities. If the care is complex and adaptive it will mould itself to the shape of the community and have a very different shape from one community to the next.*

different environments, populations and community facilities. If the care is complex and adaptive it will mould itself to the shape of the community and have a very different shape from one community to the next. The wheel may not need reinventing, but it definitely needs redesigning.

For example, in the community in which the EPICS project was piloted there was a predominantly white population with very few people from other ethnic backgrounds. There was a strong religious, charitable culture. When the project was rolled out into a new locality there was a significant Pakistani population, which was close-knit, and the whole community had a strong commitment to social welfare. The third phase included not only a Pakistani community but also a West Indian one in a town with a strong, traditional manufacturing background that was being replaced by high-tech IT industry. Each locality of the EPICS project required designing from scratch even though it was within the one umbrella organization. Identifying the strengths in each community through its cultural diversity gave the flexibility and adaptability that was the bedrock of success in each area.

Consequently, visitors to the project were advised to take EPICS tools and design and grow their own unique system, one that would exactly fit their communities and their resources, and solve their unique problems. This did not preclude sharing and learning from each other but it was essential that our visitors had a truly embedded wish to understand what it was that shaped and drove the observed models. It is not possible to design and make an integrated care system as such. It emerges from creating values and purpose, sharing knowledge and learning, and developing mutual trust – attractors of a complex system.

A shared vision is literally the prime tool in the project: the lever that sets the ball rolling.

Developing a shared vision

In failed transformations, you often find plenty of plans and directives and programmes, but no vision.

John P. Kotter, Professor of Leadership,
Harvard University

Every organization and system of care will ask itself why are we here? What is our purpose? How will we achieve our goals? Without answers to these questions the organization loses its identity and cannot function as a system – a set of processes with a common purpose. If there is a vacuum of purpose then the organization or team will flounder. It will not know which direction it should take, and individuals and groups will fill the void by setting their own agendas and going off in separate directions. It then becomes difficult to get them to pull together. Often the team or organization falls apart. It will exist but not function.

Often the vision is assumed – 'we all know why we are here' or 'we are all working for the health service or social services'. Yet, on digging deeper, it soon becomes apparent that all those involved have different perceptions of why they are there. This is not surprising when everybody has a personal vision of what they want to achieve for themselves and the way they work. For some this vision may not be explicit, nevertheless it is strong, built up over many years of experience and practice and sometimes peppered with more than a touch of cynicism. People coming from different professional and organizational backgrounds with their separate cultures are bound to have different views and so a differing professional vision. In the absence of a cor-

Winning the hearts and minds of individual people to get genuine commitment means addressing all their own individual visions and values.

porate purpose, individual visions take over and, if strong personalities are involved, conflict ensues.

The more disciplines involved, the more organizations drawn in to the new system, the more boundaries there are to cross. The more boundaries, the more individual and corporate visions there are to be addressed in order to fashion a new shared purpose. This seems such a daunting task that the temptation is for managers to go away and write the vision themselves, and then, as if coming down from the mountain, to tell everybody, hoping the organizations will buy into it. If this imposed corporate vision fails to address the many personal visions, there will be no true commitment from the individuals involved in the change. Winning the hearts and minds of individuals to get genuine commitment means addressing all their own individual visions and values. The alternative is just to try to motivate people from the top, but this is rarely sustainable over time. Ideally, everybody must see their thumb-print on the process and feel some ownership of it. If the new system or organization fails to live up to its stated vision and it clashes with personal visions, even more cynicism and disaffection ensues.

Successful delivery of care across communities with differing organizations and professional disciplines is difficult but it can be facilitated through complex adaptive systems modelling. Self-organizing groups and adaptive teams need to have a common vision and purpose, so that even when they are working independently they are still connected to the whole. In this way they foster a sense of their own value and strengthen their commitment to the goal. This is something that is difficult to achieve in traditional hierarchical organizational models.

Creating shared values

Underpinning the purpose are the values that the team or organization holds, both as individuals and jointly. The values are a statement about the important aspects of achieving the purpose. They may include the kinds of relationship that are fostered with the older person, the way people work together, the accessibility of services and the way in which professionals develop and support each other. The chosen values need to be made explicit and transparent, and then woven into the tapestry of the day-to-day workings of the new system. The core values for professionals most frequently expressed in EPICS were around caring, both for the older person and for each other. This meant everybody being valued.

It all takes time and there are no satisfactory shortcuts.

As the EPICS project rolled out to new areas, the experience was that, if you started with all the different professionals and managers expressing their own personal and organizational beliefs, it was not too difficult to draw up a common set of values to which everybody could sign up. It was then easier to draw up a statement with objectives for how the purpose could be realized. This process was not without its difficulties and pitfalls. Although this does all take time, it is vital; and there are no satisfactory short cuts.

It required several days of workshop time over a period of months (with other positive activities in between) to develop an understanding of other people's roles and their organizational cultures. However, the EPICS teams did discover some early paybacks. The initial workshops often removed constraints in communication, and professionals started to interact more easily from an early stage. But the greatest

---

NEW VALUES FOR EPICS

- customer focused + participation
- shared responsibility
- open access
- trust
- more creativity
- confidentiality
- caring for staff – social concern
- everybody valued
- learning together

---

benefit was that the teams gained the confidence in each other to be proactive and able to respond to a changing environment more quickly.

The EPICS experience was that it was helpful to have an external facilitator (with an understanding of a systems approach), at least for the workshops on value setting and the drawing up of the initial purpose statement. This allowed the leaders to take a full part and for everybody to have equal status. Any sensitive issues could be handled more easily once the ground rules of the interactions had been established and the facilitator was seen to be fair and independent. Thereafter, it was not always so necessary to have external facilitation (unless a particularly sensitive issue arose) because the behaviour patterns of mutual respect had been established.

Once the values and purpose have been drawn up they must be nurtured and managed. If neglected, they will wither and die. It is important that they are revisited

---

Values should not be left 'on the shelf'

On visits to hospitals and other organizations, members of the EPICS team were interested to find out if the exercise of creating shared values had been carried out, to confirm the purpose of their work, and whether this had generated a strategy. Almost invariably care teams would answer that they had not been involved in any such exercises and did not know explicitly the purpose of the organization for which they worked. However, when the same question was put to senior managers, they would confirm that there was a mission statement and a strategy document. When asked if they were available the reply was frequently: 'Oh, it's on a shelf somewhere…I'll look it out and show you next time you come.'

Once the values and purpose have been drawn up they must be nurtured and managed. If neglected they will wither and die.

regularly by all concerned to see if they are still relevant.

In EPICS we actively revisited our 'values' and mission at least twice a year. Often this was done at workshops where the quality and practice of day-to-day work was reviewed to see if indeed the teams were actually reflecting the values in their work. (See chapter 9, p.237 on evaluation.)

The values changed only slowly over time – providing some stability in a rapidly changing world. On the other hand, the purpose and how to achieve it were always evolving. They could never be cast in stone.

If the purpose is being revisited regularly and is evolving it is not necessary to provide much prescriptive detail. A complex adaptive approach allows for minimum specification but needs the direction of the values and purpose.

The principal of minimum specifications suggests that managers should define no more than is absolutely necessary to launch a particular initiative or activity on its way. They have to avoid the role of 'grand designer' in favour of one that focuses on facilitation, orchestration and boundary management, creating 'enabling conditions' that allow a system to find its own form. (Zimmerman, Lindberg and Plsek 1988, p.27)

The original mission statement for the EPICS project

To optimize the health and well being of the frail older people of Marlow by timely assessments of individual care needs and provision of integrated community care, thus reducing the number of inappropriate admissions to hospital and residential care and utilizing available resources in the most efficient manner.

This statement was modified two years later at a workshop attended by representatives of all the stakeholders including users and volunteers.

The second EPICS mission statement

The Marlow EPICS is an integrated care and support system available to any person of 65 or over registered with participating GP practices to ensure the most appropriate use of health, social services and community resources in order to optimize their care within legal, budgetary and resource constraints.

The second statement was a more sophisticated version reflecting experience and greater confidence. It significantly removed one specific part of the aim – 'reducing the number of inappropriate admissions to hospital and residential care'. It was felt that this was too narrow a focus for a client-centred holistic system and had been included to reflect the funding priorities at the time.

The goals supporting the second statement were:

- to optimize choice for users and carers
- to provide a co-ordinated care and support network.

A complex adaptive approach allows for minimum specification but needs the direction of the values and purpose.

Complexity of value systems

The value system in an organization will also be a system within other value systems. For example, the EPICS value system lay within that of the local healthcare and social services and their systems lay within the county council's and the health authority's. These value systems all need to be connected if there is to be consistency in the quality of care delivered. This is a real challenge for the senior leaders. (See chapter 2, p.63 on systems.)

Successful value systems in large organizations have a central pattern running through them that allows everybody to recognize them. For example, if *caring* was a key value in the value system the commissioners would place a value on *buying* care in a caring way; the providers would *provide* care in a caring way and the professional would *practise* care in a caring way. It is not difficult to see how this could be extended to other topics, such as training and staff development. Keeping these value chains connected relies on the skill and the integrity of everybody involved, but the senior managers have a particular role as stewards of these values.

Ethics and Value Systems

Ethics is the institutionalization of the value system of a profession. It is the societal contract and the social legality that underpins the relationship between the community and the individual practitioner. Each profession has its own set of ethical standards or guiding principles that are enshrined in the values and culture of that profession. Each is very different – and some are more explicitly stated than others. The ethical tenets can be a divisive force between professions even if they are only implicit in any exchange between them. The current ethical code for social workers puts the values of the relationship with their client at the centre of their practice, possibly at the expense of the wider implications of care to that client, whereas the clinical professions will tend to concentrate on practical physical outcomes at the expense of meeting their patients' emotional needs. This highlights some of the cultural conflict that arises between healthcare and social work practitioners.

If all the agencies, the voluntary sector, the community and most importantly the older person are to work as partners in any new integrated delivery of care then there is a need for a new set of ethical codes that will reflect this.

Ethical codes have tended to focus very much on the person or group being treated or offered a service, and generally have not taken into account the needs of overall populations or communities. For example, a doctor will do everything in his power for the person he is currently seeing but will feel less responsibility for those on waiting lists or in the community. Yet in this book, and in the EPICS project, there are two new values that are not reflected in most ethical codes. The first is that the older person is a partner in the whole process, and the second is that older people will gain benefit as individuals from the outcomes of population-managed health and social care processes as they will from direct care.

If all the agencies, the voluntary sector, the community and most importantly the older person are to work as partners in any new integrated delivery of care then there is a need for a new set of ethical codes that will reflect this.

The civic model of care proposed (see chapter 3, p.86 on implementation models) suggests that there is a mutual responsibility between everybody and that everybody owns the system – this is not posited in most ethical systems. Resolving these differences will be fundamental to true partnership working.

Some organizations are facing up to these issues but are still tending to act separately and are not truly inclusive of other professional groups or the older person. Examples include the Tavistock Group, a multinational group, and the Justice in Health Care Foundation based in the USA (Berwick *et al.* 2001, see boxes). The latter has looked at the issues more from the users' perspective and includes responsibilities for the users as well as the service providers and commissioners. Coming from a healthcare focus, both tend to take a unilateral position. However, they are not discipline-specific, and so they could be embraced by all the disciplines within healthcare in a way that current ones are not, but being unrelated to other organizations outside of healthcare, they might not help in some of the deeper cross-organizational values. However both involve values about populations of people.

The Tavistock Principles

- Rights – People have a right to health and healthcare.
- Balance – Care of individual patients is central but the health of populations is also our concern.
- Comprehensiveness – In addition to treating illness, we have an obligation to ease suffering, minimize disability, prevent disease and promote health.
- Co-operation – Healthcare only succeeds if we co-operate with those we serve, each other, and those in other sectors.
- Improvement – Improving health is a serious and continuing responsibility.
- Safety – Do no harm.
- Openness – Being open, honest and trustworthy is vital in healthcare.

Principles of the Justice in Health Care Foundation

- Health – Health systems should pursue health as their primary goal.
- Access – Healthcare systems should provide care primarily according to need rather than ability to pay.
- Accountability – Consumers, providers and healthcare institutions must take responsibility for health and healthcare resources with which they are entrusted.
- Choice – Consumers must have the real ability to choose their treatments and providers, in order to seek the best value in healthcare for themselves.
- Education – Education of consumers, providers and institutions regarding value and quality in healthcare is necessary for responsible and informed health choices.

There is a great need to explore these same ethical codes with older people themselves, on a wider front and using complex system thinking.

Leadership skills

Leadership is the art of creating the context and environment in which change for the better can be achieved. And self-evidently leadership is a fundamental tool for any organization, even if it has a culture of 'self-leadership'. According to Hammer (1996), the role of a leader is to:

- enable the creation of the vision and purpose
- foster a true commitment to the goals
- ensure that all parts of the processes are integrated into the whole.

Leadership is the art of creating the context and environment in which change for the better can be achieved.

Leaders are the guardians of the values. Leading complex adaptive systems requires skills possibly not usually recognized in managers. Enabling staff to be self-organizing and flexible to meet fast-changing situations means being able to let go of being in charge all of the time.

Leaders are the guardians of the values.

Maintaining the connectedness between all the parts is a major responsibility of the leader in a complex

> ### Key leadership behaviours in complex adaptive systems
>
> - develop open networks of communication
> - gain commitment through a culture of caring
> - develop people
> - recognize and show compassion for fears
> - ensure that leadership occurs throughout the organization
> - welcome diversity, question everything and generate new perspectives through contention and positive conflict
> - develop strategies, practices and goals on an ongoing basis, based on shared values
> - articulate and interpret common experience valuing everybody's contribution
> - contain anxiety and have the courage to be confident
> - legitimize the rapid uncovering of errors and use these as a positive learning experience
> - celebrate achievements.

adaptive system. The leader will spend much time managing the context of the changing environment. Included in this are the political and financial factors. A good leader will try to ensure that the right conditions exist to train and develop others within the organization so that they can work independently. The leader will be seen as serving others in the organization rather than as the master whom others serve (Plsek and Wilson 2001).

> **The leader:**
> - manages context and relationships
> - creates conditions that favour emergence and self-organization
> - lets go of 'figuring it all out'.
>
> (Zimmerman *et al.* 1998)

Within the complex systems that have self-organizing parts there will inevitably be tensions between those parts. For example, there may be creative tensions with teams having different ideas and priorities as to how to proceed as well as competition for limited resources. The skill of the leader will be to use these tensions creatively and maintain the diversity that will stimulate breaking new ground. It is rare that any one idea is completely right, or any other completely wrong. Leaders will be faced with continual challenges:

- how to give direction without giving directives
- how to lead by serving
- how to maintain authority without having control
- how to set direction when the future is unknown.

In a complex adaptive system creativity and innovation are most likely to emerge precisely at the point of greatest tension, i.e. on the edge of chaos. The chaos manager must recognize the 'forks in the road' and create a context supporting the new line of development by finding interventions that transcend the paradoxes or make them irrelevant.

Learning how to let go

One lesson of leadership was brought home to me in an abrupt and somewhat painful way in the early days of EPICS. The ideas of integrated systems and patient involvement were simmering away within me from the mid-1980s. Three or four years later, a group of interested people were drawn together to see if these ideas could be put into action. The decision to proceed with EPICS was given and, with great enthusiasm, the initial planning was started.

However, after some months the enthusiasm waned and little progress was being made. The meetings had lost their excitement and I could not understand why. When I started listening to what people were saying they were describing it as 'Chris Foote's project' and everything was being deferred to me. On reflection, I had to admit that it was vitally important to me and that when I was buried I wanted 'EPICS' carved on my chest. All those ideas were mine weren't they and didn't I have right to own it? Slowly it dawned on me that I was the problem and that if my style of leadership persisted then we would get nowhere very fast.

> It was a difficult and painful process to let go of my 'baby' and let others adopt it, own it and shape its growing up. For some months I had genuine feelings of loss. But not surprisingly the project gained momentum again. There was a renewed buzz to all the activity as all the other members of the team went off and developed the ideas in ways I had not dreamed. The various team members were now asking not for direction or permission but for advice and help in 'how to do' rather than 'what to do'. EPICS became self-organizing with several projects all being executed at the same time rather than following the linear piecemeal approach I had originally taken. From this time, the phrase EPICS-r-Us, parodied from the famous toy retailer, became currency within the project.
>
> Christopher Foote

The point is made above that an adaptable self-organizing system that is flexible enough to meet fast-changing situations requires leadership throughout its levels. This means that the traditional leadership role has to be dispersed throughout the whole organization. This cannot be achieved through a central command-and-control model. In practical terms this means that leadership skills have to be fostered in the several parts of the system.

Trust becomes a key ingredient if the whole process of leadership is to be delegated throughout the organization. This is a break from conventional wisdom whereby leadership is assumed to come only from the top. It makes two assumptions – first, that those at the top are prepared to let go and encourage leadership throughout the organization, and second, that those who are not normally in leadership roles are prepared to take them on. This is not always quite as easy as it seems. In command-and-control type organizations the culture is to wait and be told what to do. People lose their initiative and become paralysed when they are expected to take the lead in breaking new ground. Leadership has to be nurtured and become part of the ethos of the whole team.

Learning how to lead in a complex adaptive system

A year after the EPICS pilot project had been successfully launched, I was recruited to the post of Project Manager. Coming from a social work background and direct from managing a large Age Concern organization in central London, there were high expectations of me to facilitate the integration of social services and the voluntary sector into the system.

I had been accustomed to being accountable to a board of management, although self-motivating where management and service development were concerned. After a month I found myself getting angry and frustrated because I was unclear about what was expected of me; what were the limits of my responsibility; to whom I was accountable. No one was telling me what I should be doing. I appeared to have a responsibility to the EPICS project board as an officer; to the Hospital Directorate for Elderly Care Services which, in its turn, was accountable to the Directorate for Hospital and Community Services. My Line Manager was the Business Manager of the Elderly Care Services Directorate. The Co-ordinator running the EPICS system in Marlow was line-managed by the Trust's Nurse Manager, but was responsible to me (see line management chart on p.145).

I felt as if I had a lot of responsibility but little authority. I had no designated professional mentor. At critical times my rational judgement was overwhelmed. I vented my angry feelings on the champion of the system, Dr Chris Foote. This was after he had let go of his 'ownership' of EPICS in order to allow it to grow to independence. He wanted me to put my own thumb-print on the developing project. Because he was able to take an overview of the whole system he enabled me to take on the culture of 'leadership and delegation' within EPICS. This allowed me to stand back and be more objective about the dynamics and the relationships. I found my own professional mentor in the manager of the social services Team for Older People. The EPICS team and members of other disciplines in the system also became my personal support network, including colleagues from the voluntary sector.

Christine Stanners

Team building

Teamwork is undoubtedly the underlying tool that makes integrated care tick. Most organizations are dependent on groups or teams to achieve their goals. Good teams will have common goals and realize that their individual skills contribute to these in

Teamwork is undoubtedly the underlying tool that makes integrated care tick.

an interdependent manner, and that personal success is dependent on how well teams work together. Much of health and social care depends on good team-working. But even within individual organizations it is not easy to work in multidisciplinary teams. Working across organizational boundaries can be even more taxing. Much lip service is given to good team-working in older people's care, but it is surprising how little time and effort is given to developing robust teams that are able to work together creatively.

In integrated care, teams working across boundaries are most often thrown together and just told to get on with it. There is remarkably little training and virtually no team management or support on an ongoing basis. So it is hardly surprising that conflicts arise within teams, conflicts that are not only personally painful but also reduce team effectiveness (Ovretveit 1993). If cross-functioning organizations do not have a strategy for team-working, it is likely that joint senior management teams will not function well as teams themselves; and if this is the case it makes it difficult for other teams to function well, especially when competing agendas put the loyalties of team members under pressure.

Good team-working for integrated care requires:

- a shared set of explicit values and ground rules for team behaviour that are formulated by the team themselves

- a clear joint purpose and goals for the team

- a feeling of mutual support based on trust and caring for each other

- all the team members to be fully involved and participative

- a recognized and agreed decision-making process that allows all the members to take part

- the team to communicate openly and fully with each other and information to be freely available within the team

- team members to feel that they can express themselves openly and disagree with each other without losing the support and trust of the team

- the team to be able to resolve internal conflict itself, even if it requires facilitation, and not to have the resolution imposed

- the team to have a strong sense of commitment to the goal and to each other, thus raising morale, keeping the team together and lowering staff turnover

- the team to learn together and develop together

- the team to celebrate together.

Role conflict

In a setting of integrated care some of the problems of conflict can be prevented by careful and sensitive handling of the roles of the team members by the managers in each of the organizations contributing members to the team.

ROLE INCOMPATIBILITY

This is not uncommon in integrated teams and is most frequently seen when a team member has professional accountability to one manager and organizational accountability to another. When apparently incompatible decisions need to be made the team member will inevitably be torn between the two.

> An example of role incompatibility occurred when the leader of a multidisciplinary team (comprising nurses, social workers and therapy staff) who was a nurse went on maternity leave. Her replacement was the social work member of the team.
>
> The nurses felt unable to accept her as the team leader, saying that they could not be professionally accountable to her as they had been to the previous leader.

These tensions can be reduced by clear structuring of the team, making explicit the avenues of professional responsibility and organizational accountability, and ensuring that these are recognized by the entire team, both individually and as a team. If the team see the professional and the organizational managers relating and working well together as a team, they are more likely to internalize the tensions more satisfactorily.

ROLE AMBIGUITY

Some of the pressures put on staff to be multi-skilled and to work in a variety of settings may possibly lead to feelings of ambiguity about any new role. The old roles were very clearly defined and staff may feel lost in the new looser structure. There is

> *Some of the pressures put on staff to be multi-skilled and to work in a variety of settings may possibly lead to feelings of ambiguity about any new role.*

sometimes a lack of clarity as to what their new role is and to whom they are accountable. Lack of structured feedback reinforces this feeling of ambiguity. Again, this can be reduced by clear communications and being given well-defined tasks.

ROLE OVERLOAD

When individual team members, with their various professional skills, are working in an unstructured situation with feelings of incompatibility and ambiguity, overload is likely to occur. It will frequently fall on any member of the team who is compensating for the reduced performance of the team overall. Not uncommonly it falls on a team leader who is not getting sufficient structured support from the professional and organizational managers and is having to take responsibility across a wide range of disciplines and organizations.

ROLE UNDERLOAD

This can be disheartening for some team members who may feel undervalued if they are not fulfilled and are not achieving their expectations. This may be occurring because they are uncertain of their role or have not been properly trained, or when they have developed new competencies and skills that are not being acknowledged by greater responsibility.

The stress that role conflict causes can be considerable, but can be reduced by ensuring:

- that within the team there is clarity of roles, and that guidelines and acknowledged care pathways are used where these are appropriate

- that the team have access to professional and organizational support when they are unable to resolve role issues

- that the managers ensure that the team has the right skill mix and competencies to meet the goals so that unnecessary pressures are not put on other members of the team

- that the team has proper induction and training programmes

- that there is good exchange of information within the team, and effective communication of team results and evaluation

- that the team are kept fully informed of any potential organizational changes so that these are not perceived as threats

- that the successes of the team are acknowledged.

Directed creativity

Creativity, particularly if directed, is a dynamic generative tool essential if an organization is to grow and flourish.

Whilst EPICS was being developed, one of the more difficult tasks was to persuade team members that some things could be done better in a different way. Thinking had become tram-lined because 'that was the way it was always done'. One of the first priorities at the early workshops was to free up individual creativity by removing constraints on thinking.

> *Creativity, particularly if directed, is a dynamic generative tool essential if an organization is to grow and flourish.*

One of those constraints was the people themselves. Many felt that they were incapable of being creative. They needed to become aware that everybody was creative in some aspect of their lives. It might be in their pastimes and hobbies or the way they managed with their families, but wherever it was it existed and it did not need to be compartmentalized. In fact, the process of looking outside their working lives for examples of creativity was in itself being creative. Nor was it necessary to think that being creative meant that you had to invent something completely new. It simply had to be a new way of solving a problem for that team or system.

The professionals at the workshops were asked to review the current situation of older people's care and hear experiences from older people and from professional colleagues. To hear different points of view was in fact creative if this meant putting oneself into other people's positions and seeing the same problem from another perspective.

Finding new ways of thinking

The next stage was to generate escape from current models of thinking. There are numerous tools to facilitate this; two exercises useful in EPICS workshops were 'if we were…' and asking 'wicked questions'. (For further exercises see Appendix 10.1 at the end of this chapter.)

'IF WE WERE...'

Here the teams were asked to imagine that they were from a discipline other than health or social work but addressing the same problems. For example, suppose they were a team from a high street bank, how would they deal with the problem of community care? Ideas that were generated on one occasion included 'automatic tills' at convenient places such as day centres or shopping malls where older people could get advice and easier access to services. Records would be kept on smart cards (rather like electronic bank cards) to which users and professionals alike could have access. Similarly, users would be sent 'accounts' of their health status from time to time and so know what their healthcare balance was.

In another scenario, teams were asked to be a football management team. This time they said they would need a trainer to get everybody as fit as possible and a training ground to do this on. Also everybody would need to know the rules of the game and how it was played in order to participate fully and play constructively. Sport and games are supposed to be fun so it was important to make health and healthcare as enjoyable as possible!

WICKED QUESTIONS

These are the questions that you almost dare not ask because they challenge inherent, and apparently unassailable, assumptions about the way things are currently done; and if the questions were valid it would make the natural order of things unstable and threatening for everybody. Yet it is in these areas of uncertainty that complex adaptive systems thinking comes up with possible creative solutions.

Suppose the team are challenged by the wicked question 'Why do people have to be in hospital to be discharged from hospital?' The whole idea sounds ridiculous – they *are* in hospital so of course they must be discharged from hospital. But for many older people the processes of discharge involve the community and the care it provides and may have nothing to do with the core activities of the acute hospital. They are two separate systems which at the time of discharge are managed as one. They have different priorities and cultures, and so frustrations and conflict arise. Suppose that the community teams took the patients over and took control of the discharge in their own setting or that the community-based teams came into the hospital and took over for a day or two prior to the patient leaving and so be in control of the situation and not feel under pressure from another system.

Another wicked question could be 'How do you run a health and social care system for older people with no older people in it?' Again, an apparently contradictory question that challenges. Older people are 'people' first and foremost; and if we were to rid ourselves of ageist ideas and not label them as old, what kind of system of care could we and they devise that would keep them young in spirit at least?

Whenever this exercise has been played out at workshops completely different patterns of care and social responsibility have been drawn up. And those things in society that make people older than they need be have disappeared!

Other wicked questions can be 'How would you admit older people to hospital if all the accident and emergency units in the country were abolished?' Or 'How would you negotiate with the residents of a nursing home who have run amok with all the kitchen implements and say that they want to take the home over and run it for themselves?'

Once these new ideas have been generated they need to be gathered in and refined. They can then be expanded and given some detail so that it is possible to implement them. The implementation can take the form of a PDSA cycle (Plan, Do, Study, Act) as a small experiment and implemented on a larger scale if the pilot is successful.

PDSA (Plan, Do, Study, Act): A clinical improvement tool

...but the key point is that nothing in a system of care will change until something starts changing.

Paul Plsek, Senior Fellow,
Institute for Healthcare Improvement, Boston, USA.

There are nearly always tensions in the system that if addressed will result in improvement. They come from a variety of quarters. It may be the clinician introducing a new service, a social worker seeing the need for a day centre in a locality or it may arise from a complaint or investigation. Frequently the tension arises externally as a performance indicator or review of some kind. Or it may be the result of implementing the National Service Frameworks, for example.

Wherever these tensions come from, the changes that they dictate have to be put in place. It is often not sensible or possible to put in wholesale changes even if they are mandated. Working with complexity means it is not possible to know with certainty what will work in any given situation. But complex adaptive systems cope best with small-scale changes that can be put in place quickly, often as the result of changing external needs. A series of small experiments that can subsequently be more widely implemented will have an impact on the total system.

A method of doing this is the 'model for rapid cycle improvement'. Having chosen a problem where there is significant tension and selected the site and the team most appropriate to undertake the project, the next step is to ask three important questions.

1. AIM: What are we trying to accomplish?
    For example, how do we reduce the trolley wait times for elderly people in the A&E department by 50 per cent? Or, how can the care plans in nursing homes be improved?

2. MEASUREMENT: How will we know if there has been an improvement?
    For example, measure the trolley waiting times before and after the intervention. Assess the care plans against standards over time.

3. CHANGE: What changes can we make that will result in an improvement?
    For example, put in place a specialist elderly care team in A&E. Put in place a training programme for home staff.

The next stage is to undertake a quick, small-scale project as an experimental test for change.

- PLAN
- DO
- STUDY
- ACT

First, **PLAN** the change process that is proposed. Then **DO** it. Assess it by **STUDY** and measurement. Then **ACT** on the results. The action may be:

- to extend the project because it has been successful against the agreed measured standards
- to change the project because it has not been as successful as desired and repeat the cycle
- to abandon the project altogether because it will never be successful.

It is important to keep the pace of these cycles as fast as reasonably possible. The more cycles there are, the more chance to adapt and the more learning of the system behaviour occurs, so that continued commitment to change is more likely. These multiple small changes can then become the basis for the emergence of major change (Plsek 1999).

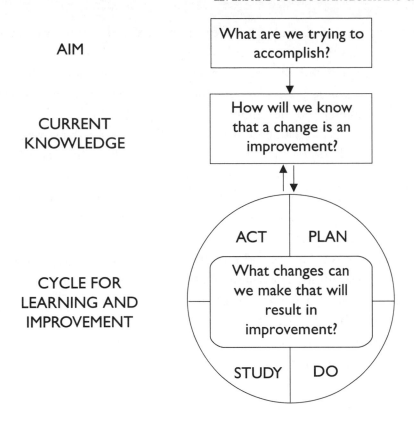

Figure 10.1 PDSA learning cycle

The 'Balance-of-Care' approach

This tool has been developed and refined over the last 25 years; it is a realistic way to develop a whole-systems approach to designing care in a given locality (Forte and Bowen 1997). It assumes that the immediacy of problems is around older people's healthcare. The basic tenet is simple. Estimate the amount of dependency there is in a given population of older people and see what options will provide an acceptably high quality of service. The balance-of-care approach uses a computer-based decision-support model that incorporates a wide range of options from home care through to acute hospital care. The range of services will include those already available and those that can be planned for. A central feature is to match these options to the finances and resources available, currently and in the future, and enable cost-effective decisions to be made. The modelling is dynamic and interactive and allows a variety of possible solutions to be considered and the choices 'balanced' against each other in the light of values and the resource availability of the locality.

The population to be studied may be either a part or the whole of a community of older people, depending on the specific initial questions being asked of the model. If, for instance, the study is about the needs for short-term and respite care in the community, the population will be community-based. But if it is about delayed discharges from hospital, then it will be the hospital-based population of older patients. However, being a whole-systems model, the solutions will involve outcomes that affect both the hospital and the community.

When it comes to estimating dependency, different people have very different measures, so the methodology must be agreed by everybody at the outset. For hospital-based patients the preferred tool is the appropriateness of admission and the appropriateness of stay protocols (Lang *et al.* 1999). Both assess the appropriateness against validated criteria for admission to (and stay in) an acute hospital. The assumption is that for those patients who do not meet these validated criteria, admission to the acute hospital was avoidable and that the older person's needs could be met by other more suitable facilities. The same applies to the inappropriateness of their stay in an acute hospital ward when alternative settings would be more effective.

A core theme of the balance-of-care approach is the involvement of all the stakeholders throughout the process from start to finish. A series of workshops provides the settings for an in-depth, ongoing dialogue as the project unfolds. Early data is presented to refine the questions being investigated, as well as to explore the range of emerging solutions. It is important to involve the older person and their community. Some of the balance-of-care workshops were specifically convened with the sole purpose of gathering older people's views and experience.

The essential steps are:

1. Identify all the key players including patients and patient organizations (both in the hospital and the community) so they can be involved in the planning and own the process from the start. The process is an iterative one with all the key players being involved throughout.

2. Select and agree the assessment tools and methodology.

3. Identify other forms of care as an alternative to admission for those patients who may not have needed acute hospital care. This may be from a range of care in the community or admission to a non-acute facility.

4. Identify alternatives for those patients not requiring ongoing acute care. These range from short-term and longer-term rehabilitation in various settings (including the community and the patient's own home) to various types of longer-term care.

5.   Encourage the participants at all the workshops to think systemically and to be as creative as possible.

6.   Identify the structures and processes needed to implement one or two pre-selected models and to provide a comparison of potential costs, which can then be weighed against those of existing care models. Other constraints, such as the availability of staff and transport requirements, can be identified and built into the equation.

7.   This analysis provides the basis of an ongoing evaluation system to provide evidence that the quality of care has improved and to generate a strategy for continuous improvement.

The approach gives leverage for change by presenting information that is relevant to the locality. This is certainly a powerful way of engaging professionals, especially clinicians. Another important leverage point is that the analysis develops the solutions as it progresses in a way that enables them to be subsequently implemented. The wide variety of stakeholders involved from all the agencies (including voluntary groups and the older people themselves) leads more easily to integrated, whole-systems solutions. These solutions will also include how the services are to be commissioned and provided.

Learning and training together

Learning and training jointly with other people is a powerful lever for changing ourselves, individually and as groups. It improves co-operation and joint working. It is also a way of developing a shared meaning and a shared language. Developing and 'growing' people are strong attractors in any complex adaptive system. Learning new things is a way of ensuring the tension and instability necessary for change in both people and organizations, keeping them at the edge of chaos and encouraging creativity and innovation.

A complex adaptive organization has always to be learning to have the ability to adapt. If learning does not take place it will not survive. When the organization or team stops learning then somebody else has to tell it what to do (the essence of command and control), and immediately it ceases to be a complex adaptive system!

A complex adaptive organization has always to be learning to be able to adapt.

Learning in a complex adaptive organization is characterized by:

- a culture of enquiry and asking questions, rather than the instant provision of answers

- ready availability of information

- individuals and teams being valued as part of the knowledge base and regularly consulted

- individuals feeling fulfilled because they are achieving new capabilities (i.e. the range of possibilities within a person to change to meet new opportunities and challenges) rather than just being trained in competencies for the sake of the organization (Fraser and Greenhalgh 2001)

- a robust appraisal and mentoring system that provides feedback loops for personal development

- a performance evaluation with shared reporting and goal-setting

- time set aside for learning together on a regular basis

- problems and situations needing resolution being presented as stories and histories to show their complex nature; the subsequent analysis and teasing out of the story for its meaning being done on a form of multidimensional model similar to the assessment and evaluation systems.

After the information systems, the training programme became the second highest priority in the development of EPICS. A series of workshops was undertaken. These initially focused on learning about systems and systems thinking and then creating the values and principles that were to drive the project forward. There was little problem in attracting participants from any of the agencies (possibly not unconnected to our having begged, borrowed or otherwise acquired funds to pay for a pleasant venue and good lunch!). Some local firms, including Rank Xerox and Amersham International (as it was then), were very generous in allowing us to use their training facilities and letting their training managers and consultants facilitate the workshops.

Links with other training organizations and teams can also be fostered. Local universities can assist in some of the analyses of the evaluation and help set up the patient satisfaction questionnaires. This has the added advantage of giving the organization a very stimulating outside influence.

Involving the older person in learning and training is extremely important and has been discussed in chapter 8. Some older people came to the workshops and the team spent considerable time visiting older people's clubs and organizations. This was not only to inform them about EPICS but also to encourage them to take part in any preventive programmes. This provided the opportunity for older people to give feedback about themselves and the programme they wanted.

Benchmarking and networking

There are two ways of benchmarking to gauge the success of an initiative. There is the mechanistic search for applicable standards from other projects, or there is the more interactive approach which involves making visits to other sites to observe and learn from other people's experience.

> *There are two ways of benchmarking to gauge the success of an initiative. There is the mechanistic search for applicable standards from other projects, or there is the more interactive approach which involves making visits to other sites to observe and learn from other people's experience.*

The EPICS team put much emphasis on the second kind of benchmarking. Reciprocally, other teams were encouraged to visit the EPICS pilot site to see what was happening there. With the promotion of 'Beacon' sites of excellence this has become a much more common practice in the UK.

Much benchmarking is done in a very random manner, based on a few visits and possibly some talks and lectures. It is important that the benchmarking exercise is structured so that the visiting team can see more than the 'nuts and bolts'. The aim should be to gain understanding of the principles and values driving the initiative. And the team should be made aware of any other underpinning processes that make the site successful.

Consequently the site to visit has to be chosen with care. It is important to know that it is among the best for the purposes of the visit, and by what criteria it is judged to be so. If nationally selected (as with the Beacon sites) this is relatively easy but otherwise a bit of research always pays. It is always worth contacting the site to clarify what it is they can offer, and to let them know what the visiting team's expectations are. These should be made explicit through the following processes.

Before the visit

- The visiting team should have a clear idea what problems in their own older people's care system they are trying to address through the visit. This will almost certainly require the team to meet in advance to define and map the problems.

- The multidisciplinary team members should identify which area of interest each will focus on most appropriately.

- They will then seek out their counterpart on the visit.

- It is important to determine what data they would like to acquire.

- They should agree what methods they will use to evaluate the site. This should relate to the visiting team's own evaluation systems, using the same measures and scales of assessment if possible.

- The visiting team should identify as many of the standards used by the host site as possible and compare them with their own.

- They should agree what kind of record will be made of the visit and who will co-ordinate any report.

During the visit

- Talk with individual members of the 'home' team matching professional disciplines.

- Observe the other team actually performing. Practical demonstrations are worth hours of talking.

- Before the team leaves it is worth meeting on the site and exchanging information to see if any areas have not been covered. There may then be time to fill the gap. It is always better to do this before leaving rather than on the journey back.

- Make sure that leaflets and literature from the host site are collected.

After the visit

- Meet as soon as possible after return, while issues are still fresh in the mind, for a debrief.

- Map out the care processes that have been observed and compare them with the in-house practice. Compare data and standards. Draw up action plans from what has been learned.

- See what tensions for change have been created.

Structuring visits like this makes sure they will be beneficial to all those involved.

When visitors came to EPICS, they were able to see the co-ordination centre in action and the IT systems being used. It was always the policy to get EPICS practitioners (including volunteers) to make the presentations and be directly involved with visitors. This gave the visitors a dynamic insight into the project, and it was highly valued. It also gave the EPICS team members confidence in presenting and it showed that they (and their work) were respected and valued by 'the management'. And, as they were party to all the discussions, they gained new information and knowledge. It was always a reciprocal learning process which more than made up for the time and planning that went into hosting the visit.

Overview

These tools and levers are at the heart of the change process that occurs within a complex adaptive system. They fashion the attractors that drive the whole process. The vision and values are what give independent agents in the integrated care process a common direction in which to travel together. Leadership at every level is what enables and initiates change throughout the system. Without learning taking place it is not possible for a complex adaptive system to adapt and change. Without adaptation and change the systems will disintegrate.

These processes can only thrive if there are robust and healthy relationships promoting good team and group working. These same relationship skills will bind the teams together to form a flexible coherent whole.

The tools are not only the levers for change but they also provide the 'glue and the grease' that keeps the machine structurally sound and moving without seizing up.

Chapter 10 – Headline points

- Involving the hearts and minds of individual people to get genuine commitment means addressing their own individual vision and values.

- It all takes time and there are no satisfactory short cuts.

- A complex adaptive approach allows for minimum specification but needs the direction of values and purpose.

- Once the values and purpose have been drawn up they must be nurtured and managed. If neglected they will wither and die.

- If all the agencies, the voluntary sector, the community and most importantly the older person are to work as partners in any new delivery of care, then there is a need for a new set of ethical codes that will reflect this.

- Leadership is the art of creating the context and environment in which change for the better can be achieved.

- Leaders are the guardians of the values.

- Teamwork is undoubtedly the underlying tool that makes integrated care tick.

- Some of the pressures put on staff to be multi-skilled and work in a variety of settings may possibly lead to feelings of ambiguity about any new role.

- Creativity, particularly if directed, is a dynamic generative tool essential if an organization is to grow and flourish.

- A complex adaptive organization has always to be learning in order to be able to adapt.

- There are two ways of benchmarking to gauge the success of an initiative. There is the mechanistic search for applicable standards from other projects, or there is the more interactive approach which involves making visits to other sites to observe and learn from other people's experience.

APPENDIX 10.1

Two exercises that develop insights into your systems

Exercise 1: Who are you connected to?

At a multidisciplinary or multi-agency team meeting or workshop, ask the members to identify:

a)   All the *external* 'customers' of the team and how the team relate to them and identify what service they provide for them.

b)   All the *internal* 'customers' of the team and what service they provide for each other and how they communicate with each other.

Draw the networks for all to see.

Though this exercise appears simplistic, it is often the first time that the team members have rationally thought through who all the individuals are that the team network with. Once the networks are identified it is also possible to formulate clearly the services provided across the networks. It will show the complexity of the relationships involved and it is the start of developing a team-based mind map of the networks that the team has. Questions emerge naturally as to how these are to be fostered and developed.

Exercise 2   The "...ing game"

At a team or departmental meeting or workshop ask the members to identify all the processes that occur whilst providing the services for the customers. Ask them to write on 'post-it notes' the associated verb of part of that process. An easy way is to remind people that any thing ending in 'ing' is part of the process such as assessing, note keeping, treating, discharging, etc. Having brainstormed all the processes in whatever order get them to put the 'post-it notes' in the sequence that it is thought they occur. Do not worry if some processes occur at the same time: connect them as parallel lines the ends of which can be drawn to meet at one point.

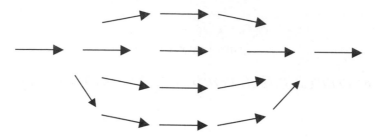

Figure 10.2 Parallel and synchronous processes

Put these on a wall or a flip chart page. It is amazing how often this has to be changed! (At this stage do not worry about *where* these take place – this exercise is primarily about process and not structures.) Even this alone can be very revealing to team members. For some of them it is the first time that they have appreciated the full range of the team's or department's activities!

The next stage is to identify all the people involved in each part of the process. Write their titles on a different coloured 'post-it note' and align them near the relevant process on the process map. *Now* do the same for the place where the process takes place on yet different 'post-it notes'.

Ask the attendees to:

- identify any waiting, delays or holdups in the whole system from the process map

- identify where there is any unnecessary repetition of activities or tasks

- identify those areas where there are similar processes being carried out by different people and where these could be performed by a single person (the assessment process is an obvious example but some therapies could be similarly rationalized)

- identify all the unnecessary processes that have been done historically, are no longer required and give no value to the whole process

- identify all the 'handoffs', that is, the passing of the older person or the process from one person to another, and reduce these wherever possible. This will speed up the processes and reduce the risk of mistakes occurring through gaps in communication.

Only when these processes have been redesigned should they be aligned to the structures and places where they are to occur. This gives the opportunity for designing creative use of structures and facilities.

The object is not only to understand the processes but also to improve the quality of the service by reducing delays and waste in the delivery of care.

References

Berwick, D., Davidoff, F., Hiatt, H. and Smith, R. (2001) 'Refining and implementing the Tavistock principles for everybody in health care.' *British Medical Journal 323*, 616–620.

Forte, P. and Bowen, T. (1997) 'Improving the balance of elderly care services.' In S. Cropper and P. Forte (eds) *Enhancing Health Services Management*. Buckingham: Open University Press.

Fraser S.W. and Greenhalgh, T. (2001) 'Coping with complexity: educating for capability.' *British Medical Journal 323*, 799–803.

Hammer, M. (1996) *Beyond Reengineering: How the process centred organization is changing our work and our lives*. London: HarperCollins

Lang, T., Liberati, A., Tampieri, A., Felin, G., Gosalves, M., Lorenzo, S., Pearson, M., Beech, R. and Santos-Eggiman, B. (1999) 'A European version of the Appropriateness Evaluation Protocol.' *International Journal of Technology Assessment in Health Care 15*, 185–197.

Ovretveit, J. (1993) *Decision and conflict in teams in Coordinating Community Care*. Buckinghamshire: Open University Press.

Plsek, P. (1999) 'Quality Improvement methods in clinical medicine.' *Paediatrics 103* (Suppl. E) 203–214.

Plsek, P. and Wilson, T. (2001) 'Complexity, leadership and management in healthcare organizations.' *British Medical Journal 323*, 746–749.

Zimmerman, B., Lindberg, C. and Plsek, P. (1998) 'Tales of Complexity.' In *Edgeware: Insights from Complexity Science for Healthcare Leaders*. Irving, TX: VHA Inc.

Further reading

Hooper, A. and Potter, J. (2000) *Intelligent Leadership – Creating a Passion for Change*. Random House Business Books.

This book makes a bridge from complexity theory to the practical implementation of some of the leadership issues needed for complex change. There is emphasis on the human factors that make leadership a success.

Katzenbach, J.R. and Smith, D.R. (1996) *Wisdom of Teams*. London: McGraw Hill.
Katzenbach, J.R. and Smith, D.R. (1999) *The Discipline of Teams*. New York: John Wiley & Son.

These two books are complementary and provide and excellent background to team working. There are numerous exercises and examples to help build effective teams.

Nelson, E.C., Batalden, P. and Ryers, J.C. (eds) (1998) *Clinical Improvement Action Guide*. Joint Commission on Accreditation in Healthcare. Illinois.

A clear exposition of the PDSA cycle and benchmarking as well as other improvement techniques, with lots of examples and forms that could easily be adapted.

Ovretveit, J., Mathias, P. and Thompson, T. (eds) (1997) *Interprofessional Working for Health and Social Care*, London: Macmillan.

There are valuable chapters that more specifically address the health and social care issues about team construction and training.

Plsek, P.E. (1997) *Creativity, Innovation, and Quality.* ASQC Quality Press.

A very practical and entertaining book bristling with good ideas that can be easily used.

Senge, P. Kleiner, A., Roberts, C., Ross, R. and Smith, B. (1994) *The Fifth Discipline Fieldbook: Strategies and Tools for Building a Learning Organization.* New York: Doubleday.

All the Fifth Discipline books emphasize the importance of purpose-setting through shared values. This one gives useful practical examples and further reading.

Wheatley, M. (1999) *Leadership and the New Science: Discovering Order in a Chaotic World.* Berret-Koehler Publishers.

This book addresses leadership through the lens of complexity and emphasizes the styles of leadership propounded in 'Edgeware': letting go, developing the context, and fostering relationships. The book is a good read, and read anything else from Margaret Wheatley that you can.

Chapter 11

The New Professionals

New Ways of Working Together
for Integrated Care

Professionals profess. They profess to know better than others the nature of certain matters and to know better than their clients what ails them or their affairs.

Everett Hughes, Chicago School of Sociology

The ultimate sign of a serviced society is a professional saying 'I'm so pleased with what you've done'. The demise of citizenship is to respond 'Thank you'.

John McKnight, Professor of Urban Studies,
Northwestern University, USA

In this chapter we consider the role of the professional in complex adaptive systems and their relationships with the older person and with other professionals. The nature of the conflicts that have arisen through clinging to rigid professional boundaries and the damage to the interests of older people are discussed. The attributes needed in the new professionals who will work in integrated care systems are outlined.

Professionals traditionally stand apart. They stand apart from their clients and patients and they stand apart from those in other professions. They stand apart from the client because they are the 'experts' and are there to meet an actual or perceived need that they think the client cannot meet for themselves. The professional has the training that gives him the legitimacy to meet that need. The assumption is that the client has no knowledge or experience in the defined area of need. As a result, a dependency ensues. The client is dependent on the professional, and the professional dependent on the client to create the need for his professionalism. As in organizational systems, this creates an addictive behaviour between the two (see chapter 2, p.57). In many circumstances the professional even creates the need just by being there to provide a service. A carer accustomed to using their common sense may lose their confidence and self-determination once they have the experience of support from a social worker, for example, and become dependent on them for decision-making.

Professionals stand apart from each other in a variety of ways. They will wear different uniforms or instinctive clothing styles which define them as a group. They will frequently use a professional language and jargon that makes them sound different. The type and style of records each profession keeps is very different and for the most part not shared. Mostly they will not entrust their work to others without retaining direct supervisory control. Each profession has its own set of standards for training and accreditation. The legal status of the professions and their accountability in law is different. For example, social workers do not have the same protection of confidentiality in giving evidence as the medical profession. Professional political agendas, often driven by the need for power and control, reinforce the separateness of the professions even further.

There have often been good reasons why this has happened. The protection of the public has been at the heart of the legislation that delineates professional boundaries and standards. Along with this, technological developments have required increased need for expertise, making it impossible for the individual to practise outside his normal field. The philosophical and cultural differences between organizations are considerable and are epitomized by contrasting the medical and social models of care (see chapter 2, p.59 on systems and chapter 3, p.86 on implementation models).

Relationships with older people

Professional styles and attitudes that separate the client from the professional and put the older person in the subservient role will prevent a system of care from becoming truly integrated.

Professional styles and attitudes that separate the client from the professional and put the older person in the subservient role will prevent a system of care from becoming truly integrated. In this day and age many older people will not accept this role. They want to be fully informed and more involved in decision-making. Those older people who are unable to stand up for themselves will increasingly have advocates and family who will do so on their behalf. Failure to recognize this can cause an atmosphere of mistrust and confrontation, which makes interaction between client or patient and the professional more difficult and likely to fail. It also makes the risk of subsequent complaint higher, and this in turn encourages defensive behaviours to compound the problem – the 'vicious cycle'! What is more important is that the problems of the older person are not properly addressed and so become even more difficult to resolve as time goes by. Delays caused through the failure of professional systems mean the older person's condition deteriorates further and the cycle of waste and duplication is perpetuated.

Inter-professional relationships

With a divide already existing between the professional and the older person the provision of an integrated service becomes even less likely when the professions act separately. Even if professionals wish to practise in a true multidisciplinary manner they have many hurdles to overcome. Professional sensitivities are never far from the surface and defensive behaviours with low trust and poor communication will drive practitioners into professional corners.

There has been much in the past to suggest restrictive practices have taken place between professions (Kelly 1998). This inability to work truly together has been

In EPICS there were initial problems between the occupational therapists and the rest of the team over the urgent supply of aids to daily living such as walking aids, commodes, etc. The occupational therapists felt that by allowing the EPICS team both to assess and to provide equipment they would lose control. After some negotiation the EPICS co-ordinators were able to build up a small stock of aids that they could use independently.

After a period the occupational therapists were able to concentrate on those cases that were complex. Their continued association with EPICS gave them direct access to other parts of the service, such as to the EPICS reserved place in the day hospital and facilitated access to social services. The arrival of an EPICS co-ordinator who was herself an occupational therapist did a lot to promote trust, and further improve relationships between the occupational therapists and EPICS.

self-defeating for all concerned. It has caused much repeat work, for example in assessments, where each profession has insisted on following its own assessment process, not trusting that of the others (see chapter 4, p.100 on assessment). It has resulted in delays when each profession has undertaken work to suit their service demands in pace and time, and has failed to meet the real needs of the older person. When professions have not been truly synchronized the piecemeal service they provide has caused unnecessary 'hand-offs', where work is passed from one professional to another with an increased chance of error. As all know, poor communication between professionals is common.

Most professionals, given the opportunity to reflect on this, recognize the unsatisfactory service they are providing and the unnecessary stress this puts on the client or patient, not to mention the stress put upon both themselves as individuals and the professional relationships within which they work. Everybody is a loser in this situation.

In summary, if a truly integrated service is to be delivered, the 'silo' mentality of professionals resulting in defensive behaviours needs to change, as do personal and professional attitudes. This is not easy. Many professionals find it difficult to share and work together. They have often built personal and professional defences to protect themselves from being overwhelmed by the volume of work expected of them and the

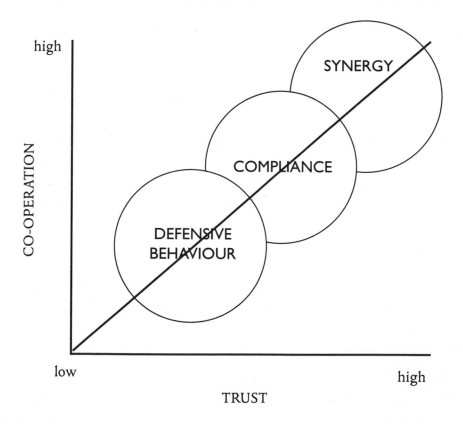

Figure 11.1 Levels of communication (Covey 1992)

potential threats of litigation from professional error. A complex adaptive system approach helps them to work with rather than against the tension.

Blurring the boundaries

Those professionals who find it the easiest to work across boundaries are usually mature, supportive people who are very aware of the social interaction between individuals and groups. They will communicate in a very open, truthful manner. They are often people with a lively curiosity who are keen to learn and experience new professional situations. They are aware of their own feelings and can handle them appropriately.

Such professionals rarely apportion blame and are capable of seeing the situation from the point of view of others. They are flexible, confident in their own abilities, aware of their limitations and, being keen to learn, are not afraid to ask for help. People with these skills and insights are usually self-motivated and have a high level of commitment to the project in hand. They are innovative and open to new ideas and have the optimism to face challenge when these ideas are implemented. Perhaps the greatest skill these complex but adaptive people have to offer is the ability to foster these skills in others, creating a generative environment. Needless to say, they will have the ability to make good and healthy professional relationships.

Once they are committed to the personal challenge to change, their further development will require sensitive facilitation. Often a peer acting as a role model can be helpful, and the availability of a secure environment will help ensure their further development and sustain their optimism. Of course, few people will have the whole range of these skills and aptitudes but one or two such people in each team can be catalytic to the success of an integrated care project. Their personal confidence gives the team stability and security because of their ability to live with uncertainty and with the minimum specifications that managing a complex adaptive system entails.

There has been increasing recognition that these emotional characteristics are what make for success in building relationships that facilitate good outcomes. Often the inability to manage personal emotional behaviour results in defensive behaviours in the individuals themselves and in those with whom they relate. The following domains of emotional behaviour have been recognized (Goleman 1998) as being key to self-understanding and professional expression:

- self-awareness – how you feel; why you feel that way
- self-regulation – how you manage yourself
- motivation – personal, emotional commitment
- empathy – connecting with other people
- social skills – making and sustaining productive relationships.

Customarily, the role of the professional has been to undertake the full range of tasks within their profession; if they have delegated, it has been to a another person within their own profession. With tight professional boundaries and the mechanistic approach of a linear, hierarchical system this appeared to be the best way to retain control. (See chapter 2, p.59 on systems.) However, following the convention that about 80 per cent of all activities are common and only 20 per cent are specialized, the greater part of their work could be done by another professional group with minimal further training.

> *Customarily, the role of the professional has been to undertake the full range of tasks within their profession; if they have delegated, it has been to a another person within their own profession.*

An example of this overlap of competencies arose in the EPICS project when one of the doctors' practices was planning to become a locality commissioner. In order to protect their budgets they decided that only clinically qualified staff could refer older people through EPICS for treatment and healthcare interventions. Until then, older people and their carers and families, social workers and housing wardens, were all able to access the EPICS resources. This change would have undermined one of the key values of EPICS – equal access for all. If the gate-keeping function were to be exercised by healthcare practitioners it would have meant inevitable delay in response. In order to provide evidence to defend the value of having a policy of open referral, it was decided to audit the referral patterns of the social workers to the EPICS system. It turned out that their referrals for healthcare interventions had been very clinically appropriate, in fact more so than those of the GPs, nurses and physiotherapists. The GPs could generally manage the clinical situation themselves through their own networks and their referrals to the system were for those problems they could not solve. These were mainly concerned with the social care of patients. The social workers referred those problems they could not manage which were the clinical or healthcare problems. But at the diagnostic levels of handicap and disability, the social workers were as competent at making a clinical assessment as the health professionals. It did not take a clinical qualification to identify when a client was having falls, or had a continence problem, for example. The social workers were also shown to be as competent at undertaking some assessments of daily living as the occupational therapists, and as competent at carrying out mini mental tests as the community psychiatric nurses.

There was also an attempt to evaluate whether there was any difference in outcome between a case referred by a client themselves (or their family), and one referred by the GPs. What emerged was that it was the assessment following referral that was important in affecting the outcome. The source of the referral had little relevance. With some initial difficulty, the GP practice managers were persuaded of the counter-intuitive nature of what they were proposing and that the delays caused by gate-keeping would in fact increase budget costs rather than contain them.

These simple audit exercises demonstrate the importance of evaluation and knowing what is happening in the system.

The roles of the new professionals

The new professionals will be working within a complex adaptive system. This will mean letting go of control in the traditional sense of total professional authority. Instead, they will work in groups that are self-organizing, needing to be flexible and responsive to rapid change in both their clients and the teams in which they work. They will move from a task-orientated work pattern to one of shared competencies, providing expert care themselves for more complex, less common and difficult situations. To enable this to happen the professional will have to develop different skills from those in which he will have been traditionally trained.

> *The new professionals will be working within a complex adaptive system. This will mean letting go of control in the traditional sense of total professional authority.*

The instigator and steward of procedures and standards

The majority of tasks will be shared within the professional domain. The new professionals will be responsible for deciding who within the teams will undertake which procedures and in what situation they are appropriately carried out. It is the new professional's responsibility to set the standards and see that they are met. This can only be done in an environment of trust and collaboration that engenders an openness and explicitness of practice. Central to this will be a shared or joint record-keeping system and the regular exchange and feedback of information.

The innovator of new techniques and professional change

The new professional will have his antennae out looking for new and best practice from elsewhere. He will be the one reading the expert journals in his speciality, going to speciality conferences and networking with other service and academic departments. He may undertake research and will certainly validate new practice within the area in which he works. He will take the lead in promoting change in professional practice and ensuring it dovetails with the processes of other professions. He will be all the time furthering his own learning and development.

The trainer and facilitator of practice

A physician when asked how he wished to be remembered answered: 'As a teacher – for my patients, my colleagues and my students.' So it must be for the new professional. He will be a trainer for his own profession enabling individuals to be more independent in their practice, and for other professions so that they can work more interdependently. As a facilitator he will encourage others to assume responsibility for working in areas new to them although within their competence. He will take pride in seeing others grow in professional skills and stature.

There are three groups of people not normally included in the context of professional teaching. They are the older person, their carers and volunteers. If they are all to be seen as integral and equal members of the team they too must develop new skills. Training older people requires a new approach from the professionals. They must see them as partners and be aware of the barriers to equal partnership created by the use of exclusive language and jargon. Experiential training methods may be new to older people accustomed to being 'taught', but the EPICS experience was that older people were avid learners and keen to acquire knowledge, new skills and competencies. (See chapter 8, p.209 on involving users and chapter 10, p.296 on levers and tools for integration.)

> *Training older people requires a new approach from the professionals.*

Many volunteers are themselves older people, or are carers or ex-carers with experience in helping others to manage the systems of care. Nevertheless, the EPICS volunteers appreciated further training and the acquisition of new skills, and this was an important factor in retaining their help.

The volunteers in EPICS were trained in a range of skills: to be discussion group leaders; to give presentations and talks; to run information desks; to produce publicity materials and displays; to carry out quality assurance interviews. They were given skills training in working on a phone link for socially isolated older people. This included listening skills, avoiding prescriptive advice, and the identification of those who needed help from the EPICS professionals. Those with a disability acted as trainers for the staff, for example in wheelchair handling or working with people with a hearing problem. They acquired basic computer skills by working in the EPICS office and gained the confidence to go on public training courses. They were included in training by the NHS Trust's IT department.

The older volunteers were more often able to see things from the older person's point of view and demonstrated intuitive skills in relationship building. Training with volunteers requires the professional to view them as equals. The new professional will value this as a two-way process of learning.

The evaluator

As in any complex system the feedback loops (see chapter 1, pp.54–5) are critical in sustaining the system's viability and adaptability to change. The new professional will have a key role in ensuring that the professional area for which he is responsible is properly monitored. Done in an open and explicit manner and involving everybody in a non- threatening way, evaluation can become a very powerful learning opportunity for all.

> Evaluation can become a very powerful learning opportunity for all.

The current information systems are mostly centralized to meet the needs of a hierarchical 'command-and-control' system and are not structured to provide data for evaluation to individuals. It is essential for the new professional working in a flexible and self-organizing way to have up-to-date information about organizational and personal performance shared openly with him if he is to be able to meet agreed targets and be self-monitoring of his own practice.

The supervisor

The style and nature of supervision is a potential area for confusion and conflict. It means different things to different people. Ordinarily the word means overseeing, or a responsible person inspecting the work of someone with less responsibility, but in the caring professions it has come to mean the process through which support, guidance and increasing insight are gained by all workers. 'Supervision is the process of reflecting on what you are doing with the help of another, in order to help you to do it better' (Atherton 1987, p.1). In a clinical setting supervision can mean directly observing and guiding practice. The health service culture is for practitioner autonomy. As a generality their work is not supervised on a case-by-case basis. Often the only time work is looked at is when something is going wrong. In a social work setting, supervision is the instrument through which individual practice and caseload is monitored, and professional development fostered.

This is an example from EPICS of what can go wrong:

A new manager with a strong social work background was appointed within EPICS to lead the team of co-ordinators, all of whom were general nurses. After some months the new manager suggested that she was going to institute 'supervision' for the team without really telling them what she intended to do. The co-ordinators in turn did not ask her she meant by 'supervision'. Clinical governance was still only a gleam in senior managers' eyes at this time.

The co-ordinators began to smoulder with the thought that a social worker would supervise them as nurses. They valued their professional autonomy and perceived that the manager's role was going to be too controlling and rigid and that their professional autonomy would be threatened. This was also their perception of social work supervision, whereas the manager felt she was going to provide managerial monitoring and supervision.

Inevitably this was very counter-productive for some months to good team functioning. This professional threat was very real to all concerned. Despite support and advice the issue was only resolved by the manager being promoted to another post elsewhere.

With hindsight this situation should not have even been allowed to start. If the situation had been anticipated, as it should have been, then the definition and the various types of supervision could have been explained to the whole team.

Supervision will strengthen team-working and enable more effective practice. It has four major outcomes:

- allows the professional to provide a better service to the older person

- provides a field for learning and professional development

- provides emotional support and the reduction of work-related stress

- ensures that goals and standards of the team and organization are being met.

But since multidisciplinary and multi-agency staff will come to it from very different perspectives, the processes of supervision need to be examined together and made explicit. The structural components need to be in place to facilitate complex working and relationships. They are important in making complex and sometimes uncertain processes robust. Supervision is a continuous process for the delivery of care. It may be part of other processes such as that for clinical governance or those which will be set up under the new General Council for Social Care, but is not the same. Nor is it the same as appraisal or assessment of the individual practitioner. Though they may all be linked, they are separate.

> *Since multidisciplinary and multi-agency staff will come to it from very different perspectives, the processes of supervision need to be examined together and made explicit.*

Team-working in complex adaptive systems

Accountability

Team members will need to know to whom they are accountable and how they are accountable if they are to work in a supportive environment that allows them to be creative and take a degree of risk. The traditional line management approach to accountability does not accord with practice in complex adaptive systems: supervision for the new professional will need added dimensions. It may be that the professional is *organizationally* accountable to the team leader who may come from another profession or organization, but *professionally* accountable to a superior from the same profession. Professionals are also accountable for their day-to-day work to the multidisciplinary team of which they are members.

Being accountable to a team gives the opportunity for complex interactions, but it does need structuring, which will rarely happen constructively by chance alone. Setting the ground rules for working together and sharing feedback in a team setting is a challenge that needs to be formally addressed by the team of new professionals. (See chapter 10 on levers and tools for integrated care.)

Delegation

> *Delegation becomes an essential skill for the new professional working in complex adaptive systems.*

Delegation becomes an essential skill for the new professional working in complex adaptive systems. It is at the core of networking with other practitioners. It brings together in one process many of the newer, non-traditional skills for working described above. The art of delegation is a truly creative process. It is not just telling someone else to do something and then just expecting them to do it – the 'command-and-control' model. This frequently results in a 'shifting the burden' archetype when the delegated task does not give the expected results. Or if an error occurs, blame is put on the delegatee with subsequent stress, bad feeling and cynicism between both parties that makes further attempts at delegation nigh impossible.

There is a sensitive balance between control and trust. Letting go of control lets people self-manage with more emphasis on assessed results than on how they were achieved. The trust has to be mutual: the person doing the delegation has to have confidence in the other to undertake the task, and the delegatee needs to have trust in the delegator. Both must agree the limits of the delegated action, and the feedback loops must be such that help can be asked for. There are several steps to delegating successfully, and much of the responsibility for success lies with the professional doing the delegating rather than with the one undertaking the delegated tasks.

The delegating professional must ask which of his or her current tasks would be better done by somebody else to improve the quality of service to the older person. Some questions to be asked are:

- If someone else provides the service will it reduce delay?

- If somebody else, already engaged in the care process, were empowered to carry out the next task in the sequence of care would this reduce a 'hand-off' and so lessen the chance of error in the transfer of care?

- Would it reduce the number of people the older person had to deal with?

The delegating professional will not feel 'unwanted' if they move into the new roles described above of being an innovator, teacher and evaluator and are allowed more time to undertake the more complex tasks appropriate to their skills and experience.

The task that might be delegated having been chosen, the person who could do this needs to be identified. For this to happen the flow of process of care needs exploring and understanding to know what should be done in what sequence and by whom. If care pathways already exist, these may be a starting point. Those undertaking a delegated task will need to develop a commitment to it and will need to understand fully the benefits to the older person, the team and themselves. Ideally, they should feel more fulfilled and excited by the prospect of an expansion of their role. In order not to overburden the delegatee, current tasks may need to be prioritized and some delegated to others within the overall system of care. Rationalizing the process in this manner should improve the quality of care for the older person.

- The identified professional's competence to undertake this new task needs to be assessed and if necessary, training given.

- The necessary support needs to be put in place for the professional before they start the new task. This will involve identifying a supervisor, allocating time and resources.

- The evaluation and feedback processes need to be explicit and shared with those to whom the professional is accountable.

HOW WILL THEY KNOW THEY ARE SUCCEEDING?

> *In a dynamic team which is regularly reviewing the processes of care, and has a shared commitment to improving the quality of care, delegation should be easily accomplished.*

In a dynamic team which is regularly reviewing the processes of care, and has a shared commitment to improving the quality of care, delegation should be easily accomplished. But true delegation does not come easily and needs persistence and practice. Doing it within professions has problems but these are multiplied across professional groups and (exponentially) across organizations. Nevertheless, the benefits in improving care are so real and cost-effective that it is worth all the effort put into it. The more boundaries that are crossed the more difficulties there are, but the greater the potential benefits. The temptation to achieve quick results and shortcut the implementation is a sure recipe for failure.

An example: The Community Falls Team

For two years the physiotherapy manager of the team had been frustrated by her inability to motivate people to work together more closely and share some of the tasks of assessing and rehabilitating older people who had fallen or were known to be at risk of falling. As a result she knew that assessments were being duplicated and that there were inherent delays in providing a service, during which time the patients had more unnecessary falls. Then, unexpectedly, two of her colleagues (one an occupational therapist and the other a chiropodist) approached her and independently suggested that their current way of working was inappropriate and not effective. They asked why they did not have joint working with rehabilitation assistants trained to be multi-skilled. Their joint commitment led to training programmes being set up to provide the rehabilitation assistants with a range of skills over time. Even so, there was a diversity in the range of skills each assistant already had, depending on the service background they came from and how many modules of training they had undertaken. The manager emphasizes that the training takes time. But now with the diversity of experience it is possible for the individual requirements of each older patient to be matched with the skills available. The delays and hand-offs have been considerably reduced.

Guidelines, protocols and care pathways (drawn up by the relevant professionals) gave the assistants confidence to act on their own and know their limitations. Each assistant has a supervisor who acts as a professional mentor, but they also have open access to the other expert professionals at any time if there is a need. A weekly meeting of the team to report on their caseload means they share expertise and learn from each other. It has also brought the expert professionals together in a more cohesive way as they develop shared guidelines and developing training programmes. This internal realignment has also made them focus on their external networks and how they and the assistants will work with professionals outside the falls team with staff in day hospitals, residential homes and the accident and emergency departments.

The added bonus was that morale improved for everybody, as did staff recruitment.

The 'new professional' manager

Over and above their role as leaders, managers will require new skills to manage in a complex environment. Traditionally, in healthcare particularly, the management task has been seen as administrative, ensuring that existing processes are sustained. This has not been conducive to change. This role will succeed in a mechanistic, predictable environment, but leaves managers de-skilled in a fast-changing, unpredictable environment that is driven by rapid advances in technology, information systems and consumerism. It is not surprising that many are so pressurized and stressed, perhaps more so than the practitioner for whom they are managing. They have diktats from above to deliver outcomes from systems that they and others do not understand. The practitioners make demands on them for more resources for systems of care that are patently wasteful. Pressure from their superiors to provide instant results for political and financial reasons forces them to adopt quick fixes that will backfire and make the situ-

> The new professional manager must be a systems thinker, understanding systems and their behaviours.

ation worse. Caught in this crossfire they will need new skills to survive. The new skills will make them the catalysts for change.

The new professional manager must be a systems thinker, understanding systems and their behaviours. The traditional administrative approach is a reductionist one of understanding by simplifying, but in reality the new professional is managing complexities in a complex environment and should understand them. Without this skill it will not be possible to grasp the current patterns of systems and see what intervention and behaviour changes can produce sustainable results.

The new manager will need to truly understand people and how and why they behave the way they do. On the one hand, people are the greatest force for change, and on the other, provide the greatest resistance to change. Enabling people to change their behaviour to achieve positive outcomes is the greatest challenge for the new managers. The skill lies in their ability to draw out an inner commitment from people rather than impose an external motivation. The new professional manager will have the socialization of the team as a responsibility. This means fostering the values of caring for each other. It will mean celebrating the good times and supporting those who are having a bad time.

Many of the professionals will have strict processes of continuous professional development and systems for practice governance. Managers who are not practitioners themselves do not have similar skills-oriented appraisal, and most of their assessments are done through management by objective with, in the health services, a performance-related award scheme attached. Though there are numerous courses for managers, evaluation of them as a method of learning and personal and organizational improvement has been disappointing. Managers will need to develop an inner need to want to learn the burgeoning science of management. The best learning takes place in a context of service delivery. Grabbing at the most recent management fad is

> The systems-skilled manager will appreciate that the spaces in the system provide the context in which to manage.

often the result of the need for a training quick fix. Managers need to own the training process of which they are part and not have it imposed. They will have an understanding of the training and in which way they will learn best.

Managers will need to be able to manage the spaces within their systems. This concept may seem odd to the traditional manager who is used to managing structures, resources and budgets – things that are on the whole tangible. But if he is systems-aware, he will realize that the connectedness of the structures is as important as the structures themselves. The systems-skilled manager will appreciate that the spaces in the system provide the context in which to manage. Ensuring shared values (and from that a shared purpose) will enable a shared direction even if people are self-organizing. The new professional will actively manage the networking and communication systems between the parts, ensuring feedback of results and outcomes, and so build the feedback loops that are instrumental to an organization that is learning through experience and reflection. The manager will be a role model in bringing people and ideas together, putting people in touch with each other so that they can interact and self-generate new ideas and approaches to mutual problems.

New managers will be takers of measured risk that allows for experimentation and innovation. In this environment they will be supportive if, in good faith, the experiment fails but lessons are learnt for ultimate success.

The new manager will not wish to be isolated from the older person who is the client but will encourage direct contact both formally and informally. So often, the only contact for the traditional manger is when things go wrong and there are complaints. In the spirit of a person-centred service the new manager will have real 'hands-on' experience of older people beyond that of formal groups and meetings. The new manager will foster diversity within their area of responsibility. Uniformity is the hallmark of a machine-like state, whereas diversity is that of the organic system. (See chapter 2, p.59 on systems and chapter 10, p.282 on levers and tools.)

Overview

As Mark Twain said, 'It is those damned humans again'. It is the humans involved that create both the problems and the solutions. They are themselves complex systems, and the manager and practitioner who does not take account of this does so at their professional peril. Navigating within complex systems will need a range of skills not traditionally taught or intuitively acquired. They are about a new relationship with the older person – a relationship that generates mutual co-operation and mutual responsibilities through mutual trust. In this relationship the older person and the practitioner learn from each other. This is not so radical that many of the professionals most admired do not do it already. But for some it is a difficult transition from letting go of control and command to a freer generative relation-

> *The new skills will enable the new professionals to redesign the relationships they have with older people and the relationships they have with each other.*

ship. Those people who do find it difficult but who are willing to try will need support and encouragement as they learn.

The same principles will apply for the professionals working together. The new skills will enable the new professionals to redesign the relationships they have with older people and the relationships they have with each other. They will reinforce the ability to put themselves in the other person's shoes and understand the problem from their viewpoint.

Chapter 11 – Headline points

- Professional styles and attitudes that separate the client from the professional and put the older person in the subservient role will prevent a system of care from becoming truly integrated.

- Customarily, the role of the professional has been to undertake the full range of tasks within their profession; if they have delegated, it has been to another person within their own profession.

- The new professionals will be working within a complex adaptive system. This will mean letting go of control in the traditional sense of total professional authority.

- Training older people requires a new approach from the professionals.

- Done in an open and explicit manner and involving everybody in a non-threatening way, evaluation can become a very powerful learning opportunity for all.

- Since multidisciplinary and multi-agency staff will come to it from very different perspectives the processes of supervision need to be examined together and made explicit.

- Delegation becomes an essential skill for the new professional working in complex adaptive systems.

- In a dynamic team which is regularly reviewing the processes of care, and has a shared commitment to improving the quality of care, delegation should be easily accomplished.

- The new professional manager must be a systems thinker, understanding systems and their behaviours.

- Managers will need to be able to manage the spaces within their systems.

- The new skills will enable the new professionals to redesign the relationships they have with older people and the relationships they have with each other.

References

Atherton, J. (1987) Workbook on Professional Supervision in Group Care (Unpublished) Bedford: Bedford H.E. College.

Covey, S.R. (1992) *The Seven Habits of Highly Effective People.* London: Simon and Schuster.

Goleman, D. (1998) *Working with Emotional Intelligence.* London: Bloomsbury Press.

Kelly, A. (1998) 'Concepts of professionals and professionalism.' In A. Symonds and A. Kelly (eds) *The Social Construction of Care.* London: Macmillan.

Ovretveit, J. (1997) 'How to describe interprofessional working.' In J. Ovretveit, P. Mathias and T. Thompson (eds) *Interprofessional Working for Health and Social Care.* London: Macmillian.

Further reading

Goleman, D. (1996) *Emotional Intelligence.* London: Bloomsbury Press.

Goleman, D. (1998) *Working with Emotional Intelligence.* London: Bloomsbury Press.

Both these books relate the importance of how the emotional skills of those working in organizations leads to success or failure. Emotional Intelligence *describes some of the science in a readable form, and the second book its application in the workplace.*

Illich, I., Zola, I.K., McKnight, J., Caplan, J. and Shaiken, H. (1987) *Disabling Professions.* London: Marion Boyars Publishers.

This short book takes a sharp look at all the professions and their relationships to the public. It is still quite disturbing in its truth and accuracy despite being written 30 years ago. Every professional should read it.

Chapter 12

Changing Places

The Way Ahead for the Care of Older People

If an organization is perfectly determined it has no choice but to accept the overriding institutional norms on the assumption they are immutable: such an organization is paralysed, has no choice, can make no decisions and the structure, once set, remains in place.

Richard Butler, Reader in Organizational
Analysis, University of Bradford

In this chapter we review the concepts of structures and distinguish between their hard physical and their softer process attributes. The suggestion is that viewing the systems as processes will free thinking to create innovative ways of doing things. The chapter looks at hospital-based and community-based processes that relate to health and social care and suggests some alternative approaches. The ultimate basis for providing integrated care for older people is the community model, which integrates the micro-community of the older person, the community of care and community of practice, all of which lie within the community of living.

Structures and organizations are important to everybody. People think in terms of structures and organizations. The more mechanistic the thinking, the more likely those structures and organizations are to have a definite, physical form that can be seen and touched. These physical elements (buildings, people, equipment) then assume the role of being the banner for the values and purpose for which they were intended. Over time the physical structure assumes an increasing importance in its own right and the values and purpose become blurred and difficult to recall. The hospital that becomes the health temple or the church that relies on its fabric for its faith are examples. It may or may not be surprising how few hospitals have a clear, well-understood clinical strategy other than some vague aspirations, and then have an implicit purpose imposed on them by others over which they have no control. All of this is embedded, symbolically, in the nature of the physical structure. Any attempt to change the character and substance of that structure is met with indignation by the local community as a threat to the subsumed values it represents. This makes change difficult when everything is literally cast in stone.

People think in terms of structures and organizations. The more mechanistic the thinking the more likely those structures and organizations are to have a definite, physical form that can be seen and touched.

Humans are structures as well. The recent publicity for a return to the old-fashioned matron, a human structure embodying all that is felt to be good about nursing, is another example of such structural and mechanistic thinking. The mists of time have blurred the image of the command-and-control icon of years ago. People have not thought through what image the rest of the nursing profession must have if all that is good is to be embodied in one figure. Will this make the rest of the profession 'bad' or 'not so good' in some way? The perceived need to return to this mechanistic way has been the failure of the evaluation systems for managing the ward environment. (See chapter 9, p.225 on evaluation.)

Structures are more than this. The definition of a structure, in organizational terms, is an enduring set of decision rules provided by an organization.

But structures are more than this. The definition of a structure, in organizational terms, is an enduring set of decision rules provided by an organization (Butler 1991). This more cryptic meaning of structure widens the whole context of what is a structure. Now things such as strategies, guidelines, care pathways, assessment processes and training programmes all come within the definition of a structure. Not just buildings, people or equipment. But because these cannot be seen or touched and they appear more fluid, there is an inherent component of uncertainty and ambiguity. For those who are more comfortable thinking in a mechanistic way this can be difficult, and even for the complexity thinker it can be challenging on occasion. Perhaps 'managing by reports' is an unconscious, archetypal behaviour reverted to as a way of handling this difficulty. The ideas and rules are entombed in the physical paper that provides the physical structure which people find easier to manage. The production of a report implies that something has been achieved with those ideas.

Nevertheless, encouraging the use of this wider definition of a structure could be the key to unlocking the problem of crossing the physical boundaries that constrain the development of innovative structures. If structures were a set of decision rules that drove a process, then they need not be dependent on any one physical building or person to give them an identity.

For example, if rehabilitation is merely viewed structurally as the rehabilitation ward and its staff, it is those physical components that give it its identity. This thinking means that when the service is expanded or changed similar structures are built or existing ones enlarged in the same mould. If, however, rehabilitation is seen as a set of decision-making processes and principles with guidelines, protocols, assessment tools and the skills and competencies required to undertake it, it is not so dependent on the physical assets of the ward for its identity. Now the question of where it is best undertaken is possible because this new definition does not contain the physical constraint of it only being on a ward and in a hospital. Choice is now available. It may be that it is best done in a ward, but it may also be done in the person's home or a residential home or a leisure centre, wherever is appropriate. Given this freedom the decision choice is made from creating values, finding the evidence, validating clinical practice, assessing feasibility and then choosing the options where rehabilitation may best be done. Viewing it only as a physical structure just means employing an architect and builder to replicate it in much the same form that already exists. And the all-important need to review all the care processes is never even addressed.

This example is relatively simple but, when the service involves several organizations, numerous structures and lots of boundaries, then it becomes considerably more complex. And that is when it can only be managed by complex adaptive thinking.

When this 'new view' of structures (being more than simply the sum of their physical parts) is applied to elements in the overall care of older people, all sorts of problems can be addressed, and solved in new ways.

Problems in the acute hospital

The current problems that acute hospitals face could be categorized into the following areas:

- referral
- admission
- inpatient care.

Problems in the referral process

What can be done to help the referrers, mainly GPs, to assist in the triage process before the patient arrives in the accident and emergency department? Any prior assessment information that is available can only help.

At the time of the referral, GPs usually want to know the assessment and treatment options available for the patient on that day. Some patients are sent to hospital because that information is not accessible; the GPs then have no option but to send them to hospital as emergencies because the hospital is only geared to managing unplanned work through the emergency system. In South Buckinghamshire a helpline for GPs was provided. The telephone was manned by a patient manager, who had a secretarial background. This manager managed the beds, the outpatient service, admissions to day hospital and the domiciliary consultation service. She was able to tell the GP all the options for care available. Sometimes the GP would be prepared to wait for a day or so for a bed if the patient's condition was not too acute. The patient would be managed by the GP at home in their own bed, and so was saved a prolonged wait in the admissions unit until a bed became available. Sometimes an urgent day hospital assessment or outpatient visit was all that was required. If keeping the patient at home was a realistic option, then a domiciliary consultation was appropriate. If the GP required clinical advice, then the patient manager always had a senior geriatrician available to speak to the GP.

The experience was that, given this information, GPs made good triage decisions. Working with GPs in this way the patient manager could resolve most of their requirements herself and there were only two or three calls per day that were sent through to the on-call geriatrician. The GP still remained in charge and always had the option of insisting on admission if thought necessary. This advice and information service prevented the 'shifting the burden' archetype that is unavoidable under many of the current situations where the GP is not enabled to remain in control.

When this hospital-based system was linked with the EPICS co-ordinator and the community-based triage system, it became a very powerful tool for triaging older patients and reduced some of the demand on the hospital admissions system.

Problems in the admission process

Many of the present systems of admission are perfectly designed to funnel patients through a single entry point (the accident and emergency department) if their needs are unplanned. Hence the long trolley waits so frequently reported in the media. Wherever funnelling occurs, queuing is inevitable if the capacity does not exactly meet the demand. As in a funnel, only a very small additional flow rate results in overflow and queuing. The three options to address this are to turn down the tap of demand, to improve the throughput by providing more facilities or additional funnels, or a combination of both.

REDUCING THE DEMAND

Almost certainly demand only needs to be reduced by 15–20 per cent to make systems that have queuing problems flow better (Bagust, Place and Posnett 1999). This should not be an exercise to stop older people who need to come to hospital from being seen. Nor should it be used as a route to be discriminatory. It is a challenge to provide viable alternative options of care to meet everybody's assessed needs. Demand reduction is a complex process that requires the whole panoply of preventive and chronic disease management as well as the referral system changes described above.

ALTERNATIVE TRIAGE AND DIFFERENT ADMISSION SITES

Part of the problem with the system is that the 'funnel is not the right type for the flow'. Accident and emergency departments are not specifically designed to meet the complex needs of older people. And if nobody knows how best to handle them waiting will be inevitable. The option is either to change the services by putting in a multidisciplinary team (including a social worker with knowledge of community-based services) or to provide alternative triage and admission facilities in a geriatric assessment unit. There are examples of day resource units based on acute hospital sites that are very skilfully managing the triage and admission processes in parallel and in association with other hospital services (Vaughan and Lathlean 1999a).

COMBINATION OF BOTH CAPACITY AND DEMAND

In practice, making small changes in managing both the capacity and the demand is a more realistic approach than just containing demand or expanding capacity singly. Doing a bit of both controls the reinforcing loop of increasing demand, and the balancing loop of constraining capacity.

Problems in inpatient care for older people

It is generally recognized that hospital is not necessarily a safe place for older people and that their needs are frequently not met. Much needs to be done to improve hospital care for older people. Recent years have seen specialist wards for older people reduce in numbers or disappear altogether. The trend has been to treat all older people in the integrated model on general wards. Older people are a heterogeneous group with a wide range of different needs. For many, the benefit of being treated on specialist surgical, orthopaedic, cardiac or gastro-enterology wards far outweighs the potential risks. But for those frail elderly with multiple and complex needs the situation is different. They are probably better treated on wards with dedicated, specially trained staff. These wards have been shown to provide better care with overall reduced lengths of stay (Landefeld *et al.* 1995).

The quandary is how to provide a service to meet the needs of all older people who are in hospital and what the nature of the hospital geriatric service is to be. It is not possible for all older people in hospital to be under the care of the geriatric services with their present resources.

REDESIGNING INPATIENT CARE

There is no doubt that well-planned and targeted hospital geriatric services are more effective in meeting older people's needs. What has been shown to be most effective is the delivery of a whole-system model of care that includes the following components:

- a comprehensive assessment

- the delivery of care to meet the needs identified from the assessment by a specialist older persons' care team, ideally by the team who performed the assessment

- ongoing review and care in the community by committed and specialist multidisciplinary services from all the statutory agencies and community services.

Any one of these alone is unlikely to have any significant impact on improving services for older people. To achieve a whole-systems approach in a hospital setting, a network and web of older people's services might prove to be the preferred model. The specialist team and the ward where the patient is being cared for are central to this, providing outreach and cross-specialty working across the hospital, and at the same time encouraging other specialty groups to network into them.

To underpin this strategy the hospital will require:

- An assessment and screening programme of older people across the whole hospital that is also part of a community-wide assessment process. The screening is to identify at the earliest opportunity those who would particularly benefit from specialist older people's services. The assessment is also crucial to the early planning of discharge arrangements.

- Nominated link workers in all the specialties to link with the elderly care teams. This is in addition to the elderly care team linking directly to other disciplines such as orthopaedics, surgery and general medicine, as often happens now. Combining these link workers into a wider-based older people's team will make them considerably more committed and effective. The inclusion of specialist geriatric nurses based in the hospital in the link teams has been catalytic in some hospitals to improving the networks. Many hospitals already have linked social workers who have more than proved their worth. In some places links have also been extended to other members of the community social teams.

- Local psychiatric departments. These are sometimes forgotten in this link process as they are often on a different hospital site. Without their assistance many of the mental health needs of the older people in hospital are ignored. Cross-specialty training of specialist registrars and ward nurses has been a practical way of fostering understanding and developing shared skills.

- Hospital-based training programmes for elderly care. All the link workers and the specialist team could contribute to these, so the whole system is learning. This will further cement the team together.

- A hospital-based evaluation system specifically for elderly care. This will help keep a check on the ongoing situation of the whole hospital and how it can be improved. The overview of this ought to rest with the specialist team and its managers.

The National Service Framework rightly stresses the importance of ensuring a positive experience as well as dignity and privacy across hospital services for older people (Department of Health 2001). However, these outcomes will only occur if the right services are delivered by the right people to the right older person. They cannot be prescribed like a tablet. If they are not being delivered, it is because other systems are not in place and an integrated service across the hospital is not provided. Staffing levels have to be adequate; ward and hospital environments must be appropriate. But these elements alone are not sufficient. The professional pride and self-esteem that staff require (particularly if recruitment is a priority) will only come when they see that they are doing a good job.

The way forward is to integrate the services for older people across the whole hospital, connecting it to the community and social care systems. Once again it cannot be over-emphasised that this does not happen by chance. It requires leadership and vision.

Alternative sites for unplanned care

If other options do not exist for the 20 per cent or so of elderly people who do not require admission to an acute hospital but do need medical care, or if they do exist but referrers do not know how to access them, then this 20 per cent will still be inappropriately admitted to an acute ward. Among these alternatives Vaughan and Lathlean (1999b) include:

- Admissions to intermediate care beds in other hospitals (usually community hospitals) for such presenting conditions as urinary tract or mild chest infections that cannot be managed at home. A wider range of patients could be admitted if the staff acquire additional skills such as the administration of appropriate intravenous medication. Medical support and support from the specialist geriatric team is essential if high standards of care are to be maintained. Likewise, admissions to these alternative beds should not jeopardize access to investigations when they are necessary.

- Admissions to nursing homes for unplanned care. Many homes successfully look after their permanent residents who become unwell or deteriorate. On other occasions they will admit dependent patients for convalescence, rehabilitation or respite care.

- Managing older people in their own homes, provided the skills and resources can be brought to them. Many areas now have rapid-response teams who can first, triage these patients and then provide care support and rehabilitation for varying lengths of time. In EPICS this was rarely more than two weeks, in other schemes it may be up to six weeks.

The success of these alternatives to admission to an acute hospital does depend on the quality of the triage and assessment process both prior to and after admission. Most of these systems are very successfully nurse-led but the staff need the assurance of knowing that they have wholehearted medical support and back-up. The quality of care can only be maintained if there are enough staff skilled in older people's care. Also there have to be resources for assessment and rehabilitation together with links to community and social care to complete the discharge process.

The close links these alternatives have to the local community is their great strength. Most older people prefer to be treated in or near their local community, or at home. But this should not be viewed as an opportunity to provide them with low-quality care or as a cheap way to solve the expensive problem of the misuse of acute hospitals. Done less than well, it may actually worsen that problem by increasing readmissions. Also referrers may avoid the facility because of low standards and still send every case to the acute hospital.

Rehabilitation

Rehabilitation is the very essence of older people's care. It is an attitude of mind as much as anything; an attitude of belief that the situation of a handicapped, disabled or disadvantaged older person can always be improved. Because it is so important that the older person believes this too, this positive attitude must be nurtured in them if they do not already have it. This shared belief is the cornerstone of the rehabilitation partnership.

> *Rehabilitation is the very essence of older people's care. It is an attitude of mind as much as anything.*

Rehabilitation is more than the functional status of the patient: it involves their minds as well as their bodies. The *Oxford English Dictionary* includes 'restoring to a proper, former condition' as one of the definitions of rehabilitation. Taken in this wider context, rehabilitation will include:

- rehabilitating the older person

- rehabilitating the older person's environment

- rehabilitating their relatives and carers by providing respite as well as new and shared skills to cope and support

- rehabilitating the staff, in the sense of learning from the older person and the event.

Rehabilitation can take place after an acute illness or event (such as a stroke or a hip fracture); it also plays an important role in chronic disease management (such as arthritis). It takes place in a variety of settings from the acute hospital wards to specialist rehabilitation wards, community hospitals, the patient's own home, residential and nursing homes and in outpatient settings such as day hospitals. With imagination there are many other community settings in which it could take place. With imagination it is ubiquitous.

This multiplicity of delivery sites and the complex nature of the rehabilitation process sometimes make it difficult to see how all the possibilities and opportunities can be grasped. Intermediate care, both in the USA and the UK, has encouraged the development of alternative sites of care to the conventional rehabilitation settings. 'Step-down' facilities that provide some rehabilitation and re-enablement in residential homes instead of hospital-based settings are becoming more common (Younger-Ross and Lomax 1998). But what is becoming apparent is that the intensity of rehabilitation varies between sites. The result is that multiple levels of rehabilitative care are now available. If this is the case, how is it best to choose the right place for the individual older person to get the right care? Providing a framework for rehabilitation that recognizes the inevitability of these different levels of care might help.

The multiple-level model of rehabilitiation

A model of rehabilitation using multiple levels has been conceived following some of the work done by the Balance of Care team when they, too, were faced with advising on the distribution of both patients and resources in particular localities (see chapter 10, p.293). This model has three levels:

- convalescence

- generic rehabilitation

- specialist rehabilitation.

CONVALESCENCE

This apparently outdated concept was raised several times by older people's focus groups when they were approached for help in planning intermediate care services. They very clearly stated that this was so that they remained dependent for as short a time as possible and could start looking after themselves at the earliest opportunity.

It has also come back into vogue in official thinking. What the older people felt they needed was some space and time in which to regain full strength and ability after an acute event such as an operation or illness, especially as lengths of hospital stay were forever shortening, and particularly with the increasing amount of 'day surgery'. Convalescence is already made available for many older people. Ward managers will keep an older person in hospital for an extra few days, a daughter will take an elderly parent to her house for recuperation, or the older person will organize extra care at home for a time. The new definition of convalescence emerging was 're-habilitation that required no skilled professional input and facilitated the older person to regain full functional capability as soon as possible'.

> *Convalescence is 'alive and well' and there is a perceived need for it.*

This level of help could be provided in the older person's home (with short-term home care), in a relative's home or by means of a short stay in a residential home. It could also involve the help of a wide range of volunteers and community-based staff.

Convalescence is 'alive and well' and there is a perceived need for it, so structuring it and planning for it would cater for those patients who would otherwise receive it inappropriately in acute wards and rehabilitation settings.

GENERIC REHABILITATION

The older people at this level are defined as those for whom there is no major need to learn new functional skills to regain independence. They need to relearn or reinforce old skills through the help of skilled rehabilitation staff (usually generalists). Another major goal is frequently the regaining of confidence. This rehabilitation could then be planned for in 'step-down' and other intermediate care settings such as community hospitals, day hospitals, other community settings, or even in older people's own homes.

SPECIALIST REHABILITATION

This would be for older people needing to learn new skills that they would not previously have been expected to have, for instance following a stroke or an amputation. Many of these older people will have complex needs and sometimes multiple major pathology requiring regular supervision from a range of disease specialists usually found only on an acute hospital site. In this model, rehabilitation is undertaken by specialist staff, such as neuro-physiotherapists, and may embrace a wider range of available staff (psychologists, dieticians, technicians, etc.). The inherently unstable nature of these older people and their complex needs means that an acute hospital is normally the site of choice.

A similar hierarchical model has also been proposed elsewhere with three tiers of need and service (Bowman 1999). The levels in this alternative model are described as:

- recuperative
- restorative
- reconstructive.

They have very similar definitions to the levels of need identified by the Balance of Care team. However, a fourth level was added that described the necessity of rehabilitating the environment of the older person as well. This was called 'reconciliatory rehabilitation', recognizing that it overlaps all three of the other levels.

These two models help in stratifying both the needs of the older person and the delivery of a rehabilitation service, assisting planners of intermediate and other care services in deciding where it is best placed. There is obviously overlap and flexibility between the levels, and it is important not to shoehorn the older person into a particular level with too rigid criteria because of service needs rather than clinical or social need. The success of such a multilevel approach will depend upon a robust assessment process that also ensures that any underlying reversible medical conditions are not overlooked. But it does bring with it the potential advantage of considering a wider range of alternative sites for care delivery, also the involvement of more people than are usually associated with the rehabilitation process. This can include acute care teams, residential and nursing homes, day facilities, the person's own home and leisure facilities in the local community, for example.

The pace and environment of rehabilitation for older people may be critical to success.

The pace and environment of rehabilitation for older people may be critical to success. The provision of a range of settings in different environments and with different staff will better address the complexity of older people's rehabilitation needs.

Rehabilitating rehabilitation: A whole system within integrated care

The rehabilitation services should be viewed as a whole system within the overall system of integrated care. All rehabilitation will need to be connected across all the sites in which it takes place, irrespective of the agency within which they are based. What might be helpful in achieving this are:

- a district-based rehabilitation strategy, jointly owned by all the agencies, and linked into the other older people strategies

- a common assessment system that links to a single district-wide assessment scheme

- a broadly unified approach to therapy across sites and based on guidelines

- multi-skilling some of the generic rehabilitation staff and then ensuring the right skill mix appropriate to the patient's needs and the site

- a common evaluation process with agreed rehabilitation outcome measures

- joint multidisciplinary training across all sites

- a co-ordination and information system that can track individual people through the rehabilitation system and align their needs to the availability of the service, ideally linked to the wider information systems.

Long-term care

One of the legacies from the workhouse era has been the attitude and approach taken to long-term care; though there are signs it may change, much of that culture remains. More recently, long-term care has been viewed as long-term institutional care, either in residential or nursing homes. The assumption was that, once admitted, the older person stayed until they died, as occurred in the workhouse. Effectively this was long-term parking. Nursing homes do, for the most part, provide much kinder care in a more acceptable environment but this attitude still prevails. One of the secondary outcomes is that nursing homes are themselves isolated from the rest of the community and social care systems and, to a large part, from the rest of the healthcare system. There is often difficulty in getting primary care teams to be involved in anything other than opportunistic care. There is remarkably little input from the hospital elderly care team, and what there was decreased even further when hospital long-stay wards closed at the time that responsibility for long-term care was transferred to social services. In the same vein social service input to individual residents is withdrawn once the older person is admitted and settled.

Long-term care has been viewed as long-term institutional care.

The aphorism 'manage long-term care well and the rest of the care system will manage itself' has more than a little truth in it. Complex modelling (Millard and McClean 1994) suggests that one years occupancy of a long-term care bed has a value of about 30–40 acute care admissions to an acute ward (assuming the average length of stay in a long-term bed is two years and an acute bed is two weeks). The numbers for acute care admission will more than double if the length of stay drops to seven days.

Social care is not so easily compartmentalized, but it is highly likely that the impact of long-stay use on shorter-term community care will be of the same order as in healthcare. There is an enormous imperative to ensure that the best use is made of the long-term resources for the sake of the older person and the overall system. Increasing the number of long-term beds is not sufficient if the demand increases, because rehabilitation and preventive care is not available (Audit Commission 2000).

The secret is to provide the best-quality care management for the individual older person in long-term care. Because this is all a complex and adaptive system the emerging systems behaviour will be that there is less demand for long-term beds. More appropriate use of them will also improve access to those older people who do need them (Challis *et al.* 2000). Meta-analysis of complex assessments and rehabilitation shows that admissions to long-term care can be prevented or delayed.

Changing long-term care

THE CARE HOME

Earlier in this chapter, the significance of 'structure' was discussed; the question can be asked whether separating in people's minds the physical structures of long-term care from its processes and invisible structures would help in reframing the context and give a different perspective. If long-term care was no longer defined just as the care home but as the care provided, perhaps this would suggest possibilities for alternative sites for care (Kane 2000). As importantly, would this then also allow alternative ways of using the nursing home?

> Could the long-term system become its own 'staging post and waiting room' rather than the hospitals?

To some extent this is already happening as a few nursing homes provide respite care and various forms of intermediate care. But there is little doubt it could be expanded further. Could some nursing homes, as happened in some of the long-stay hospital wards before they closed, provide the space and skills to assess the needs of people who need long-term nursing care but are currently waiting for this in hospital? In other words, could the long-term system become its own 'staging post and waiting room' rather than the hospitals?

This presupposes a competent assessment process is in place to prevent existing or potential residents from being deprived of appropriate medical or rehabilitative care. This is to ensure that their capabilities for living in a less dependent way have not been overlooked. It is to be hoped that the wider common assessment process and the more readily available complex geriatric assessment will ensure this is less likely to happen. For the future, there are already some exciting projects that are linking these homes to hospital geriatric departments and other rehabilitation facilities. They use telemedicine links to prevent inappropriate admission from homes to hospital and to give some rehabilitation support to the home's nursing staff (Pallawala and Lun 2001).

Some care homes are developing outreach services to the community and providing day care as part of the package offered to people requiring long-term care but not full-time residence in the home. Since the 1930s and before, charitable foundations (such as the Licensed Victuallers homes in Buckinghamshire and the Great Hospital in Norwich) have offered a whole range of accommodation on the same site. Some of the more innovative private nursing homes in the UK and the USA are providing this range of services also. The residents would move through the system from independent living through supported living in bungalows to residential and nursing care according to their changing needs.

There are potential advantages and disadvantages to the older residents of these homes. The potential advantages include the improved skill of staff in assessing and making care plans and the possibility of an environment that is more enabling than the conventional home. If there is more support for staff, there may be a reduced likelihood of unnecessary admission to hospital for sub-acute illness. The disadvantages centre around the home not being a home. That is, it takes on an even greater medical function and loses the capability to provide focused, personalized care with dignity in a homely environment. The managers of such experiments will have to take care to balance the needs of all the residents, both short-term and long-term. The old geriatric ward environment of the past does not need reinventing.

If community care were to be a truly integrated part of long-term care, then a true partnership could be developed with the nursing homes, residential homes and sheltered housing to provide supported living in the community and the older person's own home.

COMMUNITY CARE

If community care were to be a truly integrated part of long-term care, then a true partnership could be developed with the nursing homes, residential homes and sheltered housing to provide supported living in the community and the older person's own home. In many parts of the UK, what spare capacity there is in the whole system lies in the sheltered housing stock; and there is an opportunity for creative use of this resource. For example, a local housing association invited EPICS to run a volunteer information centre and phone link from one facility and planned to bring therapists, a chiropodist and a local council officer as an advice worker for the whole local community. It was also planned to invite the Health Promotion Team to have a role. (An EPI-Centre in fact!)

The experience from EPICS was that use of the community rapid response teams was invaluable in maintaining people in these environments, especially if there were sudden and unexpected changes in their condition that did not require acute hospital care.

Innovative primary care

Nowhere will all these changes have a bigger impact than on the primary care teams. The traditional opportunistic approach to the care of individuals, which has served well in times past, will no longer be sufficient alone. Managing populations for the benefit of the individual and individuals as parts of a population is the tension and paradox that the primary care trusts will face. That population may be those on a waiting list for surgery or the residents of a nursing home or the case-load of a community nurse. How will a GP care-manage a patient list of approximately 2000 (the population for which he is responsible) of whom about 350 will be over 65 years old and about 70 of those will be frail elderly?

This will require innovative and creative solutions using complex adaptive systems thinking. Certainly the GP will not be able to do it alone, and there will be a need for sophisticated team-working with shared responsibility once more based on shared values and an agreed purpose (Iliffe, Patterson and Gould 1998). Under these circumstances can the patient list remain the province of the GP alone? Common record-keeping across the disciplines (tied to an information system that provides decision support and supports the knowledge base about the older person) will be critical to the success of any future developments.

Older people's participation in, and ownership of, these new schemes may be one of the bigger hurdles to jump. Some innovative schemes that do this already exist. They also harness the resources and skills of older people to help each other and the population overall. Some practices have practice participation groups and elderly volunteers who support their peers. Disease-specific support groups can provide mutual support and help. But there still remains much antipathy by many members of the primary care team to the older person who behaves other than the socially acceptable archetype of an independent (i.e. dependent!) older person.

The community

...all evidence indicates that the activities that have helped people most are those that have evolved out of a philosophy of self help, mutual support and communal solidarity.

David R. Buchanan, community health educator

As the EPICS project in South Buckinghamshire matured and rolled out to new areas the nature of its purpose subtly and significantly changed. The more that creative solutions were developed (both for individuals and populations of older people) the more the local communities were drawn into the care network. The churches supported the telephone links, the pubs provided emergency meals-on-wheels, local volunteers provided shopping and visiting services, pharmacists and shops provided specialist services for older people. The police became more involved with home security, and local industry and businesses provided a range of support to both older people and the EPICS project. The local newspapers reported the development of EPICS and were encouraged to print articles that were of interest to the older population specifically.

Growing into the community

None of this had been planned at the outset of the EPICS project. But, as more and more innovative solutions for individuals and groups of older people were created, the more the community was drawn into the project and came to underpin it. In practice there was often no choice to do otherwise because EPICS lacked the funds to undertake all these activities itself. But in the long run this proved to be the best way forward in any case: not only did it make the EPICS project more robust by integrating it into the community, but it also helped EPICS break out of both the eligibility-led social care model and the prescriptive healthcare model and move into the civic model. The concept that EPICS was caring for older people by supporting the community to be a place of spiritual, social and physical well-being became an overarching goal. The original goal of integrating the care services now sat within this higher purpose.

The diversity of the local population provided a challenge for integration. There were problems in understanding and recognizing the needs of the older people from the ethnic groups in the community. Treated as partners in the projects, they were willing participants in helping develop integrated services for their mini-communities. Volunteers recruited from the different groups, and bilingual health workers, social workers and development workers from the Carers Centre helped with the integration (see chapter 8, p.201 on involving the users).

These community developments had not been anticipated; with hindsight it was seen that they were emergent properties of the complex adaptive system of community care. The starting vision had been robust and sound enough to embrace change as the project progressed. It was tuned to the edge by its diversity and connectedness, and grew from the multiple and simultaneous actions of many people: a process that could only flourish in an atmosphere of openness and trust (see chapter 2, p.60 on systems).

The whole systems of communities

Understanding the complexity of relationships that the design of this new care demands is the key to enabling it. Not only is there a need to see the community as the overall context in which all this happens but also to understand that, like all systems, there are communities within communities. A family will be a community within the community of a street, the street will be a community within a locality and the locality within a district. The older person will always be part of one of these communities unless they really are totally isolated.

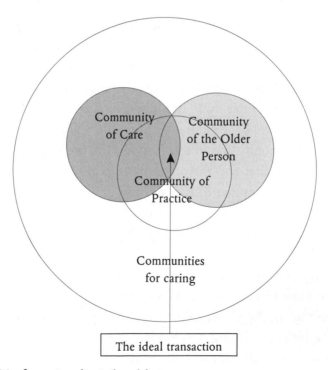

Figure 12.1 Communities for caring: the civil model

There are other communities as well. There are the communities of care that include all the voluntary organizations, good neighbours, churches and mosques, families and carers. Likewise, there are the communities of practice where the professional involved in care will be able to express the new relationships that will enhance working together. The professionals will only survive the complexity and the apparent ambiguity of the new systems if they are supportive of each other in a way that provides robust, interdependent working practices. The best teams care for each other.

Figure 12.1 depicts the relationships of communities to each other. At the centre, where they all overlap, is the point of synergy where the total power of community is released.

Overview

The care of older people is in need of total redesign if it is to meet both the goals of being truly person-centred and the challenges of an ever older and more informed population of older people. There is not a single piece of care provision that will not be affected by this. The traditional approach has been to develop and build the physical structures, then add the processes, and finally try to get the older person to fit the service. Breaking this mould will not be easy. But removing the physical structures, the buildings, the people and the equipment from our mental models and substituting the invisible structures (such as purposes, guidelines, and care pathways) opens up the opportunity to stimulate new patterns and relationships of care. The physical structures can then support rather than dictate how care is to be delivered.

Acute care has to find new ways of working with primary care and the community to rationalize the hospital referral and admission processes so that appropriate older people are not kept waiting for care or denied admission from waiting lists. Once in the hospital the care they are offered has to be designed and delivered to meet their needs, and be of high quality. Many of the current problems of acute hospital care are of the hospital's own making in that the clinicians and managers have 'perfectly designed' the systems to create these problems. (See chapter 2, p.51 on systems models.)

Long-term care must shake off the strait-jacket of just being institutional care in isolated settings. Long-term care involves everybody. The acute hospital helps by reducing disability and its involvement in chronic disease management. Primary and community care provide ongoing supervision in a variety of settings that include the person's own home, supported accommodation, residential and nursing homes. The social services will need flexible care management with ready access to complex assessments and support from clinical colleagues.

The community provides the backdrop for all this by defining the context of care through its social values and the commitment each has for the other. For any given older person the community and not the service agencies will dictate the quality of their lives and foster their strengths and aspirations. The community needs to be supported into a cohesive, caring structure and given some shape in the same way that acute and long-term care needs to become more flexible.

None of this can happen across all the parts without a shared purpose, leadership, shared assessment and evaluation systems and an information system that shares and passes on knowledge of each individual older person wherever they are in the system.

Chapter 12 – Headline points

- People think in terms of structures and organizations. The more mechanistic the thinking the more likely it is that those structures and organizations will have a definite, physical form that can be seen and touched.

- Structures are more than this, however. The definition of a structure, in organizational terms, is an enduring set of decision rules provided by an organization.

- Rehabilitation is the very essence of older people's care. It is an attitude of mind as much as anything.

- The pace and environment of rehabilitation for older people may be critical to success.

- Convalescence is 'alive and well', and there is a perceived need for it.

- Long-term care has been viewed as long-term institutional care.

- Could the long-term system become its own 'staging post and waiting room' rather than the hospitals?

- If community care were to be a truly integrated part of long-term care, then a true partnership could be developed with nursing homes, residential homes and sheltered housing to provide supported living in the community and the older person's own home.

References

Audit Commission (2000) *The Way to Go Home: Remedial and rehabilitation services for older people*. London: The Audit Commission.

Bagust, A., Place, M. and Posnett, J.W. (1999) 'Dynamics for bed use in accomodating emergency addmissions: A stochastic simulation model.' *British Medical Journal 319*, 7203, 155–158.

Bowman, C. (1999) 'Rehab for older people needs rehab.' *Health and Ageing*, November.

Butler, R. (1991) 'The institutional model of organisation' In *Designing Organisations*. London: Routledge.

Challis, D., Mozly, C., Sutcliffe, C., Bagley, H., Burns, A., Huxley, P. and Cordingley, L. (2000) Dependency of older people admitted to care homes.' *Age & Ageing 29*, 3, 255–260.

Department of Health (2001) *National Service Framework for Older People*. Standard 4 – General hospital care. London: Department of Health.

Kane, R.L. (2000) 'Changing the image of long-term care.' *Age & Ageing 29*, 6, 481–483.

Landefeld, C., Palmer, R., Kresevic, D., Fortinsky, R. and Kowal, J. (1995) 'A randomised trial of care in a hospital medical unit especially designed to improve the functional outcomes of acute ill older patients. *New England Journal of Medicine 332*, 1338–1344.

Millard, P.H. and McClean, S.L. (1994) *Modelling Hospital Resource Use: A different approach to the planning and control of healthcare systems*. London: Royal Society of Medicine Press.

Pallawala, P.M. and Lunn, K.C. (2001) EMR based telegeriatric system. *International Journal of Medical Informatics 61*, 2–3, 229–34.

Vaughan, B. and Lathlean, J. (1999a) *Intermediate care: Models in practice*. London: Kings Fund Publishing.

Vaughan, B. and Lathlean, J. (1999b) *Intermediate care: A directory of developments*. London: Kings Fund Publishing.

Younger-Ross, S. and Lomax, T. (1998) 'Outlands: five years on.' *Managing Community Care 6*, 1, 37–40.

Further reading

Audit Commission (1997) *The Coming of Age: Improving Care Services for Older People*. London: Audit Commission.

Audit Commission (2000) *The Way to Go Home: Rehabilitation and Remedial Services for Older People*. London: Audit Commission.

Both these important publications from the Audit Commission stress the value of a structured approach to older people's care. They emphasize the need for assessment and rehabilitation in providing better care for the older person to meet their wishes and in so doing prevent the unnecessary use of long-term care. They stress that this is also more cost-effective. The data they present shows the large variation in use of services and their availability across the UK.

Buchanan, D.R (2000) *An Ethic for Health Promotion: Rethinking the Sources of Human Well-being.* New York: Oxford University Press.

A philisophical reappraisal, based on evidence, of changing health promotiopn from a prescriptive approach to developing self-organizing civic communities to control their own health. Implicit throughout the book is the complex adaptive systems approach.

Calkins, E., Boult, C., Wagner, E.H. and Pacala, J.T. (eds) (1999) *New Ways to Care for Older People: Building Systems Based on Evidence.* New York: Springer Publishing Company.

As the title suggests there are numerous examples from the USA of new models of care. The problems and solutions appear very similar to those in the UK.

Iliffe, S., Patterson, L. and Gould, M.M. (1998) *Health Care for Older People: Practitioner Perspectives in a Changing Society.* London: BMJ Books.

Written from the perspective of primary care, this book centres on the primary care team approach and the changes required in primary care to meet the challenges of older people's care. It discusses community health and social services as well as screening and hospital discharge.

Kane, R.A., Kane, R.L. and Ladd, R.C. (1998) *The Heart of Long-term Care.* New York: Oxford University Press.

This comprehensive book examines the issues of long-term care in all its dimensions, including community care and chronic illness as well as institutional care. Again, the lessons from the USA are applicable in the UK.

Pietroni, P. and Pietroni, C. (eds) (1996) *Innovation in Community Care and Primary Health: The Marylebone Experiment.* London: Churchill Livingstone.

This very far-reaching experiment in providing care differently and involving people in a variety of ways can work. The authors include some alternative therapies in their approach. There are very good chapters on professional collaboration and training together with an excellent chapter on self-care and patient participation. This book is very inspiring and a must for all those interested in new ways of working and not just for primary care.

Vaughan, B. and Lathlean, J. (1999) *Intermediate Care Models in Practice.* London: Kings Fund Publishing.

This book from the Kings Fund gives a comprehensive list of models from throughout the UK There is some evaluation data included for most of them.

Chapter 13

Integrating Care at the End of Life

So little done, So much to do.

Cecil Rhodes – his last words

People who have to confront death directly –
for example, those with terminal illness or the very old –
do so with the added burden of so much denial around them.

Tom Kirkwood, Professor of Biological
Gerontology, University of Manchester

In this chapter we look at the end of life in the perspective of a continuum between life and death. We stress that the end of life can no longer continue to be ignored as one of the taboo issues of our modern society. Managing dying and the end of life well is the log that needs to be moved to help the log-jam of problems currently in the care systems.

To die well is to live well.

Two things are certain in life as we know it: birth and death. Birth marks the start and death, inevitably, the finish; as such they define life or at least the temporal part of it. If life is important, then these two events are fundamentally important. If this is the case, why is the end of life so ignored by most of us and swept aside as if it did not exist? The easy answer is to say that the materialistic values held by much of society have given an artificial sense of continuity, as if life is a machine that will continue for ever, and, if it should break down, can be repaired and continue.

> *The enormous achievements of medical science in the last 50 years have engendered the false expectation that everything is treatable and curable.*

Modern medicine has fostered this attitude further. The enormous achievements of medical science in the last 50 years have engendered the false expectation that everything is treatable and curable, and that life ought to be infinite.

Three major UK textbooks on general and elderly medicine refer only to palliative care for terminal cancer and make only passing reference to the care of those dying from other causes. The implication is almost that it is all right to die from cancer but nothing else. On closer inspection, there is specifically no mention of terminal care for the three other most common causes of death (heart, respiratory or cerebrovascular disease), fuelling the perception that death from these causes must be an error and a fault of the medical system. Basically, death is just a statistic in these books. If it is not being taught, perhaps it is not surprising that care of the dying has been ignored. Dying is still a taboo subject for most patients and professionals alike. Even the National Service Framework for Older People provides no specific standards for the end of life and dying. Nor is it mentioned in the action plans supporting the National Service Framework.

If death is viewed as a system fault beyond their control, the professions will tend to withdraw from the proper care of the dying, as some have already done. It is estimated that more than half of people who die do so in some form of distress and discomfort. This is usually actual pain, but could be shortness of breath and agitation as well. This situation will not improve if the professions ignore the needs of these patients and do not become actively involved again.

This is not to imply that dying need necessarily be medicalized, but clinicians do have an important role to play. Dying has been institutionalized: whereas the vast

> *Dying has been institutionalized.*

majority of people wish to die in their own homes if possible, most die in hospital or a nursing home. Some who are dying are even shuttled from institution to institution often to suit the needs of the institution rather than the needs of the person.

As a generalization, if death is not planned for, it will be treated as an emergency. The person dying passes through the accident and emergency department with its attendant trolley waits and delays in finding a bed. If the proximity of death is not recognized, the person's needs will not be met. Often life-sustaining therapies (some of which can be invasive and involve high technology) are instituted when the chances of any worthwhile outcome are very remote. This is mostly done in good faith, when the information to make a more informed decision is not available from elsewhere. The hustle and bustle of an acute ward rarely provides the right environment for a peaceful death.

The hospice movement has dramatically improved attitudes and the provision of care for those dying from cancer under their supervision. Some of these skills have rubbed off on to others, but in a very patchy manner. Unfortunately, many of the hospices are reliant on charitable funding to maintain their services and, because cancer is so emotive a subject, they have focused on that to maintain what limited income they get. Under these circumstances it is not surprising that, by and large, they have been unable to extend their services more generally.

Diagnosing dying

Most older people will die following a chronic illness that is known to be fatal. Their deaths will usually occur fairly quickly after a period of relative stability. Though it is expected that these patients are likely to die within six to twelve months, within that time they will have an uncertain and unpredictable prognosis. Only for a minority will the process be a very gradual decline to death. These people are usually the very frail, often demented patients, many of whom will be resident in long-term care. Consequently, death should not come as a surprise to most older people, their families or carers.

It is possible to provide fairly accurate estimates of length of life for hospitalized patients using relatively simple methods that should allow time for planning, communication and ascertaining patients' and carers' wishes. Even with acute patients it is possible to make some valid prediction of outcome. Unless it is appreciated that the patient is dying (and some broad prognostic decision made), death will come as a surprise, and it will not be possible to plan appropriately. This has to be the primary concern for the doctors involved, even if they have other roles in further care, such as managing the chronic diseases and the treatment of pain and other symptoms. This is a role in which some doctors find themselves to be professionally uncomfortable, and they may require some facilitation and help, especially during their training. This is a key step to reducing a significant part of the denial of dying.

There are considerable barriers to change in this new approach. There is the fear that in 'giving in to death' reversible conditions are overlooked, or the belief that even the remotest of chances of survival are worth the trade-off for the possibility of prolonged (although poor-quality) life. Sometimes the doctor will abdicate responsibility in decision-making and provide the care, appropriate or not, and await whatever results the lottery of chance will produce.

Life is precious and not to be wasted, but nor should the opportunity of a dignified and kindly death when acceptably and properly offered. The diagnosis of dying must be made carefully and confidently on good evidence. But if most people are dying from chronic disorders, then it should be possible to make the assessment in good time so that, if an emergency occurs, decision-making can be comparatively straightforward. The proviso has to be the availability of shared information (especially if it is not the usual care team involved). An ongoing common assessment process that is networked should be of considerable value in making these decisions.

Involving the patient

> *It is difficult to involve the patient or their carers if the possibility of dying has not been considered by the medical team itself.*

It is difficult to involve the patient or their carers if the possibility of dying has not been considered by the medical team itself. If recognition of the possibility is left until the patient is near to death, the element of surprise prevents any preparation, but if the possibility has been considered in advance it should be shared with the patient and their family. This requires skilled and sensitive communication. But with care it can, and should, be achieved. Without doubt, the vast majority of patients want to be kept in the picture and expect to be taken seriously. (See chapter 8 Appendix 8.3, p.220)

They will need reassurance about their treatment and that they will be kept comfortable and not be abandoned. Sometimes they need to know that they will not be given any unnecessary treatment. Patients rarely give up all hope of improvement in the underlying condition; balancing this against reality demands delicate handling.

Care planning

This will depend not only on the diagnosis and prognosis but on the patient's wishes, the availability of resources and the choices that can be offered.

Patient choices

The preference of the majority of patients is for treatment to be near their home and community. Also, they prefer to die in their own homes if possible. However, patients

> *The advance directive provides an opportunity for the doctor, usually the GP, to talk through some of the future issues and gain understanding of the patient's perspective and values.*

are realistic and most will want comfort and to be symptom-free if possible, and they will opt for hospital or hospice if that level of care cannot be given in the home.

An increasing number of patients will have made advance directives, or 'living wills', for their care. At the very least this indicates a wish by the patient that he or she wants to be involved in the decision-making around their death. To disregard the directive is to disregard the patient. Even when a directive has been made, it is frequently not available at a moment of crisis. Often any written wishes will be locked away in a safe place. It is important, therefore, that any common patient information system should log whether any end-of-life wishes exist and where they can be found. The advance directive provides an opportunity for the doctor, usually the GP, to talk through some of the future issues and gain understanding of the patient's perspective and values.

Availability of resources

For patients terminally ill with cancer there is an ever-increasing range of resources available for care (particularly in the community). But for the older patient dying from other causes the resources are sketchy at best. There is a large element of luck in what care is available. As a result, many patients are admitted to hospital even though this is not their wish. It is rare to find cohesive plans for care of the dying older person unless the cause is cancer. If they do exist they are mostly implicit in overall plans for the elderly.

There is undoubtedly a need for planning and implementing integrated services for the older person dying from whatever cause. This applies to all areas where older people are looked after and particularly to nursing homes in which the majority of residents will die.

A trained staff (experienced in care of the dying) is essential. They need the same degree of expertise as their palliative care colleagues. You do not need to have cancer to die in pain and distress.

Teamwork

The complex needs of the dying older person will require a wide range of skills. These will cross the hospital, primary care and community interfaces, and the team may be different from patient to patient. The teams (sometimes 'actual', sometimes 'virtual') can be co-ordinated by a care manager, often a nurse, and she will need to have easy access to medical and rehabilitation colleagues. The EPICS team frequently took on this role in the early stages of dying, particularly if the patient's condition deteriorated faster than expected. The community palliative care staff was viewed very much a part of the extended EPICS team, as well as the usual day and night community nursing services. The day hospital provided a useful and convenient place for chest aspirations and abdominal paracentesis as well as transfusions when appropriate.

Good teamwork (both in hospital and the community) results in shared decision-making and the building of consensus in what might otherwise prove to be contentious cross-disciplinary issues. A robust team will provide mutual moral and professional support for each other in making what may be difficult emotional decisions. The openness of this type of teamwork is a safeguard for everybody concerned; and all concerned will need to be involved in the process at one time or another.

> *The older person and their family are at the centre of the team, always present and carrying the biggest load. They should be able to direct and feel they are in charge.*

The older person and their family are at the centre of the team, always present and carrying the biggest load. They should be able to direct and feel they are in charge whenever possible.

The specialist cancer team or the chronic disease management team will be important in providing skilled care, especially for palliation of symptoms. The specialist nurses in those teams are frequently pivotal to the team's effectiveness, with their ability to work across hospital and community boundaries. The primary care team will be managing the person on a day-to-day basis and providing essential co-ordination. The community and voluntary bodies can provide valuable care and social support. Finally, the community (with its inputs from friends, neighbours and spiritual groups) will put the whole process in a perspective of living as well as dying.

Overview

Just as managing long-term care well supports the management of the rest of the system, so managing the end of life well can support the management of long-term care. This means that in the whole system of things much more priority has to be given to managing the end of life. Dying is not an excuse to avoid difficult decisions about priorities. It is something to do well in its own right. Nor can it ever be an easy way out of providing other sorts of care. In the same way that dying gives life added dimensions, so does the care of the dying give added dimensions to the care of the living. Dying is about living well.

It is imperative that the issues around dying should be brought out into the open for both public and professional debate. Individual and community values need to be set on how it is to be addressed.

End of life management is not simply about euthanasia (though euthanasia may be part of it). The euthanasia debate has muddied the waters of 'normal' dying and taken too much of the focus away from what will inevitably be part of everyone's life. Once the other issues of dying have been resolved, and its normality accepted, many of the issues surrounding euthanasia will resolve themselves. Euthanasia is sometimes the only way that people feel they can be in charge when all that is offered is the constricting and reclusive medical model.

It is the absence of a value system around dying that has created the vacuum being filled by the euthanasia debate. Because people's end-of-life needs are not being met, it is the extremes of dying such as euthanasia that are being substituted.

Managing the end of life is probably the greatest challenge raised in this book. A 'good death' will emerge when the right 'attractors' are in place.

The major issues to be debated and implemented are:

- involving the public and developing a value system around dying; educating them about what is possible with good end-of-life care and giving them some realistic expectations of the capability of modern medicine to perpetuate life

- providing ways of involving older people individually through informed decision-making and consent about the way they are cared for at the end of their lives

- providing training and education for all professionals about high-quality end-of-life care that addresses good symptom control, enhances dignity and supports the family both during the pre-bereavement period and after the death

- ensuring that all the people involved in caring for the dying older person have access to appropriate support

- improving communication between the older person and the professionals, particularly between patient and doctor

- creating the supporting systems that will integrate good end-of-life care into day-to-day practice.

Chapter 13 – Headline points

- The enormous achievements of medical science in the last 50 years have engendered the false expectation that everything is treatable and curable.

- Dying has been institutionalized.

- It is difficult to involve the patient or their carers if the possibility of dying has not been considered by the medical team itself.

- The advance directive does provide an opportunity for the doctor, usually the GP, to talk through some of the future issues and gain understanding of the patient's perspective and values.

- The older person and their family are at the centre of the team, always present and carrying the biggest load. They should be able to direct and feel they are in charge wherever possible.

Further Reading

Lynn, J., Shuster, J. and Kabcenell, A. (eds) (2000) *Improving Care for the End of Life: A Sourcebook for the Healthcare Managers and Clinicians.* New York: Oxford University Press

A very comprehensive approach for all those involved in caring for and supporting services for the dying.

Spiro, H.M., McCrea Curren, M. and Palmer Wandel, L. (eds) (1996) *Facing Death.* Newhaven: Yale University Press.

A very thoughtful and sensitive book with a variety of topics covered, including learning how to care for the dying. The chapter on caring for those who die in old age makes the book worth having in its own right, describing SUPPORT – a Study to Understand Prognoses and Preferences for Outcomes and Risks of Treatment for those who are seriously ill.

Epilogue

Remember Emily? Meet Winifred

One Monday morning in early February, during a meeting in the co-ordinator's office, the telephone rang. We could only hear half the conversation and could not fully see the computer screen that the co-ordinator was updating as she talked. Intrigued, we waited to hear the full story. Winifred was 85, living on her own and with a son 60 miles away. Over that weekend her arthritis had become much worse and she said she could barely move around her house. Monday was the day she usually shopped and her concern was that she had no food in the house. She wondered if anybody could help with her shopping, not being able to do it herself. Two telephone calls later the co-ordinator returned to the meeting, having asked a volunteer to go round and do the shopping and see if there was anything else that she could do at the time to help. The co-ordinator had also advised Winifred that she would call in just over an hour to do a new assessment. Additionally, she had also confirmed the availability of an EPICS day hospital place for the next day.

Following the assessment, the co-ordinator organized for the rapid response team to call to put in some early morning and bedtime care for four or five days. She rang the GP and briefly discussed the situation. He advised about some short-term pain-killers and agreed that he did not need to see Winifred that day but that he would see her at the day hospital the following day with the team present.

With her pain under better control and some physiotherapy to improve her mobility, Winifred quickly returned to being independent. The day hospital organized a routine review for a month later to confirm that she had not deteriorated and didn't need more therapy. The volunteer agreed to call weekly for six weeks. The social services were able to do their assessments and organized twice-weekly home care and 'meals-on-wheels'.

This is a straightforward and probably unremarkable story. But what might have happened if EPICS had not been there?

Winifred was a very independent woman. She had already refused to move nearer her son and rarely consulted her doctor, who she thought had better things to do than see her. Without EPICS, she would probably have waited until the next day to see if her arthritis had improved before calling her doctor (the only local person she knew to call for urgent help). He would have called that day and given a prescription that she would have had difficulty in getting and probably would not have started any treatment till the following day at the very earliest. He would have asked the nurse to call the following day, who, in turn, would have requested a social worker to call. But social workers are rarely able to visit to do their own assessment for two or three days. By Thursday, the fourth day of this 'incident', Winifred could have become even more stiff and had her first fall, perhaps barely managing to get up again. On Friday, tired and hungry, Winifred could have been found on the floor by her neighbour, having fallen three or four hours before.

The neighbour has been worried about Winifred for some time and concluded that she should be in a Home, something Winifred has vehemently resisted. By now Winifred is cold and completely lacking in confidence and is only too grateful when the neighbour calls the ambulance to take her to hospital. In the acute medical ward her mobility decreases further and, despite the best efforts of the rehabilitation team, they cannot mobilize her sufficiently to regain her confidence. Reluctantly she agrees to go into a nursing home.

Though the latter part of this story is supposition, this only needs to happen in a tenth of similar cases for it to be a human and systems disaster. It is a situation recognized commonly enough in hospital A&E departments.

What are the elements in Winifred's story that made the difference?

- Winifred was central to the whole process. She was able to put her own need first and activate the system herself (the easily read EPICS phone number on her phone saw to that). The system then responded by initiating appropriate care within the appropriate timescale.

- She was involved and informed at the outset of what would happen so she knew what to expect.

- The EPICs team had easy access to other parts of the system and quickly provided the co-ordination.

- There was trust between the GP, the day hospital, the volunteer and the EPICS team, and each valued and treated the others with mutual respect.

- The communication and information was integral to the success. Winifred knew the EPICS number and that they could help. The GP and the EPICS co-ordinator exchanged information, which in turn updated their own systems. The character of the networking relationships was paramount.

- Everybody's lives were made easier and better. Winifred stayed in her own home with confidence. and without pain. The GP could plan his work for the following day rather than having to respond to an unplanned emergency. The hard-pressed A&E department did not have to deal with an avoidable case. A valuable bed (with possible ensuing bed-blocking) was kept free for a more appropriate admission. The volunteer felt valued and safe within a supported system. And the EPICS co-ordinator (not frustrated by too many organizational constraints) felt fulfilled and satisfied with a job well done.

This was complexity at work, the simple rules in action. The outcome had not been specifically planned for. In fact it would not have been possible to have predicted Winifred's specific needs in advance. Yet those needs were met perfectly. It was an emergent outcome because the conditions, context and relationships for this kind of adaptive working were in place.

This is not to say that everything in the EPICS world was perfect. Tensions and paradoxes still arose. Many of these could be handled perfectly well within the existing systems. But new ones would always crop up, especially as the project grew and developed new subsystems. The key challenges remain:

- balancing the needs of the individual against those of the population for synergistic mutual benefit; this can only be managed through complex systems thinking

- creating systems that, on the one hand, are adaptive and free (without the old 'command-and-control' ethos) and, on the other hand, still satisfy the necessary bureaucratic and legal constraints that society imposes

- creating new systems for working that maintain the integrity and diversity of the individual, both the older person and those caring for them

- reconciling the tension between the older person having control and the fear of inflationary demands on the systems

- creating a new more positive and productive approach to ageing, one that makes it more dignified, more enjoyable (joyful even) for everybody whilst recognizing the realities of growing older.

'New care for old' can only be achieved by substituting new ways of thinking for old ways. Systems thinking has to be the key to unlock the door for a better future for older people.

EPICS – A Profile of an Elderly Persons Integrated Care System in South Buckinghamshire

EPICS was a jointly-owned 'virtual' organization which brought together health and social services, local authorities and the community and, above all, the older people and their carers into an integrated system of care. It was responsible to a Project Board with all the stakeholders represented at the level of senior management, including the local housing association and voluntary organizations. It was chaired by the Chief Executive of the South Buckinghamshire NHS Trust.

EPICS aim:

- to maintain people over 65 in the community by co-ordinating flexible, responsive packages of care according to assessed needs, placing particular emphasis on speed of response to prevent *inappropriate* admissions to hospital, and residential or nursing home care, and to prevent problems becoming crises.

EPICS mission:

- to ensure older people and their carers are at the heart of planning and delivery of services

- to ensure that all sections of the community, providers and commissioners of service, work co-operatively to provide the best support possible for older people and their carers.

EPICS direct provision:

- easily accessible information

- a single point of access 24 hours a day

- self-referral by older people and their families

- swift contact and multidisciplinary assessment

- mobilization of support co-ordinated across a range of services

- an in-house team of careworkers
- no referral forms
- no charge to user
- support by volunteers through a telephone link.

EPICS in Marlow: Operational since l994. Evaluated and costed in 1997. Extended to other areas in South Buckinghamshire in 1998. Now part of the Intermediate Care Programme which has been developed on the same principles.

The integrated system: The resources of the neighbourhood, the community, statutory health and social services, housing and voluntary services were viewed as the system supporting the older person and their carers. Preventive services such as the Falls Prevention Team, and chronic disease management were also part of the system.

The co-ordination: An EPICS co-ordinator carried out initial assessments and triggered multidisciplinary responses to the older person's need, networking all parts of the system.

The careworkers: Managed by the EPICS co-ordinator, could be mobilized within minutes. There was no charge to the user.

A client database: Held basic data on all the older people in the locality registered with the participating GP practices.

A resources database: Held detailed information on community and statutory services. Developed and managed by volunteers.

An intranet system: Modelled to connect GP practices and social services through EPICS to a continuously updated client database and directory of services. This is being incorporated into the Intermediate Care Programme and will include an assessment module.

Development funding: Provided initially through revenue released from the closure of a long-stay hospital ward and Joint Finance. Subsequent resources were allocated from Winter Funding and other government initiatives directed at reducing the numbers of people on the waiting list for hospital treatment.

Operational resources: Provided by the South Buckinghamshire NHS Trust.

An evaluation carried out in Marlow to assess the effectiveness of EPICS in saving hospital bed days suggested that for those patients appropriate for referal to EPICS the average length of stay was reduced by 10 days, representing a potential saving of about

£220,000 in a year. Following this, the Marlow EPICS was commended as a model of good practice in the Audit Commission's report *Coming of Age* in 1997.

Workshops on the integrated care model attracted practitioners and managers from the UK and from Sweden and the USA.

Volunteer support: Trained volunteers ran a Phone Link supported by a care manager from the local social services and the EPICS co-ordinator. The Phone Link provided a contact for older people isolated in the community and informal surveillance for older people at risk. Daily calls could be made whilst a carer was absent.

The local community was encouraged to become part of EPICS. Churches Together developed an Extended Phone Link for longer-term contact, with their volunteers supported professionally by the EPICS Co-ordinator.

Local councils worked in partnership on events and initiatives, such as a High Street Information Desk and older people's conferences.

Commercial sponsorship: The Phone Link costs, publicity, training facilities, conference facilities, printing and expertise were provided by the local business community.

Other Models of Integrated Care

The USA

On Lok, San Francisco

In the USA an integrated care project called On Lok was started in San Francisco.

On Lok is an independent, community-based acute and long-term care scheme designed to meet the total, multiple and interrelated needs of very old, frail and disabled people. It started in 1973 and primarily serves the Chinese community, though members come from several ethnic groups. Over the years there have been many changes and developments, but essentially the service provides both medical and social care, enabling members to continue to live at home rather than going into hospital, nursing home or residential care. Members are in fact generally very disabled or in poor health, and in order to be eligible to join On Lok have to be assessed as needing the level of care provided in a nursing home.

On Lok's focus is the Day Health Centre (a cross between a day hospital and day care centre), to which everyone goes as the mainstay of their care. This is also the base for the single transdisciplinary team (including doctors), though they also work in people's own homes. The team assesses the needs of individuals for housing, home care, day care, hospital provision and medical treatment, and then provides that care. There are seven centres, some of which have supported housing schemes attached. Typically, each provides care for 100 older people, with about 60 people attending each day.

Program of All-inclusive Care for the Elderly (PACE)

This programme provides the basis for a series of replication projects, numbering about 20 fully accredited schemes throughout the US, with many more in the pipeline. Apart from the integrated system of care, the key factor about On Lok and PACE is that they are funded through a capitated budget obtained by combining Medicare and Medicaid payments. From this capitated fund, the organization is responsible for providing all the healthcare needs of its members (including nursing home care and hospital treatments). Since 1997 these payments have been incorporated into mainstream funding providing a secure funding regime for integrated care (previously the payments were specially negotiated on a one-off basis). In UK terms this is the equivalent of combining social security payments and local authority and health authority budgets.

(Contact details for PACE: National PACE Association, c/o On Lok Inc., 1333 Bush Street, San Francisco, CA 94109.)

The UK

EPICS (Elderly Persons Integrated Care System) North Kensington – The Westway Centre

In the UK the On-Lok model was taken up and developed by Helen Hamlyn, wife of the publisher Paul Hamlyn, who had experienced the frustrations of trying to access a confused and fragmented network of services when trying to set up a coherent system of care for her elderly mother. She built a new multipurpose resource centre under the Westway Flyover in North Kensington, London.

The centre offers day care, clinics, restaurant and a multidisciplinary staff team, including nurse, social worker, therapists, consultants and care workers. Key features are:

- users are involved in the management of the centre

- activities include health promotion and health checks, reflexology, massage and beauty therapy

- the home care service is integrated with day care – the same staff provide both services

- the centre is used as a training site for multi-skilled workers.

The concept was rolled out to other developments under the generic name EPICS (Elderly Persons Integrated Care System) with a national Field Officer co-ordinating information and ideas.

Derby

EPICS centres are based in six residential care homes providing integrated care to older people in their locality. This includes:

- day care, respite and short-term care with enhanced nursing beds in the home

- multifunction treatment rooms and community facilities

- a core team of staff from all the agencies (including mental health teams and pharmacists) which meets weekly with all referrals from the catchment area channelled through the team

- telephone care link line and check calls.

The Glebe Field Project, Crich, Derbyshire

A new day care and community centre on the Glebe Field adjacent to the old vicarage in Crich was opened in September 1997. It was initiated by the local GP and draws on the EPICS framework and received support from Derby EPICS. The project provides day care, therapy and nursing services, meals, information and telephone link. It is a focal point for village activities and groups of all ages. The old vicarage provides respite care, and new high-support sheltered housing is close by.

(Information on the above EPICS projects provided by Richard Hollingbery, who was Director of the Helen Hamlyn Foundation during the formulation and development of EPICS. e-mail: richbery@aol.com Tel: 01730 2267 262. The collection of the main publications relating to EPICS together with details of the above projects are available in the library at the Centre for Policy on Ageing. Tel: 020 7253 1787.)

Warwick EPICS

The Warwick District EPICS was a one-year pilot project based on two housing schemes in Leamington Spa, Warwickshire. The objective was 'to develop a system which utilises existing community resources through the development of one access point (24 hours) for information about services' using the Warwick District Council's central alarm control monitoring system. The intention was to evaluate the importance of access to information in improving decision-making by older people and professionals. It was hoped that co-ordination of a response to the information request would lead to the identification of a more effective model of joint working, which could be transferred for use in different parts of the district and in other environments.

The programme involved enhancing the information held electronically on individual clients through the central control system and in order to gain the consent of the target users, all of them residents in the sheltered housing schemes, the EPICS Co-ordinator undertook to interview them all (100). The object was to gain their consent to being included on the database and to build up a profile of their needs and circumstances as a baseline for monitoring change. This was very time-consuming, and it was only in the last months of the pilot that the task of monitoring changes in the target group of residents was implemented. A list of trigger factors for monitoring change had been identified: death or serious illness of a resident; hospital admission; admission to residential or nursing care; or someone causing considerable concern.

The pilot project also took on the task of trying to generate a common assessment process across disciplines which could be included in the client database system.

Although the time limit on the project was extended the tasks were much greater and more complex than had been anticipated.

The experience of the project team reflected some of the problems encountered in the South Buckinghamshire development:

- Effective joint working is time-consuming and difficult, and goodwill is not enough.

- Breaking across professional boundaries is hard, professionals and service providers seem only to be concerned with their own input, as if operating in a vacuum.

- Incentives for participating agencies (the pay-offs) have to be sufficiently visible for them to give the project the priority it requires.

- An assessment of local need through a 'locality' or 'feasibility' study might have focused attention, identified the specific issues to be addressed and harnessed pressure for change.

- The value of getting to know the strategy policies for the agencies in the area is vital: it is unlikely that managers will find time for the tasks of the project unless the work required fits absolutely squarely within the principal priorities of their jobs.

- Working 'bottom-up' with the staff on the ground is valuable, but high-level leadership is essential for successful implementation.

- 'Selling' a project that has no structural identity and is difficult to quantify is not easy.

(Information on the Warwick EPICS has been drawn from the Evaluator's Report by Angela Nicholls (July 2000), commissioned by the Warwick District EPICS pilot scheme. Contact Brenda Watts. e-mail: bwatts@warwickdc.gov.uk)

Rapid Response Integrated Care Services (RRICS) – Bournewood Community and Mental Health Trust, North West Surrey.

This service arose following a survey of the experiences of 40 patients, plotting their journey through the care system. It was apparent that some had not required admission to an acute hospital and could have been managed at home or in another setting. For others, discharges had been delayed for a variety of reasons.

The service was brought together by amalgamating the 'home from hospital' teams and the community rehabilitation schemes. Their roles were extended to provide help in maintaining older people at home where appropriate. Referrals were made by the GPs and community nurses through a single point of contact. The team was based in the acute hospitals and provided direct support both for the A&E department and for the wards to help people return home and facilitate early discharges.

The aims of the service are to:

- provide a 'one-stop shop' and a single point of referral
- provide dedicated consultant medical support
- increase occupational therapy and physiotherapy support
- work with all the liaison services
- link with the discharge co-ordinators, especially in the community hospital.

The team is led by the co-ordinator, who is a nurse, and has therapists, social worker and rapid response support workers all attached. The team has access to day hospital places and to consultants via emergency clinic slots.

The team links to the falls team and the community stroke services. A significant minority of patients are referred by the RRICS team for admission either to the acute hospital or a community hospital. When this occurs the team will support the ward-based staff to assess and help in the discharge when this occurs.

Immediate plans for the future are to develop a network of such services across North West Surrey based on the primary care trusts involving local communities. The aim is for the service to be linked by the electronic health record that is being developed in North West Surrey.

Evaluation

The evaluation takes several forms:

- monitoring of referrals by source and outcome
- monitoring of length of involvement by the team
- number of people maintained at home
- patient satisfaction questionnaires done independently
- cost-effectiveness by relating performance to costs per intervention.

Integrated Care at Home – Surrey Hampshire Borders NHS Trust

Following an evaluated pilot of Rehabilitation at Home in 1995 several other similar projects were set up in the trust. These projects were funded opportunistically using short-term funds from 'Winter Pressure' monies and were discontinued when funding stopped. However, a whole-systems approach was adopted when the rationalization of the community hospitals was proposed in the trust area.

The strategy

- The concept was to support acute, primary and social care to provide a seamless service for patients as they passed through the system. The patients were adults of all ages. Partnerships were developed with primary care, social services, the Acute and Community Trusts, local authorities, voluntary and private agencies.

- Guidelines, standards and care pathways were set by the clinical leadership group.

- There was to be a single telephone number contact for all referrals.

- The target of the service was to provide 30 per cent of intermediate care in the home and the remainder in either hospital or social service beds by 2001.

- The service was to be provided by six geographically based, multidisciplinary teams who are able to support each other in times of need.

- The nurse member of the team is the co-ordinator who undertakes the initial referral and care plan, and organizes the review and management of the multidisciplinary support workers.

- Consultant geriatrician support is available within two days via the day hospital.

Services provided

- Crisis response to support GPs to maintain people at home in the event of moderately severe conditions such as infections or exacerbations of chronic conditions.

- A&E discharge support to enable people to return home directly following assessment and any therapy.

- Rehabilitation packages for up to six weeks, often following early discharge from hospital.

- Early orthopaedic discharge package to enable people to return home within 3–5 days post-surgery. This involves preoperative assessment and care planning.

Training

- A collaborative project between the University of Surrey, the European Institute of Health and Medical Sciences and the NHS Trust has developed an academic training for multidisciplinary healthcare support workers and is an access to other professional training. A practical skills training manual has been developed by trust therapy staff to underpin the academic training.

Evaluation

The whole service is supported by a dynamic evaluation process and evaluates:

- access, including ensuring no age discrimination

- efficiency through the number of bed days saved and the costing of each episode

- effectiveness through therapy outcome measures and other interventions

- patient experience, with questionnaires for satisafaction and the monitoring of complaints

- health outcomes, by monitoring place of discharge and how many remain at home.

Integrated Care for the Older Person in the North West Stockholm Region, Sweden

The pressures in the Swedish healthcare system are those that are mirrored elsewhere – an increasing number of frail elderly people, a reduction in the number of hospital beds and the increasing demands of technology. All this, together with continued expectations that the hospitals will provide the care, results in pressure to promote innovative alternatives.

Healthcare is delivered locally through the local government bodies that link healthcare, social care and the local communities. Though this has advantages in many ways, it has required persistence in persuading the lay politicians that alternative schemes were viable.

The philosophy behind the schemes starting in Stockholm is:

- 'See the human being behind the problem.' That is, see the problem from her point of view and in her context. Understand the older person.

- 'Local is optimal' – make the systems community-based.

- Do all that you can to make it easier for your fellow professional and carer to fulfil her tasks in the 'chain of care'. The chain is as strong as its weakest link.

- It may be great to handle a crisis well, but it is even better to have prevented it in the first place.

- Provide care through a one-stop rapid-response system that helps the older person, the carer and the professional.

The involvement of the older person in integrated care in Stockholm is along party political lines. The social democrats and the conservative and liberal parties all send older representatives, as do the retired civil servant groups. So far they have been very supportive of the changes. Integrated systems have started or are about to start in three regions, Jarfalla, Upplands Väsby and Solna. Not only are the health and social care systems involved but so are the churches and volunteers. Volunteers are not as common as in the UK. The ethos in Sweden tends to be to rely on the statutory organizations to provide care.

Assessment and information systems exist in all the areas of healthcare, but they provide only simple data relating to admissions and readmissions to hospital and nursing homes. All the agencies are computerized, but all have different software systems.

Evaluation

The evaluation systems are currently being set up, and will include:

- monitoring of resource usage, such as hospital admissions and length of stay

- monitoring primary care usage, such as numbers of visits to the primary care team

- monitoring of admissions to nursing homes

- satisfaction surveys amongst older people and their carers, professional carers, local organizations and local government.

Acknowledgements

This book has emerged from the complexity and diversity of the working relationships that we have had with a whole variety of people over the years.

The Buckinghamshire Health Authority, the Buckinghamshire Social Services and the South Buckinghamshire NHS Trust supported and made EPICS possible. Roy Darby, Chief Executive of the Trust, chaired the Project Board and gave us the freedom to use the EPICS material in this book. The Wycombe and Chiltern District Councils contributed wholeheartedly to making EPICS a success.

The voluntary organizations involved with EPICS are too numerous to mention in full, but Age Concern, the Society of St Vincent de Paul, Churches Together, The Priory Centre in Wycombe, The South Buckinghamshire Carers Centre, Crossroads, The Chiltern Volunteer Bureau and the Bourne End Volunteer Bureau played a significant part in shaping the integrated system.

The Doctors' House Surgery, Marlow; the Hawthornden Surgery, Bourne End; the Rectory Meadow Surgery, Amersham; the Riverside Surgery and the Wye Valley Surgery, High Wycombe; the New Surgery, and the Gladstone Road Surgery, Chesham all played a major role in developing the concepts of integrated care. GPs who were instrumental in making sure EPICS was grounded in good practice were Jonathan Reggler, Angela Bishop, John Hill and Michael Bowker.

Amongst social workers whose practice and insight helped the implementation of EPICS become a reality were, notably, Judith Burton, Deirdre O'Flynn, David Morgan, Wendy Price, Talat Siddiqui and Leslie Smaje.

John Moore of Newton Software, who was committed beyond the call of duty to the IT systems development, showed a sensitive understanding of the people and the EPICS ideals that was invaluable. David Lawrence helped with the early planning and epidemiology, and Dorothea Read was a highly valued sounding board and provided much wise counsel.

The EPICS volunteers, especially the team leaders, Alison Lewis and Joy Pearce, and the late Nessie Blair, between them made true integration with the community possible.

Gordon Lewis helped launch EPICS as project manager in 1994, and much of its success rests with him. Sue Palmer, as the first co-ordinator, and Catriona Gilmour-Hamilton, Sarah Lyle, Cathy Suggate, Katarina Podeski and Joan Richardson all contributed to the creative development and day-to-day running of the project. Carole Knight and the staff of both the Chesham and Marlow Community Hospitals contributed to EPICS with loyal dedication. Cathy Ayres and the staff of the Marlow Day Hospital were catalytic to changing the approach to urgent assessment and rehabilitation.

Local businesses, particularly Nycomed (Amersham International at the time) and Rank Xerox, were generous in their support.

Our own experience in EPICS has been much enriched by the example and support of friends from abroad. Rosalie and Bob Kane have been inspirational for many years and very generous with their hospitality, and Nick Morris, now in Australia, gave us confidence to believe that EPICS could have a universal application. In 1982 the visit by Chris Foote to the Multi-Campus Division of Geriatric Medicine UCLA was the spark that set EPICS in South Buckinghamshire alight. It has been rewarding for us to support Goran Selandar and his team from Stockholm in setting up their integrated care system. We learned much from them. Bruce Penney shared experiences of the integrated care developments in Christchurch, New Zealand.

We are indebted to the team of PACE in Denver and Chicago for their enthusiastic sharing and practical demonstration of the American model of integrated care for older people. Also Evelyn Tully from Les Petits Frères des Pauvres, for facilitating a workshop on integrated care in Lille, France.

The Simple Rules for older people's care described in the book were formulated at a workshop in Missenden Abbey in 1998 when 14 groups, all involved in integrated care, wrestled with systems complexity. We thank them for their hard work. The Simple Rules belong to them.

Ronnie Moynihan steered us through the early stages of systems thinking and generating a purpose. Without him our course would not have been set.

Paul Plsek changed our world with his approach to complex adaptive systems thinking. His dynamic teaching made it all seem easy. He has been a true friend to everybody in EPICS. We hope that we have reflected Paul's considerable contribution to healthcare in this country.

We are indebted to the work of Peter Senge and his group in the Massachusetts Institute of Technology, which has informed our thinking.

Thanks go to Joan Elliott, David Raw, Susan LaBrooy, Bryn Neale, Judith Burton, John Moore, Elizabeth Ash and Paul Plsek, all of whom have read either parts or the whole of the book and given their valuable advice and recommendations, most of which have been incorporated.

We have appreciated the encouragement and guidance from Jessica Kingsley Publishers, particularly the support of Amy Lankester-Owen.

Two people deserve our special thanks for their tolerance and support during the writing of this book. Neta Foote has not only shown understanding of a workaholic husband for many years but has herself contributed directly as a GP to EPICS and particularly in the development of the Lifeplan Project, for which she must take most credit. Rob Stanners, also a long-suffering spouse, helped considerably in the various processes of putting the text together – and made wonderful seafood pasta!

About the Authors

DR CHRISTOPHER FOOTE MBA, MBBs, FRCS (Lond.)
Consultant physician in general medicine with an interest in care of the elderly

Dr Chris Foote trained at St Mary's Hospital Paddington, in the Royal Air Force and at Oxford under the supervision of Dr Lionel Cosin and Dr Leo Wolner. He obtained his MBA, in healthcare management, at the Nuffield Institute, Leeds University, in 1993.

For the last 23 years he has worked in a busy district general hospital developing services under the continuous pressure of an enlarging elderly population without increased resources. He has realized that the conventional custodial concepts of care that originated from the workhouse and still underpin much of the practice in elderly care can no longer be made to work. He believes that a completely fresh approach will be necessary to enable older people to become equal partners in a community of healthy living opportunities.

He has been working for the last 15 years on developing integrated care systems that put the older person and their carer at the heart of the process.

This work has been commended by the Audit Commission and he has been co-operating in and facilitating similar models in both Sweden and New Zealand. He has networks with the Institute of Health Care Improvements in Boston, USA, and has run several workshops both locally and nationally in Britain. He has been a member of one of the working parties for the National Service Framework Group on elderly care, the report of which was published in March 2001. Amongst other roles, he has been the lead clinician for quality improvement in the then Oxford Regional Health Authority. He is currently embarking on a new career in consultancy to facilitate integrated care across a wider population base and is a menber of the Balance of Care Team.

CHRISTINE STANNERS MA, AIMSW
EPICS Project Manager (retired April 1999)

Christine Stanners qualified as a medical social worker and spent many years in practice in hospitals, notably working with the late Dr Marjory Warren, a pioneer of geriatric medicine in the UK. She also worked as a hospital social worker alongside Dr Christopher Foote in the Geriatric Unit at Amersham Hospital, now part of the South Buckinghamshire NHS Trust.

She found that the principles taught by Dr Warren to 'put the patient first' but to see them as part of the family system have been fundamental to all her work.

After a period spent as a community social worker and tutor and CSS study supervisor at Cassio College, Watford, she took an MA in Public and Social Administration specializing in the voluntary sector.

Always interested in working with older people, she became the first Director of a new Age Concern in the London Borough of Hillingdon. After five years she moved to Camden to become Development Director of a large Age Concern running day centres, counselling and advocacy schemes and a welfare worker service. She has also been a counsellor and trainer for CRUSE Bereavement Care.

The experience she gained in managing workforces in the voluntary sector enabled her to write the voluntary sector chapter in *Good Practice in Supervision* (edited by Jacki Pritchard, published by Jessica Kingsley) in 1995.

Christine's broad base of experience has enabled her to relate to all the stakeholders developing a system of integrated care. Working as the Project Manager for EPICS in South Buckinghamshire, she implemented the ideas initiated by Dr Chris Foote, whose vision has driven the project. She has organized and given presentations to major workshops locally, nationally and internationally. These include a seminar in Lille on intergenerational working and integrated care, and in Stockholm as part of a conference on developing interactive healthcare processes with the Institute for International Research.

She has also spent time visiting and sharing experiences with integrated care projects in Denver and Chicago.

website: www.integratedcare.org.uk

Subject Index

Abbeyfield 36
access 281
　easy 85
　to local shops 204
　to social care systems 78
accessibility, to primary care 41
accident and disease prevention
　114–17
accident and emergency units 31,
　52, 56
accidental adversaries 57
accountability 281
　and scrutiny, local 21
　model 207–8
　and team-working in complex
　　adaptive systems 315
Action Points 193
acute hospital
　distress, reduction in 122–1
　problems in 326–31
　　alternative sites for
　　　unplanned care 330–1
　　problems in admission
　　　process 327–8
　　problems in inpatient care for
　　　older people 328–30
　　problems in referral process
　　　326–7
addictive behaviour 55–6
administration 165
admission process, problems in
　327–8
　alternative triage and different
　　admission sites 327
　combination of capacity and
　　demand 328
　reducing demand 327
Age Concern 115, 140, 190, 196,
　214, 242, 250, 368
　Camden 208, 210–11
　Hillingdon 207
　Slough 178
ageism, dedicated leadership to
　combat 42–3
Agewell programme 214
aim 292
　EPICS 357
alcohol use 112
All Our Futures 206
ambulance services 141
Amersham International (later
　Nycomed) 296, 369
analysis sheet for referrers 262
Anchor Trust 36
Anderson, Fergus 28
arthritis 118
Asian community
　elders 213
　and pharmacy 204
assessment 15, 19
　analysis and implementation of
　　outcomes 103–4

decision-making must be
　planned for 104
training 104
who should do it? 103–4
comprehensive old-age
　assessment 95
contact assessment 95
context of process 96–9
　place 96–7
　time factors 97
　who should be assessed?
　　97–8
　who should do the
　　assessment? 99
as core process 90
effective 85
ensuring sustainability of system
　99–101
　ownership 100
　relevance of process 101
　toolbox approach 100
evaluation processing 184–6
in example job description for
　EPICS co-ordinator 163
getting to know the older
　person 89–108
in-depth assessment 95
involvement of older person in
　91–4
and Lifeplan 78, 93–4
overview assessment 95
purpose of 94–5
reasons for undertaking 95
resource implications 102–3
　information technology 102
　relationship of assessment
　　process to care
　　management 102
　sharing resources 102
　time 102
screening 41
selecting assessment tool 104–6
　domains and subdomains of
　　care 106–7
stages of process 95–6
at-risk group 98
attitudes, examine personal 40
attractors 60
audits, clinical 241, 245, 267
Ayres, Cathy 369

balance 280
balance-of-care approach 293–5
balanced scorecard 238–49, 256–7
balancing and reinforcing loops
　51–2
Barclay Report (1982) 34
Barthel Index 96
bed blockers 37, 55
behaviour and systems 51–2
benchmarking and networking
　297–9
benefits 161
Benefits Office 143
BetterCaring 185
'Better Government for Older
　People' (BGOP) initiative 16,
　190, 206–7, 210

Beveridge, Lord 28–9
Beveridge Report (*Social Insurance
　and Allied Services*) 28–9
Bishop, Angela 368
Blair, Nessie 368
blame
　culture 50
　and dependency, vicious cycle of
　　37–9
blocked beds 36
blurred boundaries 85, 309–11
body weight 112
boundaries
　blurred 85, 309–11
Bourne End Volunteer Bureau 368
Bournewood Community and
　Mental Health Trust, NW
　Surrey (RRICS) 363–4
Bowker, Michael 368
Buckinghamshire Health Authority
　214, 368
Buckinghamshire Social Services
　368
Bucks Community Action 214
Buddha 25
burden, shifting the 53–5
Burton, Judith 368
business
　and industry, local 142
　plan 161–2

Camden Age Concern 208, 210–11
cancer 118
　availability of resources for
　　terminal care 349
capturing data 176–7
care
　community 34–6, 337–8
　as core process 90
　domains and subdomains of
　　106–7
　innovative primary 338
　long-term 335–8
　managers 35
　networks of 85
　outcomes 240–1
　planning
　　at end of life 348–9
　　how can information system
　　　support 173–4
　provision for individuals and
　　populations of older
　　people, balancing tensions
　　between 16
　relationship of assessment
　　process to care
　　management 102
　training for population-based 81
　understanding care processes
　　169
　see also integrated care; primary
　　care
Care and Repair Schemes 36–7
CareDirect 185
carers and community 16
care home 336–7
careworkers and EPICS 358
Carers Centre 250, 340

Care Standards Act 186
Care Standard Systems Ltd 186
Caring for People (DoH 1989) 191–2
Catastrophe Theory in Systems Thinking (Arnold 1998) 71, 239
CATCH UP (Co-operative Action to Change and Hurry Up Progress) 217
Centre for Policy on Ageing 362
chambers of commerce, local 142
champion, identifying 136–7
change 292
Charter for People with Disabilities (Sheffield) 218
Chesham Community Hospital 369
Chiltern District Council 368
Chiltern Volunteer Bureau 368
choice 281
Christchurch, New Zealand 369
chronic disease management 117–20
chronic disease populations, managing 81
chronic lung disease 118
chronic obstructive pulmonary disease (COPD) 118–19
chunking 61
Churches Together group 143, 359, 368
Citizens Advice Bureaux 149
Citizens' Charters 191
citizens' juries 198–9
civic model 86–7, 340
client database, EPICS 358
clinical audits 241, 245, 267
clinical risk management, how can information system help in 174–5
clinical and social care risk management 123–8
    importance of information to clinical risk management 126–8
Clinical Satisfaction Unit, NHS Trust 242
clockware and swarmware 61
'closed cases' systems for monitoring in social services 41
Cochrane Centres 233
Coming of Age (de Beauvoir) 28
Coming of Age: Improving Care Services for Older People (Audit Commission 1998) 246, 359
command-and-control systems 60
commercial sponsorship for EPICS 359
Commission for Patient and Public Involvement in Health 194
commissioning 147–8
commitment, foster visible 139
common land 56
communication(s)
    levels of 308
    strategy 19
community 339–41
    care 34–6, 337–8
    civic model 86–7, 340

as corporate relationships of caring 16
development 21
    model 201–7
growing into 339–40
hospital beds, cuts in 32
hospitals 159
leaders, local 143
as main support 34–5
pharmacists 141–2
prevention programmes 80
resources database 173–4
whole systems of 340–1
Community Care Act 1990 35, 248
Community Dependency Index 96
Community Health Councils 198
competition and co-operation 61
complex adaptive system 21, 58–63
    key leadership behaviours in 282
    team-working in 315–18
complexity
    lens 60
    vs mechanistic approach 235–6
    process 238, 243–5
    of value systems 278–9
comprehensive old-age assessment 95
comprehensiveness 280
computer training at Age Concern Slough 178
conference for older people 212–14
confidentiality 177
confusion 112
connecting
    places 167–88
    systems 179–80
consultation 21
    problems in 209–10
    public consultation and NHS 192–5
contact assessment 95
continuity of medical care in nursing homes 41
continuous evaluation process 230
continuous feedback 85–6
convalescence 332–3
co-operation 280
    and competition 61
co-ordination
    and EPICS 358
    and liaison 164
coronary artery disease 118
corporate values of organization, examine 41
cost-effectiveness of care being delivered 238, 245–6
cost comparisons 245–6
    ensuring 80
    monitoring 245
costings 236–7
    for EPIC project 254–5
Cosin, Lionel 28
creativity, directed 289–95
crisis prevention 110–29
    chronic disease management 117–20
    clinical and social care risk management 123–8

frailty prevention 111–14
disease and accident prevention 114–17
reduction in acute hospital distress 122–1
rehabilitation 120–1
critical events, reducing number of 75–6
critical incident technique 267
Crossroads 368
customer satisfaction 238
cycle of evaluation and strategy generation 232

Darby, Roy 368
database
    client, EPICS 358
    community resources 173–4
    constructing 169–70
    managing 80, 171–2
    resources, EPICS 358
data
    analysis and reporting 229
    capturing 176–7
    collection 172–6, 229
        systems 20
    systems 78
    see also information systems 185
    other data systems relating to care of older people 185
day hospitals 28, 159
death and dying 22
    care planning 348–9
    diagnosing dying 347–8
    integrating care at end of life 345–52
    involving the patient 348
    managing end of life in hospital 220
'Debate of the Age' (Age Concern England) 190, 199
decision-making
    must be planned for 104
    and planning for action 230
delegation 315–18
demand for hospital places, reducing 327
dementia 118
Department of Care for the Elderly 133, 248
dependency 19, 55
    levels of 82–4
    vicious cycle of blame and 37–9
depression 73, 112, 118
Derby EPICS centres 361, 362
designing structures relevant to needs of older person 79
destitution relief 34
development
    funding, EPICS 358
    groups 145–7
diabetes mellitus 118
diagnosing dying 347–8
Dial-a-Ride 221
direct participation of users 20
    model 195–7
direct provision, EPICS 357–8
disconnectedness 19

discrimination 16, 18
  roots of 25–45
disease and accident prevention
  114–17
Doctors' House Surgery, Marlow
  368
'doers', identify and recruit 140
domains and subdomains of care
  106–7
Dyfed 217
dying see death and dying

easy access 85
EASYcare model 105
easy information flow 85
education 281
effective assessment 85
effectiveness 267
efficiency 267
Elderly Care Directorate, NHS Trust
  250.285
electronic government 205
electronic health records 181–2
emergency
  care 26, 29–30
  system 50
Emily 12, 22, 25–6, 49, 50, 52
emotional intelligence 57
empathy 310
end of life 17
  care planning 348–9
    availability of resources 349
    patient choices 348–9
  diagnosing dying 347–8
  integrating care at 345–52
  involving the patient 348
  managing in hospital 220
  teamwork 349–50
EPICS (Elderly Persons Integrated
  Care System) project, South
  Buckinghamshire 9–11, 13,
  14, 16, 20, 42, 62, 63, 67,
  69, 78, 79, 81, 84, 86, 93,
  96–102, 105, 114, 116,
  118–20, 124–9, 134, 136–8,
  140–4, 146–54, 168–73,
  175–9, 181–2, 184, 190,
  193, 195, 196, 200, 204,
  208–10, 212, 214, 215, 222,
  225, 231–2, 235–42, 245,
  250, 253, 254, 258–60,
  273–9, 283–5, 289, 296–9,
  307, 310, 312–14, 327, 330,
  338–9, 349–50, 353–5, 368,
  369
  aim 357
  careworkers 358
  client database 358
  commercial sponsorship 359
  as complex adaptive system 59
  co-ordination 358
  costings for 254–5
  Derby centres 361, 362
  developing evaluation in 235–7
    costing the project 236–7
    mechanistic vs complexity
      approach 235–6
    sharing the information 237

  user satisfaction monitoring
    237
development funding 358
direct provision 357
evaluation 358–9
evaluation tools used in 240–6
  care outcomes 240–1
  financial and
    cost-effectiveness
    245–6
  process complexity 243–5
  user satisfaction 241–2
example of information held on
  EPICS referral screen
  187–8
example job description for
  EPICS co-ordinator 163–6
  administration 165
  assessment 163
  co-ordination and liaison
    164
  IT management 165
  monitoring and evaluation
    165–6
  other duties 166
  staff management 164–5
  strategic networking 164
Executive Group 232
hospital admission viewed from
  systems perspective 33
how can information system
  help in evaluation of 174
and information systems
  168–77
integrated system 358
interface between social services
  and EPICS 245
intranet system 358
key features 151–3
  older persons' telephone link
    152–3
  one-stop service 151–2
and local community 359
and local councils 359
management and line
  management system 146
in Marlow 358
mission 357
monitoring interviews with
  older people who had used
  EPICS 260–4
original mission statement for
  278
new values for 276
operational resources 358
organizational structure –
  EPICS-r-Us 138
practical issues involved in
  implementing 134–66
process of setting up conference
  221–2
  attracting representative
    range of participants
    222
  food, premises and facilities
    221
  publicity 221
  topic report form 222
  transport 222

working group 221
profile 357–9
resource database 358
second mission statement 278
volunteer support 359
Warwickshire 362–3
Westway Centre, N Kensington
  361
workshops 359
ethics and value systems 279–81
evaluation
  in complex adaptive system 21
  and feedback 15
  of EPICS project 358–9
    how can information system
      help in 174
  of integrated care system
    225–68
    aims 225–32
    benefits of evaluation:
      example 231–2
    cycle of evaluation and
      strategy generation
      232
    developing evaluation in
      EPICS 235–7
    evaluating in multiple
      dimensions: balanced
      scorecard 238–49
    balancing the tensions
      239–40
    evaluation tools used in
      EPICS 240–6
    making the shapes 238–9
    value compass 246
    variation 246–9
    overview 251–2
    reporting and presenting
      evaluation outcomes
      249–51
    steps in evaluation 226–30
      continuous evaluation
        process 230
      data analysis and reporting
        229
      data collection 229
      decision-making and
        planning for action
        230
      designing evaluation and
        method of
        implementation
        228–9
      identifying issue(s) to be
        evaluated 227
      identifying stakeholders
        227
      the report 229
      understanding problem and
        context 228
    where is the evidence?
      232–5
      randomized controlled trials
        234
      real evidence 234–5
      systematic reviews 233–4
  glossary of terms used in 267–8
  of IT system 180
  and monitoring 161, 165–6

evaluator, professional as 313
evidence 232–5
expertise, bringing to older person
    in community 74
Expert Patient: A New Approach to
    Chronic Disease Management for
    the 21st Century, The (DoH
    2001) 198
expert systems in chronic disease
    management 118–20
external services, purchase of 35

facilitator and trainer of practice,
    professional as 312–13
falls 73
Falls Prevention Team 358
fear 47
feasibility study, topics used in
    158–62
    background and purpose 158
    benefits 161
    business plan 161–2
    evaluation and monitoring 161
    locality 158
    management structure 161
    need for project and how it was
        identified 158–9
    opportunities 159–60
    organizational options 160–1
    products from project
        development process 160
    project initiation document
        (PID) 162
    threats/constraints 160
feedback
    continuous 85–6
    and evaluation 15
    and feed-forward 62
finance department 147
financial and/or cost-effectiveness
    238, 245–6
fixes that backfire 52–3
focus groups 200–1
    definition and steps in planning
        219
Foote, Neta 369
frail older people 17
frailty prevention 111–14
France 14, 26
'From Margin to Mainstream'
    (Joseph Rowntree
    Foundation) 190, 196–7, 206
    case studies 217–18
        Dyfed 217
        Hereford and Ware 217
        Sheffield 218
        Sutton 218
funding
    development, EPICS 358
    and resource costs 210–15
future networks 181–2

General Council for Social Care
    315
generic multi-skilled worker, older
    person and 83
generic rehabilitation 333

geographical information systems
    181
geriatric assessment 19
geriatric care and high-tech care,
    balance between 29
geriatric units 29
geriatric wards 31
Gilmour-Hamilton, Catriona 368
Gladstone Road Surgery, Chesham
    368
Glasgow 28
Glebe Field Project, Crich,
    Derbyshire 362
goals or objectives 267
good-enough vision 61
GP
    practices 159
    satisfaction questionnaire 258–9
Great Hospital, Norwich 337
Griffiths Report (1998) 190–1
groups for assessment 97–8
'Growing Old, or Older and
    Growing?' conference 212
growth, limits to 53
guidelines and protocols, creating
    79

Hamlyn, Helen 361
Hamlyn, Paul 361
Hawthornden Surgery, Bourne End
    368
heathcare services, changes in
    delivery of 29–32
health 281
    of older people 16
    poor self-perceived 112
    prevention and promotion at all
        ages, improving 72
    public 148
Health for All (HFA) 214
Health Perspectives 199
Health Promotion Unit 214, 338
heart failure 118
heating and safety in home, value of
    37
HEES (Home Energy Efficiency
    Scheme) 36
Helen Hamlyn Foundation 362
Hereford and Ware 217
higher-risk group 127
high-tech care and geriatric care,
    balance between 29
Hill, John 368
Hollingbery, Richard 362
home care, purchasing policies for
    41
Home Care MDS (minimum data
    set) 105
hospital(s)
    accident and emergency units 31
    admissions 30–1
        viewed from systems
            perspective (EPICS) 33
    care team 31
    corporate values of 41
    demand on beds 37
    geriatric wards 31
    managers 32

managing end of life in 220
    Poor Law 18, 27–8, 29
    reduction in acute hospital
        distress 122–1
    resuscitation policy 41
    services, greater demand on 30
    waiting lists 26
        monitoring and management
            41
        system 50
    ward-based care policies 41
    see also acute hospital
housing associations 36
    local 140–1
human resources 148
hypothermia 127

'if we were...' 290
impaired thinking 112
implementation models 67–88
    civic model 86–7
    integrative care management
        model 77–81
    integrative whole systems model
        69–77
    simple rules model 84–6
    valuing the older person model
        81–4
improvement 280
inclusive planning 19
independence of older people 16,
    19
in-depth assessment 95
individual risk 78
individuals and populations of older
    people, balancing tensions
    between care provision for 16
Industrial Revolution 27
information
    held on EPICS referral screen,
        example of 187–8
    importance of to clinical risk
        management 126–8
information flow, easy 85
information systems
    assessment evaluation processing
        184–6
    connecting places 167–88
    connecting systems 179–80
        intranet 179–80
    and EPICS 168–77
        capturing data 176–7
        community resources
            database 173–4
        confidentiality 177
        constructing database
            169–70
        data collection 172–6
        how can information
            benefit older person?
            173
        how can information system
            help in clinical risk
            management? 174–5
        how can information system
            help in evaluation of
            EPICS project? 174

how can information system
help in management
of project? 174
how can information system
support care
planning? 173–4
what information is needed
about older person to
deliver personal care?
173
managing database 171–2
possible alternative sources
of population data
170–1
understanding care processes
169
evaluating IT system 180
future networks 181–2
electronic health records
181–2
geographical information
systems 181
involving older people in 178
other data systems relating to
care of older people 185
overview 182–3
timely 1/5
information technology (IT) 20
evaluating system 180
management 165
as resource 102
informed views of users 20
model 197–201
'ing' game 301
initiatives on scrutiny and
accountability, national 208
initiatives for direct participation of
users
local 195–6
national 196–7
innovative primary care 338
innovator of new techniques and
professional change,
professional as 312
inpatient care for older people
problems in 328–30
redesigning 328–30
inputs 267
instigator and steward of procedures
and standards, professional as
311
Institute for Health Service
Management 194
institutions, older person and 83–4
integrated care
at end of life 345–52
levers and tools for 271–302
models of 21
other 360–7
problems in setting up 20
systems map of 48
Integrated Care at Home, Surrey
Hampshire Borders NHS
Trust 364–6
evaluation 366
services provided 365
strategy 365
training 365–6

Integrated Care for the Older
Person in the North West
Stockholm Region, Sweden
366–7
evaluation 367
integrative care management model
77–81
managed care 79–80
managed older person 78
managed population 80–1
Integrated Care Project 214
see also EPICS
Integrated Care Solution 184
integrated care system
developing structural framework
of 144–7
and EPICS 358
evaluating 225–68
setting up and sustaining 155–6
integrative whole systems model
69–77
using the model 71–6
moving crisis line up 745
moving older person line
down 72–3
reducing number of critical
events 75–6
summary 76–7
Interactive Online Solutions (IOS)
184
interface group 98, 127
Intermediate Care Programme 358
inter-professional relationships
307–9
interventions, key 112–13
interviews
with older people who had used
EPICS, monitoring 260–4
on client satisfaction, procedures
agreed for 262–4
In the Public Interest – Developing a
Strategy for Public Participation
in the NHS (NHS Executive
1998) 192, 198, 212
intranet 179–80
EPICS 358
Involving Patients and the Public in
Healthcare (DoH 2001) 193,
209
involving the users 190–222
funding and resource costs
210–15
sharing resources 212–15
example 1: conference for
older people 212–14
example 2: working in
partnership 214–15
follow-up from conferences
215
legislation 191–2
models for public participation
195–209
community development
201–7
'Better Government for
Older People' (BGOP)
206–7
locality forums 202–5

primary care groups and
trusts 205
direct participation of users
195–7
local initiatives 195–6
national initiatives 196–7
informed views of users
197–201
citizens' juries 198–9
focus groups 200–1
patients as experts 198
local scrutiny and
accountability 207–8
lay assessors 207–8
Age Concern
Hillingdon 207
Camden Age Concern
208
national initiative 208
transactional process 208–9
overview 215
problems in consultation
209–10
public consultation and NHS
192–5
iterative process 20

job description for EPICS
co-ordinator, example 163–6
Joseph Rowntree Foundation 196
junior doctors, working hours of
30, 52–3
juries, citizens' 198–9
Justice in Health Care Foundation
280
Principles of 281
justifying rationale for planning and
delivering particular types of
care 79

Kane, Bob 369
Kane, Rosalie 369
key organizations, involve all 137
key process outcomes 238
Knight, Carole 369
knowledge 167–8

Lawrence, David 368
lay assessors 207–8
leader 282
leadership 19
dedicated, to combat ageism
42–3
key leadership behaviours in
complex adaptive systems
282
learning how to lead in complex
adaptive system 285
and organizational principles,
nine emerging and
connected 60–1
skills 21, 281–5
Leamington Spa, Warwickshire
(EPICS) 362
learning and training together
295–7
legislation 191–2

leisure facilities, local 142
let go, learning how to 283
levels of communication 308
levers and tools for integrated care
271–302
benchmarking and networking
297–9
after visit 298
before visit 297–8
during visit 298
creating shared values 275–81
complexity of value systems
278–9
ethics and value systems
279–81
developing shared vision 274–5
directed creativity 289–95
balance-of-care approach
293–5
finding new ways of
thinking 289–91
'if we were...' 290
wicked questions 290
PDSA (plan, do, study, act)
cycle 291–3
exercises that develop insights to
your systems 301–2
'ing' game 301
what are they connected to?
301
leadership skills 281–5
learning and training together
295–7
overview 299
team building 285–9
role conflict 287–9
tools that are levers of change
272
Lewis, Alison 368
Lewis, Gordon 368
Licensed Victuallers care homes,
Buckinghamshire 337
Lifeplan Project 370
assessment 78
Lille, France 369
limits to growth 53
local business and industry 142
local chambers of commerce 142
local community
and EPICS 359
leaders 143
local councils 36
and EPICS 359
local housing organizations 140–1
local initiatives
in community development
202–3
for direct participation of users
195–6
locality 158
forums 202–5
local initiatives 202–3
Older Persons Action Groups
(OPAGs) 203–5
groups 145
local leisure facilities 142
local religious organizations 143
local scrutiny and accountability 21
model 207–8

local shops, access to 204
London Borough of Camden 208
London Borough of Hillingdon
207
long-term care 22, 335–8
changing 336–8
care home 336–7
community care 337–8
loops, reinforcing and balancing
51–2
low(er)-risk group 98, 126–7
Lyle, Sarah 368

managed care 20, 79–80
managed older person 78
managed person 20
managed population 20, 80–1
management
of care, relationship of
assessment process to 102
chronic disease 117–20
of chronic disease populations
81
of database 80
of end of life in hospital 220
IT 165
and line management system
146
of networks 149–50
of project, how can information
system help in 174
of risk 80–1
of spatial component 80
staff 164–5
structure 161
manager, 'new professional' 318–20
Marlow, South Buckinghamshire
178, 231, 236, 278, 285,
358, 368, 369
see also EPICS (Elderly Persons
Integrated Care System)
project, South
Buckinghamshire
Marlow Community Hospital 369
Marlow Day Hospital 369
Meadow Larks 114
Meals on Wheels 221
measurement 292
mechanistic vs complexity approach
235–6
Medicaid 360
Medicare 360
memory loss 112
mental health conditions 118
meta-analysis 267
Middle Ages 56
elderly care in 26
Midlands 28
Missenden Abbey 369
mission statements 267
for EPICS project 278, 357
mobility problems 42
modelling 15, 18–19, 68–9
models
implementation 67–88
civic 86–7
integrative care management
77–81

integrative whole systems
69–77
simple rules 84–6
valuing the older person
81–4
of integrated care 21
other 360–7
for public participation
195–209
model 1: direct participation
of users 195–7
model 2: informed views of
users 197–201
model 3: community
development 201–7
model 4: local scrutiny and
accountability 207–8
model 5: transactional
process 208–9
Modernising Social Services (1998)
192
monitoring
care outcomes 240–1
and evaluation 161, 165–6
financial and cost-effectiveness
2452
interviews with older people
who had used EPICS
260–4
ongoing client satisfaction 242
process complexity 243–4
user satisfaction 237, 241–2
Moore, John 368
morbidity 17
Morgan, David 368
Morris, Nick 369
motivation 310
poor 73
Moyniham, Ronnie 369
multi-agency care 48
Multi-Campus Division of Geriatric
Medicine UCLA 369
multiple actions 61
multiple assessments 38–9
multiple diseases 112
multi-skilled worker, older person
and 83

National Assessment Framework
105, 106
National Assistance Act 1948
Part III accommodation 33–4
National Assistance Board 34
National Care Standards 200
National Health Service and
Community Care Act 1990
191
national initiatives
for direct participation of users
196–7
on scrutiny and accountability
208
National Institute of Clinical
Excellence (NICE) 208
National PACE Association 361
National Service Framework for Older
People (DoH 2001) see NSF
networking

and benchmarking 297–9
designing 150
strategic 164
networks
of care 85
future 181–2
managing 149–50
out-of-hours 150
New NHS, The (1997) 192, 202, 205
'new professional' manager 318–20
New Surgery, Chesham 368
Newton Software 368
New Zealand 14, 369
NHS 121
public consultation and 192–5
NHS Confederation 194
NHS Direct 115
NHS Executive Quality and Consumer Branch 194
NHS Net 18
NHS Plan 193, 194
NHS Trust
Clinical Satisfaction Unit 242
Elderly Care Directorate 250, 285
IT department 313
South Buckinghamshire 214, 258, 357, 358, 368
see also EPICS (Elderly Persons Integrated Care System) project, South 2Buckinghamshire
Surrey Hampshire Borders 364–6
Nicholls, Angela 363
North West Surrey 364
NSF (*National Service Framework for Older People*) 16, 39, 42, 192, 200, 329, 346
principles of 19
and status of older people 17
Standard 2 (types of assessment) 95
Standard 5 (Stroke) 73
Standard 6 (Falls) 73
nursing homes 26, 37
continuity of medical care in 41
lack of shared responsibility and risk taking in 124
Nycomed (formerly Amersham International) 369

objectives or goals 267
Office for Public Management 196
O'Flynn, Deirdre 368
old age, those entering 17
older people
care provision for 16
current issues 29–37
historical roots 26–9
and community 16
as individuals and populations, care of 16
status of 17–22
older person partnership, value of 82

Older Persons Action Groups (OPAGs) 200, 203–5
aims and objectives of local 203
examples of issues taken up by OPAGs in S Bucks 204
example of two-way process where providers seek views of users 205
one-stop service 151–2
criteria for success 151
On Lok integrated care project, San Francisco 360, 361
openness 280
operational resources, EPICS 358
opportunities 159–60
opportunity costs 268
Ordnance Survey mapping 181
organization(s)
examine corporate values of 41
involve all key 137
organizational and personal development 15
organizational and leadership principles, nine emerging and connected 60–1
organizational options 160–1
outcomes 268
care 240–1
reporting and presenting evaluation outcomes 249–51
out-of-hours network 150
outputs 268
Overview and Scrutiny Committee 207
overview assessment 95
ownership 100
Oxford 28
Oxford Brookes University 214

PACE (Program of All-Inclusive Care for the Elderly) (US) 360–1, 369
Pakistani community 273
Palmer, Sue 368
paradox 61
Paradox Relational Database 181
parallel and synchronous processes 302
Parkinson's disease 101, 118, 119, 132–3
Parkinson's Disease Management Team 119, 132–3
Parkinson's Disease Society 133
participation 14
direct participation of users model 195–7
models in strategy for developing public participation 195–209
partnership 14, 16, 21, 193
working in 214–15
Patients' Charters 191
patients
choices at end of life 348–9
as experts 198
forums 194

PDSA (plan, do, study, act) cycle 246, 291–3
Pearce, Joy 368
pedestrian crossing 205
Penney, Bruce 369
performance measures 244
personal attitudes, examine 40
personal care, what information is needed about older person to deliver 173
personal crisis, avoidance of 85
personal and organizational development 15
personal touch 149–50
person-centred care 16, 208–9
Petits Frères des Pauvres, Lille, France 369
pharmacists, community 141–2
pharmacy and Asian community 204
Phone Link 359
physical activity, low level of 112
place of assessment 96–7
plan, do, study, act (PDSA) cycle 246, 291–3
planning
and delivering particular types of care, justifying rationale for 79
inclusive 19
Podeski, Katarina 368
police 141
Poor Laws 18, 25, 27, 34
hospitals 18, 27–8, 29
Poor Law Amendment Act 1834 27
Poor Relief Act 1601 26, 27
population(s)
of older people and individuals, balancing tensions between care provision for 16
possible alternative sources of data 170–1
practical exercises 40–3
actively involve older people in deliberation 42
ensure dedicated leadership to combat ageism 42–3
examine corporate values of organization 41
examine personal attitudes 40
practical issues involved in implementing EPICS 134–66
aligning the total organization 147–8
commissioning 147–8
finance department 147
human resources 148
public health 148
public relations departments 148
changing ourselves 136
developing structural framework of integrated care system 144–7
development groups 145–7
locality groups 145
project board 144
steering groups 144–5

example job description for
    EPICS co-ordinator 163–6
initial stages 136–44
    identifying champion 136–7
    identifying and involving
        stakeholders 137–40
    confirm other person as
        major stakeholder
        139–40
    foster visible commitment
        139
    identify and recruit 'doers'
        140
    involve all key
        organizations 137
    present solutions not
        problems 137–9
neglected stakeholders
    140–4
    ambulance services 141
    community pharmacists
        141–2
    local business and industry
        142
    local chambers of commerce
        142
    local community leaders
        143
    local housing organizations
        140–1
    local leisure facilities 142
    local religious organizations
        143
    police 141
    private and not-for-profit
        sector 143–4
key features of EPICS in South
    Buckinghamshire 151–3
managing networks 149–50
    designing networking into
        the structure 150
    out-of-hours network 150
    personal touch 149–50
sustainability 153–6
topics used in feasibility study
    158–62
prevention
    of crises 110–29
    frailty 111–14
    programmes, community 80
Price, Wendy 368
primary–secondary interface,
    vicious cycle of 38
primary care
    changes in 30
    corporate values of 41
    groups and trusts 205
    innovative 338
private and not-for-profit sector
    143–4
procedure(s) 268
    and standards, professional as
        instigator and steward of
        311
process 268
process complexity 238, 243–5
processes 268
processing assessments 184–5
professionals

blurring the boundaries 309–11
and community 16
for complex adaptive systems 21
inter-professional relationships
    307–9
'new professional' manager
    318–20
relationships with older people
    306–7
roles of new professionals
    311–15
    evaluator 313
    innovator of new techniques
        and professional change
        312
    instigator and steward of
        procedures and
        standards 311
    supervisor 313–15
    team-working in complex
        adaptive systems
        315–18
    trainer and facilitator of
        practice 312–13
    working together for integrated
        care 305–22
project board 144
project development process,
    products from 160
project initiation document (PID)
    162
protocols and guidelines, creating
    79
public consultation and NHS 192–5
public health 148
publicity for EPICS conference 221
public relations departments 148

Quakers 27
qualitative and quantitative data
    228
quality of service, ongoing
    (monitoring interviews with
    older people who had used
    EPICS) 260–4
questionnaire for referrers 265–6
questions, wicked 290

randomized controlled trials 234,
    268
Rank Xerox 296, 369
Rapid Response Integrated Care
    Services (RRICS) 363–4
Read, Dorothy 368
Red Cross 143, 250
reconstructive rehabilitation 334
Rectory Meadows Surgery,
    Amersham 368
recuperative rehabilitation 334
redesigning care structures 21
referral process, problems in 326–7
referrers' satisfaction 241
Reformation, elderly care in 26
Reggler, Jonathan 368
rehabilitation 120–1, 331–5
    cuts in 32
    definitions of 331

multiple-level modes of 332–4
    convalescence 332–3
    generic rehabilitation 333
    reconstructive 334
    recuperative 334
    restorative 334
    specialist rehabilitation 333
rehabilitating rehabilitation:
    whole system within
    integrated care 334–5
Rehabilitation at Home 364
reinforcing and balancing loops
    51–2
relationships with older people
    306–7
relevance of assessment process 101
reliability of assessment tool 205
religious organizations, local 143
renal failure 118
report 229
reporting and presenting evaluation
    outcomes 249–51
residential homes 26, 37
residential nursing, purchasing
    policies for 41
resource(s)
    availability of, for terminal care
        349
    costs and funding 210–15
    database, EPICS 358
    human 148
    operational, EPICS 358
    sharing 102, 212–15
respite care 28
responsible risk taken by
    professional team, example of
    125–6
responsiveness of assessment tool
    205
restorative rehabilitation 334
resuscitation policy 41
revolving door system 31, 33, 117
Richardson, Joan 368
rights 280
risk
    factors 112
    management 80–1
        clinical and social care
            123–8
        screening 41
Riverside Surgery, High Wycombe
    368
role
    ambiguity 287–8
    conflict 287–9
    incompatibility 287
    overload 288
    underload 288–9

safety 280
    and heating in home, value of
        37
St John Ambulance 143
satisfaction
    monitoring
        referrers' 242
        user 237, 241–2
    questionnaire, GP 258–9

Saving Lives (DoH 1999) 198
scrutiny and accountability, local 21
    model 207–8
Seebohm Report (1968) 34
Selandar, Goran 369
self-awareness 310
self-help 34
self-regulation 310
self-sufficiency, older person and
    82–3
services, fitting around older
    people's needs 16
shadow system 61
shapes 238–9
shared responsibility 21
    and risk taking, lack of in
        nursing home 124
shared values, creating 275–81
shared vision 15, 19, 21
    developing 274–5
sharing
    information 237
    resources 102
Sheffield 218
Sheldon 28
sheltered housing 36
shifting the burden 53–5
short-term fixes 52–3
Siddartha 25
Siddiqui, Talat 368
Simple Rules 62, 369
    model 84–6
        avoidance of personal crisis
            85
        blurred boundaries 85
        continuous feedback 85–6
        easy access 85
        easy information flow 85
        effective assessment 85
        networks of care 85
        user focus 84–5
Smaje, Leslie 368
smoking 112
social care
    risk management 123–8
    services, changes in delivery of
        32–6
    systems, access to 78
Social Care Institute of Excellence
    (SCIE) 208
Social Insurance and Allied Services see
    Beveridge Report
social isolation 112
social policy, changes in 32
social services 26, 32, 214
    corporate values of 41
    criteria for admission 41
    external pressures on 36–7
    interface between EPICS and
        245
    systems for monitoring 'closed
        cases' 41
social skills 310
social workers 57
social work model 57
society, changes in 30
Society of St Vincent de Paul 250,
    368
solutions not problems 137–9

South Buckinghamshire 9, 13, 114,
    132, 149, 170, 184, 199,
    200, 203, 205, 214, 248,
    254, 326, 339, 358, 359,
    368, 369
    see also EPICS (Elderly Persons
        Integrated Care System)
        project, South
        Buckinghamshire
South Buckinghamshire NHS Trust
    see under NHS Trust
    see also EPICS
spaces, managing 63
spatial component, managing 80
specialist rehabilitation 333
staff management 164–5
stakeholders
    confirm other person as major
        139–40
    identifying 227
        and involving 137–40
        neglected 140–4
Stationery Office 185
status of older people 17–22
stay-put systems 36
steering groups 144–5
step-up/step-down care 26
Stockholm 366–7, 369
strategic networking 164
strategies 268
strategic planning and partnerships
    20
strategy generation and cycle of
    evaluation 232
street lamps, ill-placed 205
stress 53
stroke 73, 118
structures 268
    and way ahead for care of older
        people 323–42
Suggate, Cathy 368
supervision 313–15
supervisor, professional as 313–15
Surrey Hampshire Borders NHS
    Trust 364–6
sustainability 153–6
    of assessment system, ensuring
        99–101
    setting up and sustaining
        integrated care system
        155–6
    summary of process 153–4
Sutton 218
swarmware and clockware 61
Sweden 14, 225, 249, 359, 366–7
synchronous and parallel processes
    302
system(s) 47–8
    approach 15, 18, 46–65
        defining the problem 49–50
        to preventive care and risk
            management 19–20
    archetypes 52–7
        accidental adversaries 57
        fixes that backfire 52–3
        limits to growth 54
        shifting the burden 54–6
        tragedy of commons 56–7
    and behaviour 51–2

command-and-control 60
complex adaptive 58–63
    EPICS as 59
    evaluation in 21
    key leadership behaviours in
        282
    professionals for 21
    managing spaces 63
    overview 64
systems map of integrated care 48

Tavistock Group 280
Tavistock Principles 280
team building 285–9
teamwork
teamwork
    in complex adaptive systems
        315–18
        accountability 315
        delegation 315–18
            example: Community Falls
                Team 317–18
            how will they know they
                are succeeding? 317
    in end of life care 349–50
technical advances 75
techniques and professional change,
    professional as innovator of
    new 312
technology 75
telephone link, older persons'
    152–3
tensions, balancing the 23940
threats/constraints 160
time
    factors, in assessment process 97
    as resource 102
    to talk 40
toolbox approach 100
tools
    and levers for integrated care
        271–302
    that are levers of change 272
topic report form 222
total organization, aligning the
    147–8
tragedy of the commons 56–7
trainer and facilitator of practice,
    professional as 312–13
training
    and assessment process 104
    and learning together 295–7
    for population-based care 81
transactional process 208–9
transitional phase 17
transport 222
    systems 73
treatment, as core process 90
triage, alternative 327
trials, randomized controlled 234
trolley delay 49
Tully, Evelyn 369
tune to the edge 61

understanding care processes 169
uneven pavement 205
Union Houses 27

United Kingdom 14, 99, 332, 337, 359, 360, 361
United States 9, 10, 14, 99, 181, 210, 246, 280, 332, 337, 359, 360–1, 369
unplanned care, alternative sites for 330–1
user(s)
    focus 84–5
    involving 190–222
    satisfaction monitoring 237, 241–2

validity of assessment tool 205
value
    compass 246
    of 'older person partnership' 82
    systems
        complexity of 278–9
        ethics and 279–81
values
    corporate, of organization 41
    for EPICS, new 276
    shared 15, 19
        creating 273–81
    should not be left 'on the shelf' 277
valuing the older person model 81–4
    levels of dependence 82–4
        level 1: older person and self-sufficiency 82–3
        level 2: older person and generic multi-skilled worker 83
        level 3: older person and institutions 83–4
variation 246–9
    analysis of 248–9
    types of 247–8
vicious cycle
    of blame and dependency 37–9
    of primary–secondary interface 38
virtual organization of complex adaptive systems 20, 21
virtuous circle of improvement, creating 39
vision 268
    based on shared values 15, 19
    developing shared 274–5
    impairment 112
VOICE 194, 210
voluntary organizations 36
    corporate values of 41
voluntary services and elderly care 34
Volunteer Bureau 250
volunteer support, EPICS 359

waiting lists 26
    monitoring and management 41
    system 50
walking difficulties 112
ward-based care policies 41
Warren, Marjorie 28
Warwick District Council 362

Warwicks EPICS 362–3
Watts, Brenda 363
welfare market vs welfare state 35
West Middlesex Poor Law Hospital 28
Westway Centre, N Kensington (EPICS) 361
wicked questions 290
Winifred 22, 353–5
Winter Pressure 364
With Respect to Old Age (1990) 246
Women's Institutes 143
workhouses 27–8
working group 221
working in partnership 214–15
Working with Emotional Intelligence (Goleman) 57
workshops, EPICS 359
WRVS 143
Wycome District Council 368
Wye Valley Surgery, High Wycombe 368

Author Index

Adams, T. 1097
Akins, D.E. 129
Applegate, W.B. 121, 129
Arnold, V.I. 71, 88, 239, 269
Ash, E. 369
Association of Community Health
   Councils for England and
   Wales 199, 223
Atherton, J. 313, 322
Audit Commission 32, 36, 45, 246,
   268, 336, 343
Austin, B.T. 117, 130

Bagley, H. 343
Bagust, A. 327, 343
Baldwin, S. 32, 45, 120, 121, 130
Barclay Report 34, 44, 45
Barrett, J. 200, 223
Bartlett, H. 214, 224
Batalden, P. 110, 246, 269, 303
Bates, T. 45
Beck, J.C. 130
Beech, R. 303
Bernabei, R. 234, 268
Berwick, D. 280, 303
Better Government for Older
   People 13, 23, 206, 207, 223
Beveridge Report 28, 44, 45
Billis, D. 271
Blair, M. 129
Blair, T. 206
Blanchard, M. 73, 88
Blazer, D. 130
Blue, L. 13
Boaz, A. 210, 223
Boult, C. 131, 344
Bowen, T. 293, 303
Bowling, A. 109, 269
Bowman, C. 30, 45, 334, 343
Bradley, D.S. 189
Bragg, R. 189
Brownsell, S.J. 178, 189
Brummell, K. 129
Buchanan, D.R. 339, 344
Bula, C.J. 45, 130
Bullman, A. 166
Burckhardt, P. 45
Burnard, B. 45
Burns, A. 343
Burns, R. 129
Burton, J. 369
Butler, R. 323, 324, 343

Calkins, E. 122, 129, 131, 344
Calviou, A. 240, 268
Caplan, J. 322
Carlier, J. 189
Carver, D. 130
Catlin, P. 189
Challis, D. 336, 343
Checkland, P. 65

Chilvers, R. 233, 269
Churchman, W. 46
Clarke, C. 109
Coast, J. 31, 45
Cohen, H.J. 130
Cohen, J. 66
Collins, R. 73, 88
Continuing Care Conference 121,
   129
Cordingley, L. 343
Cosway, S. 130
Curry, S. 130

Davidoff, F. 303
Davis, C. 166, 269
Dawkins, R. 167
de Beauvoir, S. 25, 28
Delbanco, T. 190, 210, 223
Department of Health 16, 20, 23,
   104, 108, 192, 193, 198,
   205, 209, 223, 329, 343
Dewey, M. 129
Dickenson, E. 121, 130

Eakin, P. 96, 108
Einstein, A. 67
Elan, J.T. 129
Elkan, R. 117, 129
Elliott, J. 89, 369
English, P.A. 109, 130
Epicurus 220

Feinglass, J. 130
Felin, G. 303
Fenn, A. 31, 45
Figg, H. 45
Finlay, L. 166
Firth-Cozens, J. 53, 65
Foote, C. 9, 45, 284, 285, 369,
   371
Forte, P. 293, 303
Fortinsky, R. 343
Franke, T. 130
Franklin Williams, T.H. 130
Fraser, S.W. 296, 303

Gambassi, G. 268
Georgiou, A. 270
Goethe, J.W. von 134
Goleman, D. 57, 309, 322
Gosalves, M. 303
Gould, M.M. 338, 344
Graney, M.J. 129
Greenhalgh, T. 15, 23, 296, 303
Griffin, D. 66
Griffiths, R. 192, 223
Grimley Evans, J. 29, 45, 130
Grothaus, L. 269
Gruman, J. 130

Hammer, M. 281, 303
Hayden, C. 210, 223
Haynes, B. 269
Health Advisory Service 31, 45,
   122, 129
Henderson, A. 193, 223

Hewitt, M. 129
Hiatt, H. 303
Hirsch, C.H. 123, 130
Hohmann, C. 130
Holt, T. 62, 65
Hooper, A. 303
Horner, P. 45
Hughes, E. 305
Huxley, P. 343

Iliffe, S. 338, 344
Illich, I. 322
Inglis, A. 31, 45
Ingold, B.B. 31, 45
Inouye, S.K. 130
Institute for Health Service Manager
   194

Jalaluddin, M. 130
Jarrett, P. 130
Johnson, M. 45
Josephson, K.R. 109, 130

Kabcenell, A. 352
Kane, R.A. 11, 89, 109, 344
Kane, R.L. 11, 45, 99, 108, 109,
   130, 336, 343, 344
Katzenbach, J.R. 303
Kelly, A. 307, 322
Kendrick, D. 129
Kent, D. 269
Kirk, S. 200, 223
Kirkwood, T. 345
Kleiner, A. 66, 88, 166, 304
Koenig, H.G. 122, 130
Koontz, S. 181, 189
Kotter, J.P. 274
Kowal, J. 343
Kresevic, D. 343
Kydd, D. 130

LaBrooy, S 369
Ladd, R.C. 344
Landefeld, C.S. 130, 328, 343
Landi, F. 268
Lang, T. 294, 303
Lao Tzu 63, 271
Lapsley, I. 109
Lathlean, J. 327, 330, 343, 344
Laurent, S. 181, 189
Leveille, S.G. 234, 269
Lefevre, S. 122, 130
Liberati, A. 303
Lindberg, C. 61, 65, 66, 278, 303
Logerfro, M. 269
Lomax, T. 332, 343
Lorenzo, S. 303
Lunn, K.C. 337, 343
Lynn, J. 352
Lynn Beattie, B. 130

McClean, S.L. 335, 343
McCrea Curren, M. 352
McDermott, I. 47, 65
McKnight, J. 305, 322
Maclean, T. 99, 109

MacMahon, S. 73, 88
Martin, G. 130
Mathias, P. 166, 304
Meador, K.G. 130
Michel, J-P. 130
Millard, P.H. 335, 343
Miller, S.T. 129
Miser, H.J. 68, 69, 88
Montaigne, M. de 220
Moore, J. 369
Morgan, G. 16, 23, 245
Mozly, C. 343
Muir Gray, J.A. 115, 130, 233, 269
Mullen, L. 130

National Confidential Enquiry into
    Perioperative Deaths 29, 45
Naughton, B.J. 122, 129
NCEPOD 122, 130
Neale, B. 369
Nelson, E.C. 246, 269, 303
NHS Centre for Reviews and
    Dissemination 234, 269
NHS Confederation 194
NHS Executive Quality and
    Consumer Branch 192, 194,
    198, 212, 223
Nikolaus, T. 130
Nocon, A. 31, 45, 120, 121, 130
Norman, G. 109
Norman, H. 46

O'Conner, J. 47, 65
Office for Public Management 197,
    223
Oliveira, J. 256, 269
Olsen, A. 130
Olve, N. 256, 269
Ovretveit, J. 166, 225, 249, 269,
    286, 303, 304, 314, 322

Pacala, J.T. 131, 344
PACE (Programme for the
    All-Inclusive Care of the
    Elderly) 228, 269
Palfrey, C. 224, 270
Pallawala, P.M. 337, 343
Palmer, R. 343
Palmer Wandel, L. 352
Parsloe, P. 211, 223
Paterson, L. 338, 344
Patterson, C. 115, 130
Pearson, M. 270, 303
Peters, T.J. 31, 45
Philips, C. 224
Phillips, P. 270
Pietroni, C. 344
Pietroni, P. 344
Pithouse, A. 224
Place, M. 327, 343
Plescia, M. 181, 189
Plsek, P.E. 15, 23, 61, 65, 66, 278,
    282, 291, 292, 303, 304,
    369
Posnett, J.W. 327, 343
Potter, J. 270, 303
Potts, S. 130

Prescott, G. 45
Prevention of Dependency in Later
    Life Group 132

Quade, E.S. 68, 69, 88

Raw, D. 369
Rhodes, C. 345
Richardson, W.S. 269
Rittel, H. 134
Roberts, C. 66, 88, 304
Robinson, J. 129
Rockwood, K. 122, 130
Rogers, C. 166, 212
Rosenberg, W. 269
Ross, R. 66, 88, 166, 214, 224,
    304
Roth, G. 166
Roy, J. 256, 269
Royal Commission on Long Term
    Care 246, 269
Rubenstein, L.Z. 103, 109, 121,
    130, 268
Rudberg, M.A. 130
Ryer, J.C. 246, 269, 303

Sackett, D.L. 234, 269
Sagar, M.A. 123, 130
St Leger, A.S. 270
Santos-Eggiman, B. 303
Sayre, J.A. 109, 130
Schaefer, J. 130
Schneerson, D. 211, 224
Schnieden, H. 270
Scholes, J. 65
Seebohm Report 34, 44, 45
Senge, P. 66, 88, 166, 304, 369
Shaiken, H. 322
Shaw, G.B. 225
Shaw, P. 66
Sheffield Institute for Studies on
    Aging 109
Sheldon, B. 233, 269
Shuster, J. 352
Siebens, H. 130
Sinclair, A. 121, 130
Siu, A.L. 109
Skinner, A. 214, 224
Skyttner, L. 65
Smith, B. 66, 88, 166, 304
Smith, D.R. 303
Smith, R. 303
Social Services Inspectorate 36, 45,
    99, 102, 109
Soglin, L. 130
Sommers, L. 130
South Buckinghamshire NHS Trust
    31, 45
Spargo, J. 202, 224
Spiro, H.M. 352
Stacey, R.D. 66
Stanners, C. 9, 208, 224, 285, 372
Stanners, R. 370
Stewart, I. 66
Stolee, P. 130
Strauss, S.E. 269
Streiner, D. 109

Stuck, A.E. 111, 130
Stuck, W.E. 99, 109
Sutcliffe, C. 343
Svanborg, A. 30, 45

Tampieri, A. 303
Thomas, P. 224, 270
Thompson, A. 166
Thompson, T. 304
Travis, S. 45
Twain, M. 320

Vaughan, B. 327, 330, 343, 344
Venables, D. 45
Von Korff, M. 117, 130

Wagner, E.H. 117, 130, 131, 269,
    344
Wallace, J. 269
Walsworth-Bell, J.P. 270
Walthert, J.M. 130
Webber, M. 134
Webster, J. 130
Wetter, M. 256, 269
Wheatley, M. 304
Wieland, G.D. 109, 130
Wieland, P.G. 109
Wietlisbach, V. 45
Wilcock, G.K. 130
Wiley, C.E. 68, 69, 88
Williams, D. 129
Williamson, H. 224
Wilson, T. 62, 65, 282, 303
Winograd, C.H. 130

Yarnold, P. 130
Yersin, B. 45
Younger-Ross, S. 332, 343

Zimmerman, B. 61, 65, 66, 278,
    282, 303
Zola, I.K. 322